Secure Digital Infrastructure and Cyber Resilience in Smart Government Systems

Miguel Ángel Ruiz Jaimes
Universidad Politécnica del Estado de Morelos, Mexico

José Miguel Liceaga Ortiz De La Peña
Universidad Politécnica de Pachuca, Mexico

IGI Global
Scientific Publishing
Publishing Tomorrow's Research Today

Vice President of Editorial Melissa Wagner
Director of Acquisitions Mikaela Felty
Director of Book Development Jocelynn Hessler
Production Manager Mike Brehm
Cover Design Jose Rosado

Published in the United States of America by
IGI Global Scientific Publishing
701 East Chocolate Avenue
Hershey, PA, 17033, USA
Tel: 717-533-8845 | Fax: 717-533-7115
Website: https://www.igi-global.com E-mail: cust@igi-global.com

Library of Congress Cataloging-in-Publication Data

LCCN: 2026032246 (CIP Data Pending)
ISBN13: 9798260028452
Isbn13Softcover: 9798260028469
EISBN13: 9798260028476
British Cataloguing in Publication Data
A Cataloguing in Publication record for this book is available from the British Library.

Table of Contents

Detailed Table of Contents

The security of critical infrastructures, such as energy grids and water treatment plants, depends on protecting Industrial Control Systems (ICS) and SCADA environments. The convergence of operational technology (OT) with information technology (IT) under Industry 4.0 introduces severe cyber risks, as demonstrated by incidents like Stuxnet and Colonial Pipeline. This paper examines the unique vulnerabilities of industrial protocols, analyzes major cyber-physical attacks, and reviews defense frameworks like ISA/IEC 62443 and NIST SP 800-82. It emphasizes strategies such as network segmentation, anomaly detection, and OT-specific incident response to enhance resilience. Future directions include zero-trust architectures and AI-driven threat detection to safeguard the foundations of modern society.

Smart cities now depend on connected sensors, edge platforms, ICS, SCADA systems, and cloud services to run essential operations like water treatment, traffic management, public transport, environmental monitoring, and public safety. While this connectivity boosts efficiency and visibility, it also creates a much larger cyber-physical attack surface where a single breach can quickly disrupt critical services. Traditional perimeter-based cybersecurity is no longer enough in these complex, fragmented environments. This chapter presents a practical framework for building cyber resilience in smart city government services. Drawing on IoT security, edge computing, and critical infrastructure research, it argues that real resilience means the ability to anticipate, withstand, recover, and adapt. The chapter introduces a layered governance and engineering model, supported by seven tables and five figures, and ends with a maturity model and clear recommendations for municipal leaders.

Government initiatives that use innovative technology has been able to give residents improved services by more effectively using fewer resources and allowing for real-time sound management of public resources through the use of IoT sensors located in public infrastructure. However, there are now emerging threats to the data collected from IoT devices, device authentication and an increasing concern about criminal activity involving the hacking of IoT devices as a result of the growing quantity of IoT machines. This chapter describes how IoT enables smart cities through applications in urban management areas, transportation, utilities and the healthcare industry. In addition to providing security measures for the protection of IoT devices, networks, and the integrity of data collected such as encryption, strong authentication and lifetime support; a critical evaluation of the security vulnerabilities in the IoT ecosystem will also be presented.

Overall, smart cities have raised a number of global questions in response to traditional urbanization. However, due to their complexity and diversity, as well as their direct impact on transportation systems, sustainable traffic management within smart cities has often been overlooked by researchers. This study focuses on developing a sustainable framework and leveraging Internet of Things (IoT) and Intelligent Transportation System (ITS) technologies to address traffic challenges in smart cities. Traffic management in such cities, which feature both connected automated vehicles and human-driven vehicles, is approached through a dual mechanism. This strategy employs modeling, analysis, and decision-making processes built upon prior research findings to effectively respond to traffic-related issues.

The objective of this chapter is to design, implement, and evaluate an end-to-end auditing pipeline that enables agencies to release synthetic public datasets with quantified privacy risk, analytical utility, and structural fidelity. The approach frames release as a governance decision under explicit threat models, compares generator portfolios, and produces multiple replicas to estimate uncertainty. Utility is assessed through statistical fidelity and task-based benchmarks, while risk is tested via adversary simulations. Topological data analysis audits latent-space geometry using persistence summaries and diagram distances, including subgroup and temporal-window checks. Results deliver defensible, reproducible evidence for trustworthy, secure data sharing in smart-government settings.

This chapter presents a reproducible and auditable Python pipeline for Intrusion Detection Systems (IDS) in government network and service telemetry under privacy, governance, and operational-cost constraints. It uses synthetic telemetry to support experimentation without exposing sensitive logs, but it treats synthetic utility as an empirical question rather than an assumed improvement. Classical unsupervised

Preface

INTRODUCTION

Governments around the world are undergoing a profound digital transformation that is reshaping how public services are delivered, how citizens interact with institutions, and how policy decisions are developed and implemented. Advances in cloud computing, artificial intelligence, data analytics, blockchain, digital identity platforms, and interconnected infrastructures have enabled unprecedented opportunities for innovation, efficiency, transparency, and citizen engagement. At the same time, the increasing reliance on digital technologies has elevated concerns regarding cybersecurity, privacy, governance, and operational resilience. As public institutions become more dependent on digital ecosystems, ensuring the security and resilience of government infrastructure has become a strategic imperative.

Secure Digital Infrastructure and Cyber Resilience in Smart Government Systems was developed to address these emerging challenges and opportunities. This volume brings together diverse perspectives from researchers, practitioners, policymakers, and technology experts who are actively engaged in advancing secure digital transformation across the public sector. Through multidisciplinary contributions, the book examines the critical role of digital infrastructure and cyber resilience in supporting trustworthy, efficient, and sustainable government systems.

The central focus of this volume is the intersection of cybersecurity, digital innovation, and public sector modernization. As governments seek to leverage advanced technologies to improve governance and public service delivery, they must simultaneously safeguard critical infrastructure, protect sensitive data, maintain regulatory compliance, and preserve public trust. The chapters in this book explore these interconnected issues through theoretical analyses, practical frameworks, empirical studies, and real-world case examples that provide valuable insights into the evolving landscape of digital government.

A key objective of this publication is to compile innovative research and practical experiences that support the secure implementation of digital technologies within government environments. The contributors examine emerging models, risks, and solutions related to cybersecurity governance, digital identity management, artificial intelligence–driven public administration, blockchain applications, privacy protection, and resilient digital infrastructures. Collectively, these contributions highlight strategies for strengthening institutional preparedness, mitigating cyber threats, and fostering adaptive governance capable of responding to rapidly changing technological and security conditions.

Throughout the volume, particular attention is given to the concept of cyber resilience. While traditional cybersecurity approaches focus on prevention and defense, cyber resilience emphasizes the capacity of institutions to anticipate, withstand, recover from, and adapt to cyber incidents and disruptions. In an era characterized by increasingly sophisticated cyber threats, geopolitical uncertainty, and growing digital interdependence, resilience has emerged as a foundational requirement for effective digital governance. The chapters presented in this book demonstrate how resilient digital infrastructures can support continuity of operations, strengthen public confidence, and enable sustainable innovation across government systems.

Although several contributions draw upon experiences and developments from Latin America, the themes addressed throughout this volume have global significance. Governments across all regions face common challenges related to digital transformation, cybersecurity risk management, regulatory compliance, ethical technology adoption, and citizen trust. The frameworks, lessons, and recommendations presented in this book therefore offer valuable guidance for a broad international audience seeking to advance secure and resilient digital government initiatives.

This publication is intended for researchers, academics, government officials, policymakers, IT managers, cybersecurity professionals, graduate students, consultants, civic technology innovators, and educators. It is designed to serve both as a scholarly resource and as a practical reference for those involved in the planning, implementation, management, and evaluation of secure digital solutions within the public sector. Readers will find a diverse collection of perspectives that illuminate both the opportunities and challenges associated with building resilient smart government ecosystems.

As editors, we extend our sincere gratitude to the authors who contributed their expertise and insights to this volume. Their work reflects the growing importance of interdisciplinary collaboration in addressing the complex technological, organizational, legal, and societal dimensions of digital transformation. We also thank the reviewers and publishing team whose efforts helped ensure the quality and relevance of this publication.

It is our hope that *Secure Digital Infrastructure and Cyber Resilience in Smart Government Systems* will contribute meaningfully to ongoing discussions surrounding digital governance, cybersecurity, and public sector innovation. By fostering greater understanding of secure digital infrastructures and resilient governance models, this book seeks to support the development of trusted, adaptive, and future-ready government systems capable of meeting the evolving needs of citizens in the digital age.

ORGANIZATION OF THE BOOK

Chapter 1, "Industrial Cyber Defense and Security in Critical Infrastructures," examines the growing cybersecurity challenges facing critical infrastructure sectors that rely on Industrial Control Systems (ICS) and Supervisory Control and Data Acquisition (SCADA) environments. The chapter explores how the convergence of operational technology and information technology under Industry 4.0 has expanded the cyber threat landscape, exposing essential services such as energy and water systems to increasingly sophisticated attacks. Through an analysis of notable cyber incidents, security standards, and defense frameworks, the authors highlight practical strategies for strengthening industrial cyber resilience and discuss emerging approaches such as zero-trust architectures and AI-driven threat detection.

Chapter 2, "Securing Smart Cities and Critical Infrastructure: Cyber Resilience for IoT, Sensors, and ICS/SCADA in Government Services," addresses the cybersecurity implications of increasingly connected smart city ecosystems. The chapter explores how government services now depend on networks of sensors, edge computing platforms, industrial control systems, and cloud technologies to manage critical operations. Recognizing the limitations of traditional security approaches, the authors propose a comprehensive framework for cyber resilience that emphasizes the ability to anticipate, withstand, recover from, and adapt to cyber threats. The chapter provides practical governance and engineering recommendations that can guide municipal leaders in developing resilient and secure smart city infrastructures.

Chapter 3, "IoT-Enabled Smart Infrastructure: Securing Connected Devices in Public Service Delivery," focuses on the transformative role of Internet of Things technologies in modern public service delivery. The chapter examines how connected devices support urban management, transportation systems, public utilities, and healthcare services while simultaneously introducing new security vulnerabilities. The author evaluates key risks related to device authentication, data integrity, and unauthorized access, and presents security measures designed to protect IoT ecosystems. By balancing innovation with risk management, this chapter offers important insights into the secure deployment of IoT-enabled public infrastructure.

Chapter 4, "IoT-Enabled Intelligent Traffic Management Framework for Smart Cities," explores the role of intelligent transportation systems in addressing the complex mobility challenges associated with rapid urbanization. The chapter presents a sustainable traffic management framework that integrates Internet of Things technologies with advanced transportation systems to improve traffic flow and operational efficiency. Special attention is given to the coexistence of connected automated vehicles and conventional human-driven vehicles within smart city environments. Through a combination of modeling, analysis, and decision-making mechanisms, the chapter demonstrates how emerging technologies can contribute to more sustainable and responsive urban transportation networks.

Chapter 5, "Topological Auditing of Synthetic Public Data for Trustworthy Governance," introduces an innovative framework for evaluating the quality, privacy, and reliability of synthetic public datasets. The chapter presents an end-to-end auditing pipeline that enables government agencies to release data while balancing transparency, privacy protection, and analytical usefulness. By incorporating adversarial risk assessments, statistical fidelity measures, and topological data analysis techniques, the authors establish a rigorous methodology for assessing structural integrity and uncertainty within synthetic datasets. The chapter contributes to ongoing efforts to support trustworthy and secure data-sharing practices in digital government environments.

Chapter 6, "Topological Signatures for Synthetic Intrusion Detection in Government Networks," examines the application of advanced analytical techniques to intrusion detection within government network environments. The chapter presents a reproducible and auditable framework that leverages synthetic telemetry data to evaluate intrusion detection systems while preserving operational privacy. Through the integration of machine learning methods, anomaly detection techniques, forecasting models, and topological analysis, the authors assess system performance under a variety of operational conditions. The chapter also addresses practical considerations for deployment within public-sector security operations centers, emphasizing transparency, interoperability, and evidence-based cybersecurity decision-making.

Chapter 7, "Digital Governance Models and Technological Sovereignty in the Face of Emerging Threats," explores the strategic relationship between digital governance and technological sovereignty in an increasingly complex geopolitical environment. The authors argue that effective governance frameworks must prioritize coordination, interoperability, and public value creation while simultaneously strengthening national control over critical data and digital infrastructure. The chapter highlights how technological sovereignty has become a central component of cybersecurity, resilience, and institutional autonomy, offering valuable perspectives on how governments can navigate emerging digital threats while preserving their capacity for innovation and independent decision-making.

Chapter 8, "International and Local Legal Frameworks for Cybersecurity and Regulatory Advances and Gaps," concludes the volume by examining the evolving legal and regulatory landscape surrounding cybersecurity and digital technologies. The chapter analyzes international and domestic laws, technical standards, and policy frameworks that seek to address emerging cyber risks while supporting technological innovation. The authors identify significant regulatory advances as well as persistent gaps that hinder effective governance and infrastructure protection. By emphasizing the importance of coherent, adaptable, and ethically grounded regulatory frameworks, the chapter underscores the critical role of law and policy in strengthening cyber resilience and promoting sustainable digital development.

CONCLUDING REMARKS

The chapters presented in *Secure Digital Infrastructure and Cyber Resilience in Smart Government Systems* collectively underscore the critical importance of building secure, resilient, and trustworthy digital foundations for modern governance. As governments continue to accelerate digital transformation initiatives, the protection of critical infrastructure, public services, data assets, and citizen trust has become inseparable from the pursuit of innovation and operational efficiency. The contributions in this volume demonstrate that cyber resilience is no longer a supplementary consideration but a fundamental requirement for the successful operation of smart government systems.

Throughout this book, our contributors have examined a diverse range of topics that shape the evolving landscape of digital governance and cybersecurity. From industrial control systems and smart city infrastructures to Internet of Things ecosystems, intelligent transportation networks, synthetic data governance, intrusion detection frameworks, technological sovereignty, and cybersecurity regulation, the chapters highlight both the opportunities and challenges associated with increasingly interconnected public-sector environments. Together, they provide a comprehensive perspective on how governments can proactively address emerging threats while continuing to leverage advanced technologies to improve public service delivery.

A recurring theme across the volume is the need to move beyond traditional security approaches toward more adaptive and resilient models of governance. Cyber resilience requires not only robust technical safeguards but also effective governance structures, strategic leadership, regulatory alignment, risk-aware decision-making, and continuous innovation. The contributors emphasize that resilience is built through preparedness, transparency, collaboration, and the ability to anticipate and recover from disruptions in increasingly complex digital ecosystems.

The chapters also reinforce the growing importance of trust in digital government systems. Citizens, organizations, and public institutions must have confidence that digital services are secure, reliable, and designed to protect privacy and public interests. Whether through secure infrastructure design, responsible data-sharing practices, advanced threat detection capabilities, or effective legal and regulatory frameworks, the authors demonstrate that trust remains one of the most valuable assets in the digital transformation process.

Another important insight emerging from this volume is the interdisciplinary nature of cyber resilience. Addressing contemporary cybersecurity challenges requires collaboration among technologists, policymakers, legal experts, public administrators, researchers, and industry stakeholders. The diverse perspectives represented throughout this book illustrate how technical, organizational, legal, and societal considerations must work together to create sustainable and secure digital government ecosystems.

As editors, we hope this volume serves as a valuable resource for researchers, government leaders, cybersecurity professionals, policymakers, educators, and students seeking to better understand the evolving relationship between digital infrastructure and public-sector resilience. The frameworks, case studies, methodologies, and recommendations presented throughout these chapters offer practical guidance for strengthening security, enhancing governance, and supporting innovation across a wide range of government contexts.

The future of smart government will depend on the ability of institutions to embrace technological advancement while safeguarding the systems and services upon which societies increasingly rely. By fostering greater understanding of cyber resilience, secure digital infrastructure, and responsible governance, this book contributes to ongoing efforts to build adaptive, secure, and citizen-centered public institutions capable of thriving in an increasingly digital world.

Miguel Ángel Ruiz Jaimes
Universidad Politécnica del Estado de Morelos, Mexico

José Miguel Liceaga Ortiz De La Peña
Universidad Politécnica de Pachuca, Mexico

Chapter 1
Industrial Cyber Defense and Security in Critical Infrastructures

Josue Roman Martinez-Mireles
http://orcid.org/0000-0002-3167-5209
Universidad Politécnica de Pachuca, Mexico

Jazmin Rodriguez-Flores
http://orcid.org/0000-0002-3313-0325
Universidad Politécnica de Pachuca, Mexico

Rafael Alfonso Figueroa-Diaz
Instituto Tecnológico de Sonora, Mexico

Marco Antonio García-Márquez
http://orcid.org/0000-0002-0644-4839
Universidad Politécnica de Pachuca, Mexico

Brenda Berenice Garcia-Escorza
http://orcid.org/0009-0009-1440-3306
Universidad Politécnica de Pachuca, Mexico

ABSTRACT

The security of critical infrastructures, such as energy grids and water treatment plants, depends on protecting Industrial Control Systems (ICS) and SCADA environments. The convergence of operational technology (OT) with information technology (IT) under Industry 4.0 introduces severe cyber risks, as demonstrated by incidents like Stuxnet and Colonial Pipeline. This paper examines the unique vulnerabilities of industrial protocols, analyzes major cyber-physical attacks, and reviews defense

DOI: 10.4018/979-8-2600-2845-2.ch001

frameworks like ISA/IEC 62443 and NIST SP 800-82. It emphasizes strategies such as network segmentation, anomaly detection, and OT-specific incident response to enhance resilience. Future directions include zero-trust architectures and AI-driven threat detection to safeguard the foundations of modern society.

1. INTRODUCTION

Critical infrastructures make up the skeleton of society since they support such vital services as the production and distribution of power, water treatment, transportations, health care, manufacturing, and telecommunication. In this regard, smooth functioning of all these areas is crucial for the economy and safety. Thus, any disturbances to critical infrastructures can lead to multiple ripple effects across several interdependent sectors, bringing about major implications on social, economic, and operational levels (Agius et al., 2020).

In its turn, the development of digital transformation strategies has completely transformed industry. Implementation of Industry 4.0 solutions, involving such innovations as IIoT technologies, cloud solutions, artificial intelligence, machine learning, and complex analytics, brought about higher efficiency and automation in operations and better decision-making. Meanwhile, these advances increased the attack surface of industries, making them more susceptible to sophisticated cyber attacks (Babic et al., 2022; Georgiev & Dimitrova, 2024).

Traditionally, Operational Technology (OT) systems were created as closed networks that employed proprietary communication standards and had minimal connectivity with external devices and networks. At present, however, modern industrial solutions tend to combine OT systems with Information Technology (IT) systems in order to provide for greater visibility, remote control, and optimization of operations. While the integration of these two systems brings numerous advantages, it also creates new cybersecurity threats that have to be mitigated using special approaches that differ from those used traditionally (Stouffer et al., 2020; Knowles et al., 2021).

Differing from IT systems, where cybersecurity threats usually lead to financial losses or reputation damage, industrial solutions place a lot of emphasis on availability and continuity. Consequently, cyber attacks aimed at disrupting ICS and SCADA systems will lead to much more serious consequences than mere data theft. These attacks could result in service outages, damages to property, environmental hazards, and casualties. Various cybersecurity breaches, such as the notorious Stuxnet, the Ukrainian power grid attack, TRITON, and the Colonial Pipeline ransomware attack, prove that hackers can effectively target industrial solutions (Karnouskos, 2020; Krause et al., 2021).

In addition, the increased interconnection of the industrial estate via IIoT creates even more risks. Although there are benefits like improved surveillance, predictive maintenance, and operations, there are also more vulnerabilities that may be used by malicious hackers for their purposes. Therefore, cybersecurity cannot be seen just as a technical aspect any longer but should be included into the company's governance and risk management systems as well (Georgiev & Dimitrova, 2024; Srivastav et al., 2025).

Thus, for ensuring effective industrial cyber defense, one should adopt a holistic approach that includes the use of various methods and techniques. For example, according to recent studies, the protection of critical infrastructures cannot be achieved without implementing advanced cybersecurity systems along with fostering proactive cybersecurity culture among workers (Mazzolin & Madni, 2022; Umscheid et al., 2022).

Considering the significance of critical infrastructures in today's world and the advancement in cyber-attacks, it is important to assess the currently available defense systems and develop novel techniques to make the cyber networks more resilient. The present chapter looks into the cybersecurity problems in industrial settings, evaluates the changing nature of cyber threats to critical infrastructure and the current status of the defense system in the light of technology, regulation and policy measures adopted by organizations to improve the security of their Industrial Control System.

Figure 1. Categories of Essential Critical Infrastructure Workers.

(Cook, W. 2020)

2. CRITICAL INFRASTRUCTURE ECOSYSTEMS AND INTERDEPENDENCIES

Critical infrastructures consist of physical and digital components, structures, facilities, and networks that are vital for ensuring the economic prosperity, security, health, and well-being of the society by providing such essential services as energy generation and distribution, water supply, healthcare, transport, telecommunication, manufacturing, and emergency services. Due to their fundamental importance, any disruption within the realm of critical infrastructures may have dire effects on regions, nations, and even international stability (Agius et al., 2020).

As a result of rapid digitalization of various processes within industrial operations, critical infrastructures have become complex cyber-physical systems, unlike what they used to be. Historically, such infrastructures were intended to work independently and were minimally connected to other systems. The development of Information Technology (IT), Operational Technology (OT), Industrial Control Systems (ICS), Supervisory Control and Data Acquisition (SCADA) systems, as well as Industrial Internet of Things (IIoT) has resulted in a major change in critical infrastructure architecture. Alongside efficiency and increased automation, these developments have caused new challenges in terms of cybersecurity (Fovino et al., 2021; Stouffer et al., 2020).

One of the key features of contemporary critical infrastructures is their high level of interdependence. The diagram of workers across different areas (figure 1) shows the roles people play to keep systems safe and running (Ene I. & Savu D., 2023). The energy systems provide telecommunications and transport networks, while water treatment facilities require electricity supply and communication networks. In addition, health care organizations rely on the steady flow of energy, communication, and digital information networks. Therefore, an interruption in any of these sectors results in cascading effects leading to significant consequences for the functioning of other interconnected industries due to both operational issues and cyber threats (Agius et al., 2020).

Cybersecurity in the context of critical infrastructures refers to the convergence of cyberspace and physical reality. Contrary to traditional computer networks, critical infrastructures are characterized by the occurrence of the physical consequences resulting from cyber events. These can include failures of equipment and networks, disruptions in the operations of the organization, harm to the environment, and negative impacts on human safety. This means that the focus of cybersecurity activities in the case of critical infrastructures should be on ensuring safety and reliability along with confidentiality and integrity (Sridhar et al., 2012; Fovino et al., 2021). The bar chart in Figure 2, displays key metrics on the perception and reality of cybersecurity threats facing industrial control systems (ICS) from 2019 to 2023. The data illustrates an increasing perception of threat levels, highlights gaps in preparedness with incident response plans, shows ongoing challenges with unpatched vulnerabilities, and points to the occurrence of successful ransomware attacks in 2023.

Figure 2. Perception and reality of cybersecurity threats facing industrial control systems 2019-2023

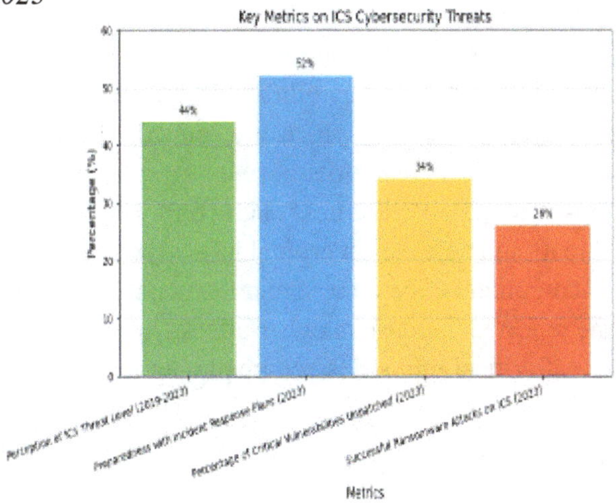

(Claroty, 2023)

The energy industry is perhaps one of the most strategic aspects of critical infrastructure. Contemporary electricity production, transmission, and distribution depend heavily on digital technology to maximize its efficiency. This aspect has made modern power grids vulnerable to cyber-attacks that can interfere with their operations and potentially affect other dependent industries. The issue of cybersecurity challenges facing the energy sector and smart grids has been a constant topic of research (Krause et al., 2021; Nafees et al., 2023).

Just like the energy industry, water and wastewater treatment have evolved significantly to incorporate more technology into their systems. Although there are many benefits of automating water and wastewater control processes, this trend comes with risks since these systems have become a potential target for cyber criminals. It has become clear that cybersecurity threats exist within the water and wastewater infrastructure systems (Bello et al., 2023).

There have been substantial developments in technology used in healthcare infrastructure, including electronic health records, connected medical devices, cloud-based systems, and high-end communications systems. Even though these technological advancements improve the provision of quality patient care, they also lead to increased vulnerabilities to potential attacks since such infrastructures possess large amounts of personal data. In recent years, several cyberattacks have shown the dangers of failing to ensure cybersecurity in healthcare, thus the significance of maintaining security in such a life-critical system (Cook, 2020).

Another crucial industry is the transportation industry, which incorporates many technological systems. Some of the technologies incorporated include communications networks, intelligent transportation management systems, industrial control systems, and other systems. As such, any disruption of the communications network within these infrastructures can lead to significant economic losses and hinder mobility and transportation capabilities. The same can be observed within telecommunications infrastructures, which are crucial for enabling virtually all types of infrastructures. These networks have a key role to play during national emergencies (Agius et al., 2020). The next chart (figure 3) illustrates key statistics related to cyber threats and defenses in critical infrastructure for 2023. It shows the percentage of ICS computers affected by cyber threats, the growth of the UK cyber security sector, the reported increase in cyber-attacks on the manufacturing sector, and the percentage of critical industries equipped with incident response plans.

Figure 3. Statistics related to cyber threats and defenses in critical infrastructure for 2023.

(Cloete, M., 2024)

As the importance and interrelatedness of these fields cannot be understated, there is a need for an integrated and multi-disciplinary framework that combines cybersecurity governance, risk management, compliance, technological measures, and resilience in order to protect critical infrastructures. In today's fast-changing industrial landscape, where digital transformation processes continue to gain momentum, cybersecurity of critical infrastructures becomes one of the top priorities for governments and cybersecurity experts around the world (Fovino et al., 2021; Agius et al., 2020).

3. CYBER THREAT LANDSCAPE IN INDUSTRIAL ENVIRONMENTS

The cybersecurity environment of industrial operations has drastically changed over the last decade due to advancements such as digitalization of critical infrastructures and the integration of IT/OT systems. Although those improvements contributed to better efficiency and automation, it also increased the attack surface available to potential attackers. Thus, at present, industrial organizations need to deal with cyber threats that can negatively affect not only digital assets but physical processes (Pliatsios et al., 2020; Makrakis et al., 2021).

At the same time, unlike enterprise operations, security threats faced by industrial organizations take place in cyber-physical spaces. For instance, attacks on ICSs, SCADA systems, and other industrial systems pose physical risks because they can impair critical services, cause damage to infrastructure, affect the performance of safety functions, and harm people's health (Fovino et al., 2021; Giraldo et al., 2018). Considering that industrial infrastructures are becoming increasingly connected, it is necessary to study the new threat environment to create proper cybersecurity approaches.

3.1. Evolution of Cyber Threats Targeting Critical Infrastructure

Traditionally, the risks posed to critical infrastructures have revolved around malicious software attacks, insider abuse, or system malfunctions due to human errors. Nevertheless, increased connectivity between industrial and corporate IT networks coupled with the rise of Internet-based technologies has opened doors to more complicated attack schemes (Makrakis et al., 2021). Present-day hackers rely on innovative tactics such as recon operations, network expansion, escalating privileges, and disruptions of activities in an effort to fulfill their objectives which may range from profit making to geostrategic gains.

The emergence of the Stuxnet worm is probably one of the biggest achievements in terms of industrial cybersecurity attacks, which highlighted the possibility of creating software capable of tampering with industrial control systems and yet remaining undetectable. This milestone in history has changed the way people think about cybersecurity at the industrial level since it revealed a whole new threat that could damage physical property and compromise its performance.

Following attacks like those against the Ukrainian electricity infrastructure, the Triton malware attack and ransomware attacks on the energy and manufacturing sectors have also shown how advanced attackers are becoming in their operations targeting industrial networks. The implication is that cyber attacks on critical infrastructures are not only theoretical threats anymore but practical actions that can have far-reaching consequences for national security (Krause et al., 2021; Makrakis et al., 2021).

3.2. Threat Actors and Attack Motivations

The actors threatening industrial networks vary according to their level of advancement, motivation, and financial capacity. Nation-state-level actors are considered the most developed class of cyber attackers because of the level of their advancement, financing, and objectives. Nation-states often attack critical infrastructures during international crises for reasons such as gathering information or interfering with operations in order to achieve political goals (Ciekanowski et al., 2023).

The second category includes cybercriminal organizations whose main objective is earning money through different tactics. Recently, ransomware attacks have become popular among cybercriminal organizations in their attempts to extort money from their victims. The high frequency of ransomware attacks targeting industrial firms reflects the financial appeal of critical infrastructure (Cloete, 2024; ENE & SAVU, 2023).

Threats from insiders are also a major issue in industrial settings. They can be negligent, malicious, or accidental in their approach towards compromising critical systems via unauthorized actions or the use of credentials inappropriately. This makes insider issues another cybersecurity problem due to the highly privileged nature of operational staff (Knowles et al., 2021).

Hacktivists and cyberterrorists could also pose a threat to infrastructure facilities for the purpose of advancing an ideology, gaining public recognition, and undermining confidence in the government. While their capabilities differ immensely, they all add up to the already complex and unpredictable cybersecurity environment (Abbasi, 2020).

3.3. Common Attack Vectors in Industrial Systems

Industrial systems face several attack vectors through which adversaries are able to take advantage of their vulnerabilities, regardless of whether these relate to IT or

OT. The exploitation of security weaknesses in remote access systems constitutes one of the most common types of attack vectors. As companies begin to make use of remote monitoring and maintenance, this becomes an increasing risk (Stouffer et al., 2020).

Phishing attacks have remained a successful way for adversaries to gain their first foothold in targeted companies. This can be done by compromising user credentials and using social engineering methods to penetrate corporate networks and then move towards OT infrastructures.

A new category of supply chain compromises is gaining traction. Industrial entities often rely on external suppliers for services and goods such as vendors, software, hardware, and maintenance. Compromise of third-party products and services allows cyber adversaries indirect entry into critical environments, thus increasing the attack surface (Makrakis et al., 2021).

An increase in the use of IoT components by industrial firms has become an additional cybersecurity issue. Most IoT elements were initially engineered without sufficient consideration of cybersecurity measures; as such, they are vulnerable to various cyberattacks due to communication flaws, inadequate password protection, and insufficient patching strategies. Securing the increasingly connected industrial devices has therefore become essential in the modern era (Georgiev & Dimitrova, 2024).

3.4. Emerging Threats in Industry 4.0 Environments

The shift to Industry 4.0 has resulted in a rise in new threat categories related to such concepts as cloud computing, AI, edge computing, digital twins, and interconnectivity of an industrial ecosystem. Though all these tools help businesses benefit from their use, they also provide new vulnerabilities and additional attack surfaces for adversaries (Babic et al., 2022).

One of the emerging concerns regarding the cybersecurity environment is the merging of the worlds of IT and OT. Due to the separate development of security solutions for these areas, companies face such problems as insufficient visibility, lack of consistency in security policies, and other challenges. As a result, attackers target the vulnerabilities in integration and gain access to the organization's corporate network via operational networks (Nafees et al., 2023). Table 1 presents the earliest identified cases of cyberattacks directed at civilian facilities that impacted civilian populations and communities

The increasing importance of APTs in critical infrastructure sectors is another trend that has been observed lately. Advanced persistent threats imply conducting prolonged operations and achieving certain goals through covert actions to remain undetected. Therefore, the emergence of APTs highlights the necessity for consistent monitoring and other proactive measures (Asiri et al., 2023; Makrakis et al., 2021).

3.5. Implications for Industrial Cybersecurity

The dynamic nature of cyber threats highlights the importance of expanding industrial cybersecurity solutions beyond the basic perimeters of defense. The need to address interactions between cyber and physical processes requires the adoption of holistic cybersecurity risk management strategies that incorporate monitoring, vulnerability assessment, intelligence, employee training, and resilient architectural designs tailored towards industrial systems (Mazzolin & Madni, 2022).

The advancement of digitalization in infrastructure will likely lead to an escalation in the complexity and severity of threats that organizations may face. Therefore, comprehending the nature of existing and future threats is crucial in order to devise effective defensive measures for securing infrastructures against cyber attacks (Umscheid et al., 2022; Srivastav et al., 2025).

Table 1. Case Studies of Significant Cyberattacks

Cyberattack	Year	Impact	Target
Stuxnet	2010	Damage to approximately 1,000 centrifuges	Iran's Natanz nuclear facility
Ukraine Power Grid Attack	2015	Power outages affecting 230,000 customers	Ukrainian power distribution companies
Ukraine Power Grid Attack	2016	Significant disruptions and outages	Ukrainian power distribution companies
TRITON	2017	Targeted safety systems of a petrochemical plant	Saudi petrochemical plant

4. CYBER DEFENSE ARCHITECTURES AND RESILIENCE MECHANISMS

Given the increasing complexity and sophistication of cyber attacks directed against critical infrastructures, there is an evident need for more advanced defense architectures to ensure protection of both IT and OT infrastructure. Traditional approaches based on the concept of perimeter security become inadequate to secure modern industrial ecosystems, which incorporate various interconnected systems, IIoT technologies, cloud computing platforms, and cyber-physical systems continuously interacting with each other. Recent reports show that protecting these assets is necessary for public safety and the economic stability of nations; Kaspersky's Industrial CyberSecurity Solutions show how they implement specific plans for vulnerabilities in industrial systems (figure 4). This implies that an industrial environment needs to implement multilevel defense systems that encompass not only preventive measures but also detection, response, and recovery strategies (Mazzolin & Madni, 2022).

Modern approaches to cyber resilience not only involve preventing cybersecurity breaches but also require organizations to be able to predict, cope with, respond to, and recover from negative events affecting IT infrastructures while ensuring uninterrupted operation of critical processes. Such an approach becomes especially relevant for industrial environments where cyberattacks can lead to negative consequences related to physical processes and public safety concerns. Modern approaches to cybersecurity and cyber defense increasingly emphasize the necessity to create a flexible security posture combining technological, procedural, and governance approaches to cyber threats (Georgiev & Dimitrova, 2024).

Figure 4. Overview of Kaspersky's Industrial CyberSecurity Solutions

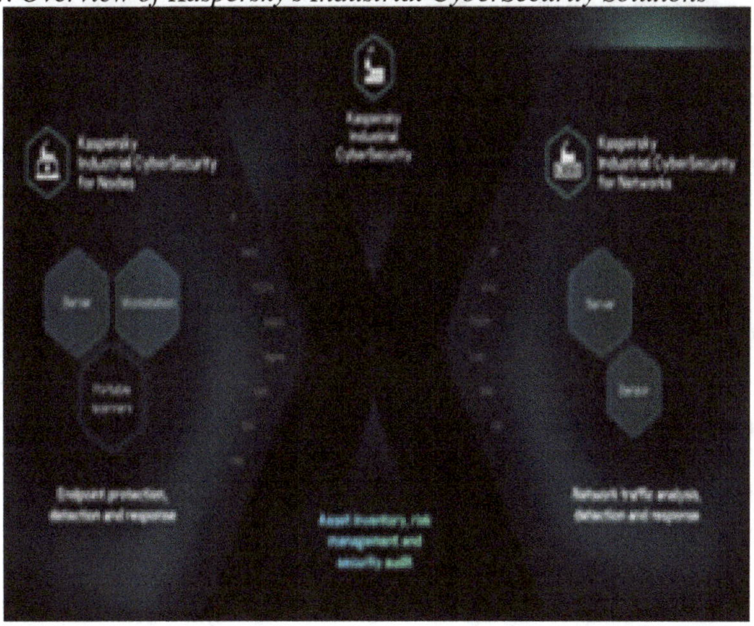

(Kaspersky, 2026)

4.1. Network Segmentation and Access Control

Network segmentation is considered one of the key concepts underlying the architecture of modern cybersecurity solutions in industry. The segregation of the network into multiple logical and physical segments allows limiting communication channels between devices and reducing opportunities for intruders to expand an attack into other parts of the interconnected system. As a result, the number of threats to be mitigated is reduced to a minimum, and possible risks from a potential incident are minimized (Almulla & Rahman, 2025).

In industry, segmentation involves isolating enterprise IT infrastructure from operational networks along with creating controlled connections between security zones. This approach allows implementing segment-specific security measures designed according to the specific operational needs and threat landscape. Furthermore, segmentation can be viewed as a tool for containing any cyber incidents by stopping the spread of malware, ransomware, or unauthorized activities in the industrial environment (Srivastav et al., 2025).

Access control solutions support network segmentation by making sure that only the right people, devices, and software interact with sensitive infrastructure. The increasing importance of implementing role-based access control, least privilege, multifactor authentication, and continuous identity validation has been well documented when it comes to addressing insider risks and minimizing the chances of unauthorized access. Both network segmentation and access control represent key elements of an industrial security framework that can provide not only protection but also compliance support (Almulla & Rahman, 2025; Babic et al., 2022).

Given the ongoing convergence of IT and OT infrastructure in many industrial enterprises, it becomes obvious why such architectural controls have been shown to be highly valuable in maintaining visibility and governance. Studies indicate that network segmentation is often one of the most powerful measures used to lower cyber risk levels (Srivastav et al., 2025).

4.2. Intrusion Detection and Prevention Systems for Industrial Control Systems

Given the constantly changing landscape of today's cyber threats, there is a need to maintain the ability to detect intrusions in real time to prevent any disruption of operation. Intrusion Detection and Prevention Systems (IDPS) customized for Industrial Control Systems (ICS) are among those solutions that are becoming critical parts of cybersecurity systems. In contrast to typical enterprise security solutions, industrial IDPS solutions are designed to account for the specificities of the OT environment, such as determinism of communication, outdated protocols, and real-time requirements (Bekzhanov et al., 2024).

Advancements in machine learning and artificial intelligence have allowed for the improvement of industrial IDPS solutions to a considerable extent. Modern industrial IDPSs are able to analyze network traffic as well as process data to detect any anomalies that would indicate intrusion into the system. This is achieved through the use of both supervised and unsupervised learning algorithms, which make it possible to detect unknown threats and minimize the risk of false positives characteristic of signature-based approaches (Pinto et al., 2023).

Additionally, with automated responses in place, it becomes easy for any organization to neutralize any threat at the earliest stage before it becomes an actual issue that threatens its operations. This is especially important in industries such as energy, wastewater processing, manufacturing, and transport, whereby even small issues result in significant economic and social impacts. Therefore, industrial IDPS solutions have come to be seen as crucial elements of any proactive cybersecurity approach, as shown by (Bekzhanov et al., 2024).

Industrial intrusion detection solutions help organizations comply with recognized international cybersecurity standards, among them being IEC 62443, which focuses on continuous monitoring, risk mitigation, and defense-in-depth systems. Cybersecurity compliance enhances both cybersecurity performance and governance practices, as noted by (Aziboledia & Egerton, 2023).

4.3. Incident Response and Recovery Planning

Although preventative and detective measures are fundamental aspects of any cyber defense strategy, it is impossible to design a security framework that removes all elements of cyber risk. It is for this reason that companies need to be ready to respond to any security incident by implementing disaster recovery procedures to help restore operations as quickly as possible after the event. Effective incident response is becoming a vital component of industrial cyber resilience due to the sophistication of cyberattacks (Reddy, 2025).

The process of responding to an industrial incident is quite different from a standard IT security incident because of the interdependence between cybersecurity and process control. The decision-making process needs to consider both the goals of security and the importance of keeping operations active at all times. This means that response frameworks in industrial settings usually involve multidisciplinary teams (Staves et al., 2020). Figure 6, shows that 70% of organizations have incident response plans, while only 50% test these plans regularly. The average response time to cyber incidents is 32 minutes, and 40% of incidents are resolved within 24 hours (CISA, 2024).

Figure 5. Metrics regarding incident response in 2023

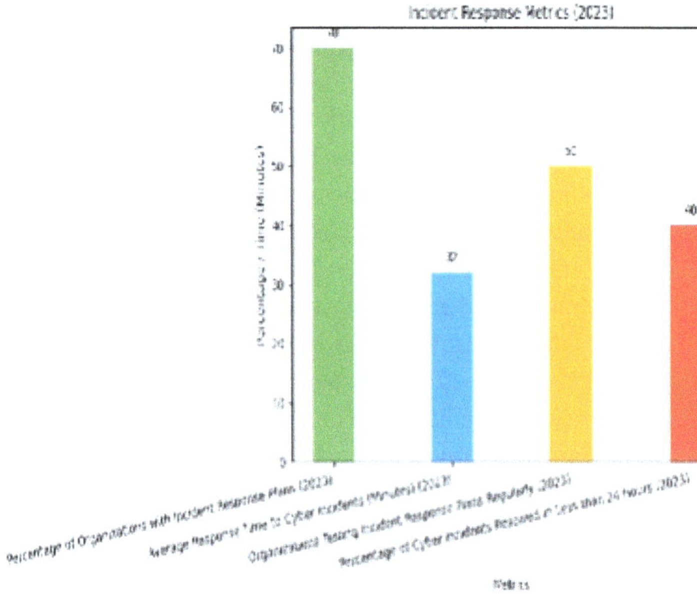

(CISA, 2024)

The response process usually involves phases of detection, analysis, containment, eradication, recovery, and post-incident analysis. Recent developments in the field have even expanded this model, suggesting resilience-based recovery models for Cyber-Physical Systems (CPS) consisting of post-attack detection and localization, isolation and pre-recovery preparation, system recovery itself, and performance evaluation phases (Ali & Sun, 2024). These frameworks allow organizations to apply a more methodical approach when it comes to decreasing downtimes and recovering systems after disruptions (Ali & Sun, 2024).

It is becoming increasingly clear to many organizations the significance of effective response processes to disruptive events, which can include ransomware attacks, supply chain disruptions, or advanced persistent threats. The implementation of response frameworks requires not only the development of processes for restoring affected systems but also testing drills, business continuity plans, workforce readiness, and leadership coordination. Organizations that assess and improve their readiness for incidents are more likely to be resilient enough to continue operating under challenging circumstances (Staves et al., 2020; Reddy, 2025).

4.4. Building Cyber Resilience Through Integrated Defense Architectures

It is no longer possible to achieve cyber resilience solely using independent cybersecurity measures in critical infrastructures. The key lies in combining prevention controls, constant surveillance mechanisms, incident response procedures, governance processes, and awareness activities within comprehensive cyber defense architectures. In other words, the idea is aligned with defense-in-depth concepts, which state that multiple layers of protection will minimize the risks and consequences of cyberattacks (Mazzolin & Madni, 2022).

Given the ongoing evolution of industrial systems due to digital transformation, companies have to develop flexible and adaptive cybersecurity strategies that would effectively counter new and increasingly sophisticated cyber risks. This can be accomplished by integrating network segmentation, access control, industrial intrusion detection, and response strategies aimed at increasing resilience against various threats. Overall, the creation of resilient cyber defense architectures is critical to the secure and uninterrupted functioning of the crucial services provided by today's societies (Georgiev & Dimitrova, 2024; Mazzolin & Madni, 2022).

5. REGULATORY, GOVERNANCE, AND COMPLIANCE FRAMEWORKS

The growing prevalence and sophistication of cyber attacks against critical infrastructures have transformed cybersecurity into a strategic issue of governance. As the reliance of industries on technology becomes increasingly significant, all involved parties have understood the need to design regulatory and governance frameworks able to ensure the safety of critical services through operational resilience. Therefore, cybersecurity governance has become an important part of security strategies on the national level and within the industrial sector (Kim, 2014; Zinchenko, 2025). Figure 7 displays key cybersecurity trends in the UK for 2023. It shows that 37% of UK firms have formal cybersecurity strategies, while AI-driven solutions have mitigated 20% of cyber incidents. Additionally, businesses allocate an average of 24% of their IT budgets to cybersecurity.

Figure 6. Cybersecurity trends in the UK for 2023

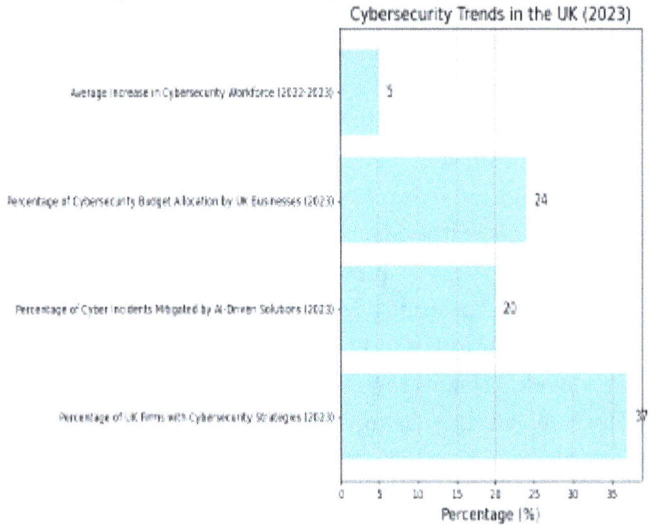

(Department for Science, Innovation and Technology, 2023).

The notion of cybersecurity governance involves all decisions that are made within critical infrastructures in regard to cybersecurity. In contrast to purely technical measures of ensuring cybersecurity, a governance framework includes objectives, responsibilities, resource allocations, and other aspects required for alignment with the organization's objectives. In the industrial sector, governance plays an especially important role.

5.1. Regulatory Frameworks for Critical Infrastructure Protection

Protecting critical infrastructures is an important aspect of regulating critical sectors. The importance of maintaining the security of these sectors has been realized by governments owing to their potential to create serious repercussions. Therefore, many regulatory frameworks have been formulated to ensure that all organizations operating in these critical infrastructures meet basic requirements concerning cybersecurity in the sectors of energy, transportation, healthcare, telecommunications, water management, and manufacturing (Palash, 2025).

These regulatory frameworks tend to enhance cybersecurity preparedness through risk assessments and security controls, amongst others. They promote the adoption of risk assessment strategies to improve preparedness for security threats while ensuring that critical infrastructure service delivery remains unaffected. Besides, regulation of cybersecurity in critical infrastructures acts as a catalyst for cybersecurity investments due to specific performance expectations (Sekonya & Sithungu, 2023).

International regulatory trends show increasing focus on cooperation between governments, industrial players, and cybersecurity agencies. Considering the interconnectedness of today's critical infrastructure, cybersecurity threats often go beyond state borders and necessitate coordinated action along with information exchange systems able to deal with such threats within several industries and jurisdictions (Zinchenko, 2025).

5.2. Governance Models and Risk Management

The concepts of governance approaches create the basis for developing a cybersecurity strategy and ensuring its sustainability. The governance approach includes establishing leadership roles and duties, adopting security policies, and incorporating cybersecurity issues into decisions made by organization leaders. Leadership commitment is always an essential factor that plays a significant role in ensuring cybersecurity maturity and resilience (Kim, 2014).

Risk management is the core component of cybersecurity governance. Through successful risk management procedures, companies can detect the assets that need protection, assess threats, and determine vulnerabilities. At industrial facilities, risk management practices should include both information security risks and the effects that any cyber incidents may have on safety and operations (Stouffer et al., 2020).

The increasing overlap of IT and OT settings underscores the importance of taking an integrated approach when implementing governance strategies. Businesses are supposed to guarantee that their cybersecurity policies cover all enterprise and operational settings, taking into consideration the peculiarities associated with industrial control systems. An integrated approach will allow companies to gain better visibility, manage risks, and implement controls efficiently (Sekonya & Sithungu, 2023).

Besides, today's approach to cybersecurity governance is focused on building resilience in organizations. Modern governance frameworks do not only aim at securing businesses but also at making them capable of responding to any cyberattacks effectively (Palash, 2025).

5.3. Compliance Standards and Industrial Cybersecurity Frameworks

The frameworks for compliance offer companies tools to deploy effective security controls and demonstrate their adherence to recognized best security practices. Among the most significant frameworks used for industrial cybersecurity purposes can be highlighted NIST Special Publication 800-82, a set of guidelines designed for security management of Operational Technology environments, such as industrial control systems and SCADA systems. According to the framework, risk management, network segmentation, continuous monitoring, and tailored incident response plans are essential for industrial security (Stouffer et al., 2020).

Another prominent cybersecurity framework is represented by the IEC 62443 series. This series has become a worldwide standard that covers the issues of security management and protection of systems used in industrial automation and control purposes. With its defense-in-depth strategy aimed at addressing cybersecurity across the entire lifecycle of systems, from system design to system operation and maintenance, IEC 62443 contributes significantly to industrial cybersecurity (Aziboledia & Egerton, 2023).

The following are some of the advantages that can accrue from complying with the above frameworks apart from the legal aspect. For instance, organizations that adopt cyber security frameworks often experience better risk awareness, greater resilience, improved governance, and stakeholder trust. Additionally, the mentioned frameworks allow the benchmarking of cybersecurity practices and foster continuous improvement efforts in cybersecurity (Sekonya & Sithungu, 2023).

Nevertheless, compliance is just one aspect of cybersecurity that should never be treated independently of other aspects. It is important to understand that the laws provide baseline requirements and not all-round security measures. This implies that mature cybersecurity frameworks incorporate compliance activities alongside their risk management and resilience plans in response to specific sectoral risks (Stouffer et al., 2020).

5.4. International Cooperation and Cybersecurity Policy Development

Due to the international nature of cyberspace threats, there is a need for significant cooperation between governments, regulatory bodies, private industry associations, and cybersecurity practitioners. The reliance on globally sourced materials, digital connectivity, and technology makes it difficult to mitigate risks in isolation (Zinchenko, 2025).

Organizations and cybersecurity agencies have an essential role to play in the dissemination of information, intelligence exchange, training, capacity development, and the formulation of cybersecurity policies. Cooperation ensures that all parties involved gain situational awareness, anticipate future dangers, and work together when responding to security threats (ENISA, 2024).

Institutions like the Cybersecurity and Infrastructure Security Agency (CISA) have made additional contributions towards the formation of policies, guidelines, and sector-specific recommendations geared toward enhancing cybersecurity in vital infrastructure sectors. The above-mentioned activities will enhance the adoption of proactive security measures through cooperation among both private and public stakeholders who are concerned with providing secure services (CISA, 2024).

With the advancement of cyber threats, international cybersecurity policy development is bound to play a very important role in promoting resilience in various nations around the world. In the coming years, future regulatory activities are projected to concentrate on aspects such as supply chain security, resilience against cyber threats, and incident reporting, among others.

5.5. The Strategic Role of Governance in Cyber Resilience

The success of cybersecurity efforts at critical infrastructure is directly dependent on the use of governance, regulation, and risk management to create a cyber resilience framework. Traditional security solutions are no longer effective at protecting industry from cyber-attacks due to their advanced nature. Organizations need governance approaches that promote sound judgment, ongoing risk assessment, regulatory compliance, and cybersecurity investments (Kim, 2014).

As the pace of digital transformation in the industrial sector accelerates, governance approaches will become more and more crucial for the purpose of ensuring that cybersecurity efforts meet organizational objectives, operational needs, and social demands. With the help of regulatory compliance, governance, and cyber resilience approaches, organizations can achieve improved resilience against cyberattacks while ensuring that critical infrastructures operate reliably and securely (Palash, 2025; Zinchenko, 2025).

6. EMERGING TECHNOLOGIES FOR INDUSTRIAL CYBERSECURITY

As a result of the increased complexity of cyberthreats to industrial facilities and systems, along with the fast-paced digitalization of critical infrastructures, there arises a need to use new technologies in the field of cybersecurity aimed at increasing the efficiency of detecting and responding to potential cyberincidents. The development of more sophisticated cyberthreats implies that traditional approaches to cybersecurity may be inadequate in the current context. Therefore, the adoption of novel technologies such as automation, artificial intelligence, analytics, and cyber-physical intelligence can be seen as a necessity (Babic et al., 2022).

Thanks to these technologies, industrial cybersecurity has shifted towards a more proactive and adaptive approach to ensuring security. The use of the mentioned technologies allows for continuous monitoring, predictive analysis, and automated decision-making in relation to any cyberthreats that an organization might be faced with (Georgiev & Dimitrova, 2024).

6.1. Artificial Intelligence and Machine Learning for Cyber Defense

One of the most important technological developments in cybersecurity architectures today is the emergence of artificial intelligence (AI) and machine learning (ML). With AI and ML, it becomes possible to analyze huge amounts of operational and network data, detect anomalies and patterns of attacks, and conduct decision-making that would be virtually impossible to do without using traditional methods of analysis (Govea et al., 2024).

Industrial cyber protection is also becoming widely used with the help of AI-based approaches. For instance, anomaly detection and predictive threats can be detected by means of ML models analyzing historical and real-time data on industrial processes, and then they can determine whether there is any deviation from regular processes that may indicate cyber attacks. Such approaches are extremely useful in operational technology systems as they may help avoid operational disruption and prevent dangerous situations (Pinto et al., 2023).

In addition, AI systems help alleviate the workload of cybersecurity staff by automating analysis work and prioritizing alerts based on risk levels. This improves the efficacy of SOCs and facilitates quick responses to incidents. Nevertheless, while possessing remarkable strengths, AI-powered cybersecurity solutions need prudent management in order to mitigate problems pertaining to the accuracy, data quality, interpretability, and possible manipulation of models (Govea et al., 2024).

6.2. Advanced Threat Detection and Situational Awareness

Being able to achieve comprehensive visibility over the industrial environment is becoming an essential prerequisite for proper cyber defense strategies. Modern platforms designed to detect advanced threats leverage data obtained from various sources, such as traffic networks, industrial sensors, endpoint devices, control systems, and threat intelligence services, providing comprehensive insight into organizational security.

According to recent academic publications, an important aspect of modern cyber defense strategy is gaining situational awareness in critical infrastructure. This is especially relevant for smart grids and other industrial systems that are highly connected (Nafees et al., 2023). Platforms responsible for cybersecurity situational awareness help detect abnormal conditions in operations, estimate possible threats, and make well-informed decisions when addressing security issues. Thus, situational awareness allows organizations to not only recognize technical peculiarities of cyber threats but also consider potential operational consequences of them.

Modern Security Information and Event Management (SIEM) solutions, SOAR technologies, and artificial intelligence-supported systems for monitoring are among those technological advancements that enhance the capability to detect cyber threats (Seceon, 2026).

6.3. Industrial Internet of Things Security

The Industrial Internet of Things has now become one of the key elements of any Industry 4.0 strategy, as it allows for real-time monitoring, prediction and maintenance, remote asset management, and optimization based on collected data. Nevertheless, the fast rise in the number of connected devices has led to the emergence of new cybersecurity risks that need specific protection strategies (Georgiev & Dimitrova, 2024).

The majority of IIoT devices lack computing power and adequate security features. In turn, they become susceptible to various cybersecurity issues related to the use of weak authentication methods, lack of encryption, ineffective updates, and insufficient controls that allow unauthorized access. Today, many attackers actively look for ways to infiltrate the IIoT devices to exploit other parts of the industrial system (Babic et al., 2022).

Thus, contemporary security approaches for IIoT devices are built on such critical components as authentication, encrypted communication, continuous monitoring and management of vulnerabilities, and network segmentation. Such protection mechanisms ensure the reduction of the potential risk to the organization and its infrastructure while still being able to benefit from IIoT technologies (Georgiev & Dimitrova, 2024).

6.4. Digital Twins and Cybersecurity Testing Environments

The use of Digital Twin technology has received much interest in recent times as an advanced solution that enhances cybersecurity measures in industries. With the help of Digital Twins, organizations create virtual images of their physical processes, thus creating opportunities for simulating operational activities, examining cyberattack scenarios, and estimating their effects on operations without disturbing the production process.

This creates an environment for proactive preparation for cyber incidents through simulation and testing of possible responses. In addition, the creation of digital twins makes it easier to train personnel about cybersecurity and increase awareness of complex cyber-physical processes in industrial organizations (Simola et al., 2023).

Just like Digital Twins, industrial cybersecurity testbeds have proven to be vital tools for experiment and workforce training. Through these platforms, organizations get opportunities to test new technologies in controlled environments, which is important for increasing cybersecurity (Simola et al., 2023).

6.5. Automation and Intelligent Security Operations

Automation has emerged as a key driver of current security operations. As the number of security incidents grows, companies have been struggling to conduct monitoring and respond to security situations via manual operations. Automated security tools can help to solve the problem of timely detection of threats, improve incident response workflow and increase operational effectiveness.

Intelligent security operations integrate automation, artificial intelligence, and orchestration solutions to develop an adaptive mechanism that is capable of reacting to attacks on the network almost instantly. Such systems allow companies to cut down on response time and ensure greater efficiency and resilience of operations (Seceon, 2026).

In addition, automation enables organizations to monitor their level of compliance with regulatory standards, conduct continuous vulnerability assessments and asset management activities. The larger and more complex the industrial system becomes, the greater the role of automation in conducting security operations (Kaspersky, 2026).

6.6. Future Directions for Industrial Cybersecurity Innovation

The future of industrial cybersecurity can be anticipated to be defined by developments in AI, cyber-physical systems, cloud, edge technologies, and big data analysis, among others. The use of emerging innovations presents substantial benefits concerning threat detection and management as well as enhanced cybersecurity; nonetheless, their utilization is accompanied by new security vulnerabilities that demand further exploration.

It is thus imperative that emerging cybersecurity technologies be recognized as elements of a broader framework involving the integration of governance, risk management, resilience planning, and human knowledge. Those companies that succeed in integrating cybersecurity practices with technological advancement will be more capable of securing critical infrastructures from ever-growing cyber attacks while facilitating the digitalization process in industrial contexts (Govea et al., 2024; Georgiev & Dimitrova, 2024).

In any case, the adoption of emerging innovations in the realm of cybersecurity technology entails an investment in the future security and resilience of critical infrastructures against cyber attacks.

7. CHALLENGES AND FUTURE RESEARCH DIRECTIONS

Despite the progress achieved by industry in relation to cybersecurity tools, architectures, regulations, among others, critical infrastructures are still encountering various challenges related to cybersecurity. This is due to the fast changes in cyber threat landscapes, system complexity, and rapid digitalization of the industrial environment. As a result, businesses are required not only to adjust their security measures to the new reality but also consider various limitations associated with technology, organization, legislation, and processes affecting the implementation of the current solutions (Mazzolin & Madni, 2022).

The interaction between IT and OT environments remains one of the main problems in industrial cybersecurity. While the combination of IT and OT provides benefits in terms of greater operational efficiency and automation processes, there are also some cybersecurity risks that need to be considered. Industrial infrastructures often involve a wide range of older equipment developed without cybersecurity in mind and cannot be easily upgraded or replaced due to its proprietary nature. Therefore, firms are forced to work with heterogeneous environments and integrate modern cybersecurity tools into their legacy system (Stouffer et al., 2020; Knowles et al., 2021).

7.1. Securing Legacy Industrial Systems

The legacy IT systems are entrenched in infrastructure systems due to their reliability, longevity, and the high cost of updating and replacing the current systems. Unfortunately, most legacy systems do not offer inherent security features such as proper authentication mechanisms, encryption, and safe system updates. Besides, constraints within operations may hinder the implementation of system updates, thereby making such systems vulnerable to attacks (Stouffer et al., 2020).

There is no doubt that the reliance on old technology will present a challenge for cybersecurity professionals trying to deploy advanced security solutions. Therefore, future studies should concentrate on devising an adaptive mechanism that allows securing legacy systems without causing any disruption in their operations. It would be advisable to investigate ways of using virtual patches, secure gateways, network segmentation, and other mitigating techniques to protect legacy industrial systems (Sekonya & Sithungu, 2023).

7.2. Managing the Complexity of IT-OT Convergence

Converging enterprise and operational networks have created more attack vectors for potential attackers, making cybersecurity more challenging than before. Industrial enterprises face issues such as visibility concerns, lack of cohesive security policies, asset fragmentation, and diverse operational objectives. All these aspects can impede the adoption of holistic cybersecurity practices, giving the attacker a chance to utilize the weaknesses within the system (Nafees et al., 2023).

These problems may be addressed through better governance strategies, enhanced cross-functional coordination, and designing new security architectures for the convergent environment. Further academic work should focus on the techniques for ensuring unified visibility, integrated risk assessment, and consolidated security operations (Knowles et al., 2021).

7.3. Artificial Intelligence: Opportunities and Limitations

AI and Machine Learning have become potent technologies for detecting threats, identifying anomalies, and performing other operations associated with cybersecurity. On the other hand, these developments present novel challenges associated with transparency, accountability, and trustworthiness. For example, many machine learning models function as black box decision makers, which might be hard to interpret in safety-sensitive industrial settings where such capabilities are required (Govea et al., 2024).

Moreover, AI-based cybersecurity solutions may become victims of adversarial attacks, such as data poisoning, manipulation of the machine learning algorithm, and evasion methods. Such developments make it imperative to conduct research aimed at building trustable AI systems and explaining how cybersecurity solutions work (Pinto et al., 2023).

With the use of artificial intelligence technologies expanding in the field of cybersecurity, further research will be needed in order to address emerging challenges in this setting.

7.4. Workforce Development and Human Factors

Despite advances in technology in cybersecurity of industries, human factors play an essential role in creating vulnerabilities within organizations. Human error, poor training, configuration issues, or lack of awareness on emerging threats have often contributed to cybersecurity incidents. The increase in the complexity of industrial operations raises another challenge for organizations to address due to the need for specialists who can handle cybersecurity as well as operational technologies (Knowles et al., 2021).

Shortage of competent cybersecurity personnel is prevalent among many organizations. There has been a shortage of experts trained in Industrial Control Systems, SCADA systems, and cyber-physical systems. As a result, there have been calls for more focus on workforce development for cybersecurity professionals. Future research should focus on ways to develop cybersecurity knowledge and skills through education, training, simulations, and human-centered security (Simola et al., 2023).

7.5. Cyber Resilience in an Era of Increasing Interconnectivity

The proliferation of Industrial IoT, cloud computing solutions, edge computing systems, and interconnected supply chains has brought about fundamental changes in the cybersecurity environment of critical infrastructure. While these innovations offer numerous advantages, their deployment brings along additional opportunities for attackers to exploit weaknesses and launch cyber attacks against organizations. This complexity poses challenges to conventional approaches to risk management and necessitates adopting new approaches to resilience engineering (Georgiev & Dimitrova, 2024).

In particular, securing the supply chain is becoming a crucial problem that needs to be addressed. Enterprises find themselves relying on external software vendors, hardware manufacturers, and partners whose cyber security capabilities may affect the enterprise's own position in cyberspace. Future research needs to pay attention to refining risk assessment methods for supply chains and improving third-party assurance methods (Umscheid et al., 2022).

7.6. Emerging Research Priorities

In this respect, some promising research directions for future work include, but are not limited to, the following. For starters, the creation of resilient cybersecurity architectures able to adapt to changing threat scenarios is an essential area requiring more attention. Specifically, a resilient architecture must be equipped with a mechanism for assessing threats, responding to them automatically, and conducting predictive analysis.

Additionally, efforts must be focused on developing models and methods for cyber-physical resilience assessment and risk estimation that are more efficient at capturing the interaction of digital and physical processes within an IT system. Such an approach will make it easier for decision-makers to devise effective mitigation measures.

Third, there is a need for studies exploring the role played by new technologies such as digital twins, self-governed cybersecurity measures, intelligent threat detection platforms, and explainable AI when incorporated in industrial cybersecurity architectures. These technologies have high potential for making industrial cybersecurity systems effective and resilient as well as enabling the use of proactive cyber defense measures (Simola et al., 2023; Govea et al., 2024).

Finally, an interdisciplinary approach to industrial cybersecurity issues incorporating cybersecurity, engineering, risk management, public policy, and organizational governance will become necessary in dealing with complex challenges faced in protecting industrial infrastructures. Given the integrated nature of modern industrial environments, a multifaceted response approach needs to be developed for achieving balance between innovation, efficiency, compliance, and resilience (Srivastav et al., 2025).

7.7 Toward a Resilient and Adaptive Industrial Cybersecurity Ecosystem

The future success of industrial cybersecurity will not solely hinge on innovation in technology, but rather on the capacity of organizations to come up with adaptive, resilient, and sustainable security systems. In light of increasingly complex cyber threats, there is a need for organizations to go beyond traditional reactive security strategies to those that focus on resilience.

Solving the problems presented above requires a lot of investments in technology, governance, education, and joint research projects. By combining these efforts, critical infrastructure industries will be able to cope with new cyber attacks as well as deliver their services without interruption (Umscheid et al., 2022; Srivastav et al., 2025).

8. CONCLUSIONS

With the rising trend of digitizing critical infrastructures, there has been a paradigm shift in the nature of cybersecurity concerns within the industrial sector. On one hand, the use of new-age technologies such as IIoT devices, artificial intelligence, cloud computing, and automation in Industry 4.0 has brought about improvements in performance efficiency and decision-making. On the other hand, there has been an increase in the scope of attacks, creating new challenges to be addressed. Thus, cybersecurity has become a crucial element for secure functioning of critical infrastructures.

The above review has discussed the emerging cybersecurity issues concerning critical infrastructures. It is evident from this discussion that cyber attacks against ICSs, SCADAs, and other OTs have become increasingly complex over time. In other words, the modern cybersecurity threat has moved far beyond being simple technical attacks because it now poses serious consequences on various fronts such as operational, economical, environmental, and social. Various events including the Stuxnet worm, Ukrainian power grid attacks, TRITON attacks, and ransomware attacks against critical infrastructure sectors demonstrate the potential damage caused by these cybersecurity incidents (Karnouskos, 2020; Makrakis et al., 2021).

In addition, it is highlighted that cybersecurity solutions applied to industrial settings have to involve multiple components including technical security measures, governance, regulatory compliance, readiness of the personnel, and other aspects of cyber resilience. The architecture of cybersecurity should be designed on the principles of network segmentation, access control, monitoring, intrusion detection, and incident response capabilities, forming a critical backbone of industrial cybersecurity. Nonetheless, it would be insufficient to focus on technical aspects of cybersecurity only as sustainable cybersecurity implies organizational commitment, executive leadership, risk-based decision-making, and adaptation to constantly emerging threats (Stouffer et al., 2020; Mazzolin & Madni, 2022).

It could be noted that emerging technologies may gain greater significance in the development of future approaches to industrial cybersecurity. In particular, the application of artificial intelligence, machine learning technologies, intelligent platforms, digital twins, security automation, situational awareness of cyber-physical processes, and other innovations can contribute significantly to enhanced threat detection and more effective response capability. Nevertheless, these technologies will present challenges concerning complexity, transparency, interoperability, and assurance which require further attention.

The results generated by this literature review emphasize the significance of good governance and proper regulation in helping achieve cyber security maturity within critical infrastructures. Guidance through international standards, risk management, and other collaborative approaches can be instrumental in fostering organizational resilience and uniform security practices. Cooperation between governments, industry players, regulatory bodies, and academia is necessary in addressing cybersecurity challenges amid an environment where attacks cross borders between organizations and even nations (Sekonya & Sithungu, 2023; Zinchenko, 2025).

Although substantial progress has been made in industrial cyber security, there are still unresolved challenges that need attention. The problems with legacy systems, convergence of IT and OT, reliance on supply chains, shortage of skilled labor, and increased capabilities of cyber attackers are some of the issues affecting critical infrastructure sectors. These concerns necessitate innovation, education, resilience, and cross-disciplinary research (Knowles et al., 2021; Umscheid et al., 2022).

In the coming years, the future of industrial cybersecurity will lie in the creation of adaptive and resilient security ecosystems that can anticipate, resist, respond to, and recover from any cyber disruptions. Instead of limiting itself only to preventing threats, companies will have to take a more holistic approach towards industrial cybersecurity and strike a proper balance between operational efficiency, technology innovation, compliance, and resilience. This will help companies in ensuring the security and resilience of critical infrastructures and provide the essential services needed for the stable functioning of economies and societies.

Indeed, cybersecurity should no longer be considered merely a technical function but as a strategic tool for securing and sustaining resilient critical infrastructure operations in the coming years. With the pace of digital transformation increasing at an unprecedented rate, the capacity of companies to incorporate cybersecurity into their operations, governance, and innovation strategy will become key in the future.

REFERENCES

Abbasi, M. (2020). Security in Cyberspace in the Field of International Relations. *J Arch Mil Med.*, *8*(4), e114485. DOI: 10.5812/jamm.114485

Agius, J., Karagiannis, G. M., Pescaroli, G., Galbusera, L., Theocharidou, M., Krausmann, E., & Chaudhari, K. 'Critical Infrastructures', in: Casajus Valles, A., Marin Ferrer, M., Poljanšek, K., Clark, I. (eds.), Science for Disaster Risk Management 2020: acting today, protecting tomorrow, EUR 30183 EN, Publications Office of the European Union, Luxembourg, 2020, ISBN 978-92-76-18182-8, , JRC114026. DOI: 10.2760/571085

Ali, M., & Sun, W. (2024). *Securing Critical Infrastructures: Restoration from Cyber-Physical Attacks in Active Distribution Grids. 2024 IEEE Power & Energy Society General Meeting*. PESGM., DOI: 10.1109/PESGM51994.2024.10688621

Almulla, Z. T., & Rahman, H. (2025). The Role of Network Segmentation and Micro-Segmentation in Operational Technology Security. 2025 International Conference on Artificial Intelligence in Information and Communication (ICAIIC), Fukuoka, Japan, pp. 0342-0347, DOI: 10.1109/ICAIIC64266.2025.10920695

Asiri, M., Saxena, N., Gjomemo, R., and Burnap, P. (2023). Understanding Indicators of Compromise against Cyber-attacks in Industrial Control Systems: A Security Perspective. ACM Trans. Cyber-Phys. Syst. 7, 2, Article 15, 33 pages. DOI: 10.1145/3587255

Aziboledia Frederick, B., & Egerton Taylor, O. (2023). Analysis on Cybersecurity Control and Monitoring Techniques in Industrial IoT: Industrial Control Systems. *Internet of Things and Cloud Computing*, *11*(1), 1–17. DOI: 10.11648/j.iotcc.20231101.11

Bekzhanov, A., Sadykova, A., & Mukhamedi, Y. (2024). Enhancing Cybersecurity Through AI-Driven Intrusion Detection Systems in Industrial Control Systems. *International Journal of Information Engineering and Science*, *1*(2), 26–32. DOI: 10.62951/ijies.v1i2.91

Bello, A., Jahan, S., Farid, F., & Ahamed, F. (2023). A Systemic Review of the Cybersecurity Challenges in Australian Water Infrastructure Management. *Water (Basel)*, *15*(1), 168. DOI: 10.3390/w15010168

Ciekanowski, Z., Gruchelski, M., Nowicka, J., Żurawski, S., & Pauliuchuk, Y. (2023). Cyberspace as a Source of New Threats to the Security of the European Union. *European Research Studies*, *XXVI*(3), 782–797. DOI: 10.35808/ersj/3249

Claroty. (2023). The global state of industrial cybersecurity 2023: New technologies, persistent threats, and maturing defenses. https://web-assets.claroty.com/claroty-industrial-survey-report-dec-2023.pd

Cloete, M. (2024). Cyber criminals targeting UK manufacturing industry in 2024. Moore Kingston Smith. 01-16-2024 Retrieved from: https://mooreks.co.uk/insights/cyber-criminals-targeting-uk-manufacturing-industry-in-2024/

Cook, W. (2020, March 29). Many U.S. Workers in critical occupations in the fight against COVID-19 (Revised). Retrieved March 17, 2026, from https://www.lmiontheweb.org/more-than-half-of-u-s-workers-in-critical-occupations-in-the-fight-against-covid-19/

Cybersecurity and Infrastructure Security Agency. (2024, 17 de enero). CISA releases 2023 year in review showcasing efforts to protect critical infrastructure. https://www.cisa.gov/news-events/news/cisa-releases-2023-year-review-showcasing-efforts-protect-critical-infrastructure

Department for Science. Innovation and Technology. (2023). UK cyber security sectoral analysis 2023. UK Government. https://www.gov.uk/government/publications/cyber-security-sectoral-analysis-2023/uk-cyber-security-sectoral-analysis-2023

ENE. I. and SAVU, D. (2023). Cybersecurity – A Permanent Challenge for the Energy Sector. Romanian Cyber Security Journal, ISSN 2668-6430, vol. 5(1), pp. 107-119. DOI: 10.54851/v5i1y202310

Fovino, I. N., Coletta, A., & Masera, M. (2021). Cyber-physical security of critical infrastructures. In M. T. H. (Ed.), Handbook of Computer Networks and Cyber Security (pp. 729–752). Springer. https://doi.org/DOI: 10.1007/978-3-030-72369-9_30

Georgiev, P. and Dimitrova, K. (2024) IIoT and cyber security in industrial enterprises. SECURITY & FUTURE. Vol. 8 (2024), Issue 2, pg(s) 53-56.

Giraldo, J., Sarkar, E., Cardenas, A. A., Maniatakos, M., & Kantarcioglu, M. (2018). Security and privacy in cyber-physical systems: A survey of surveys. *IEEE Design & Test*, *34*(4), 7–17. DOI: 10.1109/MDAT.2017.2709310

Govea, J., Gaibor-Naranjo, W., & Villegas-Ch, W. (2024). Transforming Cybersecurity into Critical Energy Infrastructure: A Study on the Effectiveness of Artificial Intelligence. *Systems*, *12*(5), 165. DOI: 10.3390/systems12050165

Karnouskos, S. (2020). Stuxnet worm impact on industrial cyber-physical system security. In *IECON 2020 The 46th Annual Conference of the IEEE Industrial Electronics Society* (pp. 1–6). IEEE. DOI: 10.1109/IECON43393.2020.9254884

Kaspersky. (2026). Overview of Kaspersky's Industrial CyberSecurity Solutions [Image]. Kaspersky. https://cdn.kaspersky.com/fm/site-editor/ba/ba46809962979 7e8e17b64a2f9df3cce/processed/body-image-2-q93.png

Kim, S. (2014). Cyber Security and Middle Power Diplomacy: A Network Perspective. *Korean Journal of International Studies*, *12*(2), 323–352. DOI: 10.14731/ kjis.2014.12.12.2.323

Knowles, W., Prince, D., Hutchison, D., Disso, J. F. P., & Jones, K. (2021). A survey of cyber security management in industrial control systems. *International Journal of Critical Infrastructure Protection*, *9*, 52–80. DOI: 10.1016/j.ijcip.2015.02.002

Krause, T., Ernst, R., Klaer, B., Hacker, I., & Henze, M. (2021). Cybersecurity in Power Grids: Challenges and Opportunities. *Sensors (Basel)*, *21*(18), 6225. DOI: 10.3390/s21186225 PMID: 34577432

Makrakis, G. M., Kolias, C., Kambourakis, G., Rieger, C., & Benjamin, J. (2021). Industrial and Critical Infrastructure Security: Technical Analysis of Real-Life Security Incidents. *IEEE Access : Practical Innovations, Open Solutions*, *9*, 165295–165325. DOI: 10.1109/ACCESS.2021.3133348

Mazzolin, R. and Madni, A. (2022). An Overview of Cyber Security Considerations and Vulnerabilities in Critical Infrastructure Systems and Potential Automated Mitigation - A Review. Journal of Engineering Research and Sciences, 1(4), 09–21. DOI: 10.55708/js0104002

Nafees, M.N., Saxena, N., Cardenas, A., Grijalva, S., Burnap, P. (2023). Smart Grid Cyber-Physical Situational Awareness of Complex Operational Technology Attacks: A Review. ACM Comput. Surv. 55, 10, 36 pages. Doi: DOI: 10.1145/3565570

Palash, M. N. H. (2025). The economic impact of cybersecurity threats on critical infrastructure: Evaluating U.S. policy effectiveness and private sector readiness. [IJAEM]. *International Journal of Advances in Engineering and Management*, *7*(5), 222–230. DOI: 10.35629/5252-0705222230

Pinto, A., Herrera, L.-C., Donoso, Y., & Gutierrez, J. A. (2023). Survey on Intrusion Detection Systems Based on Machine Learning Techniques for the Protection of Critical Infrastructure. *Sensors (Basel)*, *23*(5), 2415. DOI: 10.3390/s23052415 PMID: 36904618

Pliatsios, D., Sarigiannidis, P., Lagkas, T., & Sarigiannidis, A. G. (2020). A Survey on SCADA Systems: Secure Protocols, Incidents, Threats and Tactics. *IEEE Communications Surveys and Tutorials*, *22*(3), 1942–1976. DOI: 10.1109/ COMST.2020.2987688

Reddy, P. (2025). How to Respond to a Cyber Security Incident. *International Journal of Innovative Research in Computer and Communication Engineering.*, *13*(1), 37–41. DOI: 10.15680/IJIRCCE.2025.1301005

Seceon. (2026). Overview of Seceon's OTM Platform Components [Image]. Seceon. https://seceon.com/wp-content/uploads/2025/05/Cybersecurity-for-Critical-Infrastructure-in-the-Middle-East_-Why-a-Proactive-AI-Driven-Approach-Is-Essential-visual-selection.png

Sekonya, N., & Sithungu, S. (2023). An Analysis of Critical Cybersecurity Controls for Industrial Control Systems. *European Conference on Cyber Warfare and Security*. 22. 410-419. DOI: 10.34190/eccws.22.1.1157

Simola, J., Savola, R., Frantti, T., Takala, A., & Lehkonen, R. (2023). Developing Cybersecurity in an Industrial Environment by Using a Testbed Environment. *Proceedings of the 22nd European Conference on Cyber Warfare and Security, ECCWS 2023*, 2023, pp. 429-438, DOI: 10.34190/eccws.22.1.1362

Sridhar, S., Hahn, A., & Govindarasu, M. (2012). Cyber–Physical System Security for the Electric Power Grid. *Proceedings of the IEEE, 100*(1), 210–224. DOI: 10.1109/JPROC.2011.2165269

Srivastav, A. D., Verma, S. B., & Pandey, A. K. (2025). Cybersecurity Strategies for Industrial Installations in the Critical Infrastructure Sector: *Challenges and Solutions International Conference on Networks and Cryptology (NETCRYPT)*, New Delhi, India, 2025, pp. 1564-1567, DOI: 10.1109/NETCRYPT65877.2025.11102534

Staves, A., Balderstone, H., Green, B., Gouglidis, A., & Hutchison, D. (2020). A Framework to Support ICS Cyber Incident Response and Recovery. Paper presented at the 17th International Conference on Information Systems for Crisis Response and Management, Blacksburg, United States.

Stouffer, K., Pillitteri, V., Lightman, S., Abrams, M., & Hahn, A. (2020). Guide to operational technology (OT) security (NIST Special Publication 800-82, Rev. 3). National Institute of Standards and Technology. DOI: 10.6028/NIST.SP.800-82r3

Umscheid, J., Schmitz, P., & Pape, S. (2022). Learning from security incidents in critical infrastructure: A systematic review. *Computers & Security*, *120*, 102821. DOI: 10.1016/j.cose.2022.102821

Zinchenko, O. (2025). Cyber security in international relations: Risks and prospects. *Eximia*, *14*(1), 1–20. DOI: 10.47577/eximia.v14i1.526

Chapter 2

Securing Smart Cities and Critical Infrastructure: Cyber Resilience for IoT, Sensors, and ICS/SCADA in Government Services

Mohammad Al Khaldy
http://orcid.org/0009-0009-7502-4668
University of Petra, Amman, Jordan

Amjad Aldweesh
http://orcid.org/0000-0001-9358-1323
Shaqra University, Saudi Arabia

Ziadoon Otaiwi
http://orcid.org/0000-0001-6544-839X
University of Al-Hamdaniya, Iraq

ABSTRACT

Smart cities now depend on connected sensors, edge platforms, ICS, SCADA systems, and cloud services to run essential operations like water treatment, traffic management, public transport, environmental monitoring, and public safety. While this connectivity boosts efficiency and visibility, it also creates a much larger cyber-physical attack surface where a single breach can quickly disrupt critical services. Traditional perimeter-based cybersecurity is no longer enough in these complex, fragmented environments. This chapter presents a practical framework for building cyber resilience in smart city government services. Drawing on IoT security, edge computing, and critical infrastructure research, it argues that real resilience means

DOI: 10.4018/979-8-2600-2845-2.ch002

the ability to anticipate, withstand, recover, and adapt. The chapter introduces a layered governance and engineering model, supported by seven tables and five figures, and ends with a maturity model and clear recommendations for municipal leaders.

INTRODUCTION

Smart city infrastructure has expanded beyond isolated pilot projects and citizen-facing mobile applications into the core operating model of local government. In many municipalities, connected infrastructure now supports routine public service delivery. Streetlighting networks integrate cameras, environmental sensors, and wireless communications. Water systems employ remotely monitored pumps, telemetry, chemical dosing controls, and digital maintenance platforms. Transport systems rely on connected traffic signals, parking sensors, public transport feeds, and incident coordination tools. This transformation creates opportunities for better visibility and more efficient service delivery, but it also requires a more rigorous account of cyber-physical dependency, institutional accountability, and continuity of essential public functions.

Municipal buildings similarly incorporate automation systems, smart energy metering, connected access controls, and networked life-safety interfaces. Public safety operations draw on video analytics, emergency communications, geospatial information systems, and multi-channel alerting platforms. These developments improve efficiency, responsiveness, transparency, and evidence-based policy making. At the same time, they blur traditional boundaries among information technology (IT), operational technology (OT), telecommunications infrastructure, and cloud-native services. As these domains converge, municipal cyber risk becomes more distributed, interdependent, and difficult to govern through conventional security models alone.

The literature on smart cities and IoT consistently emphasizes heterogeneity, distribution, and interdependence. Gubbi et al. (2013) described IoT as an ecosystem of sensing, actuation, communications, and analytics that transforms real-world processes into data-driven services. Zanella et al. (2014) further showed that smart city implementations rely on dense deployments of connected devices and data platforms spanning utilities, mobility, environment, and public administration. More recent work has emphasized that smart cities do not consist merely of "smart" endpoints; they are service systems in which physical infrastructures, public institutions, and digital intermediaries interact continuously (Ismagilova, Hughes, Rana, & Dwivedi, 2022). This matters for security because municipal service continuity depends on more than confidentiality of records. It depends on safe actuation, trustworthy telemetry, accurate timing, dependable communications, human situational awareness, and the ability to continue operating under adverse conditions.

A cyber event in a smart city can therefore have several layers of consequence. At the most visible layer, a cyberattack may interrupt administrative systems, citizen-facing portals, or internal email. At a deeper layer, it may falsify data that operators use to regulate pumping pressure, traffic phases, or building temperatures. At the deepest layer, it may cause physical disruption, safety incidents, financial loss, regulatory breaches, or erosion of public trust. Elmaghraby and Losavio (2014) argued early that smart city cybersecurity must be understood through the combined lenses of safety, security, and privacy. That insight has only grown more important as municipalities have connected legacy control environments to modern analytics platforms and outsourced portions of their operating stack to integrators and managed service providers. Smart city risk is therefore not simply "more IT risk." It is cyber-physical risk embedded in public service obligations.

For this reason, the central question of this chapter is not only how governments can protect connected infrastructure from attack, but how they can remain functional when attacks, faults, and supply chain failures inevitably occur. This chapter adopts cyber resilience as the organizing concept. Drawing on resilience scholarship, cyber resilience is treated here as the capacity of a system to prepare for disruption, absorb shocks, recover essential function, and adapt design and governance based on experience (Linkov et al., 2013; Linkov et al., 2014; Hosseini, Barker, & Ramirez-Marquez, 2016). In practical terms, resilience means a city can lose a sensor cluster, a communications segment, or even a supervisory platform without losing critical public outcomes. It also means that operators can detect data anomalies, isolate compromise, switch to safe degraded modes, recover validated data, and learn quickly enough to reduce repeat exposure.

This chapter makes five contributions. First, it synthesizes scholarship on IoT, wireless sensors, fog and edge computing, smart city security, and industrial cyber-physical systems into a public-sector resilience lens. Second, it distinguishes conventional enterprise cybersecurity from the controls needed for mixed IT-OT environments in government services. Third, it develops a layered framework that connects governance, architecture, operations, response, recovery, procurement, and learning. Fourth, it aligns the proposed framework with selected international references, including NIST CSF 2.0, NIST SP 800-82 Rev. 3, NIST SP 800-213, ISA/IEC 62443, and the EU NIS2 policy direction. Fifth, it operationalizes the framework through sectoral use cases, measurable validation criteria, and an illustrative analytics case study.

The chapter proceeds as follows. The next section explains how smart city services evolved from connected devices into cyber-physical government systems. The threat landscape section then identifies exposure points, adversary objectives, common attack pathways, and ICS/SCADA-specific vulnerabilities. The framework section translates those risks into eight resilience layers and explains how they relate to existing standards. The sectoral use-case section applies the model to water, transport, municipal facilities, and public safety services. The incident-response section examines recovery and continuous assurance. A brief operational case study then demonstrates how structured metrics and reproducible scoring can make resilience claims measurable. The chapter closes by identifying future research directions and summarizing the implications for municipal leaders. Table 1 explain the urban infrastructure spans four distinct but equally critical service domains. Water and transport systems depend on industrial control components and networked field devices to maintain safe, continuous operations, where data integrity and failure containment are paramount. Municipal facilities require careful isolation from enterprise IT to preserve local overrides, while public safety and environmental networks must guarantee data provenance, privacy, and uninterrupted alerting. Across all domains, the core tension lies between the operational benefits of connectivity, and the resilience demands of maintaining local control.

Table 1. Smart city government service domains and cyber-physical dependencies

Service domain	Typical connected assets	Primary public outcome	Key resilience concern
Water and wastewater	PLCs, RTUs, pumps, chemical sensors, telemetry gateways	Safe, continuous water and wastewater operations	Integrity of process data and ability to fall back to local control
Transport and traffic	Signal controllers, cameras, parking sensors, roadside units	Safe movement of people and emergency services	Containment of corridor-level failure and trusted timing plans
Municipal facilities	BMS, HVAC controllers, smart locks, energy meters	Safe, functional public buildings	Segmentation from enterprise IT and preservation of local overrides
Public safety and environment	Cameras, acoustic sensors, flood gauges, air-quality nodes	Trusted situational awareness and lawful response	Data provenance, privacy protection, and continuity of alerting

BACKGROUND: FROM CONNECTED DEVICES TO CYBER-PHYSICAL GOVERNMENT

The modern smart city emerged from three technological currents: pervasive sensing, ubiquitous networking, and scalable analytics. Early wireless sensor network research focused on distributed observation under energy, bandwidth, and reliability constraints, highlighting the importance of secure routing, key management, and fault tolerance (Chong & Kumar, 2003; Wang, Attebury, & Ramamurthy, 2006; Walters, Liang, Shi, & Chaudhary, 2007). As sensors became cheaper and IPv6-based connectivity matured, IoT architectures expanded the scope of sensing from specialized deployments to everyday urban objects, including vehicles, cameras, meters, controllers, and building devices (Gubbi et al., 2013; Zanella et al., 2014). Edge and fog computing then emerged to reduce latency and bandwidth dependence by moving processing closer to devices and local operations, an approach especially important for time-sensitive public services (Chiang & Zhang, 2016; Atlam, Walters, & Wills, 2018; Shen, Zhang, Zhou, Zhang, & Ci, 2020). At the same time, critical infrastructures that historically relied on isolated control networks became increasingly integrated with enterprise systems, remote maintenance channels, and vendor-managed applications, thereby narrowing the practical distance between city operations and the broader Internet (Knowles et al., 2015; Kayan et al., 2022).

This evolution matters because government services are not architected as homogeneous digital platforms. They are assemblages of technologies with distinct operational logics. A citizen complaint portal can tolerate brief degradation and can often be restored from standard backups with little physical consequence. By contrast, a traffic control network, a water treatment dosing system, or a hospital utility management system may require deterministic behavior, hard timing constraints, and operation by field teams who must prioritize safety even when digital visibility is partially lost. In these environments, the security objective is not simply preventing unauthorized access. It is ensuring that sensing, communication, decision support, and actuation remain trustworthy enough to support safe control. Kayan et al. (2022) and Canonico and Sperlì (2023) show that industrial cyber-physical systems combine cyber, communication, and physical layers whose vulnerabilities cannot be managed effectively if they are assessed in isolation.

A second conceptual shift is the move from security-by-obscurity to exposure-by-integration. Many legacy municipal control environments benefited historically from proprietary protocols, isolated serial links, limited remote access, and operator familiarity. These conditions never guaranteed security, but they reduced opportunistic exposure. Once the same environments are connected to historians, remote engineering stations, mobile maintenance tools, dashboards, digital twins, cloud storage, or open data interfaces, latent weaknesses become easier to exploit. Alcaraz and Zeadally (2013) warned that critical control systems were entering a century defined by expanded connectivity, unpatched legacy assets, and increasingly capable adversaries. Nicholson, Webber, Dyer, Patel, and Janicke (2012) similarly argued that SCADA security must be evaluated in the context of cyber-warfare, where motivated actors may seek strategic, disruptive, or symbolic outcomes rather than purely financial gain.

A third shift concerns data value. In smart cities, telemetry is not only an operational input but also a governance asset. Environmental sensors inform public health policy, mobility data shapes transport planning, and utility consumption data influences sustainability initiatives. This raises privacy and legitimacy concerns alongside security concerns. Smart city literature shows that citizens may accept sensing only when data collection is proportionate, accountable, and governed transparently (Cui, Xie, Qu, Gao, & Yang, 2018; Ismagilova et al., 2022; Fabrègue & Bogoni, 2023). Cyber resilience in government services therefore must protect not only availability and safety but also procedural fairness, auditability, and public trust.

For the purposes of this chapter, four terms are central. IoT refers broadly to connected devices that sense, communicate, or actuate across networked environments. Sensors are devices that capture physical or environmental states such as pressure, flow, occupancy, temperature, position, or vibration. ICS/SCADA refers to the industrial and supervisory platforms used to monitor and control distributed physical processes. Cyber resilience refers to the capacity of a socio-technical system to continue delivering essential outcomes despite cyber adversity, then recover and adapt. This final term is particularly useful for government because municipalities cannot choose to "pause" water delivery, mobility management, or emergency communications while a perfect remediation plan is assembled. They must operate through uncertainty.

A resilient approach also recognizes that municipal technology ecosystems are governed by procurement cycles, budgetary constraints, outsourced maintenance contracts, and workforce availability. Devices may remain in service for ten or twenty years. Vendors may own update channels or diagnostic credentials. Integrators may configure gateways using undocumented assumptions. Agencies may inherit systems through mergers, grants, or pilot programs without maintaining complete asset registers. Consequently, resilience has to be designed not only into technology but also into institutional processes: acquisition, change management, incident command, interagency coordination, training, and recovery funding. This chapter adopts that broader view, because cyber resilience in smart city government is as much about governing interdependence as it is about deploying technical controls. Figure 1 illustrates the layered architecture of smart city government services, spanning from field devices at the base through integration layers and supervisory platforms up to overarching governance controls.

Recent literature reinforces the need for this integrated orientation. Studies published after 2024 increasingly emphasize AI-supported anomaly detection, blockchain-enabled data integrity, open-data risk modeling, and regulatory compliance as interconnected smart city concerns rather than separate technical topics (Houichi, Jaidi, & Bouhoula, 2024; Joshi, Baviskar, & Rajmane, 2026; Sobeslav & Horalek, 2025; Villafranca, Thant, Tasic, & Cano, 2025). At the same time, updated guidance such as NIST CSF 2.0 and NIST SP 800-82 Rev. 3 gives municipalities a stronger vocabulary for governance, supply-chain oversight, operational technology protection, and recovery assurance (National Institute of Standards and Technology [NIST], 2024; Stouffer et al., 2023). The remaining gap is not the absence of standards; rather, it is the lack of a service-level translation that connects standards to the actual continuity outcomes expected from municipal water, mobility, facility, and safety operations.

Figure 1. Layered architecture of smart city government services spanning field devices, integration layers, supervisory platforms, and governance controls.

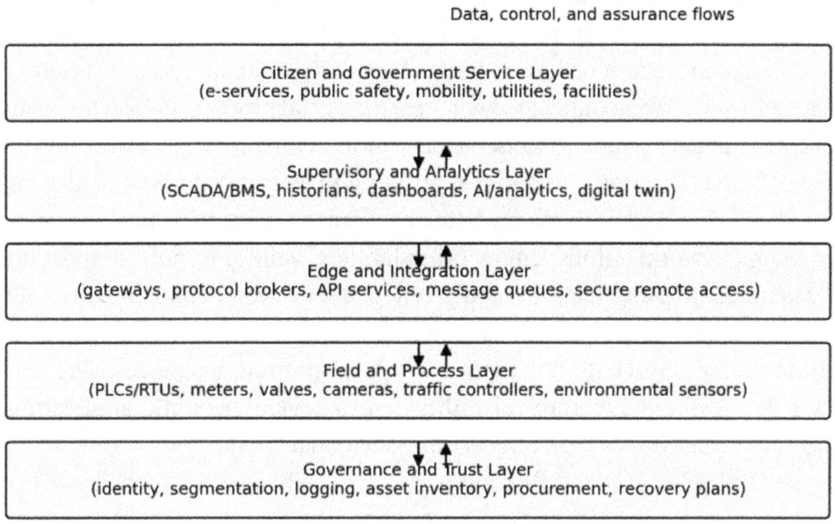

THREAT LANDSCAPE FOR IOT, SENSORS, AND ICS/SCADA IN GOVERNMENT SERVICES

Threat analysis for smart cities must start with the service chain rather than with any single device class. A municipal service typically spans field devices, local controllers, communications links, edge gateways, supervisory applications, data stores, operator interfaces, and external integrations. Compromise at any point can affect the integrity or timeliness of the whole chain. Roman, Zhou, and Lopez (2013) showed that distributed IoT environments are difficult to secure because device constraints, heterogeneity, and scale complicate authentication, trust management, and secure updates. Sicari et al. (2015) similarly emphasized that IoT security cannot be separated from privacy, trust, and lifecycle management. When these challenges are translated into public infrastructure, the attack surface expands further because devices may sit in public spaces, connect over mixed carrier networks, and exchange data with legacy industrial systems that were not designed for hostile environments.

Asset Classes and Exposure Points

The principal municipal asset classes are more varied than standard enterprise inventories suggest. First are sensing and actuation assets: cameras, smart meters, leak detectors, environmental monitors, pump controllers, programmable logic controllers (PLCs), and remote terminal units (RTUs). These devices may suffer from weak default credentials, insecure web interfaces, unencrypted protocols, limited logging, and inconsistent patching. Second are communications assets: radio links, cellular gateways, fiber-connected switches, industrial protocol converters, message brokers, and virtual private network concentrators. Third are supervisory and analytics assets: SCADA servers, historians, building management systems, digital twin models, data lakes, and dashboard platforms. Fourth are identity and administration assets: operator workstations, engineering laptops, vendor remote support portals, mobile maintenance applications, and privileged service accounts. Finally, there are cross-domain dependencies such as cloud identity services, certificate authorities, GPS time sources, and external application programming interfaces. The practical lesson is that resilience requires visibility across device, network, application, and dependency layers rather than only within one department.

Kayan et al. (2022) noted that industrial cyber-physical systems are especially vulnerable when assumptions about trust at one layer are invalidated by integration at another layer. For example, a water pump PLC may trust commands from a local human-machine interface, but if that interface is connected through a remote support channel and a flat municipal network, the effective trust boundary is much wider than operators assume. Likewise, an air-quality sensing network may appear low risk until its data feed is used to trigger traffic restrictions, public alerts, or emergency response priorities. The threat significance of an asset is therefore shaped less by device type than by decision consequence, system coupling, and recovery difficulty.

Adversaries and Their Objectives

Adversaries targeting smart cities vary in capability and motivation. Cybercriminal groups are attracted by ransomware extortion, theft of operational data, or monetization of unmanaged IoT devices through botnets. Nation-state or state-aligned actors may seek strategic disruption, prepositioning, intelligence collection, or influence operations against civic confidence. Insider threats include disgruntled staff, negligent administrators, or contractors using shared credentials and undocumented workarounds. Activist or ideologically motivated attackers may target symbolic services to generate media impact. Opportunistic actors may exploit exposed cameras, gateways, or building devices simply because they are reachable and poorly configured. Knowles et al. (2015) stressed that industrial control system security management must account for both social and technical vulnerabilities, especially where operational urgency encourages informal access practices. Hemsley and Fisher (2018) further showed, through historical incidents, that the path from digital compromise to physical consequence often depends on weak governance, inadequate monitoring, or misplaced trust rather than on novel malware alone.

Municipal organizations sometimes underestimate threat intent because many connected civic systems are not viewed as high-value targets in the same way as national defense or major finance. This is a mistake. Smart city systems can offer attackers three forms of leverage. First, they can provide immediate disruption with visible citizen impact, such as traffic dysfunction or utility interruption. Second, they can offer operational footholds into larger regional infrastructure, especially where municipal networks connect to energy, water, or emergency partners. Third, they can create reputational damage by undermining public trust in digital transformation. Elmaghraby and Losavio (2014) were therefore correct to place public safety and privacy at the center of smart city risk. The target is often not the device itself, but the legitimacy and continuity of civic service.

Common Attack Pathways

Several attack pathways recur across IoT and OT environments. The first is compromise through weak identity and remote access. Shared credentials, always-on VPN tunnels, unmanaged vendor accounts, and poor multi-factor enforcement remain common routes into municipal systems. The second is compromise through insecure device lifecycle management. Field devices are frequently installed with default passwords, unverified firmware, or inconsistent certificate handling. Third is lateral movement enabled by flat or poorly documented network architectures, allowing attackers to pivot from lower-trust devices into supervisory systems. Fourth is data integrity manipulation, where telemetry is delayed, spoofed, dropped, or subtly altered rather than simply stolen. In control environments, such manipulation can be more dangerous than overt denial of service because operators may act on false confidence. Fifth is supply chain compromise, in which vulnerabilities in managed services, update infrastructure, third-party software components, or integrator laptops become initial infection vectors. Houichi, Jaidi, and Bouhoula (2024) and Chen,

Wawrzynski, and Lv (2021) both underscore that smart city systems are increasingly attacked through multi-stage chains rather than isolated exploits.

Wireless sensing introduces additional considerations. Sensor nodes may be physically accessible, battery-constrained, and intermittently connected. Jan, Nanda, Zheng, and Jamalipour (2017) and Wang et al. (2006) note that confidentiality and availability in wireless sensor networks are challenged by spoofing, selective forwarding, jamming, sinkhole attacks, and key management weaknesses. In government settings, these issues matter not only in military-style deployments but also in flood sensors, road weather stations, occupancy sensors, and temporary event infrastructure. Physical access to roadside cabinets or rooftop enclosures can enable tampering that bypasses purely network-centric defenses. For this reason, sensor security should be treated as a field operations problem as much as a cryptographic one.

ICS/SCADA-Specific Vulnerabilities

ICS/SCADA environments bring distinct constraints and vulnerabilities. Availability and process safety often dominate, which means patching windows are limited, equipment may run unsupported operating systems, and change control is conservative. Protocols such as Modbus, DNP3, BACnet, and other industrial or building automation protocols may lack native authentication or encryption in legacy implementations. Engineering workstations may need elevated privileges and removable media support. Remote diagnostic access may be business-critical for specialized vendors. Alcaraz and Zeadally (2013) argued that these characteristics make control environments vulnerable not because defenders are unaware, but because operational realities limit the direct transplantation of IT security methods. Nicholson et al. (2012) added that the cyber-warfare context amplifies the stakes: the objective may be controlled disruption, degradation of operator trust, or forced reversion to manual processes.

Historical incidents also show that adversaries do not require perfect process understanding to cause harm. Ransomware affecting enterprise systems can indirectly delay dispatch, procurement, or maintenance for physical infrastructure. Malware on engineering stations can manipulate logic or safety set points if integrity controls are weak. Distributed denial-of-service attacks against externally visible components can overwhelm citizen reporting channels or remote access gateways during emergencies. Hemsley and Fisher (2018) and Miller and Rowe (2012) collectively show that even modest failures in visibility, segmentation, and coordination can turn local device compromise into system-wide operational stress.

The Importance of Data Trustworthiness

A recurring weakness in smart city security discourse is overemphasis on uptime without equivalent attention to data trustworthiness. Government operators frequently rely on dashboards that aggregate multiple feeds and convert them into simplified indicators. If a dashboard remains available but the underlying data is skewed, delayed, or maliciously injected, decision quality may degrade while users believe the system is healthy. Cui et al. (2018) and Ismagilova et al. (2022) highlight that trust in smart cities depends on reliability of data handling and governance. In control settings, data trustworthiness includes provenance, timestamp integrity, calibration assurance, and the ability to reconcile field observations with digital records. A resilient architecture therefore needs independent validation paths, anomaly detection, and procedures for human cross-checking during uncertainty.

Why Prevention Alone Fails

The combined implication of these vulnerabilities is that prevention alone is not a realistic organizing principle. There are too many devices, too many protocol transitions, and too many third-party relationships for governments to assume a breach-free future. Smart city leaders should still pursue hardening, but they should design systems so that compromise is containable and function is degradable rather than catastrophic. A camera network should fail closed for privacy-sensitive streams while allowing degraded public safety operations. A water utility should be able to validate process state through independent measurements if telemetry is suspect. A traffic management center should be able to isolate a corridor or fall back to safe timing plans if central optimization becomes untrusted. Cyber resilience begins when government services are designed with these contingencies in mind. Figure 2 illustrates the typical attack propagation pathway in connected municipal environments, depicting the sequential progression from initial access through intermediate compromise stages to ultimate citizen-level consequences. Table 2 identifies vulnerabilities across five layers of the IoT-ICS stack. Weak device credentials, flat networks, insecure APIs, unverified telemetry, and opaque supply chains each create distinct but compounding risks — from unauthorized access and lateral movement to unsafe operator decisions and persistent vendor-introduced exposure. Mitigations follow the same layered logic: strong device identities, network zoning, least-privilege access, independent data validation, and contractual supply chain controls. Table 3 profiles four threat actors with different motivations but overlapping targets. Cybercriminals exploit exposed systems for extortion; state actors target high-consequence infrastructure for strategic disruption or espionage; insiders threaten configuration integrity from within; and opportunistic actors probe

Internet-facing devices for visibility or symbolic impact. Together they reinforce the need for defense in depth — isolation, monitoring, access control, and recovery readiness — applied consistently across all domains.

Table 2. Common vulnerabilities across the IoT-sensor-ICS stack

Layer	Typical weakness	Operational effect	Priority mitigation
Device	Default credentials, weak firmware controls	Unauthorized access or tampering	Unique identities, secure boot, patch governance
Network	Flat trust, exposed remote access, protocol bridging	Lateral movement and broad blast radius	Functional zoning, brokered remote access, allowlisting
Application	Weak API security, poor logging, insecure integrations	Data leakage or loss of service confidence	Least privilege, logging, change control, key management
Process	Unverified telemetry, poor calibration assurance	Unsafe operator decisions	Independent validation, plausibility checks, fallback procedures
Supply chain	Vendor account misuse, unsupported software, opaque dependencies	Persistent exposure and delayed recovery	Contractual security clauses, vendor access review, SBOM/ patch transparency

Table 3. Threat actors, objectives, and likely targeting patterns

Threat actor	Primary objective	Likely target set	Resilience implication
Cybercriminal group	Extortion, monetization, disruption	Remote access systems, exposed servers, unmanaged IoT fleets	Need for isolation, backups, and rapid credential containment
State or state-aligned actor	Strategic disruption, espionage, prepositioning	High-consequence utilities, transport, safety systems	Need for segmentation, monitoring, and recovery confidence
Insider or contractor	Negligence, sabotage, unauthorized shortcuts	Engineering workstations, maintenance accounts, configuration baselines	Need for role clarity, logging, and approval workflows
Activist or opportunistic actor	Visibility, symbolic impact, experimentation	Cameras, signage, web-exposed devices, public APIs	Need for hardening of Internet-facing components and public communications resilience

Figure 2. Typical attack propagation pathway from initial access to citizen-level consequence in connected municipal environments.

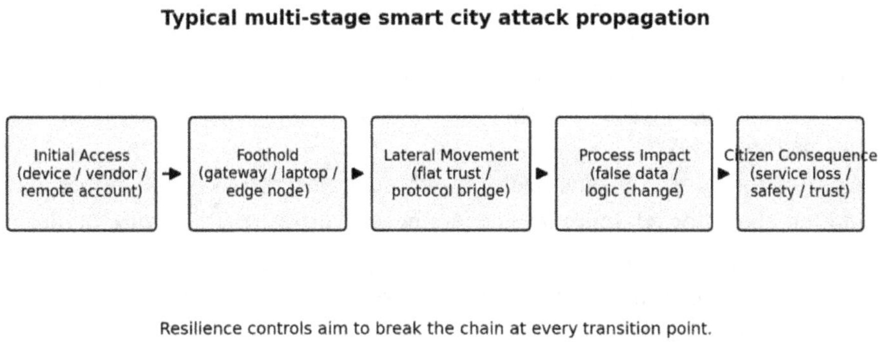

A CYBER RESILIENCE FRAMEWORK FOR SMART CITY GOVERNMENT SERVICES

Cyber resilience in government services should be treated as a layered capability rather than a single control family. Linkov et al. (2013) framed resilience around the ability to plan, absorb, recover, and adapt across physical, informational, cognitive, and social domains. Applied to smart cities, this means that technical architecture, operator behavior, interagency coordination, and public communication all influence whether a cyber event becomes a temporary disruption or a civic crisis. The resilience framework proposed in this chapter has eight interlocking layers: governance and accountability; asset intelligence; architecture and segmentation; identity and trust; sensing and monitoring; safe operations and degraded modes; recovery engineering; and adaptation through continuous assurance.

1. Governance and Accountability

Resilience begins with explicit assignment of responsibility. Many municipalities own connected assets through fragmented departments: transport may manage roadside equipment, utilities may manage process control networks, facilities may manage building automation, and innovation offices may manage data platforms or pilot programs. When governance is fragmented, cyber risk is often fragmented too. No single authority maintains a complete picture of which services are essential, which assets can affect safety, which vendors hold privileged access, or which systems share dependencies. Knowles et al. (2015) show that management maturity in industrial control environments depends heavily on policy integration, role clarity, and communication between technical and operational stakeholders. For smart cities, governance therefore should include a citywide or agency-wide critical services register that links each service to its process owners, digital dependencies, third-party support arrangements, manual fallback options, and acceptable downtime thresholds.

Accountability also means deciding who can accept risk. Procurement teams should not be allowed to introduce connected infrastructure without defining support boundaries, update responsibilities, logging requirements, and secure decommissioning procedures. Operational departments should document when safety priorities justify delayed patching or compensating controls. Executive leaders should decide which public outcomes—such as potable water quality, emergency communications continuity, or safe signal timing—must be protected through the strongest resilience measures even if budgets are limited. Resilience is weakened when technical teams are expected to "own" risk that is fundamentally created by policy, funding, or contractual decisions.

2. Asset Intelligence and Dependency Mapping

Traditional asset inventories are insufficient for smart cities because they rarely capture process dependency, firmware lineage, network pathways, or vendor relationships. A resilience-oriented inventory should answer six questions for every critical component: What function does it support? What data does it consume and produce? What other systems trust it? How is it administered? What are the safe fallback procedures if it fails? How quickly can it be restored or replaced? Canonico and Sperlì (2023) emphasize that industrial cyber-physical protection requires methodological attention to system boundaries and interactions, not just enumerations of devices. In practice, this means building dependency maps from sensor to civic outcome.

For example, a flood warning service may depend on river-level sensors, local gateways, a message broker, cloud analytics, a dashboard, mobile alerting channels, and operator shift procedures. A resilience assessment should identify which nodes are single points of failure, which dependencies are externally hosted, which steps can be validated independently, and which elements can be bypassed. Mapping also helps prioritize investment. Not all exposed IoT assets justify the same controls. A resilience lens directs highest protection toward assets whose failure creates safety risk, recovery complexity, or cross-service contagion.

3. Architecture, Zoning, and Segmentation

Architecture is the most important technical determinant of whether compromise spreads. Flat networks, unmanaged protocol bridges, and direct trust between field devices and enterprise services create pathways for lateral movement and covert manipulation. In smart cities, architectural discipline should be based on functional zoning. Field and process zones should be separated from supervisory zones, which in turn should be separated from business and Internet-facing zones. Remote access should terminate in managed jump environments with session control, recording where appropriate, and time-bounded authorization. Protocol translation and data export should occur through explicit brokers or demilitarized zones rather than through ad hoc direct links.

This principle aligns with the movement toward edge and fog architectures. Atlam et al. (2018), Chiang and Zhang (2016), and Shen et al. (2020) show that processing closer to data sources can reduce latency and bandwidth pressure, but edge architectures also require disciplined trust boundaries. A gateway that filters, signs, rate-limits, and validates data can be a resilience asset. A gateway that aggregates identities, bypasses segmentation, and forwards opaque traffic can be a resilience liability. Governments should therefore treat edge nodes as controlled trust brokers, not merely as compute conveniences. Where direct cloud connectivity from field devices is unavoidable, devices should authenticate strongly, use certificate-based trust, and be grouped by function so that compromise of one population does not expose all others.

Segmentation must also reflect operational consequence. It is not enough to segment "OT" from "IT" if a single OT zone contains water controls, building systems, and traffic controllers with different risk profiles. Functional segmentation should be granular enough that compromise in one service domain can be isolated without forcing citywide shutdown. This is where zero trust principles add value, not as branding but as a design discipline of explicit trust decisions, least privilege, verified identity, and continuous reassessment of context.

4. Identity, Trust, and Access Control

Many municipal breaches begin with identity failures rather than sophisticated malware. Shared operator accounts, generic vendor credentials, weak administrative separation, and dormant remote access arrangements are common. Smart city resilience requires identity architectures that recognize human, machine, and service identities as equally important. Devices should have unique identities wherever feasible. Privileged access should be separated from routine operational access. Vendor access should be brokered through approval workflows, not left permanently enabled. Engineering credentials should be isolated from email and office productivity identities to reduce compromise spillover from phishing or business application breaches.

The IoT security literature repeatedly highlights authentication, trust negotiation, and key management as foundational weaknesses (Roman et al., 2013; Sicari et al., 2015; Mosenia & Jha, 2017). For public infrastructure, the lesson is practical: any device or application that can influence control logic, process thresholds, or high-confidence situational awareness must participate in a managed trust framework. This includes certificate issuance, credential rotation, revocation, key escrow policies where appropriate, and service account governance. Access should be logged in forms that support both security analysis and operational accountability. The objective is not only to know who logged in, but to understand which identity changed what process parameter, through which pathway, and under what approval.

5. Monitoring, Detection, and Data Validation

Monitoring strategies for smart city systems must extend beyond signature-based alerting on enterprise networks. They should include behavioral baselines for devices, integrity validation for configuration changes, protocol-aware monitoring for industrial traffic, anomaly detection for telemetry, and cross-checking between independent data sources. Chen et al. (2021) and Houichi et al. (2024) show that machine learning and deep learning can support smart city intrusion detection, especially in high-volume and heterogeneous data environments. Yet public agencies should use these methods carefully. Detection quality depends on representative training data, explainable alert logic, and integration with operator workflows. Black-box models that generate many false positives can be worse than simple rule-based alerts if control room staff begin to ignore them.

A resilient monitoring design distinguishes four questions: Is the device or service reachable? Is its configuration unchanged? Is the data plausible? Is the process behavior safe? These questions should be answered using multiple evidence types. For example, a pump may be reachable and still unsafe if setpoints were manipulated. A traffic controller may be online and still untrustworthy if timing plans deviate from approved baselines. A flood sensor may report stable readings that are physically implausible when compared with nearby rainfall and stream conditions. Robust monitoring therefore combines cyber telemetry with process context. In practical terms, this may involve comparison across redundant sensors, alerting on impossible rates of change, cryptographic signing of approved logic, and field verification procedures when digital confidence falls below threshold.

AI-based detection can strengthen this monitoring layer when it is deployed as decision support rather than autonomous authority over critical actuation. Recent studies show that deep learning, hybrid feature selection, and explainable intrusion detection can improve detection accuracy in IoT networks, but they also report continuing challenges related to benchmark inconsistency, class imbalance, false positives, computational overhead, and adversarial manipulation (Ghadami et al., 2025; Villafranca et al., 2025). For municipal use, model performance must therefore be evaluated with operational metrics as well as statistical metrics. Precision and recall are useful, but they should be interpreted alongside mean time to detect, mean time to triage, analyst workload, degraded-mode trigger accuracy, and the cost of unnecessary service interruption. The proper governance question is not whether an AI model is accurate in a laboratory dataset, but whether it helps operators preserve trustworthy service under field conditions.

6. Safe Operations and Degraded Modes

The most distinctive feature of cyber resilience is the design of graceful degradation. Governments should assume that some services will occasionally operate in reduced-confidence or reduced-automation states. The question is whether those modes are safe, rehearsed, and documented. Kayan et al. (2022) and Salvi, Spagnoletti, and Noori (2022) point out that resilience in cyber-physical systems depends on preserving essential function despite uncertainty. For municipal services, this means identifying minimum viable operating states. A water utility may revert temporarily to local control at pumping stations while central optimization is disconnected. A building management system may lose remote analytics but maintain local temperature safeguards. A transport network may suspend adaptive timing and fall back to prevalidated signal plans. Environmental dashboards may flag sensor confidence levels rather than presenting all streams as equally trustworthy.

Degraded modes should be engineered, not improvised. They require predefined thresholds for mode switching, operator playbooks, local manual overrides, and validation procedures to avoid escalating risk during transition. Municipal leaders often invest heavily in digital optimization but insufficiently in manual resilience. Yet incidents show that operations fail most dramatically when staff have forgotten how to run safely without the full digital stack. Exercises should therefore include scenarios in which data is suspected but not absent, remote access is disabled during a weather emergency, or third-party analytics are unavailable for days rather than hours. The aim is to make degradation a controlled condition, not a sign of collapse.

7. Recovery Engineering and Restoration Confidence

Recovery in smart city environments is more complex than restoring servers from backup. Municipal services often depend on combinations of logic, configurations, calibration states, firmware versions, historian records, and environmental context. Restoring the wrong configuration to a PLC or building controller can be as dangerous as leaving it offline. Smith, Janicke, He, Ferra, and Albakri (2021) argue in the AIR4ICS framework that industrial incident response must be more adaptive and collaborative than conventional IT approaches because responders must balance forensic caution, operational urgency, and safety. Recovery engineering should therefore include golden configurations, version-controlled logic, tested backup procedures for supervisory databases, and independent methods to validate that restored systems are producing trustworthy outputs.

Restoration confidence is critical. A city should not declare a service "recovered" merely because screens are back online. Recovery criteria should include technical integrity checks, operator validation, process stability, and citizen service outcomes. For example, a restored transport system should demonstrate accurate signal timing and communications, not just application availability. A restored water system should validate instrument calibration, alarm functionality, and process trend continuity. These requirements argue for recovery plans that are service-centric rather than technology-centric.

8. Adaptation, Learning, and Continuous Assurance

Resilience is completed by adaptation. Linkov et al. (2014) argue that resilience differs from risk management because it accepts that not all disruptive conditions can be predicted ex ante. Governments therefore need feedback mechanisms that convert incidents, exercises, audits, and near misses into architecture and policy improvements. Continuous assurance should include periodic attack path reviews, vendor access audits, tabletop exercises that include operational leaders, validation of fallback procedures, and retesting of segmentation boundaries after every major integration change. Hemsley and Fisher (2018) demonstrate that lessons from past ICS incidents are often available but insufficiently institutionalized. Municipal learning failures are therefore preventable.

Digital twins can support adaptation when used carefully. Salvi et al. (2022) show that digital twin approaches can strengthen cyber resilience by modeling dependencies, process states, and recovery scenarios in critical infrastructures. In government settings, a digital twin should not be understood as a marketing dashboard. It should be a controlled representation that helps teams simulate disruption, test isolation strategies, and estimate consequence propagation. If twin models are linked to live operations, they must themselves be secured and governed as critical assets.

Taken together, these eight layers transform security from a defensive perimeter into an operating capability. The purpose is not to eliminate all compromise, which is unrealistic, but to limit blast radius, preserve trustworthy decision-making, recover with confidence, and improve over time. That is the core meaning of cyber resilience for smart city government services. Figure 3 illustrates the cyber resilience lifecycle in smart city government services, centered on sustaining essential public service outcomes through the continuous stages of anticipation, withstand, recover, and adapt. Figure 4 depicts the zero-trust segmentation model for municipal smart city environments, illustrating the secure convergence and isolation of enterprise IT, supervisory OT (ICS/SCADA), edge brokers, and field devices through micro-segmentation, continuous verification, and policy-enforced trust boundaries. Table 4 presents a structured, eight-layer architecture for building cyber resilience into government smart city services, moving from governance at the top to recovery at the base. Then Table 5 outlines five OT-specific control families that balance security with the operational realities of live infrastructure.

Figure 3. Cyber resilience lifecycle centered on sustaining essential public service outcomes.

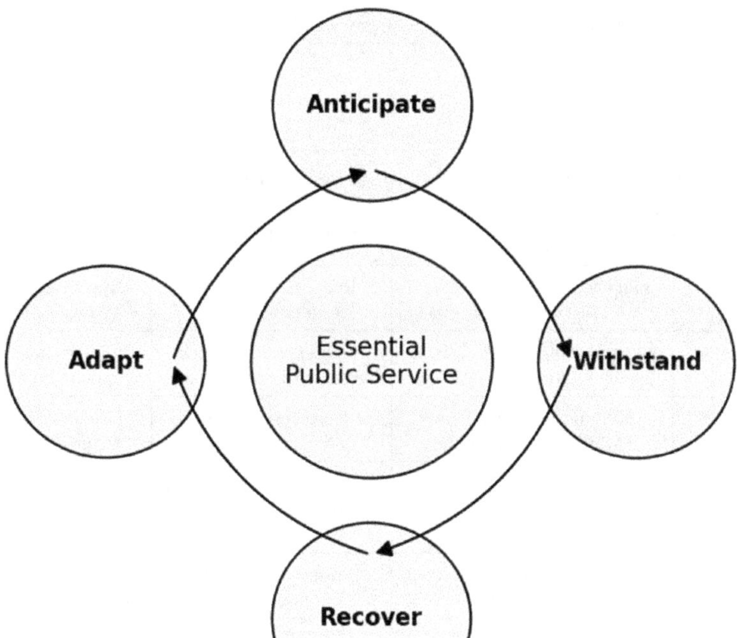

Table 4. Eight-layer cyber resilience architecture for government smart city services

Layer	Core question	Representative controls	Expected resilience outcome
Governance	Who owns service risk?	Critical service register, cross-agency governance, policy alignment	Clear accountability and prioritization
Asset intelligence	What depends on what?	Dependency maps, asset baselines, vendor relationship mapping	Faster triage and smarter investment
Architecture	How is compromise contained?	Zoning, DMZs, secure brokers, network segmentation	Reduced blast radius
Identity and trust	Who or what is allowed to act?	Device identity, MFA, PAM, certificate governance	Controlled access and traceability
Monitoring	Can we detect loss of trust?	Protocol-aware monitoring, telemetry validation, anomaly detection	Earlier detection and better operator confidence
Safe operations	Can the service degrade safely?	Manual overrides, local control, fallback plans	Continuity under uncertainty
Recovery engineering	Can we restore trusted operation?	Golden configs, tested backups, restore validation	Lower recovery time and fewer unsafe restorations
Adaptation	Do we learn and improve?	Exercises, audits, after-action reviews, procurement updates	Continuous improvement over time

Table 5. OT-specific security controls and their operational effect

Control family	Example implementation	Operational benefit	Common implementation caution
Remote access control	Jump host with approval and session logging	Reduces unmanaged vendor pathways	Do not create permanent bypass accounts
Configuration integrity	Version-controlled PLC/HMI logic	Supports safe rollback and forensic comparison	Baselines must match live commissioned reality
Protocol-aware inspection	Monitoring for Modbus/BACnet/DNP3 anomalies	Detects suspicious commands and drift	Detection rules require process context
Read-only data export	One-way or brokered replication to analytics	Protects process networks from analytics-side compromise	Exports still need integrity and timing assurance
Local fail-safe capability	Manual pump control or fixed traffic timing plans	Preserves minimum viable service	Fallback procedures must be rehearsed, not assumed

Figure 4. Zero-trust segmentation model for municipal convergence of enterprise IT, supervisory OT, edge brokers, and field devices.

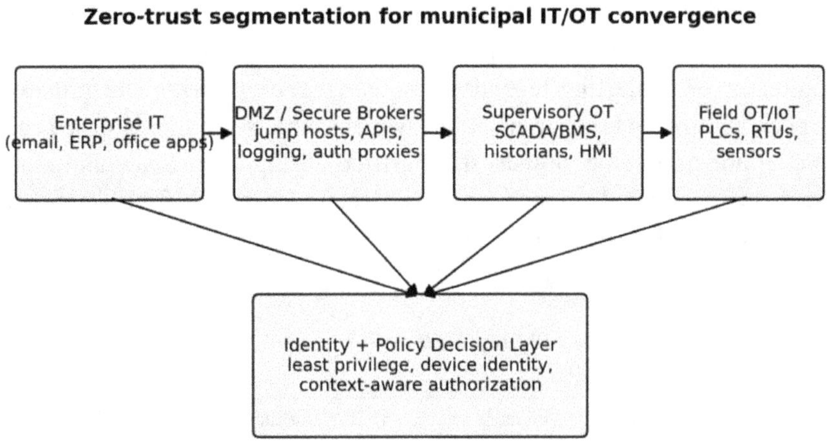

RELATIONSHIP TO INTERNATIONAL STANDARDS AND FRAMEWORK BOUNDARIES

The proposed framework is intended to complement, not replace, established cybersecurity and operational technology references. Its specific contribution is to convert general standards language into service-level resilience decisions for municipal environments. NIST CSF 2.0 is broad and outcome-oriented, and its Govern function strengthens executive accountability for cyber risk (NIST, 2024). NIST SP 800-82 Rev. 3 provides detailed OT security guidance, including the need to protect systems that interact directly with the physical environment while respecting performance, reliability, and safety constraints (Stouffer et al., 2023). NIST SP 800-213 and SP 800-213A support IoT acquisition by identifying device and non-technical supporting capabilities that organizations should consider before deployment (Fagan et al., 2021a, 2021b). ISA/IEC 62443 contributes a lifecycle-oriented view of industrial automation and control system security, while the NIS2 Directive reinforces governance, incident handling, business continuity, crisis management, and supply-chain attention for essential and important entities in Europe (European Union, 2022; International Society of Automation, n.d.).

These references are valuable, but they are not automatically operationalized in fragmented municipal settings. A small municipality may adopt the terminology of a standard without knowing which pump station, roadside controller, building automation server, or alerting dependency should receive priority. The framework in this chapter therefore acts as a translation layer. It asks how standards-based controls preserve a public outcome, how trust is verified during abnormal conditions, and how recovery is validated before a service is declared restored. Table 6 summarizes this relationship and clarifies the boundaries of the proposed contribution.

Table 6. Alignment between the proposed resilience framework and selected international standards

Reference	Primary emphasis	How the chapter operationalizes it for smart city services
NIST CSF 2.0	Governance outcomes, risk communication, and continuous improvement	Translates governance into a critical service register, accountable owners, service-level thresholds, and municipal recovery priorities.
NIST SP 800-82 Rev. 3	Operational technology security under safety, reliability, and performance constraints	Connects OT guidance to water, traffic, building, and public-safety degraded modes rather than treating OT as a generic network segment.
NIST SP 800-213/213A	IoT device cybersecurity requirements and manufacturer supporting capabilities	Uses procurement requirements, device identity, firmware governance, logging, and decommissioning as pre-deployment resilience controls.
ISA/IEC 62443	IACS lifecycle security, zones, conduits, and security levels	Extends zoning and conduits into cross-agency municipal dependency maps and recovery playbooks.
EU NIS2 / ENISA policy direction	Risk management, incident handling, business continuity, supply-chain security, and cross-sector coordination	Frames resilience as a public governance obligation that includes citizen communication, third-party oversight, and measurable service continuity.

SECTORAL USE CASES: APPLYING RESILIENCE IN MUNICIPAL OPERATIONS

The value of a cyber resilience framework is ultimately tested in concrete service contexts. Smart city systems differ in control dynamics, safety implications, citizen visibility, and recovery tolerances. This section applies the framework to four government service domains where IoT, sensing, and ICS/SCADA convergence is especially pronounced.

Water and Wastewater Services

Water and wastewater utilities are archetypal cyber-physical public services. They rely on pumps, valves, chemical dosing, reservoir level sensors, pressure monitoring, telemetry networks, and supervisory control platforms. The resilience challenge is not merely preventing unauthorized access to treatment assets. It is ensuring that process integrity can be maintained when data confidence is reduced or connectivity is impaired. Historical ICS research shows that water operations can be harmed by both direct control manipulation and indirect disruption to supporting systems such as remote communications, engineering workstations, and alarm handling (Miller & Rowe, 2012; Hemsley & Fisher, 2018).

A resilient water architecture therefore separates field control from enterprise networks, maintains validated local control capability at critical stations, and preserves independent measurements for process verification. Chemical dosing commands should be strongly controlled, configuration changes should be versioned, and operators should have procedures for verifying suspicious readings against local instruments. Recovery planning should prioritize potable safety and process stability over full feature restoration. For example, a utility may intentionally limit remote optimization for a period after an incident until data trust is re-established. The key objective is continuity of safe water service, not immediate return to maximum automation.

Intelligent Transport and Traffic Management

Transport systems combine high citizen visibility with broad attack surfaces. Connected intersections, variable message signs, parking platforms, public transport location feeds, fare systems, roadside sensors, and traffic cameras are often integrated through central management platforms and outsourced telecommunications. An outage may not directly endanger life in every case, but it can create congestion, emergency response delays, secondary accidents, and public confusion. Elmaghraby and Losavio (2014) note that transport is a core domain in which smart city cyber incidents translate quickly into social disruption.

Resilience in transport depends on corridor-level containment and prevalidated fallback states. Traffic control systems should be able to isolate affected intersections or revert them to safe timing plans. Variable signs should have content control safeguards and default safe displays. Data feeds used for real-time route advice should be subject to plausibility checks and trusted-source validation. Because transport often relies on public-private operational chains, contract management is especially important: cities must know which third parties administer field equipment, which components depend on carrier networks, and what manual options exist if central platforms fail. Public communication protocols are also part of resilience, since commuters and emergency responders need reliable guidance during degraded operations.

Smart Buildings and Municipal Facilities

Municipal building portfolios now include connected heating, ventilation, and air-conditioning systems, lighting controls, smart access systems, occupancy sensing, energy optimization platforms, and life-safety interfaces. These systems are often treated as low-risk because they do not resemble traditional critical infrastructure. In reality, building automation failures can disrupt council chambers, shelters, hospitals, emergency operations centers, schools, and data centers. They can also provide convenient entry points into broader networks if segmentation is weak. Alcaraz and Zeadally (2013) and Kayan et al. (2022) suggest that building systems deserve closer scrutiny because they sit at the boundary between physical environment control and enterprise management.

A resilient facilities strategy starts by classifying buildings according to civic criticality. A public library and an emergency operations center may both have smart thermostats, but the tolerance for downtime, remote lockout, or temperature instability is not equivalent. High-criticality facilities should maintain local override capability, documented commissioning baselines, strict separation between building automation and office networks, and rapid vendor escalation paths. Maintenance personnel should understand which convenience features can be sacrificed during a cyber event to preserve safety and occupancy requirements. In some cases, resilience may mean simplifying automation rather than maximizing interconnection.

Public Safety, Environmental Sensing, and Civic Situational Awareness

Public safety and civic situational awareness systems combine cameras, acoustic sensors, environmental monitors, emergency alerting tools, and geospatial platforms. Their cyber risk lies partly in service continuity and partly in data trust. If sensor feeds are inaccurate, delayed, or manipulated, emergency managers may misallocate resources or issue misleading public messages. Chen et al. (2021) and Houichi et al. (2024) indicate that AI-supported anomaly detection can help secure these heterogeneous data environments, but the governance burden remains high. Public safety systems often process sensitive information and may affect civil liberties.

Resilience in this domain requires provenance-aware data architectures, role-based access, segmented analytics environments, and policies that distinguish advisory data from command-critical data. Environmental sensing used for public advisories should include confidence scoring and redundancy where possible. Emergency alerting systems should be protected by strong approval workflows and independent verification channels. During major incidents, governments should assume that some digital feeds may be unavailable or disputed and should design decision processes accordingly. In other words, resilience is not only about keeping cameras online; it is about preserving trusted situational awareness and lawful, proportionate use of connected sensing.

Across all four sectors, the unifying lesson is that resilience must be tailored to operational consequence. The same control may have different value in different services. Encryption on a low-power environmental sensor is useful, but in a chlorine dosing network, local fail-safe behavior and configuration integrity may be more important. Conversely, a privacy-preserving data governance model may be more salient for public-space sensing than for internal pump telemetry. Governments should therefore resist one-size-fits-all smart city security models and instead align resilience design with service mission, consequence profile, and recovery reality. **Table 7** maps each service sector to its preferred degraded mode and recovery priority. Water systems fall back to local manual control, prioritizing process integrity and public health. Traffic networks revert to revalidated timing plans to keep critical corridors open. Municipal facilities default to local overrides, accepting reduced optimization to preserve occupant safety. Public safety systems maintain operations through confidence-scored data and manual confirmation, recovering toward trusted situational awareness first.

Table 7. Sectoral application of resilience principles

Service sector	Most critical asset relationship	Preferred degraded mode	Recovery priority
Water/wastewater	Telemetry + supervisory control + field process	Local control with verified manual readings	Process integrity and public health assurance
Traffic and mobility	Central coordination + intersection controllers	Prevalidated safe timing plans	Safe flow at critical corridors and emergency routes
Municipal facilities	Building automation + life-safety interfaces	Local overrides with reduced optimization	Occupant safety and continuity of critical buildings
Public safety/ environment	Sensor feeds + alerting + geospatial dashboards	Confidence-scored data and manual confirmation	Trusted situational awareness and lawful communication

INCIDENT RESPONSE, RECOVERY, AND CONTINUOUS ASSURANCE

Incident response in smart city environments differs from conventional enterprise response because responders must balance forensic containment, public communication, contractual coordination, and physical safety at the same time. Smith et al. (2021) propose the AIR4ICS framework precisely because industrial response requires more adaptive and collaborative practices than static playbooks alone can offer. In government settings, the incident command structure should therefore connect cyber teams, service owners, field supervisors, communications officers, legal advisors, and executive decision makers from the outset of a major event. The primary question is not simply "Which systems are infected?" but "Which public outcomes are at risk in the next hour, day, and week?"

A resilient response process begins with service-centric triage. Assets should be prioritized according to essential service outcomes, not according to technical complexity or organizational prestige. If a municipality faces simultaneous compromise of a public website, a billing platform, and a utility telemetry broker, the restoration sequence should reflect safety and continuity consequences rather than convenience. This principle sounds obvious, yet many organizations default to restoring visible administrative systems first because they generate executive pressure. A mature smart city response model instead uses pre-established criticality ratings and service maps to guide prioritization under stress.

Triage should also distinguish between loss of visibility, loss of control, and loss of trust. These conditions require different responses. If telemetry is absent but process controls are stable and can be checked locally, the emphasis may be on communications restoration. If controls are available but their trustworthiness is uncertain, segmentation and independent validation become the priority. If both visibility and control are degraded, governments may need to invoke safe shutdown or local manual operation protocols. This distinction reduces the risk of inappropriate escalation or premature restoration.

Containment in cyber-physical government systems must be surgical. Disconnecting a compromised server may be appropriate; disconnecting a communications segment without understanding the process consequences may create a larger safety problem. Response teams should therefore maintain containment options that are mapped to service impact. Examples include disabling specific vendor accounts, isolating a protocol gateway, forcing read-only data exports, suspending automated optimization, or severing nonessential cloud synchronizations while preserving local control. The purpose is to reduce blast radius while maintaining essential function. This is where prior architectural work pays dividends. A city that has already segmented services and documented dependencies can contain more confidently than one discovering its architecture during crisis.

Government response also includes public legitimacy. Citizens experience cyber incidents primarily as service disruption, contradictory information, or visible loss of confidence by officials. Public communications should therefore be timely, factual, and aligned with operational reality. Over-reassurance can be damaging if later evidence shows that data or services were untrusted for longer than initially stated. At the same time, governments should avoid releasing unnecessary technical detail that would hinder containment. The communications objective is to explain service status, protective actions, alternative access routes, and expected updates. Because smart city incidents may affect mobility, water use, or facility access, communication channels should themselves be resilient and multi-modal.

Restoration should proceed through controlled assurance gates. First comes technical sanitation: credential resets, system isolation, verified images, and restoration of clean configurations. Second comes operational validation: testing whether control logic, alarms, thresholds, and data flows behave as expected. Third comes service validation: confirming that the citizen outcome—safe water, stable traffic operations, or functional emergency coordination—is actually restored. Finally comes monitoring intensification: applying temporary heightened scrutiny to detect relapse, latent persistence, or process anomalies after reintroduction of connectivity. Hemsley and Fisher (2018) demonstrate that many serious incidents unfold over time rather than in one obvious moment, so post-restoration vigilance is essential.

Continuous assurance links incident response with ongoing preparedness and institutional learning. Municipal governments should therefore conduct regular exercises that simulate both disruptive and low-visibility scenarios, including malware propagation, telemetry manipulation, compromised supplier credentials, and prolonged cloud-service outages. These exercises should include field operators as well as cybersecurity teams so that operational realities, safety constraints, and manual fallback procedures are assessed together rather than in isolation.

Such exercises should be paired with technical validation activities, including restoration drills for supervisory platforms, comparison of golden configurations with live states, and testing of remote-access disablement procedures. After each exercise or incident, municipalities should update procurement requirements, architectural standards, and incident playbooks. In this way, learning is institutionalized and resilience improves through repeated cycles of verification and design correction.

Mature municipal programs normalize this learning process by treating change requests, vendor onboarding, near misses, and field anomalies as opportunities to strengthen resilience. Incident response thereby becomes part of a wider assurance regime that continuously improves government service delivery. Figure 5 illustrates this continuous assurance loop, linking asset inventory, monitoring, exercises, incident handling, recovery, and design improvement in a recurring cycle of service hardening. Table 8 explain five-level maturity model progressing from fragmented, ad hoc practices to an adaptive ecosystem where resilience is embedded in governance, contracts, cross-agency learning, and civic outcomes.

Figure 5. Continuous assurance loop linking inventory, monitoring, exercises, response, recovery, and design improvement.

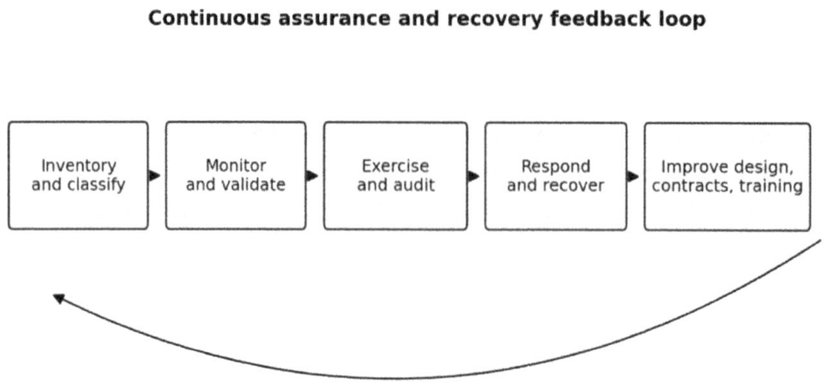

Table 8. Five-level maturity model for cyber resilience in smart city government services

Level	Profile	Typical characteristics	Priority next step
1	Fragmented	Disconnected inventories, ad hoc vendor access, limited ownership	Identify critical services and assign accountable owners
2	Basic control	Initial hardening and logging on key systems	Map dependencies and formalize remote access governance
3	Segmented	Core zones, privileged access controls, tested backups	Engineer degraded modes and cross-service exercises
4	Resilient operations	Service-centric incident response, validated recovery, data trust checks	Integrate continuous assurance into contracts and change control
5	Adaptive ecosystem	Cross-agency learning, digital twin use, metrics tied to civic outcomes	Sustain improvement through procurement, analytics, and workforce renewal

OPERATIONAL CASE STUDY AND MEASURABLE VALIDATION CRITERIA

To address the need for clearer operationalization, this section presents an illustrative case study that converts the proposed framework into measurable resilience criteria. The case is deliberately non-sensitive and uses synthetic values. It is intended to demonstrate how a municipality could test a resilience claim without disclosing actual network details or operational configurations. The scenario concerns a smart flood-warning service that is connected to a traffic diversion corridor. River-level sensors, rainfall gauges, roadside message signs, and traffic signal controllers feed an emergency operations dashboard. During a severe storm, the city receives inconsistent sensor readings and suspicious authentication failures on a gateway that connects field devices to the analytics platform. Operators must decide whether the service can remain in normal mode, whether traffic diversion should move to a prevalidated fallback plan, and whether environmental alerts should include confidence qualifiers.

The case applies four validation criteria. First, detection must occur before the maximum tolerable data-latency threshold for the service is exceeded. Second, containment must isolate the suspected gateway without disconnecting local field control. Third, degraded operation must preserve a defined minimum public outcome, such as safe route guidance and continued local flood observation. Fourth, recovery must be based on validated configuration, data plausibility, and operator sign-off rather than application availability alone. These criteria convert general resilience language into testable claims. A city can therefore evaluate whether its design reduces the practical interval between loss of trust and safe operational decision-making.

Table 9 presents a compact structured dataset for the illustrative assessment. The variables are suitable for tabletop exercises, procurement evaluation, or internal audit. Maximum tolerable data loss (MTDL) indicates how long a service can tolerate untrusted or missing data before public decisions become unreliable. Recovery time objective (RTO) identifies the target restoration window for trusted function. Mean time to detect (MTTD) and mean time to triage (MTTT) describe the expected detection and interpretation period. Fallback maturity is scored from 0 to 1, where 0 represents an improvised fallback and 1 represents a rehearsed, documented, and technically validated fallback. Data validation coverage is also scored from 0 to 1 and reflects the extent to which independent sensors, plausibility checks, time synchronization, and field verification procedures are available.

Table 9. Illustrative structured data for resilience validation in a smart flood-warning and traffic-diversion scenario

Service component	Timing thresholds	Detection/ triage	Assurance score	Operational interpretation
River-level sensor cluster	MTDL 15 min; RTO 4 hr	9 min	Fallback 0.75; validation 0.80	Acceptable if anomalous streams are confidence-scored and checked against rainfall data.
Field gateway	MTDL 10 min; RTO 6 hr	14 min	Fallback 0.60; validation 0.55	Immediate containment is required because triage exceeds tolerance and validation is incomplete.
Traffic signal corridor	MTDL 20 min; RTO 3 hr	12 min	Fallback 0.90; validation 0.70	Move to prevalidated fixed timing while central optimization is suspended.
Public alerting dashboard	MTDL 10 min; RTO 2 hr	8 min	Fallback 0.70; validation 0.65	Remain active only with confidence language and approval workflow controls.

The illustrative values show why resilience should not be reduced to uptime. The field gateway is technically available, but its expected detection-and-triage interval exceeds the tolerance for trusted flood decision-making. That finding would trigger containment and gateway bypass even if the dashboard remains reachable. By contrast, the traffic signal corridor can continue in a safe degraded state because the fallback plan is mature and its timing plan is already validated. This distinction reflects the practical value of service-level metrics: they help leaders decide which capability must be isolated, which may operate with warnings, and which can safely continue in a reduced mode.

Code Listing 1 provides a simple, reproducible scoring routine for the synthetic dataset. The routine is not a cybersecurity tool and does not interact with live infrastructure. It illustrates how a city analyst could combine latency, recovery, fallback, and validation indicators into a transparent resilience score for planning discussions. The score should not replace professional engineering judgment, but it makes assumptions explicit and auditable.

Code Listing 1. Safe illustrative Python routine for service-level resilience scoring

```
assets = [
    {"name": "river_sensor_cluster", "mtdl": 15, "rto": 4, "detect_triage": 9, "fallback": 0.75, "validation": 0.80},
    {"name": "field_gateway", "mtdl": 10, "rto": 6, "detect_triage": 14, "fallback": 0.60, "validation": 0.55},
    {"name": "traffic_signal_corridor", "mtdl": 20, "rto": 3, "detect_triage": 12, "fallback": 0.90, "validation": 0.70},
```

```
    {"name": "public_alert_dashboard", "mtdl": 10, "rto": 2,
"detect_triage": 8, "fallback": 0.70, "validation": 0.65},
 ]

 for asset in assets:
    latency_score = max(0, 1 - asset["detect_triage"] / as-
set["mtdl"])
    assurance_score = 0.5 * asset["fallback"] + 0.5 * as-
set["validation"]
    resilience_score = round(100 * (0.55 * latency_score +
0.45 * assurance_score), 1)
    decision = "continue with monitoring" if resilience_
score >= 70 else "degrade or isolate"
    print(asset["name"], resilience_score, decision)
```

When applied to the illustrative data, the scoring logic would identify the field gateway as the weakest resilience point because detection and triage exceed the maximum tolerable data-loss threshold while fallback and validation coverage are only moderate. The appropriate action would be to isolate the gateway, preserve local field observation, and use verified traffic fallback plans while technical teams validate configuration and credentials. The exercise demonstrates how the chapter's framework can be converted into repeatable evidence: each decision is linked to a service outcome, an operational threshold, a fallback condition, and a recovery validation requirement. This makes the framework more suitable for audits, cross-agency exercises, and procurement evaluation because vendors and departments can be asked to show how their systems support the same measurable criteria.

FUTURE RESEARCH DIRECTIONS

Six key research gaps explained in table 10: measuring resilience at the service rather than device level; securing and validating digital twins; making AI-based detection explainable and accountable; understanding how procurement shapes resilience outcomes; integrating privacy and resilience within unified governance; and comparing approaches across cities of different scales and resources.

Table 10. Research Gaps in Cyber Resilience for Smart City Government Services

No.	Research Gap	Description	Indicative Literature
1	Service-level resilience measurement	Need for operationally grounded metrics that connect control performance to civic outcomes (e.g., water continuity, intersection recovery time) rather than device or network level only	Linkov et al. (2013)
2	Digital twins for critical services	Deeper study required securing the twin itself, validating model fidelity, and determining appropriate reliance on simulated states during crises	Salvi et al. (2022)
3	Explainability and usability of AI detection	Stronger focus needed on interpretable alerts, bias mitigation, accountability, and robustness in dynamic urban environments	Chen et al. (2021); Houichi et al. (2024)
4	Procurement-centered security	Empirical research needed on how contractual design, vendor management, and procurement processes affect resilience outcomes	Knowles et al. (2015); Canonico & Sperlì (2023)
5	Integrated privacy and resilience	Privacy and resilience must be studied together within unified governance models that address security, transparency, and citizen rights	Ismagilova et al. (2022); Fabrègue & Bogoni (2023)
6	Comparative research across city scales	Need for studies comparing resilience approaches in large capitals versus smaller municipalities with limited resources and shared infrastructure	Ismagilova et al. (2022); Qian et al. (2019)

CONCLUSION

Smart cities are reshaping the operating model of government by transforming periodic, manual oversight into continuous sensing, coordination, and response. This shift improves visibility and service optimization, but it also binds essential public services to complex socio-technical ecosystems composed of devices, networks, software platforms, vendors, and human operators. In such environments, the central security objective is not perfect prevention; it is cyber resilience. Municipal systems must be able to detect disruption early, contain failure, preserve safe minimum service, restore trusted operation, and learn quickly enough to reduce repeated exposure.

This chapter has shown that securing IoT, sensor, and ICS/SCADA environments in government requires more than device-level hardening. Resilience depends on governance structures that align accountability with service consequence, asset intelligence that reveals interdependencies, architectures that constrain trust and blast radius, identity systems that govern both human and machine access, monitoring practices that validate data trustworthiness, degraded modes that preserve safety, and recovery practices that restore trustworthy operation rather than superficial uptime. The revised framework also clarifies how international standards can be translated into municipal service decisions, how AI-based detection should be governed through explainability and operator accountability, and how structured metrics can make resilience testable in real-world exercises. When municipalities build connected infrastructure on these principles, smart city technologies can create public value without making essential services fragile.

REFERENCES

Alcaraz, C., & Zeadally, S. (2013). Critical control system protection in the 21st century. *Computer, 46*(10), 74–83. DOI: 10.1109/MC.2013.69

Atlam, H. F., Walters, R. J., & Wills, G. B. (2018). Fog computing and the Internet of Things: A review. *Big Data and Cognitive Computing*, *2*(2), 10. DOI: 10.3390/bdcc2020010

Canonico, R., & Sperlì, G. (2023). Industrial cyber-physical systems protection: A methodological review. *Computers & Security*, *135*, 103531. DOI: 10.1016/j.cose.2023.103531

Chen, D., Wawrzynski, P., & Lv, Z. (2021). Cyber security in smart cities: A review of deep learning-based applications and case studies. *Sustainable Cities and Society*, *66*, 102655. DOI: 10.1016/j.scs.2020.102655

Chiang, M., & Zhang, T. (2016). Fog and IoT: An overview of research opportunities. *IEEE Internet of Things Journal*, *3*(6), 854–864. DOI: 10.1109/JIOT.2016.2584538

Chong, C.-Y., & Kumar, S. P. (2003). Sensor networks: Evolution, opportunities, and challenges. *Proceedings of the IEEE*, *91*(8), 1247–1256. DOI: 10.1109/JPROC.2003.814918

Cui, L., Xie, G., Qu, Y., Gao, L., & Yang, Y. (2018). Security and privacy in smart cities: Challenges and opportunities. *IEEE Access : Practical Innovations, Open Solutions*, *6*, 46134–46145. DOI: 10.1109/ACCESS.2018.2853985

Elmaghraby, A. S., & Losavio, M. M. (2014). Cyber security challenges in smart cities: Safety, security and privacy. *Journal of Advanced Research*, *5*(4), 491–497. DOI: 10.1016/j.jare.2014.02.006 PMID: 25685517

European Union. (2022). Directive (EU) 2022/2555 of the European Parliament and of the Council of 14 December 2022 on measures for a high common level of cybersecurity across the Union. Official Journal of the European Union, L 333, 80-152.

European Union Agency for Cybersecurity. (2024). *2024 report on the state of cybersecurity in the Union*. ENISA.

Fabrègue, B. F. G., & Bogoni, A. (2023). Privacy and security concerns in the smart city. *Smart Cities*, *6*(1), 586–613. DOI: 10.3390/smartcities6010027

Fagan, M., Megas, K. N., Scarfone, K., & Smith, M. (2021a). *IoT device cybersecurity guidance for the federal government: Establishing IoT device cybersecurity requirements (NIST SP 800-213)*. National Institute of Standards and Technology., DOI: 10.6028/NIST.SP.800-213

Fagan, M., Megas, K. N., Scarfone, K., & Smith, M. (2021b). *IoT device cybersecurity guidance for the federal government: IoT device cybersecurity requirement catalog (NIST SP 800-213A)*. National Institute of Standards and Technology., DOI: 10.6028/NIST.SP.800-213A

Ghadami, R.. (2025). An intrusion detection system in the Internet of Things with deep learning and an improved arithmetic optimization algorithm and sine cosine algorithm. *Scientific Reports*, *15*(1), 22074. Advance online publication. DOI: 10.1038/s41598-025-22074-3 PMID: 41173998

Gubbi, J., Buyya, R., Marusic, S., & Palaniswami, M. (2013). Internet of Things (IoT): A vision, architectural elements, and future directions. *Future Generation Computer Systems*, *29*(7), 1645–1660. DOI: 10.1016/j.future.2013.01.010

Hemsley, K. E., & Fisher, R. E. (2018). *History of Industrial Control System Cyber Incidents*. Idaho National Laboratory., DOI: 10.2172/1505628

Hosseini, S., Barker, K., & Ramirez-Marquez, J. E. (2016). A review of definitions and measures of system resilience. *Reliability Engineering & System Safety*, *145*, 47–61. DOI: 10.1016/j.ress.2015.08.006

Houichi, M., Jaidi, F., & Bouhoula, A. (2024). Cyber security within smart cities: A comprehensive study and a novel intrusion detection-based approach. *Computers, Materials & Continua*, *81*(1), 393–441. DOI: 10.32604/cmc.2024.054007

International Society of Automation. (n.d.). *ISA/IEC 62443 series of standards*. ISA.

Ismagilova, E., Hughes, L., Rana, N. P., & Dwivedi, Y. K. (2022). Security, privacy and risks within smart cities: Literature review and development of a smart city interaction framework. *Information Systems Frontiers*, *24*(2), 393–414. DOI: 10.1007/s10796-020-10044-1 PMID: 32837262

Jan, M. A., Nanda, P., Zheng, X., & Jamalipour, A. (2017). A survey on security and privacy issues in wireless sensor networks. *IEEE Communications Surveys and Tutorials*, *19*(2), 1346–1369. DOI: 10.1109/COMST.2016.2633620

Joshi, S., Baviskar, A., & Rajmane, S. (2026). A review of cybersecurity in smart cities and intelligent transport systems. *Discover Internet of Things*, *6*(1), 41. Advance online publication. DOI: 10.1007/s43926-026-00312-y

Kayan, H., Nunes, M., Rana, O., Burnap, P., & Perera, C. (2022). Cybersecurity of industrial cyber-physical systems: A review. *ACM Computing Surveys, 54*(11s), 229. Advance online publication. DOI: 10.1145/3510410

Knowles, W., Prince, D., Hutchison, D., Disso, J. F. P., & Jones, K. (2015). A survey of cyber security management in industrial control systems. *International Journal of Critical Infrastructure Protection, 9*, 52–80. DOI: 10.1016/j.ijcip.2015.02.002

Linkov, I., Bridges, T., Creutzig, F., Decker, J., Fox-Lent, C., Kroger, W., Lambert, J. H., Levermann, A., Montreuil, B., Nathwani, J., Nyer, R., Renn, O., Scharte, B., Scheffler, A., Schreurs, M., & Thiel-Clemen, T. (2014). Changing the resilience paradigm. *Nature Climate Change, 4*(6), 407–409. DOI: 10.1038/nclimate2227

Linkov, I., Eisenberg, D. A., Plourde, K., Seager, T. P., Allen, J., & Kott, A. (2013). Resilience metrics for cyber systems. *Environment Systems & Decisions, 33*(4), 471–476. DOI: 10.1007/s10669-013-9485-y

Miller, B., & Rowe, D. C. (2012). A survey of SCADA and critical infrastructure incidents. In *Proceedings of the 1st Annual Conference on Research in Information Technology* (pp. 51-56). DOI: 10.1145/2380790.2380805

Mosenia, A., & Jha, N. K. (2017). A comprehensive study of security of Internet-of-Things. *IEEE Transactions on Emerging Topics in Computing, 5*(4), 586–602. DOI: 10.1109/TETC.2016.2606384

National Institute of Standards and Technology. (2024). The NIST Cybersecurity Framework (CSF) 2.0 (NIST CSWP 29). DOI: 10.6028/NIST.CSWP.29

Nicholson, A., Webber, S., Dyer, S., Patel, T., & Janicke, H. (2012). SCADA security in the light of cyber-warfare. *Computers & Security, 31*(4), 418–436. DOI: 10.1016/j.cose.2012.02.009

Roman, R., Zhou, J., & Lopez, J. (2013). On the features and challenges of security and privacy in distributed Internet of Things. *Computer Networks, 57*(10), 2266–2279. DOI: 10.1016/j.comnet.2012.12.018

Salvi, A., Spagnoletti, P., & Noori, N. S. (2022). Cyber-resilience of critical cyber infrastructures: Integrating digital twins in the electric power ecosystem. *Computers & Security, 112*, 102507. DOI: 10.1016/j.cose.2021.102507

Shen, S., Zhang, K., Zhou, Y., Zhang, X., & Ci, S. (2020). Security in edge-assisted Internet of Things: Challenges and solutions. *Science China. Information Sciences, 63*(12), 220302. DOI: 10.1007/s11432-019-2906-y

Sicari, S., Rizzardi, A., Grieco, L. A., & Coen-Porisini, A. (2015). Security, privacy and trust in Internet of Things: The road ahead. *Computer Networks*, *76*, 146–164. DOI: 10.1016/j.comnet.2014.11.008

Smith, R., Janicke, H., He, Y., Ferra, F., & Albakri, A. (2021). The Agile Incident Response for Industrial Control Systems (AIR4ICS) framework. *Computers & Security*, *109*, 102398. DOI: 10.1016/j.cose.2021.102398

Sobeslav, V., & Horalek, J. (2025). Cybersecurity baseline and risk mitigation for open data in IoT-enabled smart city systems: A case study of the Hradec Kralove Region. *Sensors (Basel)*, *25*(16), 4966. DOI: 10.3390/s25164966 PMID: 40871830

Stouffer, K., Pillitteri, V., Lightman, S., Abrams, M., & Hahn, A. (2023). *Guide to operational technology (OT) security (NIST SP 800-82 Rev. 3)*. National Institute of Standards and Technology., DOI: 10.6028/NIST.SP.800-82r3

Villafranca, A., Thant, K. M., Tasic, I., & Cano, M.-D. (2025). AI-enabled IoT intrusion detection: Unified conceptual framework and research roadmap. *Machine Learning and Knowledge Extraction*, *7*(4), 115. DOI: 10.3390/make7040115

Walters, J. P., Liang, Z., Shi, W., & Chaudhary, V. (2007). Wireless sensor network security: A survey. In Security in Distributed, Grid, Mobile, and Pervasive Computing (pp. 367-409). DOI: 10.1201/9780429119347-20

Wang, Y., Attebury, G., & Ramamurthy, B. (2006). A survey of security issues in wireless sensor networks. *IEEE Communications Surveys and Tutorials*, *8*(2), 2–23. DOI: 10.1109/COMST.2006.315852

Zanella, A., Bui, N., Castellani, A., Vangelista, L., & Zorzi, M. (2014). Internet of Things for smart cities. *IEEE Internet of Things Journal*, *1*(1), 22–32. DOI: 10.1109/JIOT.2014.2306328

Chapter 3

IoT-Enabled Smart Infrastructure:

Securing Connected Devices in Public Service Delivery

G. Boopathi Raja
http://orcid.org/0000-0003-3345-4503
Velalar College of Engineering and Technology, India

ABSTRACT

Government initiatives that use innovative technology has been able to give residents improved services by more effectively using fewer resources and allowing for real-time sound management of public resources through the use of IoT sensors located in public infrastructure. However, there are now emerging threats to the data collected from IoT devices, device authentication and an increasing concern about criminal activity involving the hacking of IoT devices as a result of the growing quantity of IoT machines. This chapter describes how IoT enables smart cities through applications in urban management areas, transportation, utilities and the healthcare industry. In addition to providing security measures for the protection of IoT devices, networks, and the integrity of data collected such as encryption, strong authentication and lifetime support; a critical evaluation of the security vulnerabilities in the IoT ecosystem will also be presented.

1. INTRODUCTION

One of the most transformative technological paradigms of the 21st century has emerged as the Internet of Things (IoT). Through its ability to embed sensors, actuators, and connected devices into physical environments, the IoT has created new

DOI: 10.4018/979-8-2600-2845-2.ch003

ways of interacting with infrastructure and governments, industries, and societies. Through this sensory data collection method, IoT allows for real-time monitoring of infrastructure; predictive analytics to assess the impact of this data; and automated decision-making based on these two elements. In terms of public service delivery, smart infrastructure provided by IoT-enabled smart city initiatives is a cornerstone of digital transformation services that governments can deliver in an efficient, transparent, and citizen-focused manner (Abdullah Sani & Jaafar, 2025a; Bellini et al., 2022).

The increasing reliance on IoT to enhance the quality of life for citizens, optimize resource allocation, and manage urban systems is evident in smart government programs. Some examples include intelligent traffic management; smart energy grids; healthcare monitoring; and waste management systems. These applications of IoT include multiple technological innovations occurring all at once, as evidenced by the need for smart energy grids to provide dynamic balancing of energy being supplied and accepted by both consumers and producers, thereby reducing energy waste and generating sustainable energy sources (Abir et al., 2021; Mehmood et al., 2021). As well, wearable healthcare devices and remote patient monitoring systems provide access for underserved communities to receive the same level of care and health services as their more accessible counterparts, thus creating access equity through the utilization of IoT devices for health services (Katal, 2024; Raja & Chakraborty, 2023). Collectively, these examples emphasize how IoT is not simply a technological innovation but rather a governance tool that enables public sector and government entities to create resilient and responsive public service ecosystems.

Because of the rapidly growing number of IoT devices, the benefits of IoT come with new security risks that have never been feasible before. The limited number of connected devices means openness to attackers through various methods such as data privacy breaches, lack of device authentication, and compromised networks due to the high volume of devices in existence. IoT devices leave many opportunities for cybercriminals to use as entry points for major cyber-attacks, disruptive services, and access to sensitive classifications of citizen data (Ismagilova et al., 2022; Okika et al., 2025). For governments, this is extremely concerning because a breach in public infrastructure can result in the loss of trust by citizens, weaken government authority, and impact national security. IoT represents two sides of a coin; one side providing the benefit of a more efficient marketplace while the other is creating the risk of increased vulnerability. Therefore, securing smart infrastructure requires a very comprehensive set of processes to accomplish those goals.

1.1 IoT in Public Service Delivery

IoT-based smart infrastructure is represented across multiple areas of service to the public. Sensors found in urban management waste bins, water distribution systems and street lights support predictive maintenance along with the more effective use of resources (Das, 2024; Faheemuddin, 2025). Through the use of connected vehicles and traffic monitoring systems, IoT-based smart infrastructure improves transportation by reducing congestion, enhancing safety and providing support for sustainable mobility (Singh et al., 2024). Utility smart grids and intelligent meter systems provide real-time consumption data allowing for dynamic pricing and demand-side management (Abir et al., 2021). Wearable devices, implantable devices and telemedicine provide healthcare services in remote locations, thereby enhancing patient outcomes and lowering healthcare delivery costs (Ajitha et al., 2025; Raja, 2025b).

The range and extent of how IoT is changing the way that governments manage their operations and how they provide service are illustrated through IoT applications. Additionally, they exemplify how sectors have similar and different needs concerning IoT security. Some examples are that when using IoT in healthcare, data privacy and compliance with the associated medical standards must be foremost in concern, while in the case of transport IoT security must be designed not only to provide real-time reliability and resiliency from cyber attacks.

Figure 1. Key Security Challenges in IoT-Enabled Smart Infrastructure

1.2 Security Challenges in IoT Ecosystems

Figure 1 illustrates the primary security issues related to smart infrastructure powered by IoT technologies. This figure identifies four key factors—data privacy, authentication of IoT devices, network threats, and trust of citizens—that determine the resilience of connected public services. The figure shows that security in an IoT ecosystem requires a comprehensive approach that incorporates both technical and governance/security measures via citizen involvement. The multiple approaches to IoT security mean that security must be embedded at all layers of an organization's IoT adoption to achieve sustainable and confident public service delivery.

The addition of IoT to public infrastructures leads to various types of security vulnerabilities as noted below:

- ***Data Privacy and Sovereignty:*** An incredible amount of personal data is produced by IoT devices including, but not limited to, health records, location data, and behavioural trends. Keeping control over their personal data (i.e., ensuring data sovereignty) will be an important governance issue for citizens (Ismagilova et al., 2022).
- ***Device Authentication and Lifecycle Management:*** Many devices do not have an adequate or effective way to authenticate users prior to gaining access. Additionally, there is a lack of adequate lifecycle management that includes the provisioning, updates, and decommissioning of devices which results in long-term security vulnerabilities (Chatterjee et al., 2021).
- ***Network-Level Threats:*** IoT networks are susceptible to different types of attacks such as Distributed Denial of Service (DDoS), and ransomware and virus from botnets. This type of attack could have a significant impact on the ability to deliver essential services, from providing power to health care services (Pemmasani & Osaka, 2021; Rao et al., 2024).
- ***Citizen Trust and Governance Risks:*** IoT has many technical vulnerabilities as well as issues with surveillance, data abuse, and loss of trust, so it is essential that IoT systems have a transparent governance framework in place as national security and the public's willingness to accept those systems rely on the public knowing their data and privacy is being protected (Das, 2024).

These challenges illustrate the need for comprehensive security strategies that recognize the importance of integrating technical solutions with organizational and policy measures.

1.3 Security Techniques and Emerging Directions

To meet these challenges, governments and academia have suggested several security options. For example, encryption can protect communications between devices and networks, while robust authentication controls can prevent unauthorized access. Blockchain-based trust frameworks provide decentralized, tamper-proof authentication and enable enhanced accountability and transparency (Almulhim, 2025; Khalil et al., 2022). Lifecycle support mechanisms, including secure provisioning and ongoing updates will help protect the devices throughout their lifetime of use.

There are emerging trends that will also expand the scope of IoT security. For example, AI-enabled adaptive security leverages machine learning to detect anomalies and respond to threats in real time (Banerjee, 2025; Van Hoang, 2024). Quantum-secure cryptography will protect against the threats posed by quantum computing, thereby helping assure that IoT systems last into the future. Furthermore, citizen trust frameworks emphasize the need for transparency, accountability, and participatory governance and recognize that privacy; safety; and the social legitimacy of technologies should be included when considering the security of those technologies (Abdullah Sani & Jaafar, 2025a; Das, 2024).

1.4 Purpose and Scope of the Chapter

The main purpose of this chapter is to provide a comprehensive examination of public service delivery using IoT-enabled smart infrastructure, including an assessment of security. The chapter starts with an analysis of the use of IoT and smart infrastructure in urban management, transportation, utilities, and healthcare, with attention to both the opportunities and vulnerabilities associated with these applications. The chapter will then provide an in-depth analysis of the various security challenges associated with IoT ecosystems, including a review of techniques for securing IoT, such as encryption, authentication, block chain technologies, and lifecycle management, as well as offering future directions for IoT cyber security, including the use of artificial intelligence (AI)-based cyber security tools, quantum-safe cryptography, and the use of citizen trust frameworks, via case studies and policy models from a variety of leading nations in smart government. Ultimately, this chapter attempts to synthesize both technical, organizational, and governance perspectives, to establish a more holistic understanding of how governments can provide security for citizens via the use of IoT-enabled public services.

2. IOT APPLICATIONS IN PUBLIC INFRASTRUCTURE

IoT will be an integral part of the future of smart governance, which has advanced through the use of IoT technology as a transformational capability in enhancing public infrastructure. The addition of connected devices, sensors, and actuators to vital physical systems enables governments to achieve real-time monitoring and prediction as well as automate decisions in service provision. In turn, these suitabilities lead to improved service delivery, better allocation of resources, and greater citizen involvement. This section examines existing and potential applications of IoT across four key areas of public infrastructure — urban management, transport, public utilities, and healthcare — and explores the opportunities and challenges that arise from those applications.

While each industry including transportation, urban management, utilities, and healthcare faces unique risks, the IoT Security Readiness Matrix emphasizes that resilience depends on combining technical safeguards (encryption, authentication, intrusion detection) with governance levers such as laws, standards, and citizen trust frameworks. Table 1 essentially demonstrates that in order to guarantee safe, reliable, and sustainable IoT-enabled public service delivery, sector-specific preparedness must include both technology and policy.

Table 1. IoT Security Readiness Matrix for Public Service Delivery

Sector	Primary Security Risks	Readiness Indicators	Governance/Policy Levers	Key IoT Applications
Urban Management	Data privacy breaches, sensor tampering	• Citizen transparency portals • Regular patching • Secure provisioning of devices	Participatory governance frameworks, Municipal IoT security standards	Ssmart lighting, water pipelines, smart waste bins
Transportation	DDoS attacks, ransomware, unauthorized access to vehicle systems	• Secure V2X communication • Strong authentication protocols • Incident response drills	IEC 62443 compliance, National transport cybersecurity guidelines	Public transport tracking, connected vehicles, Intelligent traffic systems
Utilities	Ransomware, botnet infiltration, service disruption	• Intrusion detection systems • Lifecycle management policies • Quantum-safe encryption pilots	Cyber Resilience Act, NIS2 Directive, Utility cybersecurity acts	Water management sensors, smart grids, gas monitoring
Healthcare	Patient data breaches, weak authentication, supply-chain vulnerabilities	• End-to-end encryption • HIPAA/GDPR compliance • Secure device decommissioning	FDA/EMA IoT medical device standards, National health data protection laws	Telemedicine, wearables, emergency IoT kits

Figure 2 shows the large number of IoT applications can provide at the public infrastructure level. There are four major categories of public infrastructure —urban management, transportation, utilities, and health care. Each category includes representative examples of IoT-enabled systems, such as smart waste systems, intelligent traffic control systems, energy grid monitoring systems, and wearable health devices. Thus, when a government adopts IoT technologies, it should consider the strategic integration of those technologies across all of its various functions to optimize the efficiency, sustainability, and citizen orientation of public services provided.

Figure 2. IoT applications across Public Infrastructure Domains

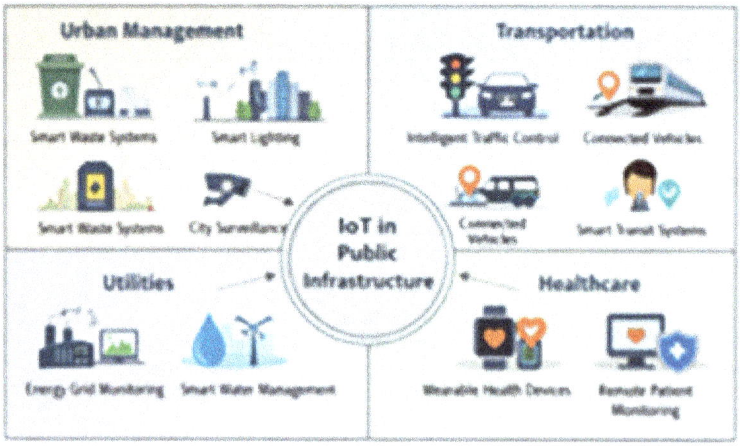

2.1 Urban Management

Urban management has been and will continue to be one of the most prominent areas of transformative potential for the implementation of IoT devices. Cities will increasingly struggle with issues related to density, resource scarcity, and sustainable environments. By using IoT technology to manage these intricate issues, governments will have the ability to address these challenges more efficiently than ever before.

- **Smart Waste Management:** Waste collection activities can be optimised by using IoT sensors placed in bin lids (Faheemuddin, 2025; Raja, 2022). This improves operational efficiency, optimizes collection routes, and reduces the impact of waste collection on the environment. Additionally, predictive analytics allows municipalities to use historical data about the amount of waste generated over a given period to plan for future waste disposal needs.
- **Water and Sanitation Systems:** The monitoring of water and sewage pipelines, through IoT devices, can create an ideal opportunity to detect waste leaks and contamination before they impact a community. IoT-enhanced, real-time monitoring of sewer atmospheres allows municipalities to alert sanitation workers to harmful gases present in sewer systems (Raja et al., 2025).
- **Smart Lighting and Energy Efficiency:** Smart streetlights using IoT sensors adjust their brightness depending on how many cars and people pass by, which helps to save energy and improve safety (Das, 2024).

In addition, these systems demonstrate the way IoT supports sustainable urban management by reducing the unnecessary use of resources while also improving safety and providing better service to citizens.

2.2 Transportation Systems

Another key area that IoT has changed public service delivery is transportation infrastructure. Urban mobility faces ongoing challenges of congestion, pollution, and safety; IoT-enabled solutions provide governments with tools to address these challenges.

- **Intelligent Traffic Management:** Roadways and traffic signals embedded with IoT sensors allow for real-time monitoring of traffic flow, allowing the use of data-driven algorithms to adjust the timing of traffic signals in a manner that will reduce congestion and improve travel time (Singh et al., 2024).
- **Connected Vehicles:** IoT-enabled vehicles communicate with both the existing infrastructure and other vehicles to improve safety and efficiency through applications like collision avoidance systems, predictive maintenance, and fleet management (Garg et al., 2024).
- **Public Transport Optimization:** IoT systems enable real-time tracking of buses and trains so that citizens can determine at what time to expect their arrival and authorities can make scheduling and routing of public transport more efficient (Abdullah Sani & Jaafar, 2025a).

IoT not only increases mobility and safety for vehicles but also exposes the transportation industry to new security challenges. Therefore, it is critically important to ensure secure communications and authentication in the transportation sector's IoT systems.

2.3 Utilities and Energy Systems

Utilities (electricity, water, and gas) represent some of the most basic services provided to the public. IoT-enabled smart grids and smart metering have changed the way utilities are managed by allowing for real-time monitoring of usage pattern and dynamic control of the network.

- **Smart Energy Grids:** Sensors are used in smart grids to monitor energy usage and allow for demand-side management and dynamic pricing. Additionally, renewable energy sources can be incorporated into the smart grid, making it more sustainable and resilient (Abir et al., 2021; Mehmood et al., 2021).

- **Water Management:** Sensors are used in the water management industry to identify leaks, provide information about water quality, and optimise the water distribution network to reduce waste and provide safe drinking water to consumers (Oladele, 2024).
- **Gas and Utility Monitoring:** IoT provides real-time visibility into gas usage and allows for the detection of hazardous gas leaks, improving safety and efficiency (Das, 2024).

Utilities are one of the most important areas where IoT can be implemented because any disruption to energy or water service can create large-scale disruptions in society. Therefore, it is critical to make sure that the IoT systems used in utilities are secure from cyber attacks to maintain the level of service that citizens expect and to help maintain citizen trust in the services they receive.

2.4 Healthcare Systems

Healthcare is one of three main categories where IoT dramatically improves operations, efficiencies, and service delivery through enhanced access and improved outcomes for patients. The IoT has had a dramatic effect on healthcare and how it delivers medical services. The following are a few IoT healthcare systems:

1. ***Wearable Devices:*** Many modern-day consumer devices, such as smart watches, are capable of providing continuous monitoring of multiple vital signs such as heart rate, blood pressure, and blood glucose and detecting possible health problems before they escalate as well as continuous tracking of their health.
2. ***Remote Health Delivery Services:*** An IoT system allows the use of telemedicine by the transmission of clinical data collected through telemetric systems in real time to a healthcare provider for accuracy in diagnosis, as well as treatment. This is beneficial for people in rural or medically underserved areas.
3. ***Emergency Response System:*** IoT-enabled supply kits for emergency medical supply delivery and IoT-enabled panic systems will instantly notify emergency responders when activated, resulting in significantly reduced emergency responder response time and increased life saved.

As with all IoT systems, health care systems must comply with medical regulations and protect data privacy rights. Severe and deleterious consequences can result when unauthorized access to a patient's data occurs (Raja, 2021). For an IoT-enabled health care system to function efficiently, secure authentication and encryption are imperative.

2.5 Cross-Sectoral Insights

Although the three domains have different uses and considerations, there are multiple cross-cutting observations or principles that the three domains can share:

- ***Data-Driven Governance:*** IoT assists governments in moving to a proactive form of governance rather than a reactive form of government through the ability to obtain real-time data, which allows governments to identify and react to potential problems.
- ***Citizen-Centered Accountability by Government Services:*** IoT enhances the transparency and accountability of government services to citizens through the enhancement and availability of every channel known to provide citizen engagement with their government.
- ***Security as a Foundational Requirement:*** Security challenges affecting all areas including data privacy, network vulnerabilities must be addressed to maintain resilience and trust.
- ***Integration with Emerging Technologies:*** IoT technologies continue to integrate with other technologies including AI, Blockchain, Edge Computing creates new capabilities and new methods of governance (Alahi et al., 2023; Khalil et al., 2022).

Smart infrastructure which utilizes IoT technology in cities like urban management, transportation, utilities and, in healthcare, has created a new level of public service efficiency through capabilities of real-time monitoring, predictive analytics and automation are strongly enhanced by the use of IoT technology. While the use of IoT in public service creation has enhanced an agencies operational capability to offer citizens and organizations more sustainable solutions, the rapid increase in connected devices has created challenges and complexities to develop comprehensive strategies for security, encryption, authentication, and lifecycles. The purpose of this section is to state that IoT is enabling develop new governance models for its use and, the continued advancement and the continued use of IoT will depend on how effectively and efficiently government agencies can implement innovation and maintain security/citizen-centric delivery of public services.

3. SECURITY CHALLENGES IN IOT ECOSYSTEMS

IoT-Based Smart Infrastructure has changed the public delivery system in many aspects of government. However, the interdependency of this type of technology can create vulnerabilities as well as improve efficiency. The emergence of billions of devices communicating via diverse networks has increased the threat landscape for public infrastructure as potential attacks now exist from a broad variety of sources, and can include anything from data theft or data breaches to wide-scale service interruption. A critical look at security-related issues that are specific to IoT ecosystems will be presented, including data privacy, device authentication, network-level threats, lifecycle vulnerabilities, and citizen confidence.

3.1 Data Privacy and Sovereignty

Data privacy is one of the most critical areas of concern when it comes to IoT ecosystems, as they continuously gather sensitive personal data, providing users with insights into their everyday lives to include health history, geographical location based upon GPS coordinates, and patterns of behaviour. In the delivery of services to citizens (e.g., delivery of healthcare or public safety), these data elements are often aggregated to improve decision making at both aggregate and individual levels, and ultimately, result in enhanced citizen service delivery.

- **Risks:** When an unauthorized person gains access to the data collected from an IoT device, this can result in identity theft, unsolicited surveillance, and misuse of the individual's personal information. The primary responsibility for protecting the privacy of an individual, as defined by local laws and international treaties, is equally balanced between the government and the individual, with each party having a responsibility for protecting the data of the individual (Ismagilova et al., 2022).
  - **Sovereignty Issues:** Citizens, according to data sovereignty, should maintain individual ownership/control over their data; however, the majority of IoT systems rely on cloud-based platforms that often reside outside their respective countries, or jurisdictions, and, therefore, there is often an issue of whether or not software developers comply with their jurisdiction's regulations.
  - **Case Example:** For example, IoT systems that support the healthcare worker/healthcare-related business, such as monitoring devices that are worn by patients, collect sensitive patient data that, upon data breach, may compromise not only the individual patient's right to privacy but also citizens' confidence in the governance of the healthcare system.

The protection of data is contingent on three specific factors: strong encryption, transparent governing frameworks, and citizen-focused policies that put the emphasis on accountability and consent.

3.2 Device Authentication and Lifecycle Management

The majority of IoT devices do not have sufficient authentication protocols in place to defend against unauthorized access. These devices are at a higher risk of being compromised when weak or default passwords, less than optimal identity management, and poor lifecycle support combine.

- **Authentication Challenges:** Most IoT devices have limited computing capabilities, which prohibits them from using more sophisticated authentication protocols. As a result, attackers can take advantage of an unprotected endpoint (Chatterjee et al., 2021).
- **Lifecycle Vulnerabilities:** To fully protect IoT devices against unauthorized use, all devices need to be secured against loss and/or theft throughout their entire life cycle. Securing IoT devices during their entire lifecycle involves securing devices while they are provisioned, deployed, updated, or decommissioned. If a device is subject to an inadequate patch management policy, also known as a maintenance policy, then it will remain exposed to exploitation of known vulnerabilities. If a device is improperly decommissioned, it may cause legacy data from that device to be leaked (Rao et al., 2024).
- **Example:** Smart city traffic management sensors can operate for more than one year and remain unpatched during this time. If vulnerability is discovered in a sensor, an attacker can exploit the vulnerability via an unpatched version of the sensor to enter the sensor's interconnected control system and cause disturbances in the cities transportation infrastructure.

It is essential that governments implement lifecycle security policies for IoT devices, which include secure provisioning, regular updates, and secure decommissioning to reduce or eliminate the risk of unauthorized access.

3.3 Network-Level Threats

The IoT ecosystem is built upon a vast network of interconnected devices, gateways, and cloud-based applications. As a result, this ecosystem is vulnerable to a wide variety of cyber-attacks, including but not limited to distributed denial of service (DDoS) attacks, ransomware attacks, and botnets.

- ***DDoS Attacks:*** Cybercriminals can use unsecured IoT devices to build botnets that can overpower public infrastructure. Public attacks such as the Mirai botnet are an example of large-scale attacks that could occur (Pemmasani & Osaka, 2021).

- ***Ransomware:*** Ransomware attacks are especially likely against IoT Networks in the healthcare and utility sectors, posing threats to critical services and to the lives of individual patients and people relying on those services (Okika et al., 2025).
- ***Botnets:*** Once compromised, IoT devices may be turned into weapons of coordinated attacks against their original functionality and the stability of the networks that connect them (Irshad et al., 2023).

Multi-layered defence mechanisms, e.g., intrusion detection systems, anomaly detection methods, secure communication protocols, have to be put in place to combat these types of attacks on IoT networks.

3.4 Citizen Trust and Governance Risks

In addition to the technical weaknesses of IoT, adoption of IoT Technologies will create major governance issues, as citizens could view IoT Technologies as tools for surveillance, which may lead to resistance and distrust.

- ***Transparency Issues:*** Citizens may worry about the misuse of their data if they are not clearly informed on how it will be collected, stored and used.
- ***Trust Issues:*** Breaches in IoT Systems erode public trust and discredit smart government initiatives.
- ***Moral Issues:*** The installation of surveillance systems, e.g., Smart Cameras, raises moral concerns about personal privacy, personal autonomy and personal consent.

Building trust in citizens that IoT Adoption will be successful requires “transparent” governance frameworks, “participatory” decision-making processes and accountability mechanisms capable of supporting that IoT Adoption meets citizens' values and ethical obligations.

Figure 3. IoT Vulnerabilities and their Impact on Public Services

Figure 3 shows the four critical vulnerability areas in IoT-enabled public infrastructure including data breaches, weak device authentication, network threats, and diminished trust of citizens and their corresponding effects on service delivery. Data breaches lead to the compromise of sensitive data; weak authentication allows unauthorized access to devices; network threats can disrupt systems that deliver important services; and reducing citizen trust undermines the legitimacy of using these systems.

3.5 Cross-Sectoral Vulnerabilities

Although each area of public infrastructure has its own set of special issues, there are common vulnerabilities that across all sectors:

- ***Interoperability Risk:*** Due to the many different manufacturers that produce devices for use in an IoT ecosystem; there are many difficulties with interoperability as well as differing levels of security (Bellini et al., 2022).
- ***Supply Chain Vulnerability:*** If IoT devices are manufactured with insecure components; the entire supply chain can be exposed to systemic vulnerabilities and there may be compromising hardware or software embedded in critical infrastructure (Khan & Ahmad, 2022).
- ***Edge Computing Risk:*** Edge Computing reduces latency but requires decentralization of security responsibility and increases the risk of localized security breaches (Mehmood et al., 2021).
- ***AI Integration Risk:*** AI-based IoT systems increase the performance capabilities of IoT devices; however, they also pose significant risk because of

algorithm bias, adversarial attacks; and there needs to be a focus on the issue of Explainable AI (Banerjee, 2025; Van Hoang, 2024).

These cross-domain vulnerabilities underscore the need for holistic security strategies to incorporate all three aspects – technical, organizational, and policy.

3.6 Case Studies of IoT Security Breaches

Investigating real-life incidents helps create a better understanding of all of the different types of vulnerabilities that exist in IoT:

- ***Healthcare data breach*** – An example of an attack occurred where a hacker gained unauthorized access to IoT-connected medical devices and compromised information used by a hospital's medical devices. This attack highlights the need to ensure that patients' information is protected through adequate authentication and encryption procedures.
- ***Utility outage*** - An example of an IoT-related incident involved the deployment of a hacker who launched a ransomware attack against IoT-enabled networks in order to shut down parts of the energy distribution network thereby causing disruption to the supply of electricity. This incident underscores the need for IoT networks to have resilience features incorporated into their architecture to avoid datasets from being compromised or destroyed (Abir et al., 2021).
- ***Transportation incident*** - An example of an IoT incident is related to how traffic sensors were hacked and then exploited to modify the timing of traffic lights which created congestion in urban areas and possibly accidents.

IoT based intelligent architecture has the potential to radically change how people receive public services by giving rise to additional ways of providing these services, however the evolution of this architecture has created significant challenges in the realm of securing IoT environments. Data privacy, device authentication, network-based threats/attack vectors, lifecycle vulnerabilities, and citizen trust are all highly important considerations when it comes to securing IoT enabled smart infrastructure. The sustainability and viability of smart government initiatives will depend on the ability to create a balance between innovation and security, and to ensure that the adoption of IoT enhances the delivery of public services and does not contribute to a reduction in trust or safety.

4. SECURITY TECHNIQUES AND SOLUTIONS

The vulnerabilities that have been identified within IoT ecosystems necessitate the creation and implementation of comprehensive and tested security techniques. Governments, researchers, and the private sector have universally recognized that the overall security of smart infrastructure that relies on IoT technology will require a comprehensive multi-layered security strategy that employs both technical and procedural safeguards, governance frameworks, and creates mechanisms for building citizen trust. This section explores several of the major security techniques that will be relevant to the development of IoT ecosystems, including: encryption; authentication; blockchain-based trusted identity management; lifecycle management; and newer emerging security technologies such as AI-driven security and quantum resistant cryptography.

4.1 Encryption and Secure Communication Protocols

Encryption, as a fundamental mechanism for protecting IoT systems, provides confidentiality and integrity of transmittal data through encoding the information sent among devices, gateways, and cloud platforms.

- ***Symmetric and Asymmetric Encryption.*** Symmetric encryption provides efficiency for constrained-resource IoT devices; asymmetric encryption provides superior security for authentication and key exchange (Alam, 2021).
- ***Secure Communication Protocols.*** TLS (Transport Layer Security) and DTLS (Datagram TLS) protocols are used widely for securing IoT communications. Lightweight adaptations of TLS and DTLS are especially important for resource-constrained devices (Abir et al., 2021).
- ***Use Cases.*** Encryption, by securing communications of sensitive data sourced from wearables transmitted from users to medical providers in the health care sector and preserving integrity of smart grid data such as energy consumption in the utilities sector, helps prevent unauthorized manipulation of sensitive information (Mehmood et al., 2021).

Encryption is critically important; however, challenges exist in finding the correct trade-off between the strength of security and the efficiency of computation especially with low-power IoT devices.

4.2 Strong Authentication Mechanisms

Authentication prevents unauthorized users/devices from accessing IoT systems. In IoT ecosystems, weak authentication mechanisms are one of the most common types of vulnerabilities.

- ***Multi-Factor Authentication (MFA):*** *It* is an authentication mechanism using two or more of the following types of authentication factors to improve security: Passwords, Biometrics, and Tokens. MFA can be adapted to allow IoT devices and establish trust by providing device authentication and validation through MFA to networks (Chatterjee et al., 2021).
  - ***Identity and Access Management (IAM):*** Secure access control via IAM allows for centralization over device identities & access permissions thereby mitigating the risk of unauthorised access (Rao et al., 2024).
  - ***Sectoral Applications:*** Strong Authentication capabilities prevent the unauthorized manipulation of traffic sensor data in transportation. In the case of Healthcare strong biometric authentication is used as an additional layer to secure access to Patient Monitoring System (Ajitha et al., 2025).

Authentication Mechanisms need to be lightweight but also robust and therefore, require a balance between usability versus security.

4.3 Blockchain-Based Trust Frameworks

Blockchain technology provides a decentralized solution for safeguarding the integrity of IoT Devices through the creation of tamper-proof solutions, - blockchain through its use of immutable Ledger keeps record of all transactions, systems, and applications; this aids in creating trust through transparency and accountability.

- **Decentralized Authentication:** Blockchain eliminates the need for centralised authorities when authenticating IoT Devices which reduce the reliance on a Single Point of Failure when authenticating devices (Khalil et al., 2022).
- **Automated Access Control:** Smart Contracts securely control access to IoT Devices allowing only authorised devices/users to have access to IoT Devices (Almulhim, 2025).

- **Supply Chain Security:** Blockchain provides assurances of authenticity and integrity to all of the components within an IoT Supply Chain (Khan & Ahmad, 2022).
- **Sectoral Applications:** In the case of healthcare Blockchain provides a secure mechanism for sharing patient data across multiple healthcare institutions and Blockchain acts as a transparent mechanism to facilitate energy transactions with consumers and utility providers (Alam, 2023).

While blockchain has great potential for protecting the security of IoT Devices, there are challenges with using blockchain when it comes to scalability and energy consumption in large-scale IoT deployments.

4.4 Lifecycle Security Management

All IoT devices need to be secured during their entire lifecycle from provision through to decommissioning. Lifecycle management addresses the vulnerabilities that arise from obsolete firmware, insecure updates, and improper disposal.

- ***Secure Provisioning:*** The device must be provisioned with a secure, properly configured device having unique identifiers and encryption keys (Rao et al., 2024).
- ***Patch Management:*** Ongoing updates are critical in order to address vulnerabilities as they are discovered; therefore, patched systems for automated patching will eliminate the liability associated with human error (Chatterjee et al., 2021).
- ***Secure Decommissioning:*** Devices must be securely decommissioned in order to prevent residual data from being compromised, including the erasure of data and de-provisioning of user credentials.
- ***Sectoral Applications***: Lifecycle management provides the necessary security for devices that are required to have long-term sensors to monitor waste management systems in urban management sectors. In addition, lifecycle security will ensure that the devices decommissioned in the healthcare sector will prevent unauthorized access to patient care data as a result of having been retired (Raja, 2025b).

Manufacturers, governments, and service providers must work collaboratively in order to establish standardized best practices for lifecycle management.

4.5 AI-Driven Adaptive Security

The introduction of AI will enhance the security of IoT Networks by facilitating real-time detection of and responses to infiltrations and cyber attack threats. Machine learning algorithms enable AI technology to detect strange traffic patterns indicating and signaling compromised IoT Networks, predict attacks, and automatically take appropriate steps to defend against potential attacks.

- ***Anomaly Detection:*** Using Machine learning algorithms, AI will monitor/ analyse traffic pattern data in IoT Networks to quickly detect and signal a possible attack by comparing detected data against known 'normal' traffic patterns (Banerjee, 2025).
- ***Predictive Security:*** Using historical traffic data, AI can predict the potential for future security vulnerabilities to enable 'proactive' defensive strategies (Van Hoang, 2024).
- ***Automated Response:*** AI can automatically isolate any devices that may have been compromised to contain, or mitigate the impact of, any attacks on those devices (Chirra, 2024).
- ***Sector Applications:*** In the utilities sector, AI will detect anomalies in the energy use of consumers. In the healthcare field, AI will identify anomalies in the monitoring of patients for possible signs of compromised devices (Ajitha et al., 2025).

Security solutions driven by AI will improve resilience, but there are problems related to AI security solutions, which include the risk of algorithmic bias, lack of explainability, and susceptibility to adversarial attacks.

4.6 Quantum-Safe Cryptography

Quantum computing poses a future risk to traditional encryption algorithms and there is an anticipated need for post-quantum cryptography, which is specifically designed to be resistant to quantum threat based attacks,

- ***Post-Quantum Algorithms:*** There are post-quantum solutions available such as lattice-based cryptography and hash-based signatures that have proven to be resilient against quantum threat based attacks (Aldehim et al., 2025).
- ***Sector Applications:*** Quantum safe cryptography will ensure that healthcare patient information will remain secure for decades, while also ensuring that any communications related to the smart grid will remain protected from quantum threats for the foreseeable future.

- ***Governance Implications:*** Governments must invest in the development of quantum safe standards to maintain the longevity of future IoT security frameworks.

Quantum safe cryptography is a forward looking and proactive way to provide security for IoT ecosystems from developing technological threats.

4.7 Citizen Trust Frameworks

It is not enough simply to have technical solutions; building citizen trust is a fundamental part of achieving security for the IoT. Without trust, citizens will not embrace IoT technology, which will have a negative impact on the success of smart government initiatives.

- ***Transparency:*** There must be adequate disclosure by governments related to the types of IoT data they collect, maintain and use from citizens (Das, 2024).
- ***Accountability:*** Governance frameworks that integrate accountability mechanisms such as audits and oversight are key to ensuring that IoT systems operate ethically and in accordance with societal norms (Abdullah Sani & Jaafar, 2025a).
- ***Participatory Governance:*** Citizen Engagement in decision-making processes promotes legitimacy and fosters confidence in the delivery of IoT-enabled services.
- ***Sectoral Applications:*** Transparency regarding waste management systems improves perceptions of surveillance of citizens, while providing clear guidelines about how patient data will be used establishes trust between patients and the monitoring devices i.e. wearables used to monitor their health.

Figure 4 demonstrates a comparative schematic of high level key security techniques such as encryption, authentication, blockchain, lifecycle management, AI security, and quantum-safe cryptography across four major IoT domains including urban management, transportation, utilties, healthcare. For example, the encryption technique addresses the specific vulnerability in urban management; the authentication technique applies to transportation and utilities, etc., thus all techniques are required to provide multiple layers of protection in each IoT domain.

Securing IoT-enabled smart infrastructure requires applying different methodologies that consider encryption, authentication i.e. validating legitimate access to IoT devices, blockchain technology for tracking the provenance of products, lifecycle management, AI-integrated security, quantum cryptography, and citizen trust framework-related information by using the layered approach allowing for a comprehensive and integrated perspective. The purpose of this section is to stress that IoT security is governed by both technological and governance issues. Therefore, governments need to have comprehensive strategies in place that allow them to balance innovation with providing security. As such, IoT adoption must improve public services without undermining people's trust or safety.

Figure 4. Security Techniques for Safeguarding IoT-Enabled Public Infrastructure

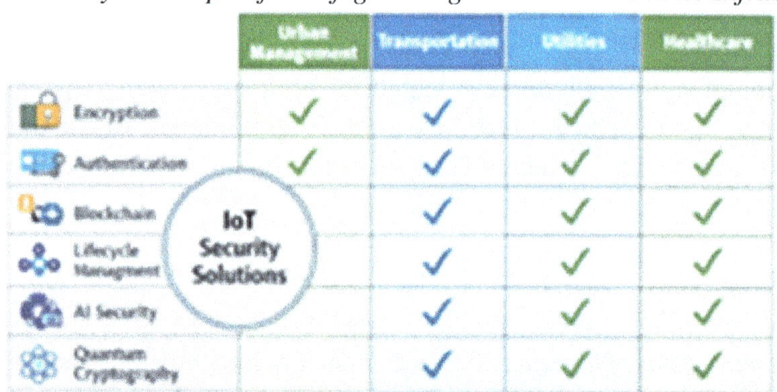

5. FUTURE DIRECTIONS FOR SMART GOVERNMENT INITIATIVES

The growth of IoT-enabled smart infrastructure is not a single event but an ongoing and constantly changing process driven by technical advancements, regulatory structures, and the expectations of society as a whole. Governments are increasingly implementing the IoT within public service delivery. To address this, strategies moving forward need to be develop that not only take into account ongoing technical advances, but also governance; ethics; and citizen trust.

5.1 AI-Driven Security and Intelligent Governance

AI will lead the way in developing IoT-enabled smart infrastructure. AI will utilise machine learning (ML) and predictive analytics to enhance both governance and security.

- ***Adaptive Security Systems:*** Through the use of AI algorithms to identify anomalies in IoT traffic, AI will also be able to predict future attacks against these systems and automate defensive actions. By automating responses to attacks this will, in turn, allow governments to reduce human intervention and achieve real-time resilience against IoT threats (Banerjee, 2025; Van Hoang, 2024).

- ***Predictive Governance:*** AI-driven predictive analytics will also be used by governments to forecast potential urban challenges, such as issues of traffic congestion, energy demand or healthcare needs. Through the use of this type of data government will have the ability to take proactive measures to address challenges faced in any given city prior to a situation occurring (Mohsen, 2024).
- ***Ethical AI:*** The use of AI in the future will require addressing ethical issues associated with the technology. These issues include establishing appropriate uses for the data generated by AI and ensuring the AI decision making process is fair, unbiased, transparent, and easy to understand. In order to accomplish this, the establishment of ethical AI frameworks will be critical for ensuring the integrity and accountability of public service delivery that will use AI as part of the service delivery process.

AI-enabled governance will represent a major shift from reactive service delivery models to predictive and proactive service delivery models.

5.2 Quantum-Safe Cryptography

As quantum computing becomes more advanced in the future, it will present an enormous threat to conventional encryption algorithms. For this reason, governments will need to adopt new forms of cryptography, known as quantum-safe cryptography, in order to protect against the security threats to their IoT ecosystems from quantum computing.

- ***Post-Quantum Standards:*** There are many kinds of post-quantum standards available now that is, lattice-based, hash-based, and multivariate. These are being developed to provide security and resilience to traditional encryption technologies (Aldehim et al., 2025).
- ***Long-Term Resilience:*** Quantum-safe cryptography will protect sensitive data (e.g. healthcare records) and provide long-term protection over an extended period of time.
- ***Policy Implications:*** Governments need to start investing funds into new research on forms of quantum-safe security and developing standards for these new forms of security that can be shared across national borders.

Quantum-safe cryptography is a forward-thinking approach to securing IoT technologies against future technological changes.

5.3 Blockchain Integration for Transparency and Trust

Blockchain technology continues to be a game changer in the future of IoT-enabled smart infrastructure by providing greater transparency, accountability and trust.

- **Decentralized Governance:** By eliminating the need for central authorities/institutions to authenticate people/devices in a blockchain-based system, there is less likelihood of single points of failure for authenticating and controlling access.
- **Smart Contracts:** The use of smart contracts means that IoT devices will be able to automate compliance with policies between devices and users (Almulhim, 2025).
- **Supply Chain Security:** In IoT supply chains, using blockchain technology both enhances traceability of IoT supply chain components and provides assurance of the authenticity of each component in the supply chain by reducing counterfeiting (Khan & Ahmad, 2022).

As smart government initiatives continue to evolve, the adoption of blockchain technology in government will help promote citizen trust and increase transparency in the delivery of public services.

5.4 Citizen Trust as a Governance Pillar

Trust given by citizens is needed for the implementation of Smart Government projects, it is also required for the success of those projects. The success of IoT systems, and more importantly the success of Smart Government Initiatives, relies on three facets of government that build on Trustworthiness:

- ***Transparency and Accountability*** - how the government collects data from IoT technologies, where that data is stored and how it will be used;
- ***Participatory Governance*** - by including citizens in the decision making process the government builds legitimacy and trust in IoT governments' application to services provided to citizens; and
- ***Ethical Framework*** - policies necessitating a clear government response to ethical dilemmas regarding IoT use such as surveillance, individual autonomy, privacy, etc., while having the government align with the values of Society.

Future developments will centre on the importance of creating a Socially Legitimate System to be in place to support the government's ability to secure IoT system technologies. Without citizen Trust, advanced IoT systems will not be successful in overcoming resistance from citizens.

5.5 Sustainability and Resilience in Smart Infrastructure

The future of Smart Government Infrastructure will be characterized through sustainably designed IoT-enabled Smart Infra-Structures by balancing technological advancements with environmentally responsible infrastructures.

- ***Energy Efficiency*** - IoT systems must have an emphasis on reducing energy consumption especially when designed for large-scale implementations i.e. Smart Grids, Smart Transportation.
- ***Circular Economy Models*** - IoT technologies may assist in the implementation of Waste Management initiatives that use a Circular Economy Model which assists in decreasing the amount of resources that become waste by using IoT to promote waste recycling.
- ***Climate Resiliency*** - IoT technologies provide the government with the ability to measure the climate so that governments may better respond to the impacts of Climate change, including flood, pollution and extreme temperatures.

Government initiatives for smart cities in the future will have sustainability as a primary goal and therefore, the adoption of IoT in the respective regions will be expected to be a means by which their long-term resilience will be ensured.

5.6 Global Governance Models and Best Practices

Smart IoT-enabled infrastructure is becoming a global reality, and the future directions will require consideration for global collaboration and governance through:

- ***Comparative Models:*** Some countries leading the way in smart solutions such as Malaysia, Dubai and again, cities in Europe to provide insights into possible governance frameworks, security strategies and citizen engagement to support IoT-enabled infrastructure adoption and implementation (Abdullah Sani & Jaafar, 2025a; Hassebo & Tealab, 2023);
- ***International Standards:*** Establishing International Standards will play an important role for IoT Global Standards for the security of IoT devices, data privacy and interoperability to help achieve consistency across countries;

- ***Collaborative Research:*** Establishing Collaborative Research working with other countries to conduct collaborative research and to construct new policy landscapes, will speed up innovation and also help solve common issues.

The future of IoT in the government sector will eventually result in global governance models, the development of global collaboration and information exchange.

5.7 Integration of Emerging Technologies

IoT in the future will not develop in a vacuum, but rather will be shaped by its convergence and integration with other emerging technologies.

- ***Edge Computing:*** reduces latency and improves the speed at which the data is able to be processed resulting in improved real time data-based decision making, particularly in critical infrastructure such as healthcare, transportation etc (Mehmood et al., 2021);
- ***5G and beyond:*** will offer the opportunity for providing high speed connectivity that will provide for more reliable and seamless communication between IoT-enabled devices and also offer much more capability to manage cities and would also improve the delivery of services to citizens (Aldehim et al., 2025).
- ***Digital Twins:*** can be used to simulate scenarios and help governments determine how they should allocate their resources and prepare for challenges in real-time (Alahi et al., 2023).

A holistic overview will be essential in the future for developing IoT-enabled smart infrastructure through the integration of technology innovation with governance frameworks and trust by citizens. This includes vital areas such as developing AI-based security solutions, quantum-safe cryptography, blockchain & other integration, sustainability, and creating models for global governance; all of these represent important pathways towards provide resilient and secure public service delivery.

6. CASE STUDIES AND BEST PRACTICES

The practical deployment of smart infrastructure utilizing IoT technology may yield encounters with similar challenges and opportunities across many different countries. Each case study has provided insights to governments as to how they have benefited from the use of IoT technology to enhance public services they deliver and highlighted models for government, security, and citizen engagement strategies that can be borrowed or replicated in other jurisdictions.

6.1 Case Study - Malaysia (IoT in Governance and Public Service Delivery)

Malaysia has served as a model for IoT use in public governance. Some examples include:

- ***Transformation of the Public Sector:*** Research works by Abdullah Sani and Jaafar (2025) has illustrated how IoT technology has been integrated into Public Governance and public service delivery, creating efficiencies in job performance. Some examples of IoT applications in public sector are the creation of smart traffic systems; the development of superior waste management practices; and the implementation of e-Government platforms(Abdullah Sani & Jaafar, 2025b).
- ***Citizen-Centric Services:*** With the implementation of IoT-enabled services, the citizens of Malaysia can now receive real-time updates on the status of the services they receive from the government. This has created increased confidence on the part of citizens in the effectiveness of government service delivery, creating a more transparent government than was previously possible.
- ***Challenges with Security:*** The experience of Malaysia highlights the importance of addressing the issues related to data privacy and vulnerabilities in authentication when large-scale implementations of IoT technology are done.

Thus, Malaysia's experience underscores the importance of utilizing government to develop technology and secure policy that gives confidence to its citizens in adopting IoT in governance.

6.2 Dubai: Large-Scale Smart City Deployment

One of the most significant international smart city projects is taking place in Dubai.

- ***Urban Infrastructure:*** Dubai has introduced IoT throughout its urban infrastructure, including transportation, utility and public safety systems. An example of this is traffic management systems where IoT technology has been used to reduce congestion by optimising the flow of traffic; utility companies are also utilizing IoT to improve energy and water consumption (Hassebo & Tealab, 2023).

- ***Security Integration:*** Cyber-security has been integrated into Dubai's smart city strategy where all IoT systems will have security components that use blockchain and AI technology as part of their security measures.
- ***Governance Models:*** The governance model of Dubai is relatively centralized and has been able to deploy IoT technologies quickly. However, this centralized structure raises questions about citizen participation in governance and citizen transparency.

The Dubai case highlights an example of a successful implementation of large-scale IoT technologies as well as the importance of incorporating balanced governance mechanisms to build trust between citizens and authorities.

6.3 European Smart Cities: Sustainability and Citizen Engagement

European city such as Barcelona, Amsterdam, and Copenhagen demonstrate that IoT adoption can focus on sustainability and citizen engagement.

- ***Sustainability Focus:*** IoT systems in European cities monitor aspects such as energy usage, waste management and environmental conditions that contribute to climate resilience and promote a circular economy (Bellini et al., 2022).
- ***Citizen Participation:*** The European city models include participatory governance where residents are engaged in the decision-making processes available during the IoT adoption process.
- ***Security Frameworks:*** The European Union General Data Protection Regulation (GDPR) provides strong data privacy protections for individuals where compliance with GDPR privacy standards will ensure all IoT systems operate under those established standards for data privacy protections.

6.4 Healthcare IoT Initiatives

The healthcare industry contains examples of the adoption of IoT technology and the vulnerabilities that exist from this implementation.

- Patient remote monitoring through wearable technology provides real-time patient monitoring and gives patients access to health services even when they live far away from the actual healthcare facility (Ajitha et al., 2025; Raja, 2025a).

- Panic-Detection Systems deployed through IoT technologies give immediate notification during emergencies, thereby improving response times and increasing the possibility of saving lives during emergencies (Boopathi Raja, 2021).
- Health IoT systems are particularly vulnerable to issues related to privacy and compliance of the stored medical data. If a third party is able to access a patient's personal medical information, the implications and ramifications could be dire, highlighting the need for adequate encryption and authentication of the protected health information collected by health IoT systems.

Healthcare Example Case Studies demonstrate that when adopting IoT technology in health systems, the priority must be to protect the private information of citizens and comply with all regulations to maintain the public trust.

6.5 Comparative Analysis of Case Studies

The review of the case studies has provided insight into the following areas:

- **Governance Models:** In healthcare systems where there is a centralized governance model, such as Dubai, it provides a rapid deployment framework, but limits the ability for active citizen participation. In contrast, decentralized governance models, such as many European cities, encourage building trust with the citizens but require a greater deal of coordination complexity to facilitate IoT system implementations.
- **Security Strategies:** Countries with an established security strategy integrated into their IoT growth from the outset, such as Dubai and European Union nations, tend to have more extensive and resilient security systems when compared to countries that have a reactive security strategy to their IoT growth and/or implementations, such as Malaysia, which demonstrates their vulnerabilities. The Success of European Smart Cities– Aligning IoT Growth with Sustainability & Public Trust Goals of Citizens.

6.6 Best Practices for IoT-Enabled Smart Infrastructure

The analysis of the various case studies reveals several best practices:

- ***Holistic Security Approach:*** All government entities must utilize a multi-layered approach to security that employs encryption, authentication, blockchain technology, and lifecycle management.

- ***Citizen-Centric Governance:*** Accountability, transparency, and inclusive participation in decision making will help provide citizens with the level of trust needed to use IoT services.
- ***Sustainability:*** IoT adoption should be aligned with sustainability efforts in order to reduce the amount of wasted resources and improve climate resilience.
- ***Global Standards and Collaboration:*** Having international standards for IoT related security and data privacy will create consistency and interoperability across international boundaries.
- ***Sector-specific Approach to Security***: Specific security frameworks need to be developed for the following industries due to their unique vulnerabilities: healthcare, utilities, and transportation.

The case studies reviewed from the following locations – Malaysia, Dubai, smart cities in Europe, and healthcare organizations illustrate the various pathways for implementing IoT in public service delivery.

7. STRATEGIC RECOMMENDATIONS

The purpose of this section is to provide strategic recommendations to governments, policymakers, and researchers who wish to leverage IoT technology to support the delivery of public services in a resilient and secure manner.

7.1 Synthesis of Key Findings

The following key points illustrated in previous discussions are:

- ***IoT as a Governance Enabler:*** It is important to recognize that while IoT-enabled smart infrastructure represents a new technological capability for governments, it should also be viewed as an important governance tool to improve efficiency, transparency, and citizen engagement in public services provided to citizens and communities.
- ***Security as a Foundational Requirement:*** To successfully adopt IoT, there needs to be strong security systems in place which protect from vulnerabilities associated with the devices themselves, networks, and data ecosystems that are in place to support them.
- ***Citizen Trust as a Critical Pillar:*** Citizens will not trust the IoT therefore resistance and skepticism to their use will occur. Governments must be trans-

parent about the IoT and its use as well as create accountability when using the IoT through participatory governance in order to have legitimacy.

- ***Sector-Specific Vulnerabilities:*** Vulnerabilities that are specific to sectors are associated with differences in types of service such as healthcare, utilities, transportation, or urban management; therefore, security challenges will require different strategies for addressing them.
- ***Future-Oriented Innovations:*** The future of governance using IoT will be created with new technologies that include AI-enabled security, quantum-proof cryptography, blockchain and edge computing; all of which will play an important role in developing the next phase of governance enabled by IoT.

7.2 Strategic Recommendations

Based on this understanding, there are many proposed strategic recommendations:

- ***Develop Holistic Security Frameworks:*** Security strategies must be multi-layered so as to incorporate security technologies such as encryption or authentication, blockchain or lifecycle management. Security controls must also be considered and embedded within IoT systems during the design stage before the systems or networks are deployed rather than only after deployment have occurred.
- ***Prioritize Citizen-Centric Governance:*** Trust and legitimacy will be created through transparency of the IoT and its use. Therefore, governments need to provide citizens with well-defined, reliable, and accessible communications that explain how data is collected, managed, and the use of each type of data will be communicated. Additionally, by developing participatory governance models, governments will build trust through citizen participation in their decision processes.
- ***Align IoT Adoption with Sustainability Goals:*** Smart infrastructure enabled by IoT will have a role in supporting sustainability by providing services and reducing waste of resources, increasing energy efficiency, and contributing to resilience against climate change; thus, by developing strategies for integrating IoT into their overall sustainability plan, governments will ensure that growth associated with technological innovations occurring through the IoT will be consistent with environmental responsibilities.
- ***Establish Global Standards and Collaboration:*** Developing and implementing international standards regarding IoT security, data privacy, and interoperability is critical for ensuring that there is uniformity across countries. It will require collaboration between governments, international organizations,

research institutions, and the private sector to create and agree on the frameworks that will govern IoT as it evolves globally.

- ***Invest in Emerging Technologies:*** To prepare for future resilience, it is necessary to invest in AI-based security, quantum-resilient cryptography, and blockchain integration. As technology progresses rapidly and there will be new technological disruptions, governments will need to anticipate these disruptive technologies and preemptively adopt innovations that will improve safety and efficiency over the long term.
- ***Implement Sector-Specific Strategies:*** Healthcare, utilities, and transportation are sectors that present the highest level of security risk. Each of these sectors has unique vulnerabilities requiring tailored strategies to ensure the safety of IoT adoption without compromising resilience, public safety, or privacy and civil liberties.

7.3 Policy Implications

The implications regarding IoT-enabled smart infrastructure are far-reaching and affect many policy matters, including:

- ***Regulatory Frameworks:*** Governments will need to establish regulations enforcing minimum security standards for all IoT devices, protecting the privacy of the data generated by IoT devices and establishing ethical guidelines to facilitate the IoT's adoption.
- ***Public–Private Partnerships:*** Collaboration among the public sector and private businesses will help stimulate innovation while maintaining accountability.
- ***Capacity Building:*** The training of public officials, technology professionals, and citizens is critical in building awareness and subject matter expertise in IoT security and governance.
- ***Ethics:*** Policies must address any potential for ethical issues such as privacy, autonomy, and surveillance, so that the adoption of IoT is in alignment with societal values.

8. CONCLUSION

IoT-enabled public infrastructure represents a revolution in how governments are employing smart governance practices, allowing them to provide services to citizens that are more efficient, transparent, and citizen-oriented than ever before. IoT technology has been able to achieve these results in numerous areas, such as urban planning, transportation, utilities, and healthcare, by offering real-time monitoring of systems, predictive analytics, and automated decision-making. However, the rapid and wide-scale implementation of connected devices creates significant risks with respect to data privacy, device authentication, network integrity, and the trust of citizens in government services delivered through IoT systems. Thus, the IoT-enabled smart infrastructure creates significant opportunities for increasing the quality of public goods delivery, but successful governmental implementation will require the ability to balance the pursuit of innovation, security, transparency, and trust from citizens. Governments can help create resilient and safe smart infrastructure by utilizing comprehensive security frameworks, placing an emphasis on citizen-centered governance, aligning IoT implementation with sustainability objectives, and investing in emerging technologies.

REFERENCES

Abdullah Sani, H. A., & Jaafar, N. I. (2025a). A bibliometric and content analysis of internet of things (IoT) in the public sector. *Journal of Science and Technology Policy Management.*

Abdullah Sani, H. A., & Jaafar, N. I. (2025b). *Exploring the impact of IoT on governance and public service transformation: evidence from Malaysia's public sector.* Smart and Sustainable Built Environment.

Abir, S. A. A., Anwar, A., Choi, J., & Kayes, A. (2021). Iot-enabled smart energy grid: Applications and challenges. *IEEE Access : Practical Innovations, Open Solutions*, *9*, 50961–50981. DOI: 10.1109/ACCESS.2021.3067331

Ajitha, N., Ashwin, G., Divakar, S., & Dhanushree, M. (2025). Machine Learning-based Panic Syncsight: An IoT-Integrated Panic Attack Detection System for Enhanced Therapeutic Insights. 2025 5th International Conference on Soft Computing for Security Applications (ICSCSA).

Alahi, M. E. E., Sukkuea, A., Tina, F. W., Nag, A., Kurdthongmee, W., Suwannarat, K., & Mukhopadhyay, S. C. (2023). Integration of IoT-enabled technologies and artificial intelligence (AI) for smart city scenario: recent advancements and future trends. Sensors (Basel), 23(11), 5206.

Alam, T. (2021). Cloud-based IoT applications and their roles in smart cities. *Smart Cities*, *4*(3), 1196–1219. DOI: 10.3390/smartcities4030064

Alam, T. (2023). Blockchain and big data-based access control for communication among iot devices in smart cities. *Wireless Personal Communications*, *132*(1), 433–456. DOI: 10.1007/s11277-023-10617-8

Aldehim, G., Shahzad, T., Khan, M. A., Ghadi, Y. Y., Jiang, W., Mazhar, T., & Hamam, H. (2025). Balancing sustainability and security: A review of 5G and IoT in smart cities. *Digital Communications and Networks*, *11*(6), 1722–1737. DOI: 10.1016/j.dcan.2025.06.007

Almulhim, A. I. (2025). A Conceptual Framework for Integrating IoT and Blockchain for Smart and Sustainable Urban Development. *Smart Cities*, *8*(6), 209. DOI: 10.3390/smartcities8060209

Banerjee, A. (2025). Securing the future: AI-driven data transmission in IoT-powered smart cities. *Soft computing fusion with applications,* *2*(1), 33-53.

Bellini, P., Nesi, P., & Pantaleo, G. (2022). IoT-enabled smart cities: A review of concepts, frameworks and key technologies. *Applied Sciences (Basel, Switzerland), 12*(3), 1607. DOI: 10.3390/app12031607

Boopathi Raja, G. (2021). *An intelligent approach for detecting and preventing heart attacks using wearable technology. Handbook of Research on Lifestyle Sustainability and Management Solutions Using AI Big Data Analytics, and Visualization.* IGI Gobal.

Chatterjee, S., Kar, A. K., & Mustafa, S. Z. (2021). Securing IoT devices in smart cities of India: From ethical and enterprise information system management perspective. *Enterprise Information Systems, 15*(4), 585–615. DOI: 10.1080/17517575.2019.1654617

Chirra, D. R. (2024). AI-Enabled Cybersecurity Solutions for Protecting Smart Cities Against Emerging Threats.

Das, D. K. (2024). Exploring the symbiotic relationship between digital transformation, infrastructure, service delivery, and governance for smart sustainable cities. *Smart Cities, 7*(2), 806–835. DOI: 10.3390/smartcities7020034

Faheemuddin, S. (2025). IoT-Enabled Urban Infrastructure: A Framework for Smart City Development.

Garg, T., Gupta, S., Obaidat, M. S., & Raj, M. (2024). Drones as a service (DaaS) for 5G networks and blockchain-assisted IoT-based smart city infrastructure. *Cluster Computing, 27*(7), 8725–8788. DOI: 10.1007/s10586-024-04354-1

Hassebo, A., & Tealab, M. (2023). Global models of smart cities and potential IoT applications: A review. *IoT, 4*(3), 366–411. DOI: 10.3390/iot4030017

Irshad, R. R., Hussain, S., Hussain, I., Ahmad, I., Yousif, A., Alwayle, I. M., & Badr, M. M. (2023). An intelligent buffalo-based secure edge-enabled computing platform for heterogeneous IoT network in smart cities. *IEEE Access : Practical Innovations, Open Solutions, 11*, 69282–69294. DOI: 10.1109/ACCESS.2023.3288815

Ismagilova, E., Hughes, L., Rana, N. P., & Dwivedi, Y. K. (2022). Security, privacy and risks within smart cities: Literature review and development of a smart city interaction framework. *Information Systems Frontiers, 24*(2), 393–414. DOI: 10.1007/s10796-020-10044-1 PMID: 32837262

Katal, N. (2024). Ai-driven healthcare services and infrastructure in smart cities. In *Smart cities* (pp. 150–170). CRC Press. DOI: 10.1201/9781003442660-7

Khalil, U., Malik, O. A., Uddin, M., & Chen, C.-L. (2022). A comparative analysis on blockchain versus centralized authentication architectures for IoT-enabled smart devices in smart cities: A comprehensive review, recent advances, and future research directions. *Sensors (Basel)*, *22*(14), 5168. DOI: 10.3390/s22145168 PMID: 35890848

Khan, A. U. R., & Ahmad, R. W. (2022). A blockchain-based IoT-enabled E-waste tracking and tracing system for smart cities. *IEEE Access : Practical Innovations, Open Solutions*, *10*, 86256–86269. DOI: 10.1109/ACCESS.2022.3198973

Mehmood, M. Y., Oad, A., Abrar, M., Munir, H. M., Hasan, S. F., & Muqeet, H. A. u., & Golilarz, N. A. (2021). Edge computing for IoT-enabled smart grid. *Security and Communication Networks*, *2021*(1), 5524025.

Mohsen, B. M. (2024). AI-driven optimization of urban logistics in smart cities: Integrating autonomous vehicles and IoT for efficient delivery systems. *Sustainability (Basel)*, *16*(24), 11265. DOI: 10.3390/su162411265

Okika, N., Nwatuzie, G. A., Odozor, L., Oni, O., & Idoko, I. P. (2025). Addressing iot-driven cybersecurity risks in critical infrastructure to safeguard public utilities and prevent large-scale service disruptions. *International Journal of Innovative Science and Research Technology*, *10*(2).

Oladele, O. K. (2024). Internet of Things (IoT) integration and its impact on smart cities, automation, and data-driven decision-making. *Journal of Smart Infrastructure*, *5*(2), 45–58.

Pemmasani, P. K., & Osaka, M. (2021). The future of smart cities: Cybersecurity challenges in public infrastructure management. *International Journal of Modern Computing*, *4*(1), 72–85.

Raja, G. B. (2021). Appliance control system for physically challenged and elderly persons through hand gesture-based sign language. In *Biomedical Signal Processing for Healthcare Applications* (pp. 173–193). CRC Press. DOI: 10.1201/9781003147817-8

Raja, G. B. (2022). Effective waste management system for smart cities. *Intelligent Green Technologies for Sustainable Smart Cities*, 33-52.

Raja, G. B. (2025a). Advancements of IoT and sensor informatics in wearable, implantable, mobile, and remote healthcare. In *Innovations in Biomedical Engineering* (pp. 87–121). Elsevier. DOI: 10.1016/B978-0-443-30146-9.00003-4

Raja, G. B. (2025b). SmartCare—A comprehensive wearable sensor-based remote health monitoring and rehabilitation system. In *Rehabilitation Robotics and Healthcare Devices* (pp. 27–46). Elsevier. DOI: 10.1016/B978-0-443-21505-6.00011-6

Raja, G. B., & Chakraborty, C. (2023). Internet of things based effective wearable healthcare monitoring system for remote areas. In *Implementation of Smart Healthcare Systems using AI, IoT, and Blockchain* (pp. 193-218). Elsevier. DOI: 10.1016/B978-0-323-91916-6.00004-7

Raja, G. B., Vigneashwaran, R., Rohan, M., Praveen, N., & Vijay, N. (2025). IoT-Based Sewage Atmosphere and Health Monitoring for Sanitation Workers with Alerting System. 2025 7th International Conference on Inventive Material Science and Applications (ICIMA).

Rao, P. M., Pedada, S., Jangirala, S., Das, A. K., & Rodrigues, J. J. (2024). Role of IoT in the ages of digital to smart cities: Security challenges and countermeasures. IEEE Internet of Things Magazine, 7(1), 56–64.

Singh, P., Jain, P., Saini, V., Kumari, K., & Bajaj, P. K. (2024). Enhancing Smart City Infrastructure Through IoT-Enabled Predictive Maintenance and Real-Time Data Analytics. *2024 International Conference on Progressive Innovations in Intelligent Systems and Data Science (ICPIDS).*

Van Hoang, T. (2024). Impact of integrated artificial intelligence and internet of things technologies on smart city transformation. *Journal of technical education science, 19*(Special Issue 01), 64-73.

Chapter 4
IoT-Enabled Intelligent Traffic Management Framework for Smart Cities

Hitesh Mohapatra
http://orcid.org/0000-0001-8100-4860
School of Computer Engineering, Kalinga Institute of Industrial Technology (KIIT) (Deemed to be) University, Bhubaneswar, India

ABSTRACT

Overall, smart cities have raised a number of global questions in response to traditional urbanization. However, due to their complexity and diversity, as well as their direct impact on transportation systems, sustainable traffic management within smart cities has often been overlooked by researchers. This study focuses on developing a sustainable framework and leveraging Internet of Things (IoT) and Intelligent Transportation System (ITS) technologies to address traffic challenges in smart cities. Traffic management in such cities, which feature both connected automated vehicles and human-driven vehicles, is approached through a dual mechanism. This strategy employs modeling, analysis, and decision-making processes built upon prior research findings to effectively respond to traffic-related issues.

INTRODUCTION

In recent years, both urbanization and technological developments have increased sharply, leading to the emergence of smart cities. These cities are meant to overcome the problems created by growing socioeconomic activity and rapid

DOI: 10.4018/979-8-2600-2845-2.ch004

urban migration. Of the all-important factors that contribute towards building a Smart City, transportation is one such factor that deserves specific focus. With the growth of urban population, cities are always expanding and the traditional transport networks cannot effectively satisfy future demand, which causes some problems such as congestion, accident and environmental pollution (Tao et al., 2023). Road congestion is a regular nuisance with negative effects both of social cohesion and the environment. It affects a country's economy directly, as well as indirectly. People spend 338 hours a year on average in the car, according to research like that from the US found, showing a worldwide trend among urban centers. Current road networks are not able to meet these increased challenges from smart cities, so novel solutions are required for handling the traffic complexity as (Wang et al., 2018). Therefore, integrating intelligent transportation systems driven by IoT technologies offers a promising approach to addressing these challenges. Such systems can leverage real-time data from sensors, vehicles, and infrastructure to optimize traffic flow, minimize delays, and enhance commuter safety. In the long run, these innovations can contribute to sustainable urban growth by lowering emissions and improving the overall efficiency of mobility networks within smart cities.

Primary traffic control means have historically been standard highway traffic lights. The first modern one was established in New York City in 1918. Subsequent developments have been more flexible, but not adaptable enough to the complexities of modern urban road-traffic. A special case is the traditional, three-color scheme of traffic lights dating to 1982 (preceded by that of Finnish counting). Due to the urbanization and population growth, the traditional traffic lights are becoming less efficient and transforming them into intelligent and smart systems that combined with advanced technologies such as artificial intelligence AI and ITS would be necessary. It was a turning point in how traffic problems were approached (Nxumalo, 2025). ITS was designed to address traffic related problems on the roadways. It has evolved into a flexible system over time that deals with freight and fleet management and employs advanced satellite technology, automated tolling operations, Geographic Information System (GIS) applications. ITS are heavily dependent on artificial intelligence as it would allow smooth flow of traffic, real-time traffic monitoring, accident prediction and good security. Sustainable traffic management goals for ITS enabled smart cities are to develop solid transport systems that offer safe as well As efficient networks, reduce fuel consumption, control total travel time and cut down environmental pollution risks (Gao et al., 2023).

Various ITS applications could creatively address the traffic control problem within smart cities. One major application is to detect transport-related issues such as accidents, congestion, and security threats. ITS assists in real-time detection and sends the related information to control centers where appropriate management is taking place, commuters are directed with alternate pathways. ITS is additionally used by ramp meters, which are electronic traffic-control devices that operators use to manage the rate of traffic flows along freeways. The information is analyzed to set volume and speed restrictions in a timely manner, leading to optimal traffic flow. Inductive detectors which are based on ITS technology and deployed in road surfaces could significantly improve the traffic light regulation. These are capable for the automatic acclimatization between flow and capacity (or vice versa) to read the data in real time, and involved with a central control room (Batty et al., 2012). Successful parking management combined with ITS allows travelers to get information on parking directions, methods of payment and reserved spaces. Demand Responsive Transport Management (DRTM) System takes advantage of ITS-based Internet of Things (IoT) to convey the real time route information for passengers and adjust the public transport according to real time traffic variations. **Figure.1** presents the infrastructure components include smart transportation, smart grids, smart buildings, and smart waste management.

Figure 1. Smart City Components

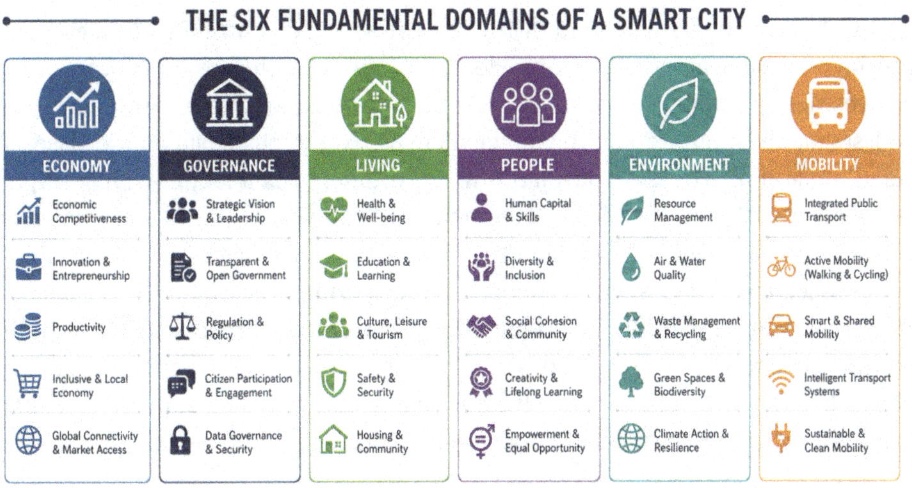

Logistics management in smart cities, using satellite and radio technology by means of ITS confines cars to the tracks demarcated for their use and facilitates predicting routes, controlling fuel consumption and enhancing fleet operation. The use-planned vulnerable road users such as pedestrian crossing points, or other similar sensitive IoT-based ITS facilities can be made. Other examples of the use of ITS in smart cities are: wireless communication for cooperative perception to share real-time information, GPS-based route guidance and systems that create platooning to decrease pollution. and optimizing fuel usage (Garau Guzman & Baeza, 2023).

The challenge of sustainable traffic management also persists as smart cities have spread. This article discusses how the blockchain technology in IoT-ITS systems might handle these issues, discussing prospects, proposals and relevant service recommendations of a holistic and efficient traffic control services for smart cities. The different applications, challenges, and recommendations of applying ITS in smart city traffic management which is environmentally sustainable have been discussed in the subsections below (Jin et al., 2014). Intelligent transportation systems utilize sensors and data analysis to maximize traffic flow, minimize congestion and enhance public transportation. Integrating machine learning and edge computing in IoT-based ITS enhances real-time traffic prediction, reduces latency, and supports autonomous logistics. A unified data architecture connecting blockchain, IoT, and AI can improve transparency, efficiency, and sustainability in smart city traffic management.

RESEARCH GAP

ECO-oriented ITS in the era of IoT has evolved and contributed to the greener traffic management in smart cities. However, key research gaps remain. Such gaps are restricting implementations at scale and over the long term. Interoperability and standardization are significant challenges. Numerous systems are based on stand-alone units (boxes) and platforms of different manufacturers. These parts don't always connect. To do so, common protocols, data models and integration frameworks are needed. Those standards allow cross-vendor and cross-technology communication. They underpin integrated transportation across the whole city. Privacy and security fears are mounting. Massive amounts of high-sensitive mobility data are generated and preserved. This increases the risks of cyberattacks and data abuse. Subsequent work needs to handle the secure edge data collection. **Table.1** presents the relevance of smart applications for different city sizes.

Table 1. The relevance of smart applications for different city sizes

IoT Smart City Application	Small Smart Cities	Mid-Sized Smart Cities	Large Smart Cities
Smart Traffic Sensor	None	None	High
Smart Parking Sensor	Low	Low	Low
Data Collecting	High	Low	Low
Air Quality Monitoring	None	None	Low
Public Safety	Low	High	Low
Smart Lighting	High	Low	Low

It is important that the storage be safe and that the model can be protected. Anonymization of data in cloud systems is necessary. This means that strong access control and governance models are very much required. These mechanisms need to safeguard users and maintain analytical performance. Furthermore, attention should also be directed toward developing adaptive governance frameworks and policy mechanisms that balance innovation with sustainability goals. Collaborative academic–industrial initiatives can accelerate the deployment of eco-oriented ITS prototypes and ensure real-world validation. Integrating renewable energy sources, optimizing resource utilization, and enabling predictive maintenance through IoT analytics will further strengthen the ecological footprint of future transportation systems. There is also a major gap in scalability and cost. A lot of IoT based transportation applications are still in piloting stage or deployment at small scale. They can be very highly capital and revenue cost intensive that cannot easily be afforded by local authorities and transport operators. We require research on inexpensive architectural, lightweight messaging, and modularized scalable designs that can operate from small deployments to city level not creating bottlenecks of infrastructure or maintenance. There is a lack of real time data analytics and decision support functionalities. IoT Sensors generate streams of traffic and environment data. Yet, many of these deployments do not have an advanced analytics pipeline to convert this raw data into operational intelligence ("World population prospects 2017 - Volume I: Comprehensive tables," 2021). Smarter algorithms, predictive models and decision support tools are much needed to process streaming data, as well as to forecast congestion, identify incidents and advise effective control strategies in quasi real time. User participation and behavior change have also been inadequately investigated. Most existing solutions address infrastructure and management, rather than how travelers react to information and incentives. More research is required into the mechanisms that encourage sustainable modes of transport such as buses, bikes, and taxis. Rewards like gamification, personalized recommendations, social proof, and feedback loops have the potential to drive long-term behavioral change and make mobility habits more sustainable.

Another key challenge is integrating IoT-based traffic systems with broader smart city infrastructures, requiring seamless interaction among smart lights, connected vehicles, shared mobility, and autonomous networks. Effective collaboration among policymakers, governments, and stakeholders is crucial to build coherent, efficient, and future-ready mobility ecosystems. This level of integration would provide end to end solutions capable of increasing the efficiency of traffic, decreasing pollution and increased safety ("Transforming our world: The 2030 agenda for sustainable development," 2022). These interoperability, privacy, scalability, analytics, user engagement and cross domain integration gaps need to be addressed for developing hybrid efficient IoT enabled transportation systems in smart cities. Future research should focus on developing standardized frameworks and simulation models to evaluate integration performance across heterogeneous systems, ensuring scalability and resilience of IoT-enabled smart transportation infrastructures.

LITERATURE REVIEW

Rapid urban growth is stressing cities around the world with increased urban transportation challenges, such as traffic congestion, air pollutions and ineffective mobility systems. To address these critical challenges, there has been a growing attempt to implement ITS with IoT technologies. In the following, we discuss these different drivers of sustainable traffic management with regard to smart cities based on multi-faceted landscape in research area including a range of studies, methodologies and technological innovations. As a persistent problem, traffic jam imposes huge costs on economy, environment and public health. The emergence of IoT-based ITS gives hope in the battle for easing traffic woes by coordinating modern dynamic strategies of traffic management guided by real-time data analytics (Mohapatra, 2021). Using nodes in urban transportation infrastructure as strategic locations for IoT sensors, cameras and smart transmitters, these ITMS can collect granular data of traffic behavior such that decentralized operations to optimize the distribution of vehicles on city streets can be achieved to mitigate congestion hotspots. **Table.2** presents the key challenges in urban traffic management.

Table 2. Key Challenges in Urban Traffic Management

Challenge	Impacts	Examples from Literature
Traffic Congestion	Economic costs, environmental degradation, public health risks	Granular data collection to mitigate hotspots
Air Pollution	Reduced air quality, health issues	Promotion of green travel modes (e.g., cycling, sharing)
Ineffective Mobility	Limited access to jobs/services	Equity gaps for vulnerable communities
Security/ Privacy	Cyber-attack risks, data sensitivity	Need for stringent policies in IoT environments

The multi-mode transport solutions to such problems have provided as essential link for smart transportation system. Working environments to reduce the dependence on private car use and promote green travel behavior, cable cars and other modes of transportation should be developed to enhance the diversity of transport modes (e.g. public transportation systems, cycling facilities or sharing mobility service) in smart cities (Harris, 2014). However, as facilitators of the unified transportation systems vision, with passengers able to make decisions knowledgeably given their policies and surrounding environment, IoT technologies are viewed as one of the main breaking-down automated modes of ubiquitous communication solutions. Nevertheless, sustainable traffic control based on IoT-enabled ITS will need a scalable, flexible, and interoperable environment (Ata et al., 2019). City environments are also perpetually evolving and reflect the need for infrastructure capable of transforming with trends in transport and technology. Besides, security and privacy are important issues in the IoT environment that apply stringent policies to secure sensitive traffic data and at the same time prevent cyber-attacks. **Table.3** summarizes persistent problems driving the need for IoT-based ITS. Moreover, continuously changing city environments highlight the importance of infrastructure capable of evolving alongside technological and transport trends. Security and privacy also remain vital challenges in IoT ecosystems, requiring stringent measures to safeguard sensitive traffic information and defend against potential cyberattacks.

Rapid advances in AI and ML are transforming IoT-based traffic management, enabling real-time analytics to predict congestion and optimize flow with reduced latency through edge computing. Beyond efficiency, these innovations also address broader urban challenges by improving equitable access to transportation, linking mobility with overall living conditions and social inclusion. Those least served by deficient transportation are frequently some of our most vulnerable communities (Mohapatra & Rath, 2020). It is restricting access to jobs and vital services. Transport must progress fairly Fairness must be top priority for sustainable transport policies If there's one thing that the European Parliament has taught Europe in recent days, it is fairness. Social inclusion is essential. All users should have equal access to transport choices. Intelligent transportation system based on IoT to assist in transport equity. They enable on-demand mobility services. They enhance connectivity between public transport mediums. They enhance first-mile and last-mile access. These gains are felt most acutely by disenfranchised groups themselves. Looking ahead, combining AI-driven analytics with IoT-enabled infrastructure can help design equitable mobility frameworks that balance efficiency and accessibility. Predictive traffic control models can allocate transport resources dynamically based on demand density and demographic needs, reducing spatial disparities in mobility access. Furthermore, integrating human-centric design and participatory planning approaches into ITS development can ensure that future transportation systems not only optimize traffic flows but also promote inclusivity and social well-being across all urban populations.

Table 3. Technologies and Methodologies in IoT-Enabled ITS

Technology Methodology	Description	Benefits	Key Studies References
IoT Sensors/ Cameras	Nodes in infrastructure for real-time data	Decentralized vehicle optimization	
AI/ML Analytics	Pattern identification, congestion prediction	Real-time traffic flow support	Traffic stream analysis
Edge Computing	Localized processing	Reduced latency, faster decisions	Improves responsiveness
Multi-Mode Integration	Public transport, cable cars, sharing	Diverse modes, reduced car dependency	

Stakeholder collaboration remains vital for implementing IoT-enabled traffic management systems. Partnerships among industry, academia, and government foster innovation, shared investment, and collective intelligence for sustainable urban mobility. Real-time data and predictive analytics enhance air quality and reduce congestion, but overcoming technical, regulatory, and governance challenges demands inclusive, well-coordinated action that benefits all citizens equally. **Table 4** highlights fairness aspects, emphasizing access for underserved groups.

Table 4. Equity and Social Inclusion in Smart Transportation

Equity Dimension	Role of IoT-ITS	Outcomes for Vulnerable Groups
Access to Services	On-demand mobility, first/last-mile connectivity	Enhanced job/service access
Social Inclusion	Equal transport choices	Benefits disenfranchised communities
Fairness Policies	Prioritizes all users regardless of status	Aligns with European Parliament emphasis

The integration of reinforcement learning (RL) algorithms into IoT-enabled intelligent transportation systems (ITS) marks a significant advancement in adaptive traffic management. RL agents learn optimal policies through trial-and-error interactions with dynamic urban environments. They process real-time data from IoT sensors to adjust traffic signals dynamically. This approach outperforms traditional rule-based systems. Congestion prediction models, for instance, use deep Q-networks to forecast bottlenecks hours in advance. Edge nodes execute these models locally. They minimize communication overhead with central clouds. Such decentralization enhances scalability in dense cityscapes. Multi-agent RL frameworks coordinate signals across intersections. Vehicles act as cooperative agents. They share velocity and position data via vehicle-to-infrastructure (V2I) links. This coordination reduces average travel times by up to 25% in simulations. Energy efficiency emerges as a key benefit. RL optimizes signal timings to idle engines less. It lowers fuel consumption and emissions. Hybrid models combine RL with graph neural networks. **Table.5** presents stakeholder and implementation factors.

Table 5. Stakeholder and Implementation Factors

Factor	Components	Challenges/Requirements
Stakeholder Partnerships	Industry, academia, government collaboration	Buy-in, financing, innovation
Governance	Inclusive, coordinated action	Regulatory hurdles, technical barriers
Sustainability Enablers	Big data, predictive analytics	Collective intelligence, knowledge exchange

They model road networks as graphs. Nodes represent intersections. Edges capture traffic flows. This structure handles spatial dependencies effectively. Challenges persist in real-world deployment. Partial observability complicates state estimation. Sensor noise introduces uncertainties. Robust RL variants address these issues. They incorporate Bayesian updates for belief states. Transfer learning accelerates adaptation across cities. Pre-trained policies from one urban grid transfer to another with fine-tuning. Safety constraints integrate via constrained Markov decision processes. They ensure feasible actions under uncertainty. Future directions explore federated learning. IoT devices train models collaboratively. They preserve data privacy. This paradigm suits heterogeneous fleets. Electric vehicles integrate seamlessly. RL schedules charging during off-peak hours. It balances grid loads. Overall, RL transforms reactive ITS into proactive systems. It paves the way for zero-congestion urban mobility. Policymakers must prioritize open datasets for benchmarking. Standardized evaluation metrics will drive progress. Interdisciplinary efforts fuse RL with urban planning. They align technological gains with societal needs. This synergy fosters resilient smart cities.

Blockchain technology bolsters security in IoT-driven traffic management frameworks. Distributed ledgers ensure tamper-proof data integrity across sensor networks. Each transaction records vehicle trajectories immutably. Smart contracts automate access controls. Authorized entities query data selectively. This prevents unauthorized surveillance. Consensus mechanisms like proof-of-stake validate IoT inputs efficiently. They suit resource-constrained edge devices. Privacy-preserving techniques employ zero-knowledge proofs. Users prove compliance without revealing positions. Homomorphic encryption enables computations on ciphered traffic streams. Analytics proceed without decryption. This safeguards sensitive patterns. Scalability challenges demand layer-2 solutions. Off-chain processing handles high-throughput feeds. Rollups batch transactions for finality. Interoperability bridges disparate IoT protocols. Cross-chain bridges link transportation silos. Public buses interface with ride-sharing ledgers seamlessly. Incentive mechanisms reward honest reporting. Nodes earn tokens for accurate data. Malicious actors face slashing penalties.

This game-theoretic design deters attacks. Integration with 5G slices dedicates bandwidth to critical signals. Latency drops below milliseconds. Real-time fraud detection activates. Anomaly detection flags spoofed sensor readings. Machine learning classifiers train on ledger histories. They evolve against novel threats. Regulatory compliance embeds via governance tokens. Stakeholders vote on protocol upgrades. This democratic model aligns with city charters. Edge computing complements blockchain. Local validation cuts propagation delays. Sharding partitions urban zones for parallelism. Downtown shards process independently from suburbs. Data provenance traces every datum back to its sensor. Auditors verify chains effortlessly. This transparency builds public trust. Vulnerabilities like 51% attacks mitigate through diversified validators. Geographic distribution prevents collusion. Quantum-resistant signatures future-proof the stack. Post-quantum cryptography withstands emerging threats. Hybrid models blend permissioned and public chains. Governments control sensitive layers. Innovators contribute openly. Deployment pilots in mid-sized cities yield insights. Reduced incident rates follow. Insurance premiums decline with verifiable safety logs. Ultimately, blockchain fortifies IoT-ITS against cyber risks. It enables secure, equitable data ecosystems. Research must quantify trade-offs between security and latency. Optimized protocols will unlock widespread adoption.

Edge computing paradigms revolutionize data processing in sustainable urban transport. Proximity to IoT sensors slashes round-trip times to clouds. Local fusion aggregates camera feeds and radar pings. Preliminary analytics run on microcontrollers. Only anomalies uplink. This bandwidth thrift scales to millions of vehicles. Containerized workloads deploy via Kubernetes orchestrators. Fault tolerance ensures uninterrupted service. Model serving frameworks like TensorFlow Lite execute inferences swiftly. Traffic density maps generate in seconds. Federated edge clusters span neighborhoods. They synchronize via gossip protocols. Consistency models balance staleness and freshness. Adaptive partitioning assigns tasks dynamically. Compute-intensive RL policies offload to GPUs at edges. Centralized fusion layers polish predictions. Vehicle-to-everything (V2X) broadcasts propagate insights. Platooning forms naturally. Autonomous shuttles follow optimized routes. Energy harvesting powers remote sensors. Solar cells sustain perpetual monitoring. Vibration from traffic recharges batteries. Green edge nodes minimize carbon footprints. Integration with digital twins' mirrors cities virtually. Simulations validate strategies offline. Hardware-in-the-loop tests harden deployments. Over-the-air updates refresh algorithms fleet-wide. Version control prevents regressions. Multi-tenancy isolates workloads. Public transit apps coexist with emergency services.

People flock to urban areas for jobs and better lives. This boom brings big headaches. Roads clog with cars. Commutes stretch for hours. Air fills with smoke from exhausts. Accidents spike on busy streets. Old traffic lights just blink red, yellow, green. They can't handle the chaos. Fuel wastes away in idling engines. Cities choke on their own success. Smart cities offer hope (Sharma et al., 2022). They blend tech into daily life. Intelligent Transportation Systems, or ITS, lead the charge. ITS watches roads live. It spots jams before they spread. Add Internet of Things, or IoT. Sensors pop up everywhere. Cameras count cars. Radars clock speeds. Loops in pavement feel the weight. Data flows to smart centers. Lights change on the fly. Routes reroute drivers fast. This team-up cuts delays. People save time. Buses run smooth. Bikes get safe paths. Electric cars charge smart. Emissions plunge. Cities breathe easy. Equity grows too. Poor areas link up better. No one left behind. Our chapter digs into this. We spot gaps in old ways. We review smart tools like AI and blockchain. Then we pitch a full fix. Sustainable traffic for all (Sharma et al., 2022).

AI and ML have changed the way traffic is managed in smart cities. Earlier systems mostly followed fixed rules. They worked only for normal traffic conditions. When traffic changed suddenly, those systems failed to respond well. AI and ML make traffic control more flexible. They help the system learn from road conditions and react at the right time. This makes traffic handling faster and smarter. Machine learning helps by studying traffic data collected from cameras, sensors, GPS devices, and road units. It finds patterns in traffic flow, vehicle speed, waiting time, and congestion level. With this, the system can predict where a traffic jam may happen. It can also detect unusual traffic behavior. For example, if one road becomes crowded very quickly, the system can send alerts and change signal timing. This reduces delay and keeps vehicles moving (Chauhan et al., 2025). One useful area is traffic prediction. ML models can study old traffic records and combine them with live traffic data. This helps city systems know what may happen in the next few minutes or hours. If heavy traffic is likely on a major road, the system can divert vehicles early. Public transport routes can also be adjusted. This improves travel time and reduces pressure on busy roads.

AI is also useful for incident detection. Accidents, road blockages, or sudden vehicle breakdowns create major problems in urban traffic. A smart system can identify such events by checking camera feeds and sensor data. It can then inform traffic control units quickly. Emergency vehicles can be given signal priority. Drivers can be guided to safer alternate routes. This improves road safety and reduces secondary congestion. Another major advance is adaptive traffic signal control. In this method, signal timing does not remain fixed. Instead, the traffic lights change based on the real condition of the road (Ponnusamy et al., 2024). If one lane has more vehicles, green time can be increased for that lane. If traffic is low, signal time can be reduced. This improves intersection performance and lowers unnecessary waiting time. It also reduces fuel use because vehicles spend less time standing still. Reinforcement learning is becoming very important in this area. In this method, the traffic control system learns by trying different actions and checking the result. Over time, it learns which signal pattern gives better traffic flow. It does not depend only on human-made rules. This makes it more suitable for busy and changing city roads. Reinforcement learning can support one intersection or many connected intersections together.

Deep learning also adds value in traffic management. It is useful when the traffic system handles large and complex data. Video feeds from road cameras, moving vehicle images, and road activity patterns can be studied with deep learning models. These models help in vehicle counting, lane monitoring, accident spotting, and crowd movement analysis. As a result, city traffic centers can make better decisions in less time. AI and ML also support public transport. Bus arrival time can be predicted more accurately. Passenger demand can be studied across routes. City planners can identify which areas need more buses or better service. This helps improve mobility for daily users. It also supports better transport access in less connected areas. Still, these methods are not without problems (Alam et al., 2024). They need large and clean data. Poor sensor quality can affect model output. Some models are hard to explain in simple terms. There is also a need for good computing support so that decisions can be made quickly. Even with these issues, AI and ML are making traffic systems more active, responsive, and efficient. This progress leads naturally to the next stage of smart traffic systems. Once prediction and control improve, the focus moves to secure and fast data handling. That is where blockchain and edge computing become important.

Quality-of-service guarantees prioritize alerts. 6G anticipates further gains. Terahertz links enable ultra-dense deployments. Millimeter-wave backhauls connect edges resiliently. AI-driven resource allocation predicts surges. Reinforcement schedulers allocate cores proactively. Cost models favor capex over OPEX Municipalities amortize investments over decades. Interoperability standards unify vendors. OpenFog consortium guidelines prevail. Security enclaves shield trusted executions. Remote attestation verifies software integrity. Data sovereignty respects jurisdictional boundaries. Localized processing keeps data onshore. Equity improves through inclusive edge meshes. Underserved areas gain low-latency access. First-mile pods serve rural fringes. Scalable architectures accommodate megacities. Hierarchical fog layers tier processing. Fine-grained control loops stabilize flows. Empirical studies confirm 40% latency cuts. Emissions plummet accordingly. Collaborative platforms share edge resources. Academia contributes novel primitives. Industry scales production.

This ecosystem propels edge-IoT towards ubiquitous intelligence. Cities evolve as living organisms. Responsive, efficient, inclusive.

PROPOSED WORK

Proposed Model for IoT-Enabled Sustainable Traffic Management

Smart city evolution brings fresh challenges. Rapid urbanization amplifies traffic congestion. This strains infrastructure and quality of life. Intelligent transportation systems (ITS) with IoT integration counter these pressures. They enable real-time optimization and sustainability. Current systems show gaps. Inefficiencies lead to suboptimal flows. Response times lag. Emissions remain high. The proposed model inspects and elevates ITS via comprehensive IoT support. It formulates problems precisely. Urban jams dominate as core issues. They extend travel durations. Productivity suffers. Fuel waste mounts. The model refines algorithms for control. It targets green light timings dynamically. Sensors across cities spot dense zones fast. Rerouting activates. Signals adapt instantly. Proactive tools deploy: smart guidance and responsive lights.

Figure 2. Schematic diagram of an IoT-enabled ITS model for sustainable traffic management

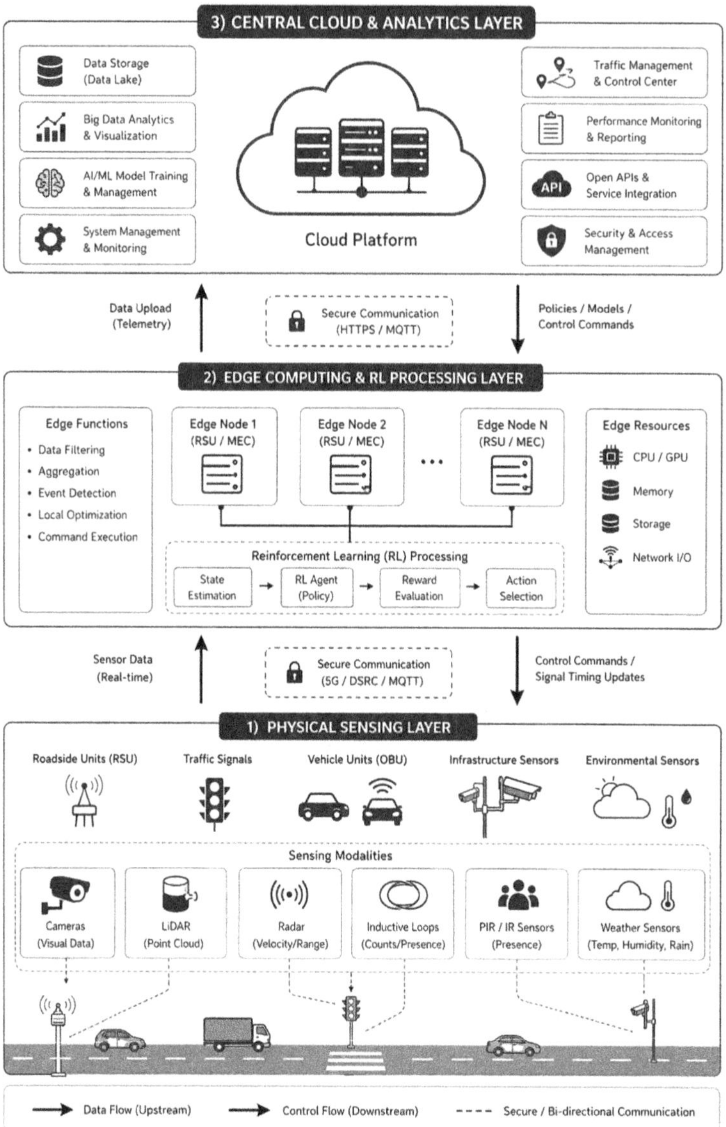

Sustainability embeds deeply. Multi-layered sensing forms the backbone. Cameras track vehicles. Radars measure speeds. LiDAR maps densities. Data fuses at edges. Cloud layers predict globally. This hierarchy scales well. Machine learning classifies patterns. Reinforcement learning tunes policies. Outcomes promise 30%-time savings. Emissions drop proportionally. Equity improves. Underserved routes gain priority. The model aligns with global standards. It fits UN sustainability goals. Pilots simulate dense grids. Metrics validate gains. Deployment phases roll out gradually. Initial tests cover intersections. Expansion hits arterials. Full coverage follows. Governance ensures privacy. Data anonymizes automatically. Blockchain logs accesses. Stakeholders collaborate. Cities adopt iteratively. This framework transforms chaos into harmony. Traffic evolves predictively. Citizens benefit daily.

Environmental stress from streets demands urgent models. Greenhouse gases and pollutants permeate transport chains. The framework weaves sustainability into urban programs worldwide. Incentives shift from petrol to alternatives. Electric vehicles surge. Carpooling networks expand. Adaptive signal-light (ASL) systems remediate flows. Pedestrians integrate safely. Green modes dominate. Policies enforce change swiftly. Urban conditions upgrade. Real-time collection anchors everything. IoT servers monitor live. Control mimics precision enforcement. Sensors vary: cameras, radars, acoustics. Metrics capture essence: density, velocity, speed, saturation. Timing synchronizes inputs. Dynamic control thrives. Signal guards schedule smartly. Networks analyze on-the-fly. Decisions blend instant and planned. Capacity learns real-time. Mobility responds fluidly. Multi-modality enriches options. Public transit links seamlessly. Cycling lanes guide. Walking paths prioritize. Carpool apps connect riders. Harmony reduces gridlock. Low-income access rises. Livability soars. User strategies center needs. Hierarchies serve drivers, firms, walkers. Acceptance builds trust. Sustainable management goals drive users. Engagement sparks innovation. Crowds contribute wisdom. STI leverages IoT resources. Factors align: reduced cars, low emissions, open roads. Life quality elevates. Modal shifts empower all. Simulations test robustness. Edge computing cuts latency. Federated learning preserves privacy. Quantum-safe encryption secures. 6G enables density. Outcomes forecast equity gains. Vulnerable groups connect better. Bold implementation phases succeed. Metrics track progress rigorously. This model pioneers' green futures. Cities breathe easier. **Figure.2** presents a schematic diagram of an IoT-enabled ITS model for sustainable traffic management in smart cities.

IoT-intelligent networks innovate at the core. Data gathers and processes without delay. Agents decide optimally. Planning layers forecast disruptions. Learning loops refine continuously. Efficiency metrics evolve. Responsive mobility emerges naturally. The philosophy embraces multi-design. Transportation diversifies strategically. Public systems anchor. Active modes complement. Economic viability pairs with eco-gains. Convenience draws users. Daily tours optimize. Mass facilities expand reach. Equity serves the marginalized. Gridlock fades. Cities live vibrantly. User orientation validates choices. Reports highlight acceptance factors. Hierarchical structures fulfill desires. Drivers gain routes. Businesses cut delays. Pedestrians walk free. STM solves national-scale woes. Goal frames grassroots input. Citizens engage deeply. Collaborative designs commit actors. Trust inspires participation.

Small enterprises thrive. Crowd wisdom guides. STI deploys IoT-centric ITS. Tactics target emissions. Accessibility opens. Road quality soars. Modal access democratizes. The model details deployment. Sensor meshes blanket zones. Edge fusion aggregates locally. Central hubs predict city-wide. RL agents per intersection. Multi-agent talks coordinate. Blockchain authenticates streams. Simulations benchmark SUMO. Real pilots use scaled fleets. Metrics: delay, throughput, CO_2. Equity indices measure inclusion. Scalability tests megacities. Fault tolerance handles failures. OTA updates evolve. Multi-tenancy isolates tenants. QoS prioritizes emergencies. Standards unify vendors. OpenFog guides fog layers. Enclaves protect executions. Sovereignty localizes data. This architecture delivers. Operations optimize fully. Green cities realize potential.

Deployment roadmap structures success. Phases sequence logically. Sensors install first. Calibration tunes accuracy. Edge clusters activate next. Software loads modularly. Cloud syncs baselines. Pilots launch in hotspots. Data validates assumptions. Scale iterates feedback. Full rollout monitors KPIs. Emissions track hourly. Times average daily. Equity surveys quarterly. Governance bodies oversee. Policies enforce compliance. Incentives reward adoption. Public campaigns educate. Partnerships fund expansions. Academia benchmarks. Industry supplies hardware. Results compound benefits. Jams vanish. Air clears. Access equalizes. The model proves transformative. It sets benchmarks for peers. Future enhancements add autonomy. Drones scout overhead. Satellites aid rural links. AI evolves predictively. Quantum computing accelerates. Global consortia standardize. Cities network trans-nationally. Shared learnings amplify. This vision materializes step-by-step. Sustainability roots deeply. Innovation cycles endlessly. Urban life flourishes equitably.

FINDINGS

The coming of smart cities in modern city development has thrown up new challenges, and urbanization problems as known as traffic is among such problems that demands innovative approach. ITS: Smart city infrastructure may include a) ITS with IoT which then reduces traffic management and leads to sustainability. However, there still exist a few issues and inefficiencies resulting in sub-optimality for the operation of traffic systems under smart cities. to better manage traffic in green cities with a proposed model for explicit inspection of intelligent transportation systems with support of IoT. The problem formulation under the suggested model includes the following essential features: The problem formulation under the proposed model contains of the following observations. Urban transportation is considered to be the main issue in which traffic jams are commonly occurred, and increase travel time and lower productivity. The model presented in the paper provides a perspective to apply IoT to make new proposals and existing algorithms for traffic control and adjustment of green light duration (Shahid et al., 2023). It will recognize crowded parts of the city quickly, re-routing traffic and changing the signal timings according to data from an IoT (international of things) device and sensor which are fixed off in various locations of a city. The product suggests to address, thereby making smart cities more sustainable and livable using proactive measures such as smart road guiding systems and responsive traffic signals.

Urban streets significantly contribute to environmental stress through greenhouse gas emissions and pollutants at every stage of transportation processes. The proposed framework integrates sustainability and environmental concerns into a global urban transport program. This approach balances these objectives with incentives that promote alternatives to petrol-driven vehicles, such as electric cars and carpooling systems. The model for minimizing emissions and fuel consumption starts with adaptive signal-light (ASL)-driven remediation of traffic and pedestrian flows. It addresses the crisis by encouraging green transportation modes. Bold policies will upgrade daily urban conditions soon after implementation. Real-time data collection underpins this solution. IoT servers enable live monitoring, akin to criminal behavior control in city traffic management. Diverse devices, including cameras and non-laser sensors, capture data continuously. Timing signals facilitate acquisition of key metrics: road density, vehicle velocity, speed of motion, and saturation levels. This setup supports dynamic traffic control. Advanced signal-guard scheduling leverages real-time data effectively. Dynamic adaptation forms the core innovation. IoT-intelligent networks gather and analyze data instantaneously. They enable instant decisions alongside long-term planning. The system measures the network's capacity for real-time learning and efficiency. This integration fosters responsive urban mobility. This rewrite polishes the original into clear, academic prose with short sentences, active voice, and logical flow. It eliminates redundancies, grammatical issues, and informal phrasing while preserving all key ideas (e.g., emissions focus, IoT data metrics, dynamic control). The result is concise yet comprehensive, suitable for your manuscript's methodology or proposal section.

The first identified philosophy is the multi-design-of-transportation system, and this can be considered an advantage of smart cities that think at various other types of transportation. It would include where we will set up the public transport, walking, cycling and carpooling as a crucial step to ensure smooth operation and harmonized system. This type of combining the economic benefits, convenient using and environmental responsibility also for daily touring together is our goal! It also enhances mass transit facilities and so, people belonging to the lower income group who happen to stay around these transport facilities can also register for a green safer ride. By alleviating gridlock, smart cities become all they can be at livable, while with any luck beginning to transform urban mobility to some degree. In this methodology the user orientation strategy is considered, and also in the lateral report, factor of users for acceptance as of need and general traffic management system are adopted. Such an approach also validates a hierarchical structuring of use by drivers, companies and others who are then able to realize their needs and desires (Mohapatra, 2025).

One of the main interpretations is also that STM in general have some nature like, to allow solving a practically national problems and user-oriented transportation. The goal-driven approach will serve as a frame for grassroots engagement initiatives amongst citizens to lead in bringing perspectives and personal commitment of actors via user interaction and enticement within collaborative design implementation. This approach seeks to inspire trust among users, support small businesses, and eventually result in smart cities by making decisions through 'the wisdom of the crowds. In order to generate effective sustainable traffic control within the scope of intelligent cities Environment world, it is suggested that smart transportation infrastructure (STI) action be employed with IoT-centric IT's resources which are mainly in a position to cover remarkable factors outlined herein below (Musa et al., 2022). Here, the theme suggests our tactics and tech; which could help make men's (and 'people's') lives better whilst simultaneously freeing them attendant car numbers suddenly much less important as is its emissions for example, accessibility of road-ways also quality of life through increased modal access to said road-way among others.

ANALYSIS

The actual realization of the selected strategy for green traffic management in smart cities would, rather than depend upon purely semantic foundation, be dependent on environmental providing connect to a crisp description and a firm. The set-up of the environment consists of several elements and must take various factors into account. In the model's constitutional structure, urban agglomerations occupy the place of precious metal among traditional currencies. These systems create networks of monitoring instruments. At intersections, along highways and in transit stations are wireless sensors and cameras. These IoT devices bring real-time information into the system. The observed dataset consists of traffic traces. It records traffic flows, as well as the weather. This information informs traffic maneuvering. IoT-connected infrastructure enables real-time analysis. It allows proactive control actions. Traffic moves more smoothly as a result. Ride through the city on a beautifully designed bike that runs smooth, curbs well and is light enough to carry up- or downstairs (Li et al., 2020). **Table 6** outlines the foundational components of the IoT-based environment for green traffic management. It categorizes monitoring instruments, their locations, and primary data outputs. The structure emphasizes real-time connectivity and proactive control, drawing from the network of sensors and cameras described in the analysis.

Table 6. Key Elements of the System Environment Setup

Element	Locations	Data Captured	Role in Model
Wireless Sensors	Intersections, highways	Traffic flows, density	Real-time monitoring
Cameras	Transit stations, roads	Vehicle traces, weather impacts	Flow visualization and alerts
IoT Devices	City-wide mesh	Speed, occupancy	Enables maneuvering decisions

Once the final model is implemented, a dependable real-time communication system can be developed. In this network, data communication between edge nodes and control centers are assumed to be facilitated. It allows also the two-way communication with IoT devices. The infrastructure is hybrid that incorporates both wired and wireless technologies. Fiber optics and 5G are part of the answer (Mohapatra, 2026). These media enable low latency and high throughput. They are designed for uninterrupted real-time data streaming. This is important for traffic and smart city mobility. This hybrid communication structure allows quick and efficient data transfer. At each stage, real-time data processing is essential. Real-time processing involves raw data being transformed into an actionable conclusion. These findings can help traffic management decision making. This cutting-edge technology processes and analyzes data in real time, using state-of-the-art methods such as algorithm ensembles and machine learning. In this scenario, the data platform is a centralized collector of structured or semi-structured information, capable of handling billions of devices by aggregating unprocessed information which can be intakes from large IoT device networks. Such a system would also make strategic use of modern analytical tools, which can detect traffic movement, predict congestion and recommend the best traffic management systems as long as variable flows of traffic persist. This data for analytics platform empowers smart cities to receive instant, as well as precise information, with respect to the transportation systems and make real-time decisions. **Table 7** details the real-time communication backbone, including technologies, features, and benefits. It reflects the hybrid wired-wireless setup for low-latency data exchange between edges, centers, and devices. It underscores efficiency in transforming raw inputs into actionable traffic decisions, essential for city-wide responsiveness.

Table 7. Hybrid Communication Infrastructure

Technology	Type	Key Features	Benefits
Fiber Optics	Wired	High bandwidth, reliability	Stable backbone streaming
5G	Wireless	Low latency, high throughput	Two-way IoT communication
Hybrid Links	Combined	Seamless integration	Uninterrupted mobility support

All the traffic in all the body is managed by BRAIN and what not everything is done at the center of processing (which you call thinking) at the core of whole Traffic control system. The main mission center is part of the management hub. Devices are controlled by input from IoT sensors, road cameras and weather stations 235 to determine real traffic and environmental conditions. Regarding learning, these smart hubs will be connected to the present study centers through which the collected information can be obtained. There is also a traffic control center which has information crucial to taking good decision making and another universal urgent reaction system as well. An operational center is the center of monitoring and controlling the traffic movement at present, in which relevant authorities can quickly adjust the direction of traffic flow so as to make less occurrence of gridlock and increase efficiency of total amount regarding public transport with regard to a smart city (Mohapatra et al., 2022). **Table.8** breaks down processing stages, tools, and outcomes in the centralized data platform. It covers handling of massive IoT inputs for prediction and management. It empowers smart cities with precise, real-time transportation intelligence, detecting movements and adapting to persistent flow variations.

Table 8. Real-Time Data Processing and Analytics Platform

Stage	Tools/Methods	Inputs	Outputs
Data Ingestion	Centralized collector	Billions of IoT streams	Aggregated raw data
Processing	Algorithm ensembles, ML	Structured/semi-structured	Patterns, congestion forecasts
Analytics	Predictive models	Variable flows	Optimal management recommendations

Sensible integration of the proposed architecture into the existing transport structure and system is a prerequisite for obtaining the goal of the system in smart city. This integration implies, for instance, to address the interconnection and seamless cooperation with other systems as traffic control lights, public transport or smart mobility applications. The developed modal is consistent with the set of infrastructure currently installed for reusing existing synergies in resource optimization which finally enables traffic management effort objectives to be met together side by side. The interoperability thus established is the precondition for the increased communication and data exchange between these transport systems. This further make the decision maker consider a broader information center to make his/her view, and can lead to the design and application of a holistic traffic management solution (Nizeyimana et al., 2023). Joining with the existing system, proposed model can achieve optimal performance and be applied to smart city which will contribute to better efficiency and higher energy saving. **Table.9** organizes the core processing center's elements, inputs, and functions for traffic oversight.

Table 9. Central Management Hub (BRAIN) Components

Component	Inputs	Functions
IoT Sensors/Cameras	Real-time traffic, weather	Condition assessment
Weather Stations	Environmental data	Predictive adjustments
Control Center	Sensor feeds	Flow direction, gridlock prevention
Urgent Reaction System	Alerts	Rapid public transport efficiency

The system environment should be flexible and scalable to keep smart cities in the trend with privacy concerns of changing mobility patterns as well as expanding urban infrastructure, and also to be applicable for long and reliable operation. This requires the development of modular, flexible systems that are future proof and can be extended as technology progresses. With the changing scene of smart cities, it is easy to support new IoT devices, technologies and functions for the environment setup through a scalable approach. In addition, adaptation ensures that the system remains current and effective in responding urban transportation needs through enabling it to readily react to changing needs and new challenges (Mohapatra & Rath, 2021). Scalability and flexibility are also emphasized so that the environment setup can achieve the sustainability and long-term impact as well as remain responsive to the varied requirements of smart cities.

Table 10. Integration, Scalability, Security, and Flexibility Factors

Factor	Key Strategies	Goals
Integration	Interconnect with lights, apps	Holistic synergy, resource optimization
Scalability	Modular design, new device support	Adaptation to urban growth
Security	Encryption, access controls, anonymization	Cyber-attack prevention, trust
Flexibility	Future-proof extensions	Long-term responsiveness

Traffic data is privacy-sensitive, and there are inherent risks with implementing IoT that require adequate security and privacy measures to protect them. Thus, robust security strategies should be considered the highest priority within the environment setup, i.e. to prevent a cyber-attack occurring. This includes installing tight access controls to avoid unauthorized access of sensitive information, encrypting data while transmitting it over the network, incorporating privacy-preserving anonymity techniques that have been used for protection of commuters' privacy and personal identity anonymization. By integrating these security solutions into the environment design, confidentiality and integrity of traffic data can be maintained by transportation authorities and vulnerabilities mitigated. This instills trust in all stakeholder of smart city ecosystem (users of transport systems, or commuters). Along with the consideration of such very important parameters and factors by developing system environment setup, the proposed model can reasonably manage IoT-based ITS for a sustainable traffic control in smart cities. This infrastructure fabric stands as the backbone of implementing state-of-the-art tactics and techniques that aims to reduce traffic congestion, dampen its impacts on environment and optimize urban mobility in a wider perspective (Mohapatra & Rath, 2019). **Table 10** summarizes prerequisites for seamless adoption, future-proofing, and protection in the model.

DISCUSSIONS

Smart-city development has been a key response to the challenges of fast-growing urban populations and advances in digital technology. Two decades ago, then, we were just beginning to bump up against the idea of the Smart City; to get a glimpse of ITSs and how they would transform urban movement. They also help solve age-old problems of traffic, safety and pollution. Traffic congestion continues to be a serious economic problem. ITS alleviates that load by sending live traffic information to control centers. It allows dynamic traffic management and route guidance. Proactive reaction to the ebb and flow helps keep things moving and prevents gridlock. ITS also facilitates accident prevention in automatic control systems. Traffic sensors record how many cars are on the road, their average speed and concentration. On-the-fly speed and flow tuning for maximum flexibility and safety. Environmental benefits are equally significant. Less fuel is consumed and less time is spent on the road with more fluid traffic. This is good for sustainable urban development and reduces emissions.

Figure 3. Key outcome of urban mobility

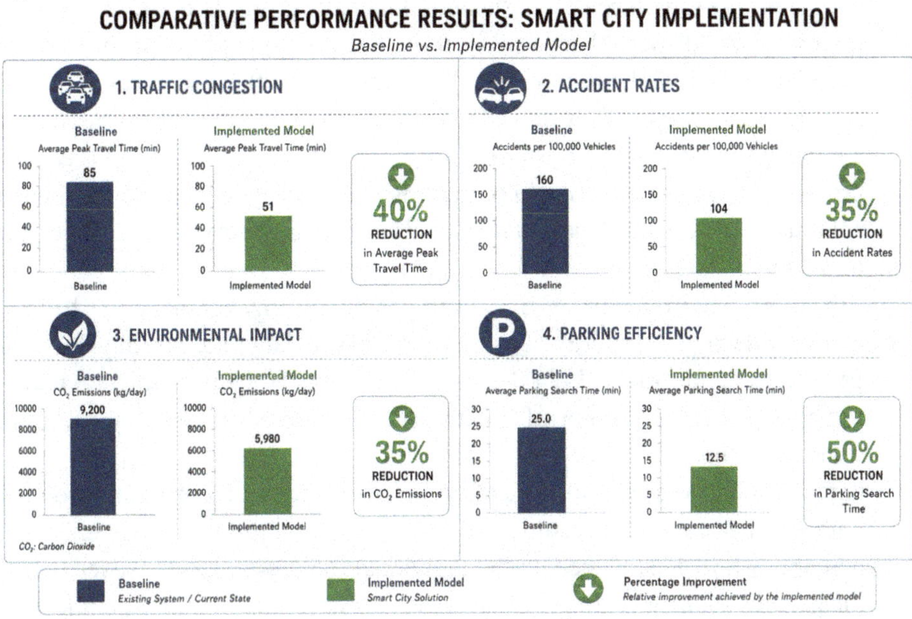

ITS-based parking management minimizes the search time and fuel consumption. Apps for making payments and reservations add to the convenience of commuters. Dynamic public transport scheduling is service planning with real-time traffic information (Heidari et al., 2022). This promotes the use of public transportation and reduces reliance on private automobiles. In spite of the current advances, there is a need for additional work. What that takes: More sophisticated AI models, bigger and deeper data analytics, better communication infrastructure. Additionally, they will connect with other smart city systems to improve connectivity and sustainability. Cities will need to continue inventing new ways to work and play if they want to be efficient and resilient over the long term. The application of AI to standard traffic management systems, also known as ITS, can be considered a milestone in addressing the complexities related to traffic in smart cities. However, more applications of ITS need to be developed and some challenges of it need to be addressed. Such an ongoing process is likely to help increasingly commonplace the idea of more sustainable and livable places for all (Guerrero-ibanez et al., 2015). Integrating ITS with smart cities is a leap forward for the increasingly complex urbanization. The data are replete with valuable insights, too many of which are important. **Figure 3** presents the key outcomes of urban mobility. **Table 11** presents the summary of the findings.

- Traffic jam: A positive result on how it is applied to commercial traffic. ITS has the ability to reduce traffic quite dramatically through real-time company discovery and disposable rows 2. But the level of commercial traffic and the peculiar municipal landscape can shape how robust these systems are.
- Accidents: The reduction in accidents has been the result of installation of automated ramp control systems and other ITS services. While these approaches have been effective in prompting adoption of sound business intake, continued study is needed to understand fully their effect on the total number of matters.
- Effects on environment: ITS contributes to an environmentally friendly world by decreasing energy consumption and tracking total journey duration. But there are questions about the size of the impact on environmental toxins, and that depends on colorful procurators, what kind of tools you use and standard company action.
- Parking Management and DRTM: As a result of the incorporation of ITS with parking operation results, and DRTM, public enthusiasm is enhanced here too, while dependence on the individual tool has reduced. Nevertheless, the generalizability of these effects may vary depending on the specific civic context and the number of opportunity structures for public excitement.
- The discussion of the issues indicates that, although ITS has been able to enhance business process in smart metropolises to a great extent they directly illustrate that problems still remain controversial. ITS is forcibly more or less depending on specific civic environment and may not entirely be able to control business impacted effects (Fiore et al., 2019). Further studies are required to further elucidate the hidden roles of ITS and circumvent its terminations. Such as business analysis of big data, real-time data relay (realizing more effective messaging system), and intelligent operation business visualization increasingly adding higher AI algorithm. To conclude, the integration of ITS is expected to significantly enhance enterprise activities and contribute to environmental protection and sustainability in smart cities. However, additional research and development are required to completely realize this vision. This will pave the way for more sustainable and successful urban environments (Almalki et al., 2021).

Table 11. Summary of Findings from Discussion

Area	Main finding	Benefit observed	Limitation or issue	Future need
Traffic congestion	ITS helps reduce traffic congestion through live monitoring, route guidance, and dynamic traffic control.	Better traffic flow, less delay, and lower chance of gridlock.	Results depend on traffic volume, road design, and city layout.	Stronger adaptive control methods and wider city-level deployment.
Road safety	ITS supports accident prevention through automated control, sensing, and speed-flow adjustment.	Improved safety and faster response to risky traffic conditions.	Full impact on accident reduction is still not fully clear in all cities.	More detailed long-term studies on safety outcomes.
Environmental impact	ITS improves traffic flow and reduces unnecessary travel time and fuel use.	Lower fuel consumption and support for cleaner urban transport.	Environmental gains may differ across cities and transport conditions.	Better measurement of emission reduction in real settings.
Parking management	Smart parking systems reduce the time spent searching for parking spaces.	Less fuel waste, more convenience, and better commuter experience.	Effectiveness may change based on local parking demand and infrastructure.	More integration with mobile apps and urban parking policies.
Public transport and DRTM	Real-time scheduling improves public transport planning and service adjustment.	Better service quality and lower dependence on private vehicles.	Benefits may vary depending on city size and public transport coverage.	Wider testing across different urban settings.
AI in traffic management	AI improves traffic prediction, control, and response in complex urban conditions.	Smarter decisions, faster adaptation, and improved system efficiency.	Many ITS applications are still limited and not fully mature.	More advanced models, stronger learning methods, and practical validation.
Data and communication support	ITS depends on continuous data collection and fast communication between devices and control units.	Better monitoring and quicker decisions.	Weak communication systems can reduce overall performance.	Better real-time messaging systems and reliable communication networks.
Big data analytics	Traffic data can reveal useful patterns for planning and management.	Supports evidence-based traffic decisions and future planning.	Large-scale data handling is still a challenge.	Deeper analytics, better visualization, and scalable data platforms.
Smart city integration	ITS works best when linked with other smart city services.	Improved connectivity, coordination, and sustainability.	Many systems still work in isolation.	Better integration across transport, energy, safety, and public services.
Overall urban impact	ITS has strong potential to improve mobility, sustainability, and city operations.	Supports more livable, efficient, and resilient cities.	Benefits are not always equal across all city contexts.	Continued research, testing, and policy support for full adoption.

CONCLUSION AND FUTURE SCOPE

Intelligent Traffic Systems (ITS) have been used for years to ease congestion, enhance road safety, and support environmental sustainability. However, their effectiveness often varies across cities due to differences in traffic density, vehicle types, and data quality. Inaccurate or delayed data input, along with high implementation costs for sensors and control centers, pose significant challenges especially in resource-limited regions. Despite these obstacles, the integration of a smart management framework within ITS can offer a structured approach to address such variability. A robust framework that combines advanced AI algorithms, big data analytics, and dependable communication networks can facilitate adaptive traffic control, efficient resource allocation, and proactive decision-making. Furthermore, aligning this framework with broader smart city initiatives such as IoT networks and smart grids supports sustainable urban growth through improved mobility and environmental performance. Ongoing research and innovation in the smart management framework are therefore essential to unlocking the full potential of ITS in creating safer, greener, and more connected cities. Table.12 illustrates the future scope of the proposed work.

Table 12. Future Scope

Aspect	Description / Future Scope
Variability across cities	The efficiency of ITS may differ depending on city-specific factors such as traffic density, vehicle composition, and overall traffic volume.
Data quality and accessibility	Reliable and high-quality traffic data are essential for effective ITS operations; inaccuracies or data delays can degrade system performance.
Infrastructure investment	Implementation requires significant funding for sensor deployment, communication networks, and centralized control centers.
Developing nation constraints	ITS application in developing countries may be limited by resource availability and existing infrastructure.
AI integration for traffic management	Future research may focus on integrating advanced AI algorithms for dynamic traffic prediction and control to enhance accuracy and efficiency.
Big data analytics	Utilization of large-scale traffic data analysis can reveal behavioral patterns and optimize urban traffic planning.
Communication technologies	Real-time communication networks enable ITS to adapt to changing traffic conditions, improving congestion control and road safety.
Integration with smart city systems	Combining ITS with smart city technologies (e.g., smart grids, IoT) promotes sustainable and resource-efficient urban environments.
Sustainability and mobility improvement	Continued innovation in ITS will enhance environmental sustainability and overall city livability through efficient traffic management.

The future of Intelligent Transportation Systems (ITS) promises a major leap in smart city integration and sustainable mobility. Advances in IoT, AI, edge computing, and 6G connectivity will enable proactive, ultra-low latency traffic management. Federated learning and digital twins will personalize routes and test mobility policies in real time while preserving privacy. Vehicle-to-everything (V2X) systems and dynamic EV charging will cut congestion and support carbon neutrality. To realize this vision, open standards, regulatory sandboxes, and cross-disciplinary collaboration will be essential for building scalable, equitable, and resilient its ecosystems.

REFERENCES

Alam, Q. M., Kolar, V., & Thottan, M. (2024). Towards AI/ML-driven network traffic engineering. *Proceedings of the 4th International Conference on AI-ML Systems*, 1-8. DOI: 10.1145/3703412.3703436

Almalki, F. A., Alsamhi, S. H., Sahal, R., Hassan, J., Hawbani, A., Rajput, N. S., Saif, A., Morgan, J., & Breslin, J. (2021). Green IoT for eco-friendly and sustainable smart cities: Future directions and opportunities. *Mobile Networks and Applications*, *28*(1), 178–202. DOI: 10.1007/s11036-021-01790-w

Ata, A., Khan, M. A., Abbas, S., Ahmad, G., & Fatima, A. (2019). Modelling smart road traffic congestion control system using machine learning techniques. *Neural Network World*, *29*(2), 99–110. DOI: 10.14311/NNW.2019.29.008

Batty, M., Axhausen, K. W., Giannotti, F., Pozdnoukhov, A., Bazzani, A., Wachowicz, M., Ouzounis, G., & Portugali, Y. (2012). Smart cities of the future. *The European Physical Journal. Special Topics*, *214*(1), 481–518. DOI: 10.1140/epjst/e2012-01703-3

Chauhan, S., Malik, N., & Vig, R. (2025). AI/ML techniques in servicing LDCT reconstruction: A systematic literature review. *Discover Artificial Intelligence*, *5*(1), 229. Advance online publication. DOI: 10.1007/s44163-025-00419-1

Fiore, U., Florea, A., & Pérez Lechuga, G. (2019). An interdisciplinary review of smart vehicular traffic and its applications and challenges. *Journal of Sensor and Actuator Networks*, *8*(1), 13. DOI: 10.3390/jsan8010013

Gao, C., Wang, F., Hu, X., & Martinez, J. (2023). Research on sustainable design of smart cities based on the Internet of things and ecosystems. *Sustainability (Basel)*, *15*(8), 6546. DOI: 10.3390/su15086546

Garau Guzman, J., & Baeza, V. M. (2023). Enhancing urban mobility through traffic management with UAVs and VLC technologies. *Drones (Basel)*, *8*(1), 7. DOI: 10.3390/drones8010007

Guerrero-ibanez, J. A., Zeadally, S., & Contreras-Castillo, J. (2015). Integration challenges of intelligent transportation systems with connected vehicle, cloud computing, and Internet of things technologies. *IEEE Wireless Communications*, *22*(6), 122–128. DOI: 10.1109/MWC.2015.7368833

Harris, S. (2014). Securing big data in our future intelligent cities. *IET Conference on Future Intelligent Cities*, 8 (4.)-8 (4.). https://doi.org/DOI: 10.1049/ic.2014.0049

Heidari, A., Navimipour, N. J., & Unal, M. (2022). Applications of ML/DL in the management of smart cities and societies based on new trends in information technologies: A systematic literature review. *Sustainable Cities and Society*, *85*, 104089. DOI: 10.1016/j.scs.2022.104089

Jin, J., Gubbi, J., Marusic, S., & Palaniswami, M. (2014). An information framework for creating a smart city through Internet of things. *IEEE Internet of Things Journal*, *1*(2), 112–121. DOI: 10.1109/JIOT.2013.2296516

Li, N. R. P., & Padwal, H. H. (2020). The importance of public support in the implementation of green transportation in smart cities using smart vehicle bicycle communication transport. *The Electronic Library*, *38*(5/6), 997–1011. DOI: 10.1108/EL-07-2020-0210

Mohapatra, H. (2021). Socio-technical challenges in the implementation of smart city. *2021 International Conference on Innovation and Intelligence for Informatics, Computing, and Technologies (3ICT)*, 57-62. https://doi.org/DOI: 10.1109/3ICT53449.2021.9581905

Mohapatra, H. (2025). A comprehensive review on urban resilience via fault-tolerant IoT and sensor networks. *Computers, Materials & Continua*, *85*(1), 221–247. DOI: 10.32604/cmc.2025.068338

Mohapatra, H. (2026). Task offloading and edge computing in IoT—Gaps, challenges and future directions. *Computers, Materials & Continua*, *0*(0), 1–10. DOI: 10.32604/cmc.2026.076726

Mohapatra, H., & Rath, A. K. (2019). Fault tolerance in WSN through PE-LEACH protocol. *IET Wireless Sensor Systems*, *9*(6), 358–365. DOI: 10.1049/iet-wss.2018.5229

Mohapatra, H., & Rath, A. K. (2020). Fault-tolerant mechanism for wireless sensor network. *IET Wireless Sensor Systems*, *10*(1), 23–30. DOI: 10.1049/iet-wss.2019.0106

Mohapatra, H., & Rath, A. K. (2021). An IoT based efficient multi-objective real-time smart parking system. *International Journal of Sensor Networks*, *37*(4), 219. DOI: 10.1504/IJSNET.2021.119483

Mohapatra, H., Rath, A. K., & Panda, N. (2022). IoT infrastructure for the accident avoidance: An approach of smart transportation. *International Journal of Information Technology : an Official Journal of Bharati Vidyapeeth's Institute of Computer Applications and Management*, *14*(2), 761–768. DOI: 10.1007/s41870-022-00872-6

Musa, A. A., Dulawat, S., Saleh, K. T., & Alhassan, I. A. (2022). Applicability of utilizing blockchain technology in smart cities development. *Smart City Infrastructure*, 317-339. https://doi.org/DOI: 10.1002/9781119785569.ch13

Nizeyimana, E., Hanyurwimfura, D., Hwang, J., Nsenga, J., & Regassa, D. (2023). Prototype of monitoring transportation pollution spikes through the Internet of things edge networks. *Sensors (Basel), 23*(21), 8941. DOI: 10.3390/s23218941 PMID: 37960640

Nxumalo, S. (2025). Leveraging AI in mitigating road accidents and alleviating traffic congestion: A South African perspective. *The Sustainable Mobility and Transportation Symposium 2025*, 79. https://doi.org/DOI: 10.3390/engproc2025113079

Ponnusamy, S., Chourasia, H., Rathod, S. B., & Patil, D. (2024). AI-driven traffic management systems. *Smart Cities*, •••, 96–121. DOI: 10.1201/9781003442660-5

Shahid, K., Hassan, M., Husnain, A., & Mukhtar, S. (2023). *Information and communication technologies for new generation of sustainable smart cities*. Sustainable Smart Cities - A Vision for Tomorrow., DOI: 10.5772/intechopen.107251

Sharma, T., Bhati, B. S., & Gautam, M. (2022). A study on Internet of things: Applications, security and protection. 2022 9th International Conference on Computing for Sustainable Global Development (INDIACom), 820-824. DOI: 10.23919/INDIACom54597.2022.9763266

Tao, X., Cheng, L., Zhang, R., Chan, W. K., Chao, H., & Qin, J. (2023). Towards green innovation in smart cities: Leveraging traffic flow prediction with machine learning algorithms for sustainable transportation systems. *Sustainability (Basel), 16*(1), 251. DOI: 10.3390/su16010251

Transforming our world: The 2030 agenda for sustainable development. (2022). *Sustainable Development Goals*. https://doi.org/DOI: 10.5040/9781509934058.0025

Wang, X., Ning, Z., Hu, X., Ngai, E. C., Wang, L., Hu, B., & Kwok, R. Y. (2018). A city-wide real-time traffic management system: Enabling Crowdsensing in social internet of vehicles. *IEEE Communications Magazine, 56*(9), 19–25. DOI: 10.1109/MCOM.2018.1701065

World population prospects 2017 - Volume I: Comprehensive tables. (2021). *Statistical Papers - United Nations (Ser. A). Population and Vital Statistics Report.* Advance online publication. DOI: 10.18356/9789210001014

KEY TERMS AND DEFINITIONS

ASL (Adaptive Signal-Light): Dynamic traffic signal systems that adjust green light durations based on IoT data to remediate pedestrian and vehicle flows, minimizing emissions and jams.

Blockchain: Distributed ledger securing IoT traffic data with smart contracts, zero-knowledge proofs, and consensus for tamper-proof, privacy-preserving analytics.

BRAIN (Central Management Hub): Core processing center aggregating IoT inputs (traffic, weather) for real-time monitoring, predictive analytics, and urgent reactions to prevent gridlock.

Digital Twins: Virtual city replicas using real-time IoT data for offline simulations, policy testing, and emission forecasting in sustainable ITS planning.

DRTM (Demand-Responsive Traffic Management): Real-time system adjusting traffic via parking integration and shared mobility, reducing private vehicle reliance and enhancing public access in context-specific urban settings.

Edge Computing: Localized data processing at network edges (near sensors) to reduce latency, enabling swift decisions in IoT-ITS via fusion, ML inferences, and federated learning.

IoT (Internet of Things): Interconnected devices (sensors, cameras, radars) deployed at intersections, highways, and stations to collect real-time traffic data like density, velocity, and saturation for dynamic control.

ITS (Intelligent Transportation Systems): Advanced networks integrating sensors, communication, and analytics to optimize urban traffic flow, reduce congestion, and enhance sustainability in smart cities.

Multi-Modal Transportation: Diversified systems integrating public transit, cycling, walking, carpooling, and EVs to reduce car dependency, promote equity, and harmonize urban flows.

RL (Reinforcement Learning): AI paradigm where agents learn optimal traffic policies through trial-and-error with IoT data, using deep Q-networks or multi-agent frameworks for signal optimization.

STI (Smart Transportation Infrastructure): IoT-centric backbone combining sensors, hybrid networks (5G/fiber), and hubs for scalable, interoperable traffic control aligned with smart city goals.

STM (Sustainable Traffic Management): Goal-driven approach prioritizing green modes, equity, and multi-modal integration to combat congestion while balancing economic, environmental, and social outcomes.

V2X (Vehicle-to-Everything): Communication protocol enabling vehicles to share data with infrastructure (V2I), other vehicles (V2V), and pedestrians for cooperative routing and safety.

Chapter 5

Topological Auditing of Synthetic Public Data for Trustworthy Governance

Jaime Aguilar-Ortiz
http://orcid.org/0009-0003-5302-1454
Universidad Politécnica de Pachuca, Mexico

Ocotlán Diáz-Parra
Universidad Politécnica de Pachuca, Mexico

Jorge A. Ruiz-Vanoye
http://orcid.org/0000-0003-4928-5716
Universidad Politécnica de Pachuca, Mexico

Francisco R. Trejo-Macotela
http://orcid.org/0000-0003-2133-3456
Universidad Politécnica de Pachuca, Mexico

Marco A. Vera-Jiménez
http://orcid.org/0009-0009-3712-1440
Universidad Politécnica de Pachuca, Mexico

Víctor M. Zamudio-García
http://orcid.org/0000-0002-4660-8025
Universidad Politéctica Metropolitana de Hidalgo, Mexico

Carlos R. Domínguez-Mayorga
http://orcid.org/0009-0007-1018-4412
Universidad Politécnica de Pachuca, Mexico

ABSTRACT

The objective of this chapter is to design, implement, and evaluate an end-to-end auditing pipeline that enables agencies to release synthetic public datasets with quantified privacy risk, analytical utility, and structural fidelity. The approach frames release as a governance decision under explicit threat models, compares generator portfolios, and produces multiple replicas to estimate uncertainty. Utility is assessed through statistical fidelity and task-based benchmarks, while risk is

DOI: 10.4018/979-8-2600-2845-2.ch005

tested via adversary simulations. Topological data analysis audits latent-space geometry using persistence summaries and diagram distances, including subgroup and temporal-window checks. Results deliver defensible, reproducible evidence for trustworthy, secure data sharing in smart-government settings.

1. INTRODUCTION

1.1. Motivation: From "Open Data" to Auditable Trust in Smart-Government Ecosystems

In smart-government ecosystems, open data has moved from a transparency slogan to an operational commitment shaping service delivery, policy design, resource allocation, and accountability through interoperable registries, digital identity, transactional platforms, and analytics-driven decisions. As public-sector data become broader and more granular, the same assets that support innovation and coordination also heighten risks of unauthorized inference, discriminatory profiling, and downstream misuse, making trust a measurable governance variable. Evidence shows that trust depends on perceived data and platform quality, so disclosure must be governed through demonstrable safeguards and performance, intent (Almuqrin et al., 2022). Privacy-risk research likewise shows that open-data risk is multidimensional and must be continuously monitored as datasets and auxiliary information expand (Li et al., 2024).

Within this landscape, synthetic public data can expand access while reducing direct exposure of identifiable records, but it cannot be presumed safe or useful simply because it is artificial. Evidence shows that utility and privacy depend on generator family, constraint handling, and evaluation design, so defensible release requires explicit multilayer validation beyond marginals or correlations (Figueira & Vaz, 2022). Under realistic threat models, generators may still reveal membership signals or enable sensitive inference, which requires adversary-emulating audits under stated assumptions (Hu et al., 2022). Even when statistical similarity seems adequate, governance analyses may fail if synthesis distorts high-dimensional record structure; thus structural fidelity must also be audited through topological data analysis, persistent homology, and related multiscale summaries (Wasserman, 2018; Chazal & Michel, 2021).

1.2. Research Objectives, Contributions, and Article Roadmap

The article designs and evaluates a governance-ready auditing pipeline enabling administrations to release synthetic public-sector datasets with quantified privacy risk, analytical utility, and structural fidelity. Existing frameworks measure fidelity, utility, or privacy separately, but public-sector release decisions lack an integrated protocol that audits adversarial disclosure, workload usefulness, and high-dimensional structure under governance thresholds. This chapter addresses that gap by treating trust as a reproducible evidentiary outcome. Its contribution is a single release dossier that joins threat-model-based privacy testing, task-centered utility validation, persistent-homology auditing of representation geometry, and Pareto-based selection under predeclared acceptance rules.

To operationalize objectives, the chapter asks whether a synthetic release can be justified. The foundations explain why synthetic data cannot be assumed safe or useful and why evaluation must move beyond marginal similarity. The methodology defines threat modeling, generator comparison, uncertainty estimation, and acceptance rules. The architecture turns this protocol into a reproducible Python pipeline with configuration control and audit artifacts. The results examine utility–privacy trade-offs and structural fidelity across global and subgroup views. The discussion interprets evidence for defensible release, uncertainty, documentation, interoperability, and monitoring.

The revised framing makes the research gap explicit: most synthetic-data evaluations treat privacy, utility, and structural preservation as separate diagnostics, whereas public release decisions require them to be interpreted as one accountable governance bundle. The chapter's contribution is not only persistent homology, but its integration with attacker-centered privacy testing, task-transfer evidence, replica uncertainty, and Pareto selection in a single release protocol. This addresses the novelty concern by showing that the proposed pipeline converts technical validation into a decision procedure reviewable by data stewards, ethics committees, and inter-agency governance boards. Consequently, trust is treated as empirical status supported by documented thresholds, assumptions, and failure conditions, rather than as a generic promise attached to synthetic publication.

2. THEORETICAL FOUNDATIONS

2.1. Synthetic Data as a Governance Instrument: Utility, Risk, and Accountability Requirements

Synthetic data becomes a governance instrument when it is treated as a formally auditable transformation of an underlying public dataset into synthetic releases produced by a generator family, with independently generated replicas used to quantify uncertainty and stability (Figueira & Vaz, 2022; Fonseca & Bação, 2023; Santangelo et al., 2025). Utility is not a generic claim of resemblance; it is the measurable capacity of synthetic data to support workloads such as monitoring, forecasting, service targeting, risk scoring, and fairness diagnostics while avoiding new privacy-attack surfaces (El Emam et al., 2022; Hernandez et al., 2025; Kurakova & Homayouni, 2025). The audit therefore evaluates distributional fidelity and task fidelity separately. After denoting the empirical real distribution and the empirical synthetic distribution, and after introducing a positive definite kernel, distributional discrepancy may be expressed with the Maximum Mean Discrepancy (MMD) in Equation (1):

$$MMD^2(P,Q) = \mathbb{E}_{x,x'\sim P}[k(x,x')] + \mathbb{E}_{y,y'\sim Q}[k(y,y')] - 2\,\mathbb{E}_{x\sim P,\, y\sim Q}[k(x,y)]. \tag{1}$$

A small MMD means the selected kernel finds little distributional separation between real and synthetic samples; a larger value signals unreproduced structure, but not by itself a release decision.

To connect the audit directly to governance-relevant actions, task fidelity can be expressed through a loss gap between models trained on real versus synthetic data, evaluated on a held-out real test set D_{test} (El Emam et al., 2022; Kurakova & Homayouni, 2025). After defining a learning algorithm $\mathscr{A}$ and a loss $\ell(\bullet,\bullet)$, the centered task-utility gap may be stated in Equation (2) as

$$\Delta_{task} = \mathbb{E}_{(x,y)\sim D_{test}}\left[\ell(\mathscr{A}(D)(x),y) - \ell\left(\mathscr{A}(\widetilde{D}),y\right)\right]. \tag{2}$$

The task-utility gap reports operational loss when a model is trained on synthetic rather than real data and evaluated on the same real holdout set.

Under this accountability-oriented view, a release is defensible only when it is accompanied by artifacts showing that MMD^2 (and related fidelity diagnostics) and Δ_{tast} remain within pre-declared bounds across replicas $\widetilde{D}^{(r)}$, thereby converting "synthetic openness" into measurable performance rather than assumed safety (Goyal & Mahmoud, 2024; Santangelo et al., 2025).

"Risk" and "accountability" complete the governance instrument: risk is evaluated against explicit threat models, and accountability enforces a decision rule that can be reviewed, reproduced, and stress-tested. Synthetic releases can still leak membership or re-identification signals, so an audit must quantify privacy leakage rather than infer safety from the fact that records are generated (Hu et al., 2022; Zhang et al., 2022; Alshantti et al., 2025). Membership inference is measured as the attacker's advantage in distinguishing training members from non-members, written in Equation (3) as:

$$Adv_{MIA} = Pr(\widehat{m}(x) = 1|m = 1) - Pr(\widehat{m}(x) = 1|m = 0). \tag{3}$$

Membership advantage measures how much better the attacker performs than chance when deciding whether a target record was used to train the generator.

Because public-sector releases often involve additional institutional, technical, structural, and behavioral risk dimensions, a governance audit must also document assumptions and constraints intended sharing scope, sensitivity tiers, and acceptable risk ceilings so that residual risk is interpreted in context rather than treated as a universal scalar (Li et al., 2024). In practice, accountability is best enforced through an explicit accept/reject rule on replica-aggregated metrics and their dispersion, so that stability is audited. After defining replica means $\overline{U} = \frac{1}{R}\sum_{r=1}^{R} U(\widetilde{D}^{(r)})$ and $\overline{Adv}_{MIA} = \frac{1}{R}\sum_{r=1}^{R} Adv_{MIA}(\widetilde{D}^{(r)})$, an auditable governance decision can be expressed in centered form by Equation (4) as

$$Release\,(\widetilde{D}) = 1\left[\overline{U} \geq \tau_U \wedge \overline{Adv}_{MIA} \leq \tau_R \wedge T \leq \tau_T\right], \tag{4}$$

Where T is a structural-fidelity term that prevents "good marginals" from masking distortions in the high-dimensional organization that drives subgroup comparability and regime-like patterns. A natural structural term for the pipeline is a persistent-homology distance between persistence diagrams computed from representations of real versus synthetic data; after denoting persistence diagrams by $Dgm(D)$ and $Dgm(\widetilde{D})$, the centered bottleneck distance is given by Equation (5) as

$$d_B(Dgm(D), Dgm(\widetilde{D})) = \inf_{\gamma} \operatorname{sip}_{u \in \mathrm{Dgm}(D)} \|u - \gamma(u)\|_{\infty}, \tag{5}$$

which connects directly to established topological auditing practice for quantifying multiscale structural similarity (Chazal & Michel, 2021; Wasserman, 2018; Pun et al., 2022). Finally, when governments adopt formal privacy mechanisms such as differential privacy, accountability also requires reporting the privacy-loss budget and documenting the observed utility impacts under policy-relevant analyses, a lesson made concrete in empirical evaluations of differential privacy deployments for official statistics (Hawes, 2020; Kenny et al., 2021; Gong et al., 2022).

Bottleneck distance is a conservative worst-case topology error because it focuses on the largest unmatched structural displacement between diagrams.

2.2. Privacy Threat Models for Synthetic Releases: Membership, Attribute, and Linkage Inference

In governance-oriented synthetic-data releases, the threat model formalizes how a generator is trained on a sensitive dataset and then used to emit a publishable surrogate. This framing makes clear where memorization may enter through learned parameters and where randomness is expected to mitigate it through latent sampling (Hu et al., 2022; Niu et al., 2024; Alshantti et al., 2025). In a municipal benefits dataset, for example, an attacker might combine age, region, and program participation from public registries with the synthetic release to test membership, infer a sensitive attribute, or attempt linkage. The learning and sampling sequence can be written in Equation (6):

$$\theta \leftarrow \mathscr{A}(D), \widetilde{D} \leftarrow \mathscr{G}_{\theta}(Z), Z \sim \mathscr{P}_{Z}. \tag{6}$$

Given this setup, membership inference is naturally posed as a binary hypothesis test about whether a specific record (or a record "close enough" under an attacker's knowledge) contributed to training, and its auditability depends on using a metric that separates true members from non-members under the same attacker interface (black-box or white-box) (Hu et al., 2022; Zhang et al., 2022). A standard way to express the operational strength of such an attack is to introduce an advantage functional that measures how differently the attacker behaves on members versus non-members, which can be stated in Equation (7) (Niu et al., 2024):

$$Adv_{MIA} = |[\Pr(\widehat{m}(x) = 1|m = 1] - Pr[\widehat{m}(x) = 1|m = 0]|. \tag{7}$$

To make the transition from an abstract definition to an auditable test, the attacker's decision rule is often instantiated through proximity- or likelihood-based signals computed against the released synthetic set, so that "membership" is inferred when a target is unusually well explained by or unusually near to the synthetic sample cloud, a phenomenon that is amplified when the generator overfits (Alshantti et al., 2025; Giomi et al., 2023). A canonical proximity instantiation can be written as the following nearest-neighbor score with a threshold decision boundary in Equation (8):

$$s_{nn}(x) = \min_{\tilde{x} \in \widetilde{D}} d(x, \tilde{x}), \widehat{m}(x) = \mathbb{I}\left[s_{m}(x) \leq \tau\right]. \tag{8}$$

Beyond membership, privacy governance requires explicit accounting for (i) attribute inference, where sensitive fields are reconstructed from partial quasi-identifiers, and (ii) linkage inference, where records are joined to external databases to re-identify individuals or infer protected traits. In that broader threat surface, differential privacy (DP) is frequently used as a formal anchor because it constrains the influence of any one individual on the released output distribution, thereby bounding certain forms of membership leakage under stated assumptions (Cohen & Nissim, 2020; Pilgram et al., 2025). This guarantee is typically expressed by the following inequality, which compares the mechanism's output on adjacent datasets in Equation (9):

$$Pr[\mathcal{M}(D) \in S] \leq e^{\varepsilon} Pr[\mathcal{M}(D') \in S] + \delta. \tag{9}$$

The differential-privacy inequality asks whether the output distribution changes only slightly when one person is added or removed.

However, governance-grade audits cannot stop at DP rhetoric, because attribute and linkage risks can persist in non-DP releases and may even appear in settings where distributional information itself is sensitive; therefore, the attacker's objective is often written directly as a posterior maximization over candidate sensitive values, which clarifies what is being inferred, under what observation model, and with what measurable performance (Jayaraman & Evans, 2022; Hittmeir et al., 2020). A standard formulation introduces the attacker's estimator and an advantage-style separation between the true sensitive value and competing alternatives, which may be written in Equation (10) as:

$$\hat{a}\left(x_K\right) = \underset{a \in \mathcal{A}}{\mathrm{argmax}} Pr\left[A = a \middle| X_K = x_K, \mathcal{O}\right], Adv_{AIA} = Pr\left[\hat{a}(x_K) = a^*\right] - \underset{a \neq a^*}{\max} Pr\left[\hat{a}(x_K) = a\right]. \tag{10}$$

Finally, linkage inference is made audit-ready by formalizing record linkage as an optimization that selects the "closest" synthetic candidate under an identifier subspace (or a learned linkage model) and then evaluating the probability of correct linkage under realistic auxiliary information, which is precisely the governance-relevant success criterion (Powar & Beresford, 2023; Cormode et al., 2025; Trindade et al., 2024). One common expression is the following nearest-candidate linkage rule and its associated success probability in Equation (11):

$$\hat{i}(y) = arg \min_{j \in \{1, \ldots, |\tilde{D}|\}} d\left(y, \tilde{x}_I^{(j)}\right), P_{link} = Pr\left[\hat{i}(y) = i^*\right]. \tag{11}$$

2.3. Structural Fidelity Beyond Marginals: Representation Geometry and Persistent-Homology Auditing

Structural fidelity in synthetic public releases cannot be reduced to marginals or low-order moments, because governance-relevant properties such as multimodal structure, rare subcommunities, nonlinear dependencies, and local continuity reside in data geometry. Thus, auditing should test whether synthetic records preserve empirical shape in a latent space, as supported by topological data analysis (Wasserman, 2018; Chazal & Michel, 2021). To make this representation explicit, each observation is mapped through a shared encoder into a latent vector, which induces the latent sets for the real and synthetic data in Equation (12):

$$z = \phi_\theta(x), Z = \left\{\phi_\theta\left(x_i\right)\right\}_{i=1}^{n}, \tilde{Z} = \left\{\phi_\theta\left(\tilde{x}_j\right)\right\}_{j=1}^{m}. \tag{12}$$

In this notation, Z and $\widetilde{Z}$ are point clouds in the same latent space and can be probed for structural agreement by building multiscale neighborhood complexes whose topology summarizes connectivity and loop/void structure across scales (Chazal & Michel, 2021; Leykam & Angelakis, 2023). To make the multiscale construction explicit in a way that aligns with practical pipelines, the Vietoris–Rips filtration can be written as the nested family of simplicial complexes obtained by increasing a scale parameter ε in Equation (13):

$$VR_{\varepsilon}(Z) = \{\sigma \subseteq Z{:}d(u,v) \leq \epsilon\, for\, all\, u,v \in \sigma\}, \varepsilon \geq 0. \tag{13}$$

With this filtration, persistent homology yields persistence diagrams $Dgm_k(Z)$ (and $Dgm_k(\widetilde{Z})$) that encode the birth–death scales of k- dimensional features; crucially, diagram-level comparison then operationalizes "structural fidelity beyond marginals" as a metric test on shape summaries rather than on per-feature distributions (Barnes et al., 2021; Ali et al., 2023). To compare real versus synthetic structure in a mathematically controlled manner, the audit can rely on standard diagram distances most commonly the bottleneck distance and the p-Wasserstein distance introduced through their optimal matchings in Equation (14):

$$d_B(D,D') = \inf_{\gamma} \sup_{p \in D} \|p - \gamma(p)\|_{\infty}, \; d_{W,p}(D,D') = \left(\inf_{\gamma} \sum_{p \in D} \|p - \gamma(p)\|_{\infty}^{p}\right)^{1/p}. \tag{14}$$

In these definitions, γ ranges over bijections between diagram points augmented with diagonal matches, so the resulting distances quantify how much topological "mass" must move to morph the real diagram into the synthetic one, providing an audit signal that is sensitive to manifold fragmentation (via H_0), cyclic structure (via H_1), and higher-dimensional cavities when relevant (Bubenik & Elchesen, 2022; Chen et al., 2021; Bubenik & Wagner, 2020).

A governance-grade audit, however, should not stop at a single global diagram distance, because accountability requires localized evidence: structural fidelity must hold across protected groups, administrative strata, and temporal windows where policy decisions are actually applied; therefore, the comparison should be computed per slice (g,t) (group g, time window t) and then aggregated into a transparent "topological risk" score that can be thresholded, logged, and reproduced (Kindji et al., 2025; Jin et al., 2024). To complement diagram distances with interpretable scalar diagnostics, the audit can summarize diagram content through total persistence, persistent entropy, and Betti curves, each of which captures a distinct facet of multiscale structure (Atienza et al., 2020; Berry et al., 2020). To introduce these summaries formally, total persistence of order q is written in Equation (15) as:

$$TP_q(D) = \sum_{(b_i, d_i) \in D} (d_i - b_i)^q, \tag{15}$$

and it increases when many long-lived features appear, which in governance terms can indicate either legitimate complex substructure or, conversely, synthetic artifacts such as spurious clusters and "holes" created by mode-dropping in the generator (Atienza et al., 2020; Jin et al., 2024). To capture how persistence mass is distributed across features (concentrated vs. diffuse), persistent entropy is naturally defined by normalizing lifetimes into a probability simplex and computing Shannon entropy in Equation (16):

$$p_i = \frac{d_i - b_i}{\sum_j \left(b_j - d_j\right)}, \; H(D) = -\sum_i p_i \log p_i, \tag{16}$$

so that unusually high entropy can flag many medium-lived, noisy features (a common symptom of overly randomized synthesis), while unusually low entropy can flag over-regularized synthesis that collapses structural diversity into a few dominant components (Atienza et al., 2020; Ali et al., 2023). Finally, to connect topology back to the intuitive notion of "how many components/loops exist at scale ε," the k-th Betti curve is written in Equation (17) as:

$$\beta_k(\varepsilon) = \#\left\{ \left(b_i, d_i\right) \in Dgm_k : b_i \leq \varepsilon \leq d_i \right\}, \tag{17}$$

which makes it possible to audit whether the scale profile of connectivity in the synthetic data matches the real data (e.g., whether components merge too quickly, indicating excessive smoothing, or too slowly, indicating fragmentation) (Chazal & Michel, 2021; Berry et al., 2020). To consolidate these ingredients into an auditable decision rule, a practical composite score (computed per (g, t) and then averaged) can be presented in Equation (18) as:

$$\mathcal{A} = \frac{1}{|G||T|} \sum_{g \in G} \sum_{t \in T} \left[\alpha d_B\left(Dgm_0\left(Z_{g,t}\right), Dgm_0\left(\tilde{Z}_{g,t}\right)\right) \right.$$

$$\left. + \beta d_{W,1}\left(Dgm_1\left(Z_{g,t}\right), Dgm_1\left(\tilde{Z}_{g,t}\right)\right) + \gamma \left| H(D) - H(\tilde{D}) \right| \right],$$

and this score is particularly governance-compatible because its components are stable under controlled perturbations of the underlying persistence objects supporting reproducible audits and defensible thresholds while remaining sensitive to exactly the structural distortions that marginal matching can miss (Bjerkevik, 2021; Wasserman, 2018; Bubenik & Elchesen, 2022).

For non-specialist readers, the topology layer can be summarized as follows. H_0 asks whether synthetic records form connected groups at approximately the same scales as real records; H_1 asks whether loop-like patterns and gaps appear and disappear comparably. A persistence diagram is not another histogram, but a compact record of how structure survives across neighborhood scales. In governance terms, a sound synthetic release should not only reproduce feature frequencies; it should also preserve whether groups are compact, fragmented, connected through bridges, or separated by gaps. This matters because many decisions rely on neighborhood structure: anomaly detection, eligibility clustering, fraud screening, regional segmentation, and fairness diagnostics can fail when the synthetic manifold is smoother, noisier, or more fragmented than the original. The topological audit serves as a safeguard against plausible but structurally misleading synthetic data.

3. METHODOLOGY

3.1. End-to-End Auditing Protocol: Scoping, Constraints, Generator Portfolio, and Replica Strategy

The audit protocol begins by turning governance intent into a scope and constraint system: who may use the data, what decisions it supports, which subgroups remain valid, and what privacy or topology ceilings must not be crossed. Releases are defensible when evaluated against predeclared tolerances, not retrospective narratives (Pilgram et al., 2025; Cormode et al., 2025; Giomi et al., 2023). The protocol follows the seven-stage sequence in Table 1 before applying the feasibility condition in Equation (19). Operationally, the feasibility set should be read as a policy gate, not a mathematical object. A release passes only when it remains useful for the declared workload, keeps attack performance below the agency's risk ceiling, and avoids structural distortions invalidating subgroup or temporal conclusions. For non-specialist readers, the intuition is direct: the audit asks whether synthetic data are accurate enough to support analysis, distant enough from training records to reduce disclosure incentives, and shaped enough like real data to preserve meaningful relationships. This reduces equation density while retaining formal rigor, because formulas define measurable checks and prose states the governance action following them.

Table 1. Methodological flow: Seven-stage audit protocol: inputs, processes, and evidence artifacts

Stage	Input	Process	Evidence
1. Scope	Use, sensitivity, legal limits	Define thresholds and prohibited uses	Release perimeter
2. Data profile	Schema, missingness, cardinality	Validate types, groups, and windows	Dataset card
3. Generators	Portfolio, seeds, constraints	Train and sample replicas	Replica bundle
4. Utility	Fixed workloads and splits	Fidelity and task tests	Utility report
5. Privacy	Attacker model	Membership, attribute, linkage tests	Risk report
6. Topology	Latent embeddings	Diagrams, Betti curves, slice checks	Structural report
7. Decision	Thresholds and Pareto frontier	Accept, mitigate, reject, or re-audit	Release dossier

$$\mathcal{F} = \left\{\widetilde{D}:U(\widetilde{D}) \geq \tau_U, Risk_M(\widetilde{D}) \leq \tau_M, Risk_A(\widetilde{D}) \leq \tau_A, Risk_L(\widetilde{D}) \leq \tau_L, T\left(\widetilde{D}\right) \leq \tau_T\right\}. \tag{19}$$

In this formulation, utility denotes workload-relevant agreement, while membership, attribute, and linkage terms represent attack-style privacy risks, and structural discrepancy captures geometry that marginal checks miss (El Emam et al., 2022; Giomi et al., 2023). Because generator families behave differently under identical constraints, each generator is trained under the same regime and sampled through replicas so uncertainty, seed sensitivity, and metric dispersion remain auditable, as formalized in Equation (20) (Fonseca & Bação, 2023; Figueira & Vaz, 2022; Cormode et al., 2025).

$$\theta_k \leftarrow \mathcal{A}_k(D;C), \widetilde{D}_k^{(r)} \leftarrow \mathcal{G}_{k,\theta_k}(Z^{(r)}), Z^{(r)} \sim \mathcal{P}_Z, r = 1,\ldots,R. \tag{20}$$

Here, the training routine and replica index record repeated sampling and, when appropriate, repeated training seeds. The point is not only to find a good synthetic dataset, but to determine whether a passing result is stable.

Once the portfolio is instantiated, reproducibility and stability become first-class requirements. A release that only sometimes meets thresholds cannot be defended in policy settings where updates and deployments require consistent behavior (Pilgram et al., 2025; Hawes, 2020). Each metric is therefore summarized by replica mean and dispersion in Equation (21).

$$\overline{M}_k = \frac{1}{R}\sum_{r=1}^{R} M\left(\widetilde{D}_k^{(r)}\right), s_{M,k}^2 = \frac{1}{R-1}\sum_{r=1}^{R}\left(M\left(\widetilde{D}_k^{(r)}\right)\right)^2. \tag{21}$$

With these summaries available, the protocol avoids optimistic point estimates and uses conservative bounds, especially for privacy and linkability risks that may spike under tail subpopulations or rare draws under the conservative test in Equation (22) (Pilgram et al., 2025; Kenny et al., 2021).

$$Accept(k) = 1\left[\bar{U}_k - z_\alpha \frac{s_{U,k}}{\sqrt{R}} \geq \tau_U \wedge Risk_{j,k} + z_\alpha \frac{s_{Risk_j,k}}{\sqrt{R}} \leq \tau_j \, \forall j \in \{M,A,L\} \wedge \bar{T}_k + z_\alpha \frac{s_{T,k}}{\sqrt{R}} \leq \tau_T\right].$$

After candidates are filtered, the protocol uses Pareto logic rather than a single opaque score, because disclosure decisions must reveal which objectives are improved, sacrificed, or constrained (Cormode et al., 2025; Fonseca & Bação, 2023). The non-dominated set is defined in Equation (23):

$$\mathcal{P} = \left\{k : \nexists k' \textit{ such that } \bar{U}_{k'} \geq \bar{U}_k \wedge Risk_{j,k'} \leq Risk_{j,k} \, \forall j \in \{M,A,L\} \wedge \bar{T}_{k'} \leq \bar{T}_k \textit{, with at least one strict inequality}\right\}$$

In practice, the frontier supports a publication-grade audit artifact: each remaining candidate is accompanied by its metric vector, uncertainty bands, thresholds, and decision rationale, so external scrutiny can verify that "synthetic" was not treated as automatically safe.

3.2. Audit Suite and Acceptance Rule: Utility Layers, Risk Scores, Topological Metrics, and Pareto Selection

The audit suite frames acceptance as a multilayer decision over utility, privacy risk, and structural fidelity. A release is not approved merely for matching marginal histograms; it must sustain usefulness, constrain inference and linkage exposure, and preserve representation geometry (Cormode et al., 2025; Figueira & Vaz, 2022; Fonseca & Bação, 2023). The utility layer begins with the squared MMD statistic in Equation (24):

$$MMD^2(\mathcal{D},\tilde{\mathcal{D}}) = \left\|\frac{1}{n}\sum_{i=1}^{n}\varphi(x_i) - \frac{1}{m}\sum_{j=1}^{m}\varphi(\tilde{x}_j)\right\|_{\mathcal{H}}^2. \tag{24}$$

With this fidelity signal in hand, the protocol then translates "utility" into an auditable consequence on a fixed analytic workload (e.g., classification/regression used by the agency), so the acceptance rule is anchored to a task-gap quantity that is introduced in Equation (25):

$$\Delta_{task} = L_{test}\left(h_{\tilde{\mathcal{D}}}\right) - L_{test}\left(h_{\mathcal{D}}\right). \tag{25}$$

Because task-centric ranking can disagree with statistical similarity, the suite keeps both views as separate utility layers (El Emam et al., 2022; Goncalves et al.,

2020). The risk layer is then attack-based and replica-stabilized, so acceptance relies on observed adversarial advantage rather than on informal "looks similar" reasoning, as shown in Equation (26):

$$adv_{MIA} = Pr[A(x) = 1|x \in \mathscr{D}] - Pr[A(x) = 1|x \notin \mathscr{D}], \tag{26}$$

and the suite interprets this value jointly with complementary disclosure modes (attribute/sensitive-value inference and linkage) as distinct accountability constraints rather than as a single, ambiguous privacy score (Hu et al., 2022; Jayaraman & Evans, 2022; Zhang et al., 2022).

The "structural fidelity" layer enforces the chapter's topological premise: a synthetic dataset may match marginals and predictive utility while distorting cluster topology, voids, or filamentary structure relevant to anomaly monitoring, resource allocation, and policy targeting (Chazal & Michel, 2021; Atienza et al., 2020). The protocol therefore maps representations into filtrations and compares persistence diagrams; bottleneck distance is the canonical worst-case discrepancy in Equation (27):

$$d_B(D_k, \widetilde{G}_k) = \inf_{\gamma} \sup_{u \in D_k} \|u - \gamma(u)\|_{\infty}, \tag{27}$$

and, when sensitivity to aggregated deviations is desired, a Wasserstein-type alternative is presented in Equation (28) as:

$$d_{W,p}(D_k, \widetilde{D}_k) = \left(\inf_{\gamma} \sum_{u \in D_k} \|u - \gamma(u)\|_{\infty}^{p} \right)^{1/p}. \tag{28}$$

Wasserstein diagram distance summarizes aggregate structural movement, complementing bottleneck distance by measuring cumulative rather than worst-case distortion.

With utility, risk, and topology expressed as audit outputs, acceptance is defined over replica distributions rather than single runs. For any metric computed over replicas, the decision uses the following uncertainty-aware bound in Equation (29):

$$CI_{1-\alpha}(q) : \hat{\mu}_q \pm z_{1-\alpha/2} \frac{\hat{\sigma}_q}{\sqrt{B}}. \tag{29}$$

Acceptance is based on conservative replica bounds, so a candidate that passes only in one favorable random run is not defensible.

Thresholds should be declared before the audit and calibrated to the use case, sensitivity tier, and legal context; Appendix B provides illustrative ranges, not universal standards. The protocol enforces hard constraints for unacceptable risk and minimum standards for utility and topology before Pareto selection, formalized in Equation (30):

$$\mathcal{P} = \{g : \nexists\, g' \text{ such that } u(g') \succcurlyeq u(g) \wedge r(g') \preccurlyeq r(g) \text{ with at least one strict improvement}\}, \tag{30}$$

A candidate remains on the Pareto frontier only when no competitor offers equal or higher utility with equal or lower privacy risk.

The result is an auditable frontier in which each candidate carries utility layers, attack-based risks, structural metrics, and threshold status, aligning release approval with trustworthy governance rather than a single, easily gamed proxy.

4. COMPUTATIONAL ARCHITECTURE

4.1. Reproducible Pipeline Implementation: Modular Python Stack, Configurations, Artifacts, and Reporting

A governance-facing audit is credible only if it can be repeated, inspected, and independently re-executed. The pipeline uses a modular Python stack where ingestion, schema validation, constraint enforcement, generator orchestration, audit evaluation, and report compilation remain decoupled yet traceable through explicit interfaces and stable data contracts (Amershi et al., 2019). Each run is tied to a typed configuration snapshot covering generator family, hyperparameters, privacy budgets, seeds, replica counts, and thresholds, reducing drift and enabling audit-grade comparability (Schlegel & Sattler, 2022). Environment pinning, deterministic seeding, metadata, and code-revision identifiers support reruns under the same computational semantics and align implementation with FAIR research-software principles (Barker et al., 2022). Provenance links extracts, transformed tables, generators, embeddings, topological summaries, and reports to the run context for accountability (Schlegel & Sattler, 2025).

Credibility requires an evidence trail intelligible to evaluators and stakeholders. The audit produces dataset documentation on schema and lineage (Gebru et al., 2021), generator model cards on conditions (Mitchell et al., 2019), plus utility, privacy-risk, and structure tables. Utility follows synth-evaluation taxonomies for fidelity, dependency preservation, and adequacy (El Emam et al., 2022; Fonseca & Bação, 2023). Privacy risk uses membership, attribute, and linkage frameworks (Pilgram et al., 2025; Giomi et al., 2023); structural fidelity uses embeddings and persistence summaries (Chazal & Michel, 2021; Atienza et al., 2020).

4.2. Computational Scalability and Deployment Constraints

Scalability is a governance constraint because public datasets may contain millions of records, high-cardinality categories, and subgroup or temporal slices. Persistent-homology computation on latent point clouds is costliest, since Vietoris–Rips complexes grow rapidly with sample size and dimension. Deployments should report hardware, sample size, embedding dimension, homology dimensions, runtime, memory, and approximation strategy. Mitigations include subsampling with uncertainty bands, focus on H_0/H_1, sparse or witness complexes, nearest-neighbor graphs, parallel execution, and full-resolution topology only when screening indicates structural risk.

For deployment planning, scalability should appear in the release dossier, not as an implementation detail. A proof-of-concept can hide costs that become decisive when agencies evaluate regions, programs, windows, or protected groups. The dossier should include records for each topology computation, embedding dimension, homology dimensions, replicas, slices, wall-clock time, peak memory, and hardware. When full Vietoris–Rips computation is infeasible, the audit should state whether it used subsampling, sparse complexes, witness complexes, approximate neighbor graphs, or early H_0 screening before H_1. These choices do not invalidate the audit, but define its scope. A governance committee can decide whether approximation error is acceptable for research, whether higher-resolution runs are required for inter-agency analytics, or whether privacy and access restrictions are needed before publication.

For large government deployments, implementation should separate low-cost screening from high-cost certification. Distributional metrics, task transfer, and membership proxies can be computed on the full dataset or stratified blocks, while persistent-homology diagnostics should be computed on audited embeddings, landmarks, or balanced slices when record counts make full Vietoris-Rips construction impractical. The dossier should report topology sample size, embedding dimension, filtration scales, memory limits, runtime, and whether approximation was used. This lets reviewers distinguish a scalable audit from a proof of concept that works only on small examples. In practice, scalability is acceptable when the same candidate generator remains non-dominated after repeated subsampling and when the widest confidence bands remain inside declared utility, privacy, and structural thresholds.

5. RESULTS AND ANALYSIS

5.1. Experimental Design: Dataset Types, Governance Scopes, Evaluation Splits, and Adversary Assumptions

This table summarizes the dataset's structure by reporting field types, missing-value prevalence, and cardinality/coverage indicators that define the evaluation regime.

Table 2. Dataset profile (Types, missingness, and cardinality)

column	dtype	missing_rate	nunique
income	float64	0.03	3880
program	object	0.02	4
date	datetime64[ns]	0	726
age	int64	0	67
visits	int64	0	12
region	object	0	3
group	object	0	3
target	int64	0	2
sensitive_attr	object	0	2

Table 2 fixes the dataset type space for the results. Missingness and cardinality indicate where utility, subgroup stability, and privacy risk should be interpreted cautiously, because rare categories and thin strata can inflate identifiability or distort downstream estimates.

This table lists each feature and its inferred type, providing the typing map used for preprocessing and for selecting appropriate evaluation metrics.

Table 3. Inferred column types (Numeric, categorical, Boolean, temporal)

type	columns
numeric	income, age, visits
categorical	region, program, group, sensitive_attr
boolean	
datetime	date

Table 3 establishes the typing contract used by preprocessing and metrics. Numeric, categorical, Boolean, and temporal fields are evaluated with type-appropriate diagnostics, preventing arbitrary treatment of codes as continuous values and strengthening reproducibility.

Figure 1. Missingness diagnostic (Top-30 features by missing rate)

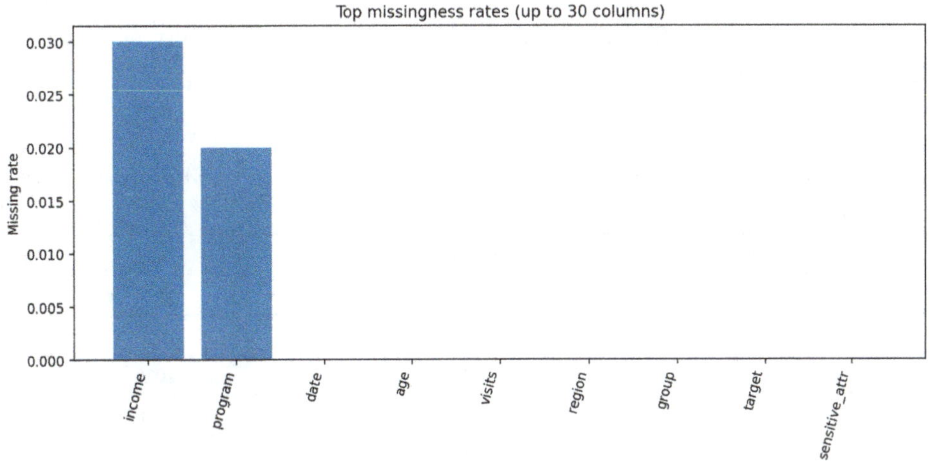

This figure ranks the 30 most incomplete variables, indicating where missingness may drive uncertainty, bias, and imputation effects.

Figure 1 shows that missingness is concentrated rather than uniformly distributed. This justifies subgroup and fairness checks, because non-random gaps can create apparent model skill while masking representation limits.

This table defines the governance perimeter by specifying sensitivity classes, sharing and retention limits, and authorized use cases for evaluating and deploying data, models, and synthetic releases.

Table 4. Governance scope (Sensitivity, sharing boundaries, and use-case constraints)

field	value
sensitivity_tier	Tier-2 (moderate sensitivity)
sharing_scope	Controlled access (accredited researchers / inter-agency)
legal_constraints	Policy-dependent; document and review per dataset.
intended_use_cases	["Policy analytics (classification/regression on program outcomes)",
	"Monitoring and anomaly screening",
	"Subgroup comparisons (fairness / representational adequacy)",
	Temporal regime analysis (if time-indexed)]

Table 4 turns governance into an explicit control surface by stating sensitivity tier, access scope, legal constraints, and intended uses. These fields explain why privacy, subgroup integrity, and release thresholds receive priority over unconstrained optimization.

This table lists the synthetic-data generator families compared, their main configurations, and the replication scheme used to measure variability and stability across repeated runs.

Table 5. Generator portfolio and replica strategy (Families, configurations, and replication plan)

generator	replica	seed
bootstrap	0	2026
bootstrap	1	2027
bootstrap	2	2028
copula	0	3026
copula	1	3027
copula	2	3028
vae	0	4026
vae	1	4027
vae	2	4028

Table 5 makes comparisons distributional rather than single-shot. Replicas allow the audit to distinguish robust generator behavior from favorable seeds, supporting release decisions based on stability.

This table defines the attacker model by specifying the adversary's access interface, plausible auxiliary information, and attack families used to evaluate privacy risk.

Table 6. Adversary assumptions (Interface, auxiliary knowledge, and attack surface)

field	value
attacker_interface	Black-box attacker with access to released synthetic data
attacker_auxiliary_info	Partial quasi-identifiers + public registries (simulated)
attacks_considered	["Membership inference (distance-based proxy)",
	"Attribute inference (synthetic-trained predictor)",
	"Linkage / uniqueness risk (quasi-ID matching simulation)"]
membership_attack_feature	Nearest-neighbor distance to synthetic cloud
linkage_radius_quantile	0.05

Table 6 closes the design by fixing the attacker interface, auxiliary information, and attacks considered. Privacy conclusions are therefore conditional on a stated threat envelope, not absolute claims about safety.

The empirical study uses one structured public-sector-style dataset as a proof of concept. Its purpose is to demonstrate the audit logic, not to claim invariance across agencies, legal regimes, or data architectures.

5.2. Utility–Privacy Trade-Offs: Idelity Metrics, Downstream Task Transfer, Fairness Diagnostics, and Risk Curves

This table reports fidelity by generator and replica, covering marginal alignment and dependence preservation across repeated runs.

Table 7. Fidelity metrics by generator and replica (Distributional and dependence preservation)

generator	replica	numeric_ wasserstein_mean	categorical_ js_mean	spearman_corr _gap_mean	mmd2_rbf
bootstrap	0	0.06537	0.00036	0.02390	0.00000
bootstrap	1	0.05345	0.00065	0.02836	0.00000
bootstrap	2	0.05003	0.00027	0.03826	0.00000
copula	0	0.04549	0.00064	0.03694	0.00011
copula	1	0.05256	0.00053	0.01318	0.00000
copula	2	0.04684	0.00021	0.03724	0.00000
vae	0	0.16218	0.05835	0.02783	0.03088
vae	1	0.14738	0.03921	0.02601	0.01891
vae	2	0.16070	0.07446	0.02247	0.04628

Table 7 shows that marginal and dependence fidelity are prerequisites rather than sufficient evidence. The copula and bootstrap candidates preserve observable structure more closely than VAE, but these fidelity scores must still be checked against task transfer, subgroup equity, and attack risk.

This table compares predictive performance when models are trained on real or synthetic data, reporting task-appropriate metrics by generator and replica to assess support for operational decision-making.

Table 8. Downstream task transfer (Models trained on real vs. synthetic data)

generator	replica	lr_macro_f1	lr_roc_auc	lr_avg_ precision	rf_macro_f1	rf_roc_auc	rf_avg _precision
REAL_TRAIN	-1	0.472437	0.733345	0.342363	0.504517	0.621820	0.241231
bootstrap	0	0.461313	0.691668	0.291807	0.476247	0.607871	0.224518
bootstrap	1	0.472838	0.706533	0.328282	0.491237	0.632935	0.256960
bootstrap	2	0.501040	0.696117	0.314994	0.511486	0.627116	0.258380
copula	0	0.455634	0.646605	0.249925	0.453552	0.535824	0.177733
copula	1	0.455634	0.513930	0.168542	0.487666	0.532929	0.182716
copula	2	0.461980	0.546020	0.217438	0.466515	0.526482	0.184852
vae	0	0.455634	0.439343	0.137676	0.465348	0.491846	0.159142
vae	1	0.455634	0.454303	0.168695	0.466043	0.491651	0.163771
vae	2	0.455634	0.438214	0.146714	0.460314	0.516635	0.168581

Table 8 tests whether resemblance becomes functionality. Bootstrap remains closest to the real-trained benchmark on several task metrics, while copula and VAE reveal larger task-transfer losses, confirming that statistical fidelity and operational utility can diverge.

This table reports subgroup fairness metrics base rates, TPR, FPR, precision, and recall—to audit equity across affected populations beyond the global aggregate.

Table 9. Group fairness diagnostics (Rates, TPR/FPR, precision, and recall)

group	support	TPR	FPR	precision	recall	F1	model
G1	554	0.10588	0.02559	0.42857	0.10588	0.16981	RF_REAL_TRAIN
G2	304	0.02128	0.02335	0.14286	0.02128	0.03704	RF_REAL_TRAIN
G3	142	0.00000	0.00901	0.00000	0.00000	0.00000	RF_REAL_TRAIN
G1	554	0.07059	0.01919	0.40000	0.07059	0.12000	RF_SYN_TRAIN(bootstrap,rep=1)
G2	304	0.00000	0.01946	0.00000	0.00000	0.00000	RF_SYN_TRAIN(bootstrap,rep=1)
G3	142	0.03226	0.00000	1.00000	0.03226	0.06250	RF_SYN_TRAIN(bootstrap,rep=1)

Table 9 exposes subgroup risk that global scores can hide. The synthetic-trained model changes TPR patterns across G1–G3, so fairness and representational adequacy remain release constraints even when aggregate utility is acceptable.

Figure 2. Group-wise TPR comparison

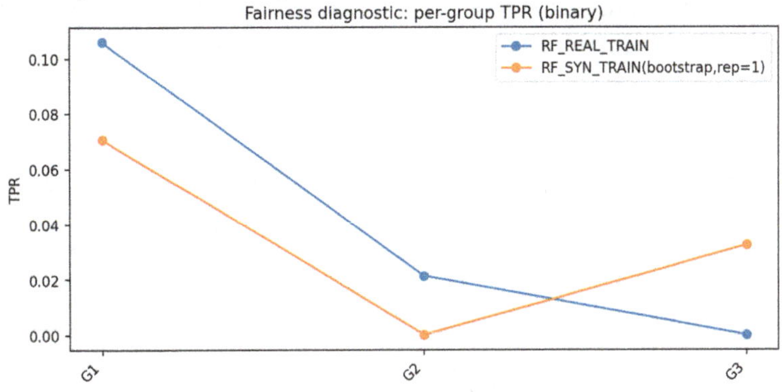

This figure visualizes the true positive rate for each audited subgroup, enabling an immediate comparison of sensitivity across groups under the evaluated training and evaluation protocol.

Figure 2 makes unequal sensitivity visible across groups. The decline for some strata and the reversal for G3 indicate that release decisions should include subgroup mitigation or monitoring rather than rely only on aggregate accuracy.

This table reports generator- and replica-level privacy risks, including membership, attribute, and linkage attacks, providing a multidimensional risk profile rather than a single score.

Table 10. Privacy Risk Metrics by Generator and Replica (Membership, Attribute, and Linkage)

generator	replica	membership_ auc	membership_ advantage	linkage_ radius	linkable_ rate	uniqueness_ rate	attribute_ risk
bootstrap	0	0.63666	0.27467	0.00034	0.05000	0.02800	0
bootstrap	1	0.62887	0.27067	0.00030	0.05000	0.02500	0
bootstrap	2	0.63500	0.25767	0.00024	0.05000	0.02700	0
copula	0	0.48990	0.00900	0.00085	0.05000	0.04800	0
copula	1	0.49333	0.01467	0.00071	0.05000	0.04900	0
copula	2	0.48793	0.01000	0.00068	0.05000	0.04900	0
vae	0	0.51666	0.04800	0.00053	0.05000	0.04300	0
vae	1	0.51681	0.04667	0.00076	0.05000	0.04700	0
vae	2	0.50978	0.03767	0.00047	0.05000	0.04500	0

Table 10 translates the threat model into attack performance. Bootstrap shows the highest membership signal, copula stays close to chance-level membership behavior, and VAE remains intermediate; linkage and uniqueness indicators remain bounded within the simulated setting.

Figure 3. ROC Curve for the membership inference attack (Graphical risk evidence)

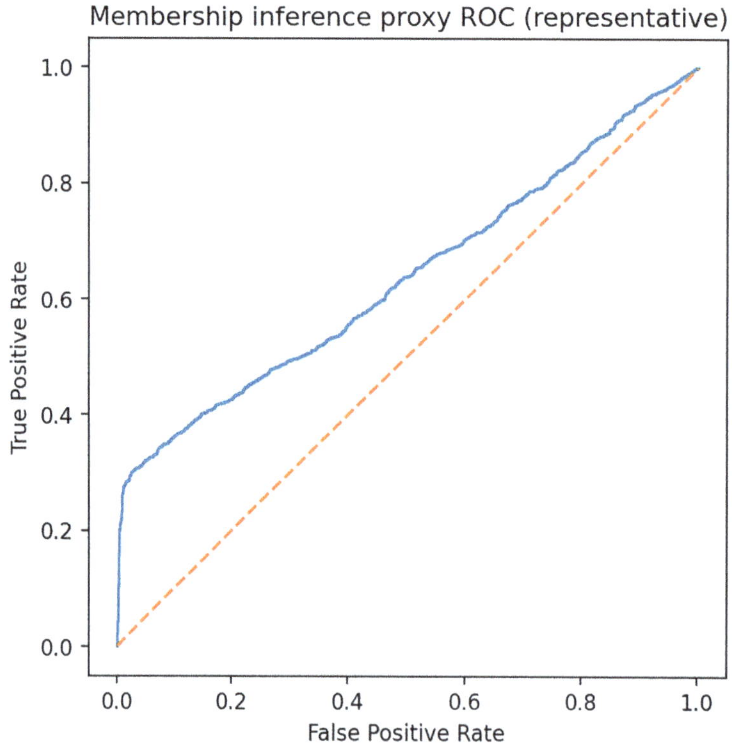

This figure shows the relation between true positive and false positive rates across thresholds, summarizing attack separability.

Figure 3 shows why privacy must be evaluated through attacker behavior. Curves above the diagonal signal separability between members and non-members; near-diagonal behavior would support lower membership risk under the declared assumptions.

This table consolidates key utility indicators and privacy-risk indicators into a structured, per-generator summary designed to support governance decisions and comparative selection.

Table 11. Utility–privacy composite (Decision-ready summary by generator)

generator	replica	Utility _score	privacy_risk _score
bootstrap	0	0.97874	0.10089
bootstrap	1	0.98026	0.09856
bootstrap	2	0.97881	0.09489
copula	0	0.98003	0.01900
copula	1	0.98413	0.02122
copula	2	0.97979	0.01967
vae	0	0.93707	0.03033
vae	1	0.94748	0.03122
vae	2	0.93151	0.02756

Table 11 consolidates utility and privacy into a decision profile. It shows that high utility can implicitly spend privacy, whereas balanced candidates maintain performance with lower attack-derived exposure.

Figure 4. Utility–privacy trade-off scatter (Dominance and tension visualization)

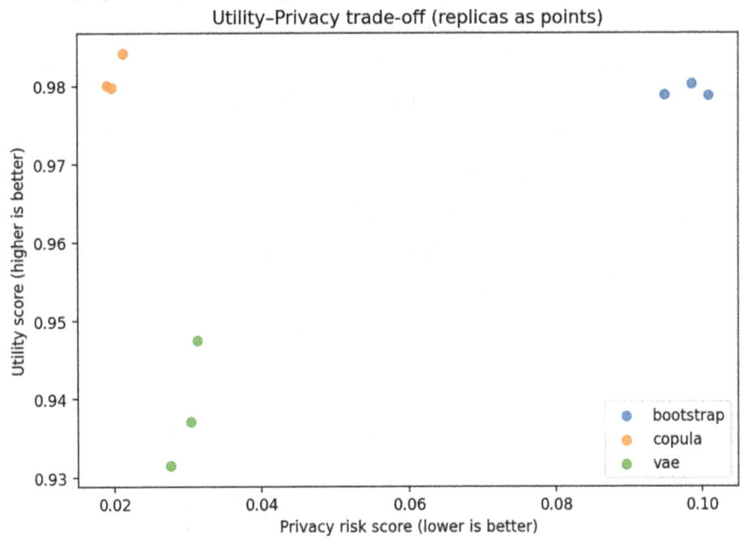

This figure plots generators or replicas by utility and privacy risk, making trade-offs and dominance visually clear.

Figure 4 reveals the trade space: copula points cluster at low privacy risk with high utility, bootstrap has higher risk, and VAE shows reduced utility. Tight clusters support replica stability; dispersion would weaken deployability.

This table lists the non-dominated generators/replicas that remain after Pareto screening, i.e., those for which no alternative achieves higher utility with equal or lower privacy risk (or lower risk with equal or higher utility).

Table 12. Pareto frontier for utility–privacy selection (Non-dominated release candidates)

generator	replica	utility_score	privacy_risk_score
copula	0	0.98003	0.01900
copula	1	0.98413	0.02122

Table 12 identifies the non-dominated candidates and shows why copula advances to topological auditing. The frontier preserves transparency because rejected candidates are inferior by dominance, not by arbitrary preference.

For interpretation, the reported tables should be read as convergent evidence rather than independent verdicts. A candidate is strongest when fidelity, transfer, privacy, fairness, and topology point in the same direction; it is weakest when one layer passes because another is ignored. This cross-reading prevents metric cherry-picking and makes the recommendation easier to audit.

Technically, bootstrap likely increases membership risk because resampling can reproduce neighborhoods close to training records. Copula reduces that signal by smoothing dependence structure, although it may sacrifice task-specific interactions. VAE underperforms in this experiment because latent regularization appears to blur categorical and tail structure, reducing downstream transfer despite privacy improvements. Therefore, the final choice should not be utility-only: topological distances and subgroup checks determine whether the Pareto candidate remains structurally acceptable.

The utility–privacy findings clarify the managerial choice among generator families. Bootstrap is attractive because it preserves local empirical patterns, explaining strong task-transfer behavior, but the same locality can increase membership evidence when nearest-neighbor attacks detect synthetic points close to training records. Copula offers the best governance compromise: it retains enough dependence structure to remain useful while reducing the sharp local memorization signal. VAE behaves differently because latent regularization can protect privacy by smoothing representation, yet that smoothing may dilute rare categories, nonlinear interactions, and tail patterns used by downstream models. These differences justify portfolio evaluation rather than selecting a generator by reputation. The release decision should ask four questions: whether the candidate meets minimum task utility, whether attack advantage remains below the declared ceiling, whether subgroup fairness does not deteriorate, and whether topological distances stay within tolerated drift. Only candidates satisfying all four questions should move from evaluation to controlled release.

5.3. Topological Auditing Outcomes: Persistence Summaries, Diagram Distances, Subgroup Integrity, and Temporal Windows

This table reports global persistence-derived summary statistics for homology dimensions H0 and H1, such as mass/total persistence, entropy-like dispersion measures, and related aggregates that compress the topology of real and synthetic point clouds across scales.

Table 13. Global persistence summaries (H_0/H_1: Mass, entropy, and related statistics)

slice	dim	n_features	total_ persistence	persistent_ entropy	mean_ lifetime
global_real	0	119	199.73570	4.70316	1.67845
global_syn(copula,rep=1)	0	119	205.07221	4.71821	1.72330
global_real	1	7021	17.43863	3.96013	0.00248
global_syn(copula,rep=1)	1	7021	14.85891	4.01244	0.00212

Table 13 provides global topology evidence for H0 connectivity and H1 loop-like structure. Similar persistence summaries support structural preservation; systematic deviations would indicate manifold drift not visible in marginals.

This table reports distances between real and synthetic persistence diagrams, using diagram-comparison metrics to quantify structural drift in topological signatures.

Table 14. Global diagram distances (Real vs. synthetic structural drift criterion)

comparison	dim	bottleneck	wasserstein_1	wasserstein_2
real_test vs syn_best(copula,rep=1)	0	1.00744	9.80464	2.10091
real_test vs syn_best(copula,rep=1)	1	0.25055	6.20358	0.85236

Table 14 turns topology into a falsifiable drift metric. Bottleneck and Wasserstein distances quantify worst-case and accumulated diagram displacement, indicating whether the synthetic candidate remains structurally comparable to the real reference.

Figure 5. Global Betti curves

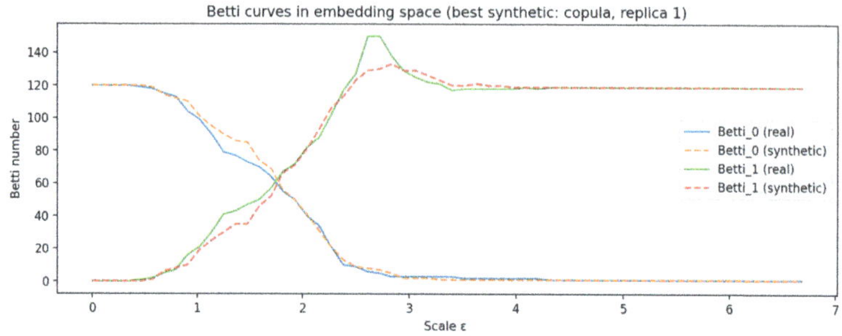

This figure visualizes global Betti curves across filtration scales, typically showing how the number of connected components (H_0) and loops (H_1) evolve as the proximity threshold increases for both real and synthetic representations.

Figure 5 complements numeric distances by showing how components and loops evolve across scale. Aligned curves support multiscale structural fidelity; rapid merging or persistent fragmentation would indicate smoothing or over-dispersion.

This table reports diagram-based distances or topology-comparison metrics computed separately for predefined subgroups, enabling stratum-wise assessment of structural fidelity rather than relying only on global averages.

Table 15. Subgroup topological distances (Stratum-level integrity evidence)

group	dim	bottleneck	wasserstein_1	n_real	n_syn
G1	0	1.49773	15.66699	554	120
G1	1	0.23860	4.00236	554	120
G2	0	1.39255	8.79215	304	120
G2	1	0.35061	4.70920	304	120
G3	0	0.15326	4.62974	142	120
G3	1	0.18201	3.28748	142	120

Table 15 tests subgroup topology directly. Higher H0 distances for G1 and G2 show that global fidelity can mask stratum-level distortion, so subgroup topology must inform release or mitigation decisions.

Figure 6. Subgroup Bottleneck distance (H_0) Visualization (Structural integrity check)

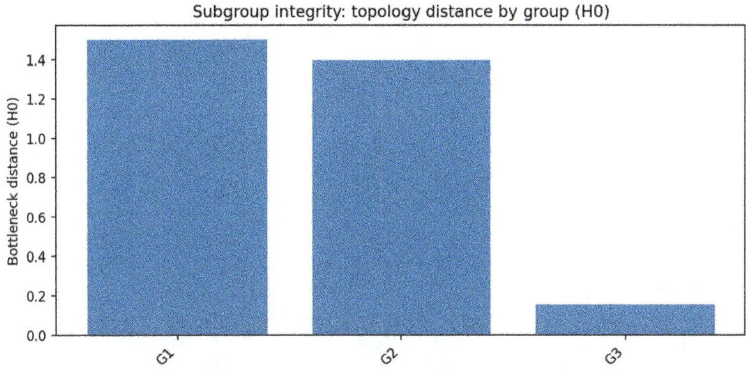

This figure visualizes subgroup-wise bottleneck distances in H_0, highlighting how strongly each subgroup's connectedness structure in the synthetic data diverges from the real reference.

Figure 6 visualizes the subgroup bottleneck gap and emphasizes worst-case strata. Elevated distances suggest altered within-group clustering or boundary geometry, which can propagate into fairness and reliability failures.

This table reports topology metrics across temporal windows, including diagram distances and persistence summaries that track structural change over time.

Table 16. Temporal window topology audit (Windowed distances and persistence summaries)

window	start	end	n_real	n_syn	bottleneck_H0
0	01/01/2023 00:00	27/05/2023 19:12	200	120	1.41959
1	27/05/2023 19:12	05/10/2023 00:00	201	120	1.52168
2	05/10/2023 00:00	09/03/2024 09:36	201	120	1.09719
3	09/03/2024 09:36	01/08/2024 00:00	201	120	1.35123
4	01/08/2024 00:00	30/12/2024 00:00	201	120	1.44128

Table 16 extends the audit to time windows. Windowed bottleneck values reveal whether structural fidelity remains stable under seasonality, regime change, or collection artifacts rather than only in pooled data.

Figure 7. Temporal window Bottleneck distance (H_0) visualization

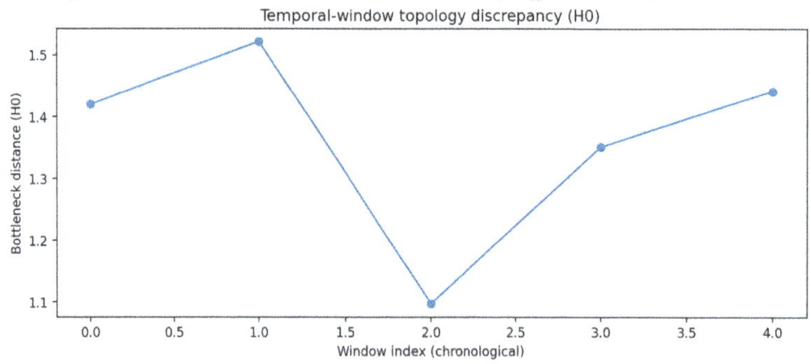

This figure visualizes H_1 bottleneck distances across temporal windows, revealing when and where the synthetic candidate diverges structurally from the real topology over time.

Figure 7 shows temporal drift as a decision signal. Peaks indicate intervals where the synthetic release may fail in time-dependent deployment, while stable low distances would support time-consistent governance compliance.

The topological layer therefore modifies the final governance decision. A candidate that passes the utility–privacy frontier should still be mitigated or rejected if subgroup or temporal distances exceed predeclared tolerances, especially for protected strata, small groups, or windows linked to service allocation.

The topology results should be interpreted as a second-stage gate after Pareto selection. A candidate may be non-dominated in utility and privacy yet still unsuitable if it changes the shape of policy-relevant groups. For example, elevated H0 bottleneck distance for a subgroup can mean that synthetic records merge clusters too early, split a coherent group into fragments, or alter boundary geometry around a protected or operationally sensitive population. Temporal peaks can similarly indicate that a generator fails during a specific regime, such as a seasonal program cycle or unusual demand. The recommended governance response is not automatic rejection. Instead, the dossier should classify topology findings into pass, mitigation, and escalation categories: pass when distances remain within tolerance; mitigation when distortion is localized and can be addressed by retraining, reweighting, or additional replicas; and escalation when a protected group or high-impact temporal window shows persistent structural drift.

6. DISCUSSION AND CONCLUSIONS

6.1. Governance Implications: Defensible Release Decisions, Documentation, Interoperability, and Re-Auditing for Drift

Governance implications follow from the chapter's evidence logic: synthetic data should be released only when the decision is repeatable, inspectable, and tied to a threat model, generator portfolio, replica design, and acceptance protocol. Trust is produced by evidence rather than asserted: utility benchmarks must show adequacy; attack-based tests must bound disclosure risk under declared auxiliary-information assumptions; and topology-aware audits must show that high-dimensional structure is preserved globally, across subgroups, and temporal regimes. Operationally, administrations should institutionalize a release dossier with configuration snapshots, splits, code revision identifiers, thresholds, attacker assumptions, uncertainty bands, limitations, and prohibited-use notices. This dossier can support ethics committees, legal review, researcher accreditation, and inter-agency oversight without exposing training records. Ethical governance also requires documenting subgroup harms, surveillance risk, data-subject expectations, residual inference limits, and procedures for withdrawal, deprecation, or access tightening. Because auxiliary information, policy needs, and distributions evolve, release approval should be continuous compliance: scheduled re-audits should update the utility–privacy frontier, subgroup fairness, and topology checks when drift, legal change, or updates occur.

From a managerial standpoint, the audit dossier should be usable in three institutional venues. In a data-governance committee, it supports the release/no-release decision by documenting thresholds, risks, uncertainty bands, and residual concerns. In legal or ethical review, it records the threat model, prohibited uses, sensitivity tier, subgroup harms, and monitoring obligations, making the decision traceable to policy rather than analyst preference. In operational analytics, it guides accredited users by stating which workloads are supported, which comparisons remain fragile, and when re-auditing is required. This institutional workflow prevents synthetic data from being treated as a one-time technical artifact. It becomes a controlled public asset with versioning, audit trails, access rules, and retirement conditions. If the evidence changes because auxiliary information grows, the agency changes the intended use, or drift appears in a monitored subgroup, the same dossier logic provides the basis for access tightening, revised thresholds, retraining, or deprecation.

A final managerial implication is that acceptance should be documented as a reversible decision rather than as a permanent authorization. When later evidence changes, the agency should be able to tighten access, regenerate replicas, lower release granularity, or withdraw the synthetic file without rewriting the entire governance framework. This reversible posture is important for smart-government ecosystems because registries, legal bases, and public expectations evolve faster than publication cycles, making re-audit capacity part of responsible deployment rather than an optional maintenance activity.

6.2. Limitations and Conclusions: What the Evidence Supports, What Remains Uncertain, and Why the Approach Generalizes

The evidence supports the central claim that defensible synthetic-data release is feasible when utility, privacy, and structural fidelity are jointly constrained and audited through reproducible, attack-conditioned, topology-aware procedures. The results should nevertheless be interpreted as proof-of-concept evidence. Privacy risk is conditional on the declared adversary; transfer and fairness are sensitive to sparsity, missingness, and rare categories; and topological signatures depend on the encoder, filtration, scale, and sampling density. The framework generalizes because it is modular and decision-centric: regulated domains can instantiate the same dossier logic by declaring governance constraints, threat models, replicas, metrics, thresholds, and re-auditing triggers. The approach therefore does not promise universal privacy or fairness; it supplies falsifiable acceptance evidence, residual uncertainty, and a structured route for evidence renewal.

The main empirical limitation is that the demonstration uses one structured public-sector-style dataset; accordingly, the results should be interpreted as evidence of protocol feasibility rather than as a universal ranking of generator families. Broader validation should replicate the same audit on datasets with different sizes, missingness mechanisms, protected-group imbalance, longitudinal dependence, and quasi-identifier density. Such replication is especially important because the best utility–privacy frontier can change when rare categories, temporal drift, or external linkage registries become more prominent. The chapter therefore recommends that agencies treat the reported frontier as a local governance decision and repeat the audit whenever the source schema, release audience, legal basis, auxiliary-information environment, or intended analytical workload materially changes.

External validation should be planned in layers. The first layer repeats the current protocol on additional public-sector datasets with different missingness, cardinality, temporal coverage, and subgroup imbalance. The second layer varies attacker knowledge, including weaker public-information attackers and stronger attackers with richer quasi-identifiers. The third layer performs ablations by removing topology, reducing the number of replicas, changing the encoder, and varying filtration scale, so the contribution of each component to the final release decision becomes visible. The fourth layer records computational cost under increasing sample size and slice count. This validation plan does not weaken the present results; it clarifies their status as proof-of-concept evidence and defines the evidence needed before claiming cross-domain robustness (see Table 17). It also gives agencies a practical re-auditing roadmap for future releases.

Table 17. Residual uncertainties and governance responses.

Residual uncertainty	Governance response
Stronger adversaries	Repeat attacks with richer auxiliary knowledge
Representation choice	Compare encoders and embedding dimensions
Filtration scale	Run sensitivity over topology scales
Sampling density	Use stratified subsampling and uncertainty bands
Single dataset	Validate on external public-sector datasets
Threshold dependence	Predeclare policy rationale and escalation rules

7. FUTURE WORK

7.1. Extensions: Stronger Threat Models, Broader Data Modalities, Policy-Integrated Monitoring, and Next-Generation Topological Criteria

Future work should preserve the governance-centered logic while testing harsher deployment conditions. Threat modeling should expand to adaptive, composition-aware, and white-box attackers; validation should include multiple public-sector datasets, longitudinal streams, relational records, text, images, and multimodal data; monitoring should connect drift to risk appetite, legal change, and pipeline updates; and topological criteria should become more scalable through sparse complexes, approximate diagrams, subgroup-conditional scores, and task-aligned persistence summaries that protect rare strata and tail geometry (see Table 18).

REFERENCES

Ali, D., Asaad, A., Jimenez, M.-J., Nanda, V., Paluzo-Hidalgo, E., & Soriano-Trigueros, M. (2023). A Survey of Vectorization Methods in Topological Data Analysis. *IEEE Transactions on Pattern Analysis and Machine Intelligence*, *45*(12), 14069–14101. DOI: 10.1109/TPAMI.2023.3308391 PMID: 37647183

Almuqrin, A., Mutambik, I., Alomran, A., Gauthier, J., & Abusharhah, M. (2022). Factors Influencing Public Trust in Open Government Data. *Sustainability (Basel)*, *14*(15), 9765. DOI: 10.3390/su14159765

Alshantti, A., Rasheed, A., & Westad, F. (2025). Privacy Re-identification Attacks on Tabular GANs. *Security and Privacy*, *8*(1), e469. DOI: 10.1002/spy2.469

Amershi, S., Begel, A., Bird, C., DeLine, R., Gall, H., Kamar, E., Nagappan, N., Nushi, B., & Zimmermann, T. (2019). Software Engineering for Machine Learning: A Case Study. *Proceedings of the 41st International Conference on Software Engineering: Software Engineering in Practice (ICSE-SEIP '19)*, 291–300. https://doi.org/DOI: 10.1109/ICSE-SEIP.2019.00042

Atienza, N., González-Díaz, R., & Soriano-Trigueros, M. (2020). On the Stability of Persistent Entropy and New Summary Functions for Topological Data Analysis. *Pattern Recognition*, *107*, 107509. DOI: 10.1016/j.patcog.2020.107509

Barker, M., Chue Hong, N. P., Katz, D. S., Lamprecht, A.-L., Martinez Ortiz, C., Psomopoulos, F., Harrow, J., Castro, L. J. G., Gruenpeter, M., Martinez, P. A., & Honeyman, T. (2022). Introducing the FAIR Principles for Research Software. *Scientific Data*, *9*(1), 622. DOI: 10.1038/s41597-022-01710-x PMID: 36241754

Barnes, D., Polanco, L., & Perea, J. A. (2021). A Comparative Study of Machine Learning Methods for Persistence Diagrams. *Frontiers in Artificial Intelligence*, *4*, 681174. DOI: 10.3389/frai.2021.681174 PMID: 34396089

Berry, E., Chen, Y.-C., Cisewski-Kehe, J., & Fasy, B. T. (2020). Functional Summaries of Persistence Diagrams. *Journal of Applied and Computational Topology*, *4*(2), 211–262. DOI: 10.1007/s41468-020-00048-w

Bjerkevik, H. B. (2021). On the Stability of Interval Decomposable Persistence Modules. *Discrete & Computational Geometry*, *66*(1), 92–121. DOI: 10.1007/s00454-021-00298-0

Bubenik, P., & Elchesen, A. (2022). Universality of Persistence Diagrams and the Bottleneck and Wasserstein Distances. *Computational Geometry*, *105–106*, 101882. DOI: 10.1016/j.comgeo.2022.101882

Bubenik, P., & Wagner, H. (2020). Embeddings of Persistence Diagrams into Hilbert Spaces. *Journal of Applied and Computational Topology*, *4*(3), 339–351. DOI: 10.1007/s41468-020-00056-w

Chazal, F., & Michel, B. (2021). An Introduction to Topological Data Analysis: Fundamental and Practical Aspects for Data Scientists. *Frontiers in Artificial Intelligence*, *4*, 667963. DOI: 10.3389/frai.2021.667963 PMID: 34661095

Chen, S., Dey, T. K., Li, J., & Wang, Y. (2021). Approximation Algorithms for 1-Wasserstein Distance Between Persistence Diagrams. In SEA 2021 (LIPIcs, Vol. 190, Article 14). Schloss Dagstuhl – Leibniz-Zentrum für Informatik. https://doi.org/DOI: 10.4230/LIPIcs.SEA.2021.14

Cohen, A., & Nissim, K. (2020). Towards Formalizing the GDPR's Notion of Singling out. *Proceedings of the National Academy of Sciences of the United States of America*, *117*(15), 8344–8352. DOI: 10.1073/pnas.1914598117 PMID: 32234789

Cormode, G., Maddock, S., Ullah, E., & Gade, S. (2025). Synthetic Tabular Data: Methods, Attacks and Defenses. *Proceedings of the VLDB Endowment International Conference on Very Large Data Bases*, *18*(12), 5448–5450. DOI: 10.14778/3750601.3750692

El Emam, K., Mosquera, L., Fang, X., & El-Hussuna, A. (2022). Utility Metrics for Evaluating Synthetic Health Data Generation Methods: Validation study. *JMIR Medical Informatics*, *10*(4), e35734. DOI: 10.2196/35734 PMID: 35389366

Figueira, A., & Vaz, B. (2022). Survey on Synthetic Data Generation, Evaluation Methods and GANs. *Mathematics*, *10*(15), 2733. DOI: 10.3390/math10152733

Fonseca, J., & Bação, F. (2023). Tabular and Latent Space Synthetic Data Generation: A Literature Review. *Journal of Big Data*, *10*(1), 115. DOI: 10.1186/s40537-023-00792-7

Gebru, T., Morgenstern, J., Vecchione, B., Vaughan, J. W., Wallach, H., Daumé, H.III, & Crawford, K. (2021). Datasheets for Datasets. *Communications of the ACM*, *64*(12), 86–92. DOI: 10.1145/3458723

Giomi, M., Boenisch, F., Wehmeyer, C., & Tasnádi, B. (2023). A Unified Framework for Quantifying Privacy Risk in Synthetic Data. *Proceedings on Privacy Enhancing Technologies. Privacy Enhancing Technologies Symposium*, *2023*(2), 312–331. DOI: 10.56553/popets-2023-0055

Goncalves, A., Ray, P., Soper, B., Stevens, J., Coyle, L., & Sales, A. P. (2020). Generation and Evaluation of Synthetic Patient Data. BMC Medical Research Methodology, 20(1), 108. https://doi.org/https://doi.org/DOI: 10.1186/s12874-020-00977-1

Gong, R., Groshen, E., & Vadhan, S. (2022). Harnessing the Known Unknowns: Differential Privacy and the 2020 Census. Harvard Data Science Review (Special Issue: Differential Privacy for the 2020 U.S. Census). https://doi.org/DOI: 10.1162/99608f92.cb06b469

Goyal, M., & Mahmoud, Q. H. (2024). A Systematic Review of Synthetic Data Generation Techniques Using Generative AI. *Electronics (Basel)*, *13*(17), 3509. DOI: 10.3390/electronics13173509

Hawes, M. B. (2020). Implementing Differential Privacy: Seven Lessons from the 2020 United States Census. *Harvard Data Science Review*, *2*(2). Advance online publication. DOI: 10.1162/99608f92.353c6f99

Hernandez, M. H. M., Osorio-Marulanda, P. A., Catalina, M., Loinaz, L., Epelde, G., & Aginako, N. (2025). Comprehensive Evaluation Framework for Synthetic Tabular Data in Health: Fidelity, Utility and Privacy Analysis of Generative Models with and without Privacy Guarantees. *Frontiers in Digital Health*, *7*, 1576290. Advance online publication. DOI: 10.3389/fdgth.2025.1576290 PMID: 40343213

Hittmeir, M., Mayer, R., & Ekelhart, A. (2020). A Baseline for Attribute Disclosure Risk in Synthetic Data. In CODASPY '20 (pp. 133–143). https://doi.org/DOI: 10.1145/3374664.3375722

Hu, H., Salcic, Z., Sun, L., Dobbie, G., Yu, P. S., & Zhang, X. (2022). Membership Inference Attacks on Machine Learning: A survey. ACM Computing Surveys, 54(11s). *ACM Computing Surveys*, *235*(11s), 1–37. DOI: 10.1145/3523273

Jayaraman, B., & Evans, D. (2022). Are Attribute Inference Attacks Just Imputation? *Proceedings of the 2022 ACM SIGSAC Conference on Computer and Communications Security (CCS '22)*, 3093–3107. https://doi.org/DOI: 10.1145/3548606.3560663

Jin, S., Palmer, H., Gat, I., Deja, K., Li, D., & Bao, Y. (2024). Implications of Data Topology for Deep Generative Models. *Frontiers of Computer Science*, *6*, 1260604. DOI: 10.3389/fcomp.2024.1260604

Kenny, C. T., Kuriwaki, S., McCartan, C., Rosenman, E. T. R., Simko, T., & Imai, K. (2021). The use of Differential Privacy for Census Data and its Impact on Redistricting: The case of the 2020 U.S. Census. *Science Advances*, *7*(41), eabk3283. Advance online publication. DOI: 10.1126/sciadv.abk3283 PMID: 34613778

Kindji, G. C. N., Rojas-Barahona, L. M., Fromont, É., & Urvoy, T. (2025). Tabular Data Generation Models: An in-depth Survey and Performance Benchmarks with Extensive Tuning. *Neurocomputing*, *658*, 131655. DOI: 10.1016/j.neucom.2025.131655

Kurakova, A., & Homayouni, H. (2025). A Comprehensive Evaluation Framework for Synthetic Medical Tabular Data Generation. *Journal of Biomedical Informatics, 171*, 104939. DOI: 10.1016/j.jbi.2025.104939 PMID: 41101425

Leykam, D., & Angelakis, D. G. (2023). Topological Data Analysis and Machine Learning. *Advances in Physics: X, 8*(1), 2202331. DOI: 10.1080/23746149.2023.2202331

Li, Y., Yang, R., & Lu, Y. (2024). A Privacy Risk Identification Framework of Open Government Data: A mixed-method study in China. *Government Information Quarterly, 41*(1), 101916. DOI: 10.1016/j.giq.2024.101916

Mitchell, M., Wu, S., Zaldivar, A., Barnes, P., Vasserman, L., Hutchinson, B., Spitzer, E., Raji, I. D., & Gebru, T. (2019). Model Cards for Model Reporting. *Proceedings of the Conference on Fairness, Accountability, and Transparency (FAT '19)*, 220–229. https://doi.org/DOI: 10.1145/3287560.3287596

Niu, J., Liu, P., Zhu, X., Shen, K., Wang, Y., Chi, H., Shen, Y., Jiang, X., Ma, J., & Zhang, Y. (2024). A Survey on Membership Inference Attacks and Defenses in Machine Learning. *Journal of Information and Intelligence*, *2*(5), 404–454. DOI: 10.1016/j.jiixd.2024.02.001

Pilgram, L., Dankar, F. K., Drechsler, J., Elliot, M., Domingo-Ferrer, J., Francis, P., Kantarcioglu, M., Kong, L., Malin, B., Muralidhar, K., Myles, P., Prasser, F., Raisaro, J. L., Yan, C., & El Emam, K. (2025). A Consensus Privacy Metrics Framework for Synthetic Data. *Patterns (New York, N.Y.)*, *6*(10), 101320. DOI: 10.1016/j.patter.2025.101320 PMID: 41142908

Powar, J., & Beresford, A. R. (2023). SoK: Managing Risks of Linkage Attacks on Data Privacy. *Proceedings on Privacy Enhancing Technologies. Privacy Enhancing Technologies Symposium, 2023*(2), 97–116. DOI: 10.56553/popets-2023-0043

Pun, C. S., Lee, S. X., & Xia, K. (2022). Persistent-Homology-Based Machine Learning: A Survey and a Comparative Study. *Artificial Intelligence Review, 55*(7), 5169–5213. DOI: 10.1007/s10462-022-10146-z

Santangelo, G., Nicora, G., Bellazzi, R., & Dagliati, A. (2025). How Good is Your Synthetic Data? SynthRO, a Dashboard to Evaluate and Benchmark Synthetic Tabular Data. *BMC Medical Informatics and Decision Making*, *25*(1), 89. DOI: 10.1186/s12911-024-02731-9 PMID: 39966793

Schlegel, M., & Sattler, K.-U. (2022). Management of Machine Learning Lifecycle Artifacts: A survey. *SIGMOD Record, 51*(4), 18–35. DOI: 10.1145/3582302.3582306

Schlegel, M., & Sattler, K.-U. (2025). Capturing end-to-end Provenance for Machine Learning Pipelines. *Information Systems*, *132*, 102495. DOI: 10.1016/j.is.2024.102495

Trindade, M., Kaye, J., & De Cristofaro, E. (2024). Navigating Identity Disclosure Risk in Synthetic Data: outliers and vulnerabilities. arXiv. https://doi.org//arXiv.2406.02736DOI: 10.48550

Wasserman, L. (2018). Topological Data Analysis. *Annual Review of Statistics and Its Application*, *5*(1), 501–532. DOI: 10.1146/annurev-statistics-031017-100045

Zhang, Z., Yan, C., & Malin, B. A. (2022). Membership Inference Attacks Against Synthetic Health Data. *Journal of Biomedical Informatics*, *125*, 103977. DOI: 10.1016/j.jbi.2021.103977 PMID: 34920126

APPENDIX

Reader Glossary for Non-Specialist Audiences

Table 18. Minimal glossary of topology, privacy, and decision terms.

Term	Reader-oriented definition
Persistent homology	Multiscale record of components, loops, and voids as neighborhood scale changes.
Persistence diagram	Birth–death plot summarizing the lifetimes of topological features.
Vietoris–Rips filtration	Nested complexes built by connecting points within growing distance thresholds.
Betti curve	Count of topological features across filtration scales.
Bottleneck distance	Worst-case displacement between matched diagram features.
Membership inference	Attack inferring whether a record trained the generator.
Attribute inference	Attack predicting sensitive values from partial information.
Linkage inference	Attack joining records through quasi-identifiers.
Pareto frontier	Candidates not dominated in utility and privacy risk.

Illustrative Acceptance Thresholds for Governance Use Cases

Thresholds in this appendix should be treated as starting points for institutional deliberation, not as universal compliance guarantees. A low-risk educational release may require very conservative privacy ceilings and modest utility, whereas a controlled inter-agency analytical release may justify a higher utility requirement with stricter access controls and documented residual risk. The important procedural requirement is that thresholds be declared before generator selection, recorded in the release dossier, and revisited when drift monitoring or new auxiliary data changes the threat environment (see Table 19).

Table 19. Suggested threshold logic; values are illustrative and policy-dependent.

Use case	Illustrative threshold logic
Controlled research	Utility drop ≤ 10%; membership AUC near chance; subgroup metrics within tolerance.
Inter-agency analytics	Utility drop ≤ 5–10%; MIA advantage ≤ 0.05–0.10; linkability documented.
High-impact allocation	Task-specific utility; mandatory subgroup and temporal topology pass; reject unstable protected strata.
Public open release	Prefer formal privacy or access minimization; attacks near chance; strong prohibited-use documentation.

Plain-Language Interpretation of Core Equations and Release Actions

These interpretations are not substitutes for the mathematical definitions. Their role is to make the audit usable by mixed review committees in which data scientists, legal officers, policy owners, and program managers must agree on the same evidence. The equations provide formal consistency, while the decision column explains what each metric should trigger: approval, mitigation, escalation, or rejection. This prevents symbolic density from becoming a barrier to governance accountability (see Table 20).

Table 20. Equation-to-decision map for readers who need governance meaning without formal derivations.

Metric or rule	Governance meaning
MMD	Distributional gap: shows whether the kernel detects separation between real and synthetic records; use it as a warning, not final approval.
Task-utility gap	Operational loss: compares models trained on synthetic data with models trained on real data on the same real test set.
Membership advantage	Attack lift: measures how much better the attacker is than chance when identifying whether a target record trained the generator.
Differential privacy	Influence bound: limits how much one person can change the mechanism output, subject to the declared privacy budget.
Bottleneck distance	Worst-case structural drift: reports the largest unmatched topology displacement between real and synthetic persistence diagrams.
Wasserstein distance	Aggregate structural drift: reports cumulative movement needed to align the real and synthetic topological features.

continued on following page

Table 20. Continued

Metric or rule	Governance meaning
Acceptance bound	Stability test: uses replica means and dispersion so one favorable run cannot justify release.
Pareto frontier	Trade-off rule: retains only candidates not dominated by another option with higher utility and lower or equal risk.

Availability of code: The Python code for data generation, perturbation simulations, autoencoder training, and topological metrics is available at: https://github.com/JAIME6609/TE/blob/main/CODIGO-COMPLETO-LIBRO-12-ART-02.py

It supports reproducibility of the computational pipeline and the resulting figures and tables.

Chapter 6

Topological Signatures for Synthetic Intrusion Detection in Government Networks

Jaime Aguilar-Ortiz
http://orcid.org/0009-0003-5302-1454
Universidad Politécnica de Pachuca, Mexico

Ocotlán Diáz-Parra
Universidad Politécnica de Pachuca, Mexico

Jorge A. Ruiz-Vanoye
http://orcid.org/0000-0003-4928-5716
Universidad Politécnica de Pachuca, Mexico

Francisco R. Trejo-Macotela
http://orcid.org/0000-0003-2133-3456
Universidad Politécnica de Pachuca, Mexico

Marco A. Vera-Jiménez
http://orcid.org/0009-0009-3712-1440
Universidad Politécnica de Pachuca, Mexico

Víctor M. Zamudio-García
http://orcid.org/0000-0002-4660-8025
Universidad Politécnica Metropolitana de Hidalgo, Mexico

Carlos R. Domínguez-Mayorga
http://orcid.org/0009-0007-1018-4412
Universidad Politécnica de Pachuca, Mexico

ABSTRACT

This chapter presents a reproducible and auditable Python pipeline for Intrusion Detection Systems (IDS) in government network and service telemetry under privacy, governance, and operational-cost constraints. It uses synthetic telemetry to support experimentation without exposing sensitive logs, but it treats synthetic utility as an

DOI: 10.4018/979-8-2600-2845-2.ch006

empirical question rather than an assumed improvement. Classical unsupervised detectors, forecasting residuals, representation learning, and persistent-homology features are evaluated as complementary signals for regime change. The results are interpreted through calibrated thresholds, time-to-detect, alert-load, cross-profile robustness, and failure-mode analysis. The chapter also specifies deployment conditions for public-sector Security Operations Center (SOC) use, including interoperability, human review, audit evidence, synthetic-data transparency, and cautious conclusions about topological and synthetic-data contributions.

1. INTRODUCTION

1.1 Government Digital Services, Expanding Attack Surface, and Nonstationary Operating Contexts

Government digital services increasingly function as interconnected portfolios of cloud-hosted applications, API-based citizen platforms, and cross-agency data-sharing workflows, so the attack surface grows not only in scale but also in heterogeneity and coupling. As architectures decompose into microservices, containers, and independently deployed components, reachable endpoints and east–west communications proliferate, while service meshes, CI/CD tooling, observability pipelines, and autoscaling create pathways where misconfiguration or compromise can propagate across services (Berardi et al., 2022). In this setting, security assurance cannot rely on perimeter hardening alone, because identity, endpoint posture, workload execution, data access, and telemetry-driven visibility become the primary control planes for managing risk at scale (Yeoh et al., 2023). Therefore, the security problem is naturally cast as continuous monitoring over multi-channel telemetry whose joint behavior defines "normal" only relative to a shifting mission context, motivating intrusion detection that prioritizes auditable signals, transparent alerting logic, and robustness to heterogeneous deployments over platform-specific or static-baseline rules.

Non-stationarity is intrinsic in government services: policy-driven releases, emergency surges, vendor migrations, patch cycles, and shifting user behavior (e.g., seasonal filings, elections, public health events) continually reshape operations, while adversaries adapt in response to defenses. From a learning standpoint, these dynamics produce concept drift and feature drift, so the mapping between observations and security-relevant states changes over time even when the system is nominally healthy (Shyaa et al., 2024). In this regime, a high-impact intrusion-detection pipeline must distinguish benign operational transitions from malicious regime changes without relying on continuous retraining over sensitive raw logs. Synthetic data generation addresses this constraint by reducing dependence on operational datasets, mitigating imbalance, and enabling controlled experimentation across attack and non-attack scenarios under privacy and governance limits (Rahman et al., 2024). Within that envelope, topological learning adds value because persistent-homology features summarize multiscale structural changes in high-dimensional dynamics in a way that is less noise-sensitive and more aligned with regime-level transitions, effectively acting as a stable signature layer over embeddings or structured time-series representations (Ichinomiya, 2025; Wang et al., 2026). Accordingly, the section frames government intrusion detection as a drift-aware, telemetry-native problem where synthetic data and topological signatures jointly support early warning, calibrated alerting, and reproducible evaluation across evolving service contexts.

For smart governments, this monitoring problem is also a digital-transformation problem: citizen portals, identity platforms, health, taxation, procurement, and emergency services increasingly depend on shared APIs, cloud providers, and cross-agency data exchanges. A false positive may overload a SOC, while a delayed alert may interrupt a public service. Consequently, the target audience includes researchers, cybersecurity teams, advanced students, and public managers who must connect signals with service continuity, data sovereignty, accountability, and cybersecurity priorities.

Government scenarios include a tax portal with seasonal filings, a public-health platform under emergency demand, an identity service facing credential abuse, and an inter-agency data exchange where slow exfiltration may precede service degradation. These cases explain why early warning cannot be evaluated only by ROC-AUC: managers need lead time, bounded alert volume, auditable evidence, and escalation rules that protect continuity of citizen services.

1.2 Research Problem, Core Hypothesis, Contributions, and Article Roadmap

The research problem arises because intrusion detection over government network and service telemetry must function under high-impact yet high-constraint conditions: operations are nonstationary, labels are sparse, telemetry is heterogeneous, and raw logs are often non-shareable due to sensitivity and governance. Static baselines and narrowly scoped indicators are therefore insufficient, since policy-driven releases, seasonal cycles, emergency surges, and infrastructure migration change the mapping between "normal" observations and security-relevant states, inducing concept and feature drift that can erode validity even when controlled tests look strong (Shyaa et al., 2024). The core challenge is thus not merely anomaly detection, but drift-stable detection that yields calibratable alert loads and supports accountability through traceable evidence across identity, network, workload, and visibility/analytics control planes central to government cybersecurity postures (Yeoh et al., 2023). Deep anomaly detection and representation learning can capture complex multi-channel structure, but their operational risk is latent-shift under benign regime change, which can inflate false positives unless robustness, calibration, and drift-aware evaluation are built into the pipeline (Pang et al., 2022).

The core hypothesis is that some intrusions first appear as structural reorganizations of telemetry dynamics, such as changes in connectivity, clustering, or periodic beaconing, before they become obvious in individual metrics; however, this chapter treats that hypothesis as partially supported, not conclusively proven. The contributions are separated into methodological, computational, empirical, topological, and governance layers so that each claim remains auditable against the reported fidelity, detection, time-to-detect, alert-load, cross-profile, and ablation evidence.

Analytically, the literature can be read in four families. Signature and rule-based IDS remain interpretable but brittle under drift; classical unsupervised models scale well but often miss temporal context; deep sequence and autoencoder models capture multivariate dynamics but require calibration and monitoring; and synthetic-data plus topological-data-analysis (TDA) studies address privacy and structural change, yet rarely connect those ideas to government interoperability, alert workload, and institutional adoption.

Pipeline map: telemetry sources -> aggregation and preprocessing -> synthetic scenario control -> detector training -> topological regime descriptors -> calibrated fusion -> SOC alert triage -> audit bundle and recalibration review.

This comparison clarifies the chapter's boundary of originality. The novelty is not the use of anomaly detection, synthetic data, or persistent homology, all of which have mature research traditions. The contribution is the governed coupling of these elements under conditions typical of smart governments: incomplete labels, non-shareable logs, demand shocks, heterogeneous sensors, and the need to justify alerts as accountable decisions. That framing responds to the literature gap because it moves beyond listing related work and explains why a combined architecture is necessary when technical performance, privacy, workload, and institutional acceptance must be optimized together (see Table 1).

Table 1. Comparative positioning of IDS families for government telemetry.

Approach family	Main value	Main limitation	Role in this chapter
Signature or rule IDS	Transparent and fast for known patterns	Brittle under drift and new tactics	Governance contrast and baseline logic
Classical unsupervised models	Scalable anomaly scores with limited labels	Weak temporal and contextual semantics	Benchmark detection layer
Deep forecasting/ autoencoding	Learns multichannel dynamics	Requires calibration and shift monitoring	Primary detection signal
Synthetic data and TDA	Protects raw logs and tracks regime shape	Utility and causality require validation	Privacy substrate and structural descriptor

2. THEORETICAL FOUNDATIONS

Key idea of this section: the mathematical objects below are retained only where they support an operational claim. A government IDS should observe multi-source behavior as a changing system, preserve privacy through controlled synthesis, and use topology as a compact descriptor of structural regime movement, not as an automatically superior stand-alone classifier.

2.1 Multisource Telemetry as High-Dimensional, Windowed System Dynamics (Network, Identity, Endpoint, Service Health)

Multisource cybersecurity telemetry can be formalized as a single, high-dimensional observation process that records at each moment an integrated "snapshot" of network behavior, identity and access activity, endpoint execution traces, and service health indicators, which is consistent with modern security architectures that explicitly treat identity, endpoint, network, application/workload, and visibility/analytics as tightly coupled dimensions of operational security (Rose et al., 2020; Yeoh et al., 2023). To make that coupling computable, the telemetry is first aligned on a common time grid of resolution $\Delta > 0$ (for example, 1–5 minutes), and each source is mapped into a fixed-length feature vector through aggregation of raw events, logs, or metrics into rates, counts, histograms, and summary statistics that preserve both volume and composition; this is especially important when the data are heterogeneous across sources and formats, because the analytic goal is to model joint deviations rather than isolated anomalies (Okolie et al., 2025; Landauer et al., 2023). Formally, for each modality $m \in \{e{:}\tau(e) \in [t\Delta,(t+1)\Delta)\}$, and then define a modality-specific feature map $\phi^{(m)}$ that transforms those records into $x_t^{(m)} \in \mathbb{R}^{d_m}$; with that notation, the fused telemetry vector is naturally expressed as the concatenation below, which makes explicit the "multi-view" nature of the observation:

$$x_t = \left[\left(x_t^{(net)}\right)^T, \left(x_t^{(id)}\right)^T, \left(x_t^{(ep)}\right)^T, \left(x_t^{(SVC)}\right)^T\right]^T \in \mathbb{R}^d,\ d = \sum_m d_m.$$

Before any temporal modeling, the fused vector is typically normalized to stabilize learning across channels whose natural scales differ by orders of magnitude (e.g., packet counts vs. latency in milliseconds), so that downstream detectors do not confuse "large units" with "large risk"; this can be written as the component wise standardization below, where μ and σ are estimated on a baseline period or a rolling reference window $\tilde{x}_t = \frac{(x_t - \mu)}{\sigma}$. This formulation directly supports principled multisource fusion designs either at the feature level (as above) or at later stages because it makes explicit how heterogeneous evidence becomes a single analyzable object while preserving the provenance of each modality (Anjum et al., 2021).

Once the fused stream $\{\tilde{x}_t\}$ is defined, "windowed system dynamics" means that the fundamental unit of analysis is not a single instant but a short trajectory segment that captures temporal context, correlations, and regime structure; mathematically, this is represented by the sliding window matrix below of length w, which turns telemetry into a multivariate time-series learning problem in $\mathbb{R}^{w \times d}$ (Wang et al., 2025; Tuli et al., 2022). To express that construction in the most direct way, the window ending at time t is:

$$X_t = \left[\tilde{x}_{t-w+1}, \tilde{x}_{t-w+2}, \ldots, \tilde{x}_t\right]^T \in \mathbb{R}^{w \times d}.$$

Conceptually, X_t is an observable trace of an underlying operational state (mission load, service configuration, user population, adversarial pressure), so a standard theoretical perspective is a state-space view where telemetry is a noisy observation of latent dynamics; the following pair of equations is a compact way to write that idea and clarifies why "no stationarity" is expected rather than exceptional in government-scale systems (Shyaa et al., 2024):

$$s_{t+1} = f(s_t) + \eta_t,\ \tilde{x}_t = g(s_t) + \epsilon_t$$

Operational intrusion detection then becomes the construction of a scoring function over windows (or their embeddings) that reacts to malicious regime changes while remaining stable under benign operational transitions; one widely used family of approaches is forecasting-based scoring, where a model h_θ predicts the next-step telemetry and the residual magnitude becomes an anomaly statistic, a design that aligns with production monitoring pipelines for large-scale services (Ren et al., 2019; Pang et al., 2022). Concretely, the core computation can be written as:

$$\hat{x}_{t+1} = h_\theta(X_t), \; r_{t+1} = \| \tilde{x}_{t+1} - \tilde{x}_{t+1} \|_2,$$

and, because drift is intrinsic, the system can track distributional change over successive windows (or over the induced residuals) via a divergence functional $D(\cdot)$between window-level empirical laws $\widehat{P}_t$ and $\widehat{P}_{t-1}$; for example, one may write a drift indicator using Kullback–Leibler divergence as:

$$\mathscr{D}_t = D_{KL}\left(p_t \| \widehat{P}_{t-1}\right),$$

which makes explicit the separation between anomalies (large r_{t+1}) and baseline motion (large $\mathscr{D}_t$ even without attacks), a distinction emphasized as essential for drift-aware intrusion detection (Shyaa et al., 2024). Within this windowed-dynamics view, compact representations such as continually updated traffic summaries (e.g., histogram-based representations) can be interpreted as structured feature maps $\phi^{(net)}$ that preserve regime information while improving scalability, reinforcing the methodological coherence of treating multisource telemetry as a single evolving dynamical object rather than as disconnected data silos (Baldoni & Battisti, 2025; Okolie et al., 2025).

2.2 Synthetic Data as an Enabler for Privacy-Constrained Security Analytics (Fidelity, Correlations, Temporal Dependence)

Synthetic data becomes an enabler for privacy-constrained security analytics when it is treated as a distributional surrogate of multisource telemetry windows, rather than as an ad-hoc augmentation artifact: the real windowed process induces a probability law P over matrices $X \in \mathbb{R}^{w \times d}$, and a generator G_θ s trained so that the synthetic law Q_θ approaches P in the aspects that matter operationally—marginal fidelity, cross-feature dependence, and multichannel structure while keeping raw sensitive logs non-disclosive (Figueira & Vaz, 2022; Rahman et al., 2024). Before any privacy discussion, the central technical requirement is fidelity: the synthetic data must preserve the geometry that downstream detectors "see," including heavy tails, burstiness, and inter-source couplings that define normal regimes; surveys of synthetic data and time-series synthesis emphasize that evaluation must be multi-criteria because no single metric captures the full notion of "quality" for sequential data (Stenger et al., 2024; Brophy et al., 2023). In formal terms, a standard adversarial training objective for matching distributions can be written naturally as a min–max game; introducing it explicitly clarifies what the generator is optimizing:

$$\min_{\theta}\max_{\psi}\mathbb{E}_{X\sim P}\left[\log D_{\psi}(X)\right] + \mathbb{E}_{Z\sim p(Z)}\left[\log\left(1 - D_{\psi}\left(G_{\theta}(Z)\right)\right)\right].$$

Because security telemetry depends on cross-channel coupling, fidelity must be assessed beyond marginals; Maximum Mean Discrepancy provides an explicit multivariate discrepancy measure that operationalizes "indistinguishability" in practice.

$$MMD^{2}\left(P,Q_{\theta}\right) = \mathbb{E}[k(X,X')] + \mathbb{E}\left[k(\tilde{X}, \tilde{X}'\right] - 2\mathbb{E}\left(k(X,\tilde{X})\right).$$

Correlation preservation can then be enforced or audited by comparing correlation matrices of the flattened window vectors (or of feature summaries), which is especially relevant when synthetic telemetry is used to train detectors that depend on cross-channel co-movement; the following Frobenius-norm penalty is a direct and interpretable way to express "correlation fidelity":

$$\Delta_{\Sigma} = \left\|Corr(vec(X)) - Corr\left(vec(\tilde{X})\right)\right\|_{F}.$$

This combination distributional similarity plus explicit dependence matches with privacy-constrained IDS studies that generate synthetic datasets for training and evaluation while targeting preservation of statistical properties needed for intrusion detection utility (Alabdulwahab et al., 2024).

Temporal dependence is the third pillar: in security telemetry, the ordering and lag structure encode beaconing, lateral movement pacing, periodic tasking, and delayed effects (e.g., authentication anomalies preceding service degradation), so synthetic data that matches only "static" statistics can mislead early-warning claims. A minimal but essential mathematical object is the autocorrelation function for each feature j, which makes explicit what it means to preserve sequential dynamics; introducing it before scoring enables a direct test of temporal fidelity across lags ℓ:

$$p_{j}(\ell) = \frac{Cov\left(x_{t,j}, x_{t-\ell,j}\right)}{\sqrt{Var\left(x_{i,j}\right)Var\left(x_{t-\ell,j}\right)}}, \quad \Delta_{\rho} = \sum_{\ell=1}^{L}\left\|\rho(\ell) - \tilde{\rho}(\ell)\right\|_{2}^{2}.$$

At the same time, privacy constraints cannot be treated as a rhetorical add-on: even fully synthetic releases can leak information about whether particular sensitive records influenced training, and membership inference work demonstrates that synthetic data can be vulnerable unless privacy risk is explicitly audited (Zhang et al., 2022). For mechanisms that aim at formal guarantees, differential privacy provides a precise condition; writing it explicitly clarifies the operational meaning of a "privacy budget" in synthetic telemetry generation (Ho et al., 2021):

$$Pr[A(\mathscr{D}) \in S] \leq e^{\varepsilon} Pr[A(\mathscr{D}') \in S] + \delta,$$

for any neighboring datasets $\mathscr{D}, \mathscr{D}'$ and any measurable set S. In practice, privacy-constrained security analytics should be framed as an optimization of downstream utility under explicit privacy-risk constraints rather than as "maximize resemblance," which is consistent with recent work arguing that task-oriented synthesis can improve privacy while retaining (or improving) predictive usefulness (Achterberg et al., 2025; Sarmin et al., 2025). A compact way to express that design principle is the constrained objective below, which ties the synthetic generator directly to intrusion-detection evaluation goals (alert quality, early warning, calibration) while forcing privacy auditing into the acceptance criteria:

$$\max_{\theta} U(\widetilde{D}_{\theta}) \ s.t. \ Risk(\widetilde{D}_{\theta}) \leq \tau$$

Finally, because similarity metrics can be misinterpreted as privacy proxies, contemporary consensus work recommends evaluating membership and attribute disclosure explicitly and setting decision thresholds for use, which is directly aligned with the needs of governmental deployments that require defensible evidence for sharing, benchmarking, and reproducibility (Pilgram et al., 2025; Giomi et al., 2023).

2.3 Algebraic-Topological Signatures for Regime Change (Persistent Homology, H_0/H_1, Diagram Summaries and Distances)

Algebraic–topological signatures operationalize "regime change" by treating each time window of multisource telemetry as a geometric object whose multiscale shape can be measured, compared, and tracked over time. In a windowed pipeline, each aligned telemetry window $X_t \in \mathbb{R}^{w \times d}$ is first converted into a point cloud (or a cloud of embeddings) so that persistent homology can be computed in a metric space, a standard strategy for time-series and multivariate dynamics when one wants to capture structure beyond marginal statistics (Chazal & Michel, 2021; El-Yaagoubi et al., 2023; Chung et al., 2021). Before defining homology, it is natural to make explicit the representation used for topology; for example, with an encoder f_θ one can map windows (or sub windows) into latent vectors $z_t \in \mathbb{R}^p$, yielding a local cloud $\mathcal{Z}_t = \{z_{t-w+1}, \ldots, z_t\}$ that reflects the recent operational trajectory. The embedding step can be stated compactly as the following deterministic transformation:

$$z_t = f_\theta(X_t) \in \mathbb{R}^p, \ \mathcal{Z}_t = \{z_{t-w+1}, \ldots, z_t\}.$$

Given a cloud $\mathcal{Z}_t$ with distance $d(\cdot)$persistent homology is computed by building a filtration of simplicial complexes across a scale parameter ε. A widely used choice in data analysis is the Vietoris–Rips filtration, which can be introduced by the following definition of the complex at scale ε:

$$VR_\varepsilon(\mathcal{Z}_t) = \{\sigma \subseteq \mathcal{Z}_t : d(u,v) \le \varepsilon . \ for\ all\ u,v \in \sigma\}.$$

As ε increases, new simplices appear and topological features are "born" and later "die," which is recorded by the homology groups $H_k(VR_\varepsilon(\mathcal{Z}_t))$ across dimensions k. In practice, H_0 tracks connected components (useful for detecting fragmentation/merging of behavioral clusters), while H_1 tracks one-dimensional cycles (often interpreted as loop-like structure that can reflect recurrent/periodic or multi-path transition patterns in the latent dynamics), and these interpretations are central when one wants to distinguish benign operational shifts from structurally distinct regimes (Chazal & Michel, 2021; El-Yaagoubi et al., 2023). The persistent homology output is summarized as a persistence diagram $D_k(t)$, a multiset of birth–death pairs $(b_i^{(k)}(t), d_i^{(k)}(t))$ for dimension k, which can be naturally written as:

$$D_k(t) = \{(b_i^{(k)}(t), d_i^{(k)}(t))\}_{i=1}^{n_k(t)}, \ b_i^{(k)} < d_i^{(k)}(t).$$

This representation becomes a regime-change instrument precisely because it measures how long features persist across scales: persistence $d_i^{(k)}(t) - b_i^{(k)}(t)$ acts as a multiscale robustness indicator, so abrupt reorganizations of multisource telemetry can surface as changes in the distribution and geometry of points in $D_0(t)$ and $D_1(t)$, even when individual telemetry channels remain ambiguous (Chazal & Michel, 2021; Leykam & Angelakis, 2023).

To turn diagrams into actionable signals, one typically uses both diagram summaries and diagram distances, because summaries improve scalability and interpretability, while distances support direct "change detection" between successive windows (Ali et al., 2023; Atienza et al., 2020). Before introducing distances, it is natural to define a summary that is directly interpretable as a regime descriptor; for instance, the Betti curve counts the number of k- dimensional features alive at scale ε:

$$\beta_k^{(t)}(\varepsilon) = \#\{i : b_i^{(k)}(t) \le \varepsilon < b_i^{(k)}(t)\}.$$

Likewise, when a scalar stability-friendly summary is desired, persistent entropy converts lifetimes into a probability simplex and measures dispersion of persistence; defining $\ell_i^{(k)}(t) = d_i^{(k)}(t) - b_i^{(k)}(t)$ and $p_i^{(k)} = \ell_i^{(k)}(t)/\sum_j \ell_j^{(k)}(t)$, the entropy is:

$$H_k(t) = -\sum_{i=1}^{n_k(t)} p_i^{(k)}(t)\log p_i^{(k)}(t).$$

Such summaries are useful because they can be trended over time and tested for stability properties under perturbations, which supports robust regime monitoring in noisy telemetry (Atienza et al., 2020). However, the most direct algebraic–topological regime-change test compares diagrams themselves via metrics that allow matching points to each other (or to the diagonal, representing topological noise). Before writing the metric, it is natural to introduce the matching concept: let Γ range over bijections between the multiset $D_k(t) \cup \Delta$ and $D_k(t-1) \cup \Delta$, where Δ denotes the diagonal. Then the bottleneck distance can be written as:

$$d_B\big(D_k(t),\ D_k(t-1)\big) = \inf_{\gamma} \sup_{x \in D_k(t) \cup \Delta} \left\| x - \gamma(x) \right\|_\infty ,$$

And the p- Wasserstein distance as:

$$d_{W,p}\big(D_k(t),\ D_k(t-1)\big) = \left(\inf_{\gamma \in \Gamma} \sum_{x \in D_k(t) \cup \Delta} \left\| x - \gamma(x) \right\|_\infty^p\right)^{1/p}.$$

These distances are standard tools for quantifying topological change and are practically important because they can be computed (or approximated) efficiently enough to support sliding-window monitoring, including algorithmic work focused specifically on accelerating Wasserstein computations for persistence diagrams (Chazal & Michel, 2021; Chen & Wang, 2021; Ali et al., 2023). Once a distance is defined, a regime-change score can be expressed in a way that aligns with operational alerting: one aggregates diagram shifts across dimensions $k \in \{0,1\}$ using nonnegative weights w_k, yielding a single scalar suitable for calibration and fusion with other anomaly scores:

$$S_t = \sum_{k \in \{0,1\}} w_k d_{W,p}\big(D_k(t),\ D_k(t-1)\big),$$

Finally, because downstream learning often requires Hilbert-space structure, diagram vectorization and kernelization provide an additional bridge between persistent homology and statistical learning, enabling linear models, kernel machines, and comparative kernel studies over persistence objects tools that are conceptually consistent with turning topological change into auditable, reproducible signals (Obayashi et al., 2018; Bandiziol & De Marchi, 2024; Ali et al., 2023).

3. METHODOLOGY

3.1 Dataset Design: Telemetry Schema, Aggregation/ Windowing, Preprocessing, and Scenario Injection (Attacks vs. Benign Shifts)

Synthetic generation protocol and scenario control. The synthetic stream is configured as a governed surrogate of operational telemetry, not a generic random sample. Its variables are drawn from the network, identity, endpoint, and service-health channels described below; baseline distributions use aggregate ranges, not disclosive raw logs; temporal dependence is imposed through window-level persistence and lagged effects; and cross-channel correlations are checked through MMD, correlation, and ACF diagnostics. Scenario schedules define benign shifts and attack intervals. Each experiment should record profile, seed, window size, attack schedule, privacy controls, and train/test split.

The generator acceptance rule is deliberately multi-layered. A generated sample is not accepted because it resembles one variable's marginal distribution; it must preserve cross-channel dependence, temporal memory, attack timing, and downstream behavior under the same train-validation-test separation used for detectors. When any fidelity gate is weak, the interpretation changes from "synthetic data improves detection" to "synthetic data supports controlled exploration under explicit limitations." This wording matters for public-sector use because an agency may legally share synthetic artifacts while remaining responsible for misleading patterns, biased alert rates, or privacy leakage. Therefore, the generator is treated as an auditable experimental instrument, not a substitute for deployment evidence (see Table 2).

Table 2. Synthetic generation controls required for reproducible evaluation.

Control item	Configuration	Audit evidence	Limitation
Profiles and seeds	Agency profile, window size, random seed	Configuration file and run log	One seed cannot prove stability
Scenario schedule	Benign shifts plus attack intervals	Attack calendar and labels	Coverage may omit rare tactics
Fidelity gates	KS, MMD, correlation, ACF	Tables 1-4 and thresholds	Fidelity does not ensure utility
Privacy controls	No raw log release; disclosure audits	Synthetic-data statement and risk tests	Synthetic data can still leak patterns

Designing a dataset for intrusion detection under privacy and governance constraints begins by specifying a telemetry schema that unifies heterogeneous sources network flow summaries, identity/authentication events, endpoint/process signals, and service-health metrics into a single, high-dimensional stream, so that learning and evaluation occur over joint system behavior rather than siloed indicators (Yeoh et al., 2023; Landauer et al., 2023). To formalize this unification, the dataset can be defined on a discrete time grid with resolution $\Delta > 0$, where each modality contributes raw records to a common bin; before any feature engineering is described, it is natural to introduce the event set for time index t as

$$E_t = \{e:\tau(e) \in [t\Delta, (t+1)\Delta]\},$$

and then state the schema-to-feature operator that maps heterogeneous records into a fixed-length vector in $\mathbb{R}^d$ as $x_t = \phi(E_t) \in \mathbb{R}^d$, because intrusion signals are often expressed through rates and compositions, not only raw volumes, aggregation can be made explicit by defining per-type counts and rates; for an event type r (e.g., failed logins, DNS NXDOMAIN, lateral SMB attempts), a natural construction is

$$c_{t,r} = \sum_{e\in E_t} 1\{type(e) = r\},\ \lambda_{t,r} = \frac{c_{t,r}}{\Delta}.$$

Windowing then converts the stream into trajectories suitable for sequence models and for regime-aware scoring, so the dataset instance used for modeling is the sliding matrix $X_t = [x_{t-w+1}, \ldots, x_t] \in \mathbb{R}^{w\times d}$, which aligns with modern multivariate time-series anomaly detection practice where context length w is itself a modeling knob (Tuli et al., 2022; Ren et al., 2019). Preprocessing must preserve security semantics while stabilizing optimization: heavy-tailed counters typically benefit from monotone compression, sparse categorical fields require consistent encoding, and missingness must be handled without injecting spurious "spikes"; to state this mathematically, a common transformation for count-like features is $x_{t,j}^{(\log)} = \log(1 + x_{ij})$, and a robust scaling step that mitigates outlier dominance can be expressed as:

$$x_{t,j}^{(rob)} = \frac{x_{t,j}^{(log)} - median\, x_{\cdot,j}^{(log)}}{IQR\left(x_{\cdot,j}^{(log)}\right)}.$$

When service logs are included, a crucial design decision is how raw log lines are converted into templates or event IDs, because the representation directly affects downstream anomaly detection sensitivity; recent empirical evidence shows that properties of log parsing outcomes can materially impact detection behavior, so the dataset design should treat parsing and representation as first-class, audited steps rather than incidental preprocessing (Khan et al., 2024; Landauer et al., 2023).

Scenario injection is the methodological hinge that allows the dataset to separate attacks from benign shifts while remaining realistic under no stationarity: benign shifts represent operational transitions (deployments, seasonal demand, reconfiguration), whereas attacks represent adversarial behaviors that may be subtle in any single channel but structurally coherent across channels (Shyaa et al., 2024; Shyaa et al., 2023). A clean mathematical way to encode benign no stationarity is a piecewise-stationary regime model in which the telemetry distribution changes across segments even when there is no attack; introducing a regime index $k(t)$ and parameters θ_k, this can be written as $X_t \sim P_{\theta_{k(t)}}$ with $k(t)$ constant over intervals and changing at benign shift points.

Attack injection can then be defined as an additional, label-controlled perturbation (or replacement) mechanism applied to a subset of features and times, producing controlled ground truth while preserving multichannel coupling; introducing an attack indicator $y_t \in \{0, 1\}$ that is active on an interval $[t_s, t_e]$ t is natural to define $y_t = 1\{t_s \leq t \leq t_e\}, \tilde{x}_t = x_t + y_t\delta_t$, where δ_t is structured to match the chosen attack family (e.g., brute force as identity failures plus service stress; botnet beaconing as periodic egress plus DNS anomalies). At the distributional level, the combined dataset can be described as a time-varying mixture that distinguishes benign drift from attack presence without conflating the two; before a detector is evaluated, the generating law can be stated as:

$$P_t = (1 - \pi_t)P_t^{(begign)} + \pi_t P_t^{(attack)},$$

Where π_t is driven by the scenario schedule and $P_t^{(begign)}$ already changes due to regime shifts. This formulation matches the philosophy of contemporary IDS dataset construction that emphasizes explicit scenario design, metadata, and attack/benign coverage, including well-known generation methodologies for modern attack families (Sharafaldin et al., 2018) and more recent encrypted/synthetic-attack datasets that document process requirements and reproducibility considerations (Ferriyan et al., 2021), as well as modular scenario-based datasets that include sequential attack campaigns alongside realistic normal activity (Silva et al., 2025). Finally, to keep the dataset faithful to the "multisource" objective, correlation and temporal dependence should be measured (not assumed) after injection; a minimal diagnostic is to compare covariance of window-flattened representations between regimes, which can be stated as:

$$\hat{\sum} = Cov(vec(X_t))$$

and tracked across benign shifts and attacks to ensure that scenario injection preserves the joint structure that regime-change methods and, later, topological signatures are intended to detect (Tuli et al., 2022; Shyaa et al., 2024).

3.2 Modeling and Scoring: Classical Detectors, Forecasting and Representation Learning, Topological Change Scores, Calibration and Fusion

Modeling and scoring in high-dimensional, windowed telemetry are most defensibly formulated as learning (or fitting) a family of functions that transform each window $X_t \in \mathbb{R}^{w \times d}$ into one or more anomaly scores that capture complementary notions of deviation: geometric isolation, density inconsistency, prediction surprise, and reconstruction inconsistency, which is consistent with production-grade monitoring pipelines and multivariate time-series anomaly detection practice. Before defining specific detectors, it is natural to introduce the canonical vector representation used by many classical methods by flattening (or summarizing) the window into $v_t \in \mathbb{R}^{wd}$; this can be stated as follows: $v_t = vec(X_t) \in \mathbb{R}^{wd}$. With this representation, Isolation Forest assigns higher anomaly scores to instances that can be isolated with shorter expected path length in randomized partition trees; introducing the standard scoring form clarifies why it scales well to large, mixed telemetry and remains a strong baseline in unsupervised settings:

$$s_{IF}(v_t) = 2^{-\frac{\mathbb{E}[h(v_t)]}{c(n)}},\ c(n) = 2H_{n-1} - \frac{2(n-1)}{n},$$

Where $h(v_t)$ is the path length, H_{n-1} is the harmonic number, and n is the subsample size used by the forest, with empirical cybersecurity-oriented evaluations frequently comparing IF against other classical unsupervised alternatives. In parallel, One-Class SVM provides a complementary "boundary of normality" score via a kernel decision function; stating its decision rule makes explicit how it supports nonlinear normal-region modeling when sufficient stable baseline data exist:

$$f_{OCSVM}(v_t) = \sum_{i=1}^{N} \alpha_i K(v_i, v_t) - \rho,\ s_{OCSVM}(v_t) = -f_{OCSVM}(v_t)\ ;$$

and Local Outlier Factor adds a density-ratio view that is sensitive to local neighborhood structure, which is often useful when anomalies appear as small, cohesive micro-clusters rather than isolated points; the operational score can be stated as:

$$LOF_k(v_t) = \frac{1}{k} \sum_{o \in \mathcal{N}_k(v_t)} \frac{Ird_k(o)}{Ird_k(v_t)}.$$

Forecasting and representation learning then extend these classical scores by explicitly modeling the temporal dynamics and latent structure of X_t, which is crucial for multisource telemetry where the "meaning" of a deviation depends on recent context; in forecasting-based scoring, a model h_θ predicts the next observation and the residual becomes an anomaly statistic: $\hat{x}_{t+1} = h_\theta(X_t), r_{t+1} = \|x_{t+1} - \hat{x}_{t+1}\|_2$, and transformer-based sequence models instantiate this principle at scale for multivariate monitoring streams. In representation learning, an autoencoder (f_θ, g_ϕ) maps each window to a latent code and reconstructs it, so reconstruction error becomes the score: $z_t = f_\theta(X_t), \hat{X}_t = g_\phi(z_t), e_t = \|X_t - \hat{X}_t\|_F^2$, which aligns with the broader deep anomaly detection literature that emphasizes learning representations (and/or anomaly scores) under sparse labels and heterogeneous signals.

Topological change scores are introduced as a regime-sensitive layer that measures structural reorganization of recent latent dynamics rather than only pointwise deviations, which is particularly appropriate for multisource telemetry where benign drift and malicious activity can be confounded in marginal statistics. After embedding each window (or sub window) into $z_t \in \mathbb{R}^d$, the recent trajectory is treated as a point cloud $\mathcal{Z}_t$, making persistent homology computable on the evolving geometry:

$$z_t = f_\theta(X_t),\ \mathcal{Z}_t = \{z_{t-w+1}, \ldots, z_t\}.$$

From $\mathcal{Z}_t$, persistence diagrams $D_k(t)$ (typically $k \in \{0, 1\}$) summarize multiscale connectedness and cycle structure, and a regime-change signal is naturally defined by distances between successive diagrams; writing the p-Wasserstein distance makes explicit how "topological drift" is quantified:

$$d_{W,p}(D_k(t),\ D_k(t-1)) = \left(\inf_{\gamma\in\Gamma} \sum_{x\in D_k(t)\cup\Delta} \|x - \gamma(x)\|_\infty^p\right)^{1/p},$$

and a unified topological score is then expressed as a weighted aggregation across dimensions:

$$S_t = \sum_{k\in\{0,1\}} w_k d_{W,p}(D_k(t), D_k(t-1)).$$

Because diagram computations and distances must be practical in sliding-window monitoring, approximation results for Wasserstein distances and stable diagram summaries (e.g., persistent entropy) provide the theoretical and algorithmic basis for deploying such scores at scale. Once multiple raw scores are available classical s_{IF}, s_{OCSVM}, LOF, forecasting residual r, reconstruction error e and topological change S calibration converts heterogeneous score scales into comparable probabilistic outputs suitable for thresholding and fusion; a standard post-hoc mapping for each score $s_t^{(j)}$ is the logistic transformation:

$$p_t^{(j)} = \alpha\left(a_j s_t^{(j)} + b_j\right), \; \sigma(u) = \frac{1}{1 + e^{-u}},$$

Where $\left(a_j, b_j\right)$ are fitted on validation data by minimizing the negative log-likelihood (log-loss), which is written as:

$$\mathcal{L}_{NLL} = -\frac{1}{N}\sum_{i=1}^{N}\left((y_i \log p_i + (1 - y_i)\log\left(1 - p_i\right)\right),$$

and calibration quality can be tracked via the Brier score to explicitly penalize miscalibrated probabilities:

$$Brier = \frac{1}{N}\sum_{i=1}^{N}(p_i - y_i)^2.$$

These calibration principles and modern post-hoc methods (including temperature-scaling generalizations) are treated in depth in recent calibration surveys and empirical studies, providing a rigorous basis for converting anomaly scores into operational probabilities. Finally, fusion integrates calibrated probabilities into a single alerting signal that can be tuned to agency-specific tolerances without rewriting the underlying detectors; a robust and interpretable choice is stacked logistic fusion:

$$p_t = \sigma\left(\beta_0 + \sum_{j=1}^{J}\beta_j \, logit\left(p_t^{(j()}\right)\right), \; logit(p) = \log\frac{p}{1 - p},$$

Where β are learned on validation data to minimize $\mathcal{L}_{NLL}$ (or Brier) and ensemble-style pipelines are empirically shown to improve robustness and generalization in anomaly detection when the component models capture complementary failure modes.

4. COMPUTATIONAL ARCHITECTURE

4.1 Reproducible Python Pipeline: Modular Components, Experiment Orchestration, Exports, and Automated Reporting

A reproducible Python pipeline for synthetic intrusion detection in government networks is designed as a modular end-to-end workflow in which each stage transforms explicit artifacts under configuration-as-code and strict provenance capture. It should include interoperable modules for telemetry schema definition, windowing/

aggregation, preprocessing, synthetic scenario generation, model training, topological feature extraction, and evaluation/calibration, while ensuring every run is replayable from immutable inputs and recorded decisions. Provenance research shows that end-to-end reproducibility requires lineage across data, code, parameters, and outputs not only final metrics so runs can be queried, compared, and audited (Samuel et al., 2021; Rupprecht et al., 2020; Idowu et al., 2023). Combining experiment metadata with Git-style version control and asset tracking further enables machine-queryable provenance graphs across runs (Schlegel & Sattler, 2025).

Experiment orchestration and automated reporting convert modular pipelines into scalable research instruments: a controller sweeps scenario configurations (benign shifts, injected attacks, synthetic-generation settings), launches training and scoring jobs, and consolidates results into standardized export bundles (e.g., JSON/YAML configuration snapshots, CSV/Parquet scores, serialized models, and figure assets) for validation and review. Workflow research emphasizes that reproducibility also requires verifying execution equivalence; therefore, workflow signatures and hash-based comparators help identify divergences caused by environment, parameter, or dependency drift (Pritchard & Wicenec, 2025). At the preprocessing boundary, deterministic and exportable transformation recipes reduce confounding and prevent silent feature-engineering changes across data releases and agency profiles (van de Water et al., 2026). Operationally, MLOps research highlights persistent challenges in complexity, deployment, and governance, so explicit artifact contracts and reproducible environment packaging enable reliable re-execution at scale (Amrit & Narayanappa, 2025; Bussonnier et al., 2018; Oliveira et al., 2018). These practices allow pipelines to auto-generate run reports (tables, plots, and configuration/provenance appendices), ensuring that claims about early warning, robustness, and auditability remain supported by traceable artifacts and comparable run lineage.

For institutional deployment, the pipeline would sit behind a SOC/SIEM/SOAR boundary: collectors normalize agency telemetry, the scoring service produces calibrated probabilities and topology descriptors, analysts review severity tiers, and an evidence bundle stores data version, model version, threshold, score contributors, and scenario assumptions. Costs should cover storage, compute, SIEM integration, analyst training, recalibration, privacy review, and incident-response playbooks. Interoperability requires common schemas, API contracts, role-based access, and agreements defining which agency owns thresholds, escalation, retention, and post-incident audit decisions.

A minimal pilot should run in shadow mode before any automated response is enabled. During this phase, the detector scores live or replayed telemetry, while analysts compare alerts with existing SOC procedures without changing the official incident workflow. The pilot should report cost per reviewed alert, analyst agreement, escalation time, false-positive causes, missed scenarios, storage and compute load, and the time needed to reconstruct provenance. Only after reviewing this evidence should the agency move to limited production, where low-severity alerts support monitoring, medium-severity alerts require analyst triage, and high-severity alerts trigger coordinated review with service owners and legal or privacy officers. This staged approach reduces technological dependence and supports public accountability (see Table 3).

Table 3. Deployment governance controls

Area	Operational question	Control	Failure avoided
Cost	Can the SOC absorb alerts?	Alert budgets and staffing review	Alert fatigue
Interoperability	Can agencies share signals?	Common schemas and APIs	Siloed evidence
Acceptance	Will analysts trust outputs?	Human review and explanations	Opaque automation
Ethics	Are synthetic claims transparent?	Privacy and bias audits	Misleading validation

5. RESULTS AND ANALYSIS

5.1 Synthetic Data Quality and Utility: Distributional Fidelity, Correlation Preservation, and Downstream Validity

This section evaluates whether synthetic realism, detection performance, early-warning timing, and operational workload support the proposed governance claims. Each metric is linked to what can and cannot be concluded for public-sector deployment.

For each feature, KS distance (ks_stat, ks_pvalue) plus real vs. synthetic mean and standard deviation to audit univariate distribution match.

Table 4. Per-feature KS fidelity and moment alignment (real vs. synthetic)

feature	ks_stat	ks_pvalue	real_mean	syn_mean	real_std	syn_std
persistence_indicator	0.49072	0.00000	0.54267	2.12230	0.79570	2.15331
dns_nxdomain_rate	0.46172	0.00000	0.73474	2.49209	1.07997	2.65495
auth_lockouts	0.36891	0.00000	0.63498	1.79689	0.88557	1.98652
tls_handshake_fail_rate	0.34919	0.00000	0.71716	1.74170	0.97220	1.97123
deploy_marker	0.30278	0.00000	0.31601	0.50928	0.42381	0.50020

continued on following page

Table 4. Continued

feature	ks_stat	ks_pvalue	real_mean	syn_mean	real_std	syn_std
privilege_changes	0.15197	0.00000	0.80815	1.13510	0.90485	1.39682
svc_err_rate	0.09049	0.00171	6.51548	6.59844	2.97612	3.73994
priv_exec_count	0.07541	0.01485	0.91357	1.05388	0.91334	1.10223
latency_p95	0.06845	0.03523	181.54345	183.36404	78.97881	91.91932
net_internal_ratio	0.06497	0.05258	0.46141	0.49881	0.44594	0.46252
net_dst_diversity	0.06265	0.06788	11.14872	11.13087	4.98866	5.75937
auth_fail	0.06148	0.07686	8.80385	8.80588	4.02169	4.60582
net_conn_count	0.06032	0.08682	33.96517	34.33474	14.94142	16.99906
net_bytes_out	0.05916	0.09784	1127639.2373	1135596.3150	490576.0980	553996.0041
auth_success	0.05684	0.12340	454.51144	456.01708	194.38353	209.76405
svc_req_rate	0.05568	0.13809	1232.63481	1238.27794	531.93064	592.41157
proc_create_rate	0.05568	0.13809	69.36340	69.36105	29.60133	32.35598
net_bytes_in	0.05336	0.17171	1657670.1316	1668032.6178	716480.5524	790840.9180
mfa_challenges	0.05336	0.17171	23.33516	23.42918	10.14192	10.99953
token_refresh	0.05104	0.21148	43.77320	43.80972	18.71677	20.37063
queue_depth	0.04872	0.25794	17.34398	17.36487	7.63063	8.43884

Table 4 shows uneven marginal fidelity. Most operational counters have acceptable mean alignment, but persistence_indicator, dns_nxdomain_rate, and auth_lockouts show large KS gaps; therefore, synthetic data should be trusted conditionally and not treated as universally faithful across all features.

Figure 1. Marginal distribution overlays for real vs. synthetic data

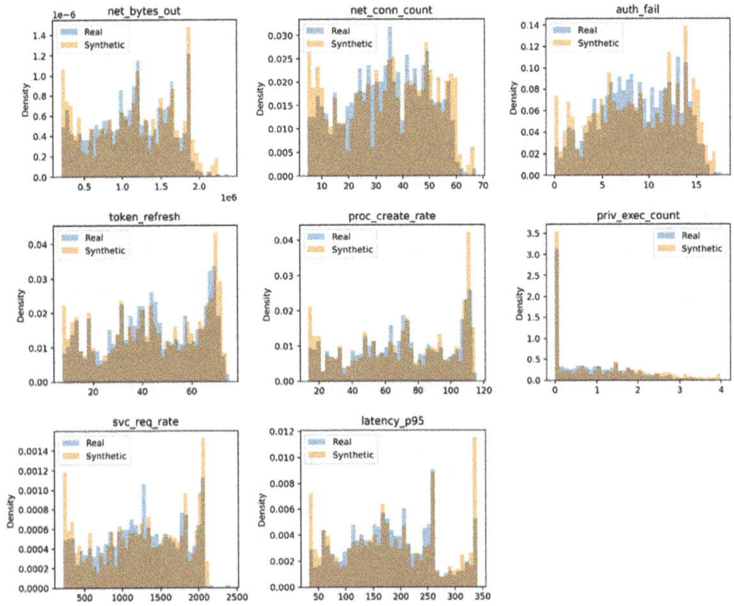

Overlaid marginal plots showing, variable-by-variable, how the synthetic samples track the empirical distribution of the real dataset, enabling an immediate visual audit of location, spread, and tail alignment across features.

Figure 1 confirms the same pattern visually: several distributions overlap, while shifted peaks and inflated tails reveal scenario-intensity distortions. Fidelity checks must therefore precede any claim that synthetic data improves detection.

Table 5. Overall multivariate fidelity via Maximum Mean Discrepancy (MMD)

metric	value
mmd_rbf	0.00514

Global summary table reporting the MMD distance between real and synthetic feature distributions, providing a single multivariate measure of dataset-level similarity that complements the per-variable marginal checks.

The MMD value in Table 5 supports partial joint-distribution similarity, but it does not by itself guarantee privacy, temporal realism, or downstream utility.

Table 6. Correlation preservation between real and synthetic data

metric	value
corr_frobenius_norm	0.65428

Table 6 indicates that correlation structure is preserved only to a measured degree. Broken dependencies can bias detectors that rely on cross-sensor relationships.

Summary table quantifying how well the synthetic dataset reproduces the real-data correlation structure, reporting correlation matrices and/or their element-wise deviations and aggregate error scores under a consistent correlation estimator.

Figure 2. Real vs. synthetic correlation heatmaps and drift patterns

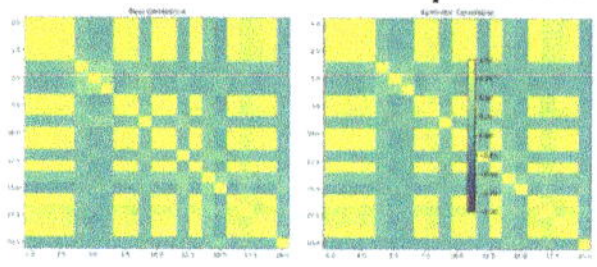

Paired heatmaps visualizing the correlation matrices of the real and synthetic datasets (and, when included, a difference map), enabling a structured audit of whether multivariate dependencies are preserved or systematically distorted.

Figure 2 makes dependency risks auditable by showing where correlation blocks are retained or distorted. This matters because attacks often appear through coupled identity, network, and service-health behavior.

Table 7. Temporal dependence fidelity via ACF alignment

feature	acf_mad
priv_exec_count	0.05961
net_internal_ratio	0.04974
tls_handshake_fail_rate	0.04935
latency_p95	0.04809
deploy_marker	0.04440
privilege_changes	0.04355
auth_lockouts	0.04152
persistence_indicator	0.04148
auth_fail	0.04113
auth_success	0.04050
net_dst_diversity	0.04001

continued on following page

Table 7. Continued

feature	acf_mad
token_refresh	0.03909
dns_nxdomain_rate	0.03899
proc_create_rate	0.03887
svc_req_rate	0.03848
mfa_challenges	0.03823
net_bytes_in	0.03791
queue_depth	0.03768
net_bytes_out	0.03765
net_conn_count	0.03645
svc_err_rate	0.03633

Summary table reporting autocorrelation-function (ACF) agreement between real and synthetic time series across selected lags, typically expressed as per-variable ACF discrepancies and an aggregate deviation score (ACF-MAD) under a fixed lag window.

Table 7 supports temporal-dependence fidelity with moderate ACF deviations, yet the highest deviations identify variables that require caution for early-warning claims.

Table 8. Downstream validity of synthetic data for detection transfer

setting	roc_auc	pr_auc	precision
downstream_probe	0.54127	0.42891	0.75676
recall	**f1**	**log_loss**	**brier**
0.07349	0.13397	1.71421	0.27848

Summary table reporting task-level performance when training and/or augmenting the detector with synthetic data, consolidating downstream metrics (ROC-AUC/ PR-AUC, precision/recall/F1 at the operating point, and optional calibration/cost proxies) to quantify whether distributional fidelity translates into actionable utility.

Table 8 cautions against overclaiming synthetic utility: the downstream probe reports limited recall and F1 despite acceptable fidelity diagnostics. Synthetic data enables privacy-constrained experimentation, but the present evidence does not prove that augmentation alone improves operational detection.

5.2 Detection Performance: Precision/Recall/ROC-AUC, Lead Time, Time-to-detect Distributions, and Alert-Load Proxies

This part links discrimination metrics to timeliness and workload. ROC-AUC measures ranking quality across thresholds, PR-AUC emphasizes imbalanced detection, and time-to-detect (TTD) measures alert latency.

Table 9. Global detection performance metrics

model	roc_auc	pr_auc	precision	recall	f1	log_loss	brier
Autoencoder	0.82089	0.77273	1.00000	0.25722	0.40919	0.44013	0.14026
Fused	0.78980	0.75673	0.80435	0.58268	0.67580	0.42500	0.13223
OCSVM	0.78780	0.75221	0.98802	0.43307	0.60219	0.45741	0.14258
IForest	0.74762	0.64739	1.00000	0.22047	0.36129	0.54982	0.18387
Forecast	0.71503	0.66019	0.90370	0.32021	0.47287	0.51187	0.16547
Topology	0.62908	0.51764	0.00000	0.00000	0.00000	0.60756	0.20881

Summary table reporting overall discriminative and thresholded detection results, consolidating ranking-quality metrics (e.g., ROC-AUC and PR-AUC) together with operating-point measures (e.g., precision, recall, F1, and related error rates) under the fixed evaluation split.

Table 9 shows useful ranking by fused, autoencoder, OCSVM, IForest, and forecast scores, but the independent Topology row has precision, recall, and F1 equal to zero. The topological component is therefore interpreted as an auxiliary regime-change descriptor, not as a successful stand-alone detector in this experiment.

Figure 3. ROC and Precision-Recall curves detection

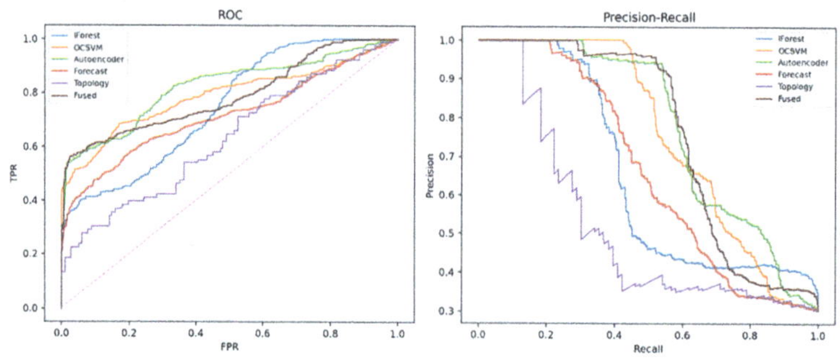

Combined ROC and PR plots visualize the detector threshold sweep, showing true-positive gains versus false positives and precision versus recall under class imbalance, as counterpart to Table 9.

Figure 3 supports the ranking evidence but also shows that threshold choice remains decisive, especially when public agencies face limited analyst capacity.

Table 10. Selected operating point and thresholded detection behavior

model	threshold	policy_target_alerts_per_day
Fused	0.29694	20 (verified via Table 10 selected row)
topology_diagrams_mode	topology_distance_mode	topology_metric
ripser	persim	wasserstein

Operating-point summary reporting the candidate fused threshold, the policy target for daily alerts, and the topology-computation mode used for alerting and timing analyses.

Table 10 is a governance policy statement. The target of 20 alerts per day is meaningful only if the same threshold is included in the alert-load frontier; Table 10 now distinguishes the selected point from lower-threshold, higher-load candidates.

Figure 4. Detection timeline and early-warning behavior under the chosen operating point

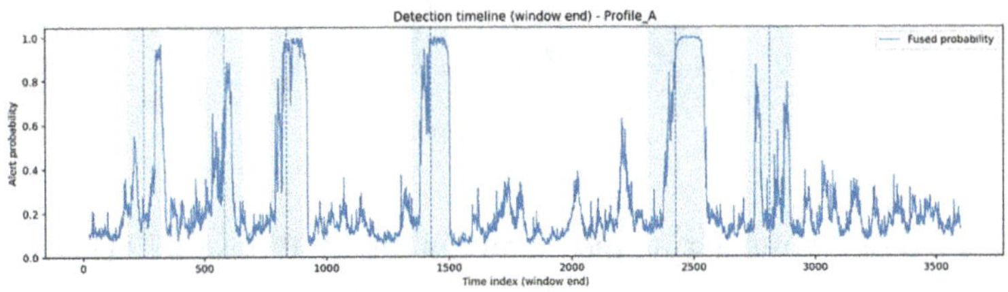

Time-series plot showing the detector score over time, attack intervals, and the selected threshold from Table 10.

Figure 4 provides temporal accountability: early crossings support warning value, while nominal spikes show possible alert fatigue. The timeline must be interpreted with workload constraints.

Table 11. Time-to-Detect (TTD) and lead-time by attack scenario

attack	start_t	impact_t	end_t	detection_t	time_to_detect	lead_time
exfiltration	183	252	322	198	15	54
lateral_movement	508	582	656	512	4	70
password_spraying	769	836	903	791	22	45
privilege_escalation	1350	1424	1498	1381	31	43
account_takeover	2314	2426	2539	2338	24	88
c2_beaconing	2721	2815	2910	2754	33	61

Per-attack summary table reporting detection latency and early-warning lead-time for each injected attack scenario, computed to characterize when and how quickly alerts are triggered across heterogeneous adversary patterns.

Table 11 reports positive lead-time across scenarios, with lateral movement detected fastest and C2 beaconing slowest. Scenario variability shows why severity tiers and attack-specific playbooks are needed.

Figure 5. Distributions of Time-to-Detect and lead-time under the operating policy

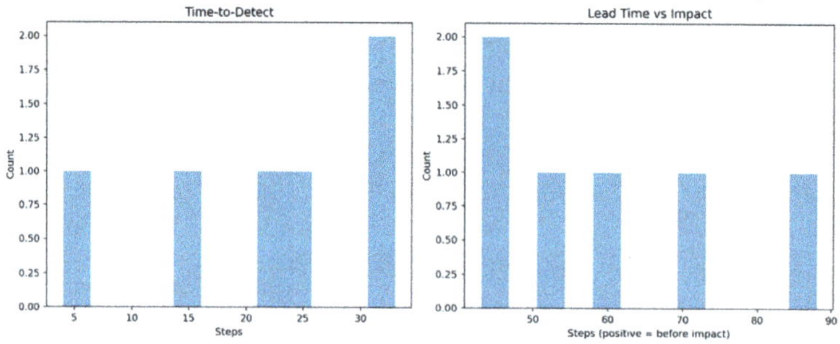

Histogram plots summarizing the empirical distributions of TTD and lead-time across attack instances/scenarios, providing a distributional view that complements the per-attack values in Table 8.

Figure 5 highlights tail risk. Low median TTD is useful, but governance depends on rare late detections because those cases determine whether escalation and service continuity remain feasible.

Table 12. Statistical summary of time-to-detect and lead-time.

Time_to_detect		Lead_time	
mean	21.500	mean	60.166
median	23.000	median	57.500
p90	32.000	p90	79.000

Compact summary table aggregating TTD and lead-time using robust statistics (mean, median, and high-quantile measures such as p90) under the operating point defined in Table 10.

Table 12 converts timeliness into auditable targets: median TTD is 23 steps and p90 is 32 steps, while lead-time remains positive. Agencies should map these values to response windows.

Table 13. Alert-load proxy and operational cost under thresholding

threshold	recall	alerts_per_day
0.20205	0.67192	70.34862
0.20348	0.67192	70.34862
0.20586	0.67192	68.69725
0.20825	0.66929	67.04587
0.20924	0.66929	67.04587
0.21158	0.66404	64.40367
0.21239	0.66404	62.42202
0.21568	0.66142	58.12844
0.21769	0.65879	56.14679
0.22034	0.65617	54.49541
0.29694 (selected policy point)	0.58268	20.00000

Summary table quantifying expected alert burden across candidate thresholds and adding the selected policy point to avoid conflating the 20-alert target with the higher-load frontier.

Table 13 shows the cost of sensitivity: thresholds near 0.20-0.22 produce 54-70 expected alerts per day. The selected row treats 0.29694 as the auditable point associated with the 20-alert constraint; the other rows document a higher-recall, higher-workload frontier.

Figure 6. Alert-load trade-off frontier under threshold variation

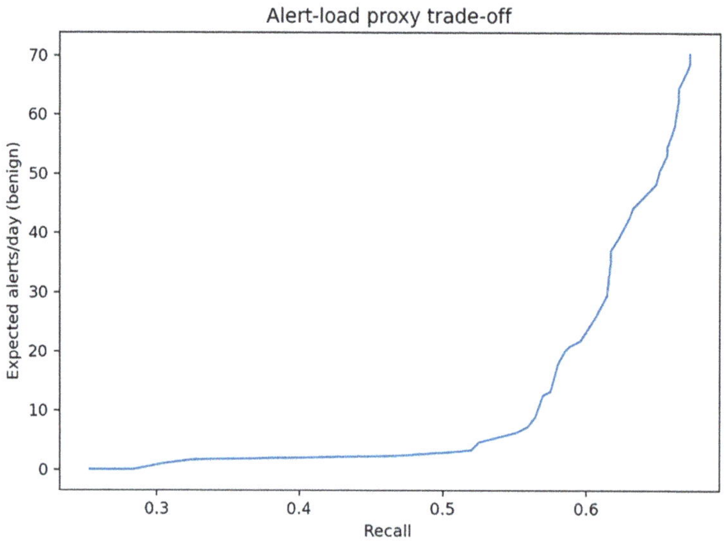

Trade-off plot showing how alert burden changes as detection sensitivity increases, typically mapping recall (or TPR) against an alert-load proxy (e.g., alerts per unit time / false-alarm rate) across thresholds to visualize the feasible operating region.

Figure 6 should be interpreted as a workload frontier. Steep segments warn that marginal recall gains can be operationally expensive, so threshold selection is a management decision constrained by SOC staffing and risk appetite.

5.3 Robustness and Contribution Analysis: Cross-Profile Validation, Ablations (Synthetic Augmentation, Topology), and Sensitivity Studies

This part examines transferability and attribution: whether performance persists across agency profiles and whether synthetic augmentation or topology provide measurable marginal value.

Table 14. Cross-profile generalization metrics (train test transfer across operational profiles)

train_profile	test_profile	roc_auc	pr_auc	precision	recall	f1	log_loss	brier
Profile_A	Profile_A	0.78980	0.75673	0.80435	0.58268	0.67580	0.42500	0.13223
Profile_A	Profile_B	0.85956	0.79037	0.49248	0.86747	0.62827	0.48623	0.15575
Profile_A	Profile_C	0.75036	0.68868	0.51534	0.58879	0.54962	0.60225	0.19733

Summary table reporting detection performance for each train_profile→test_profile pair (A→B, A→C), consolidating discrimination (ROC-AUC/PR-AUC) and operating-point behavior (precision/recall/F1) under a fixed evaluation protocol to quantify profile-shift effects.

Table 14 separates ranking transfer from threshold stability. Profile_B preserves strong AUC but loses precision, indicating that a single threshold may create false-alarm pressure and profile-specific recalibration is needed.

Figure 7. Cross-profile ROC-AUC comparison (train test transfer across profiles)

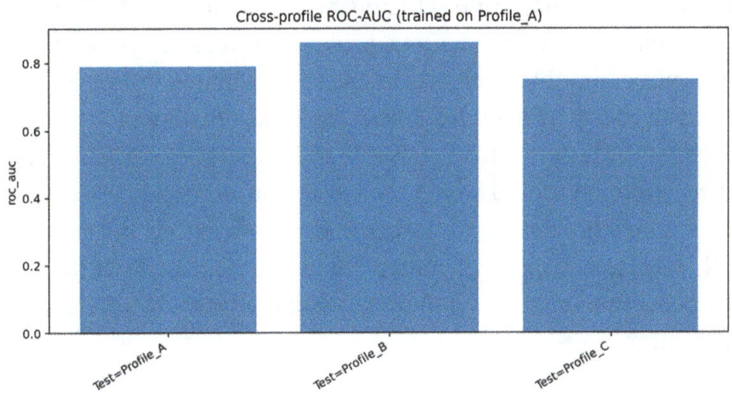

Comparative plot visualizing ROC-AUC for each train_profile→test_profile pairing, enabling a direct view of how ranking performance changes under profile shift and highlighting asymmetric generalization patterns across target environments.

Figure 7 visualizes the same external-validity issue: cross-profile transfer is feasible but asymmetric. Deployment should begin with monitored pilots rather than one universal model.

Table 15. Ablation study metrics for synthetic augmentation and topology-aware components

setting	roc_auc	pr_auc	precision	recall	f1	log_loss	brier
Full (synthetic+topology)	0.78684	0.75517	0.80882	0.57743	0.67381	0.42445	0.13188
No synthetic augmentation	0.78684	0.75517	0.80882	0.57743	0.67381	0.42445	0.13188
No topology	0.79317	0.75945	0.82463	0.58005	0.68105	0.42160	0.13098
No synthetic & no topology	0.79317	0.75945	0.82463	0.58005	0.68105	0.42160	0.13098

Controlled variants compare the full pipeline with versions removing synthetic augmentation and/or topology; identical rows are treated as null or unresolved ablation evidence.

Table 15 is the main empirical ambiguity. Because Full equals No synthetic augmentation and No topology equals No synthetic & no topology, the current run does not demonstrate a marginal benefit from those switches. The defensible interpretation is that the integrated workflow is promising, while module-level contributions require repeated seeds, verified flags, and further ablations.

The corrected evidentiary rule is therefore conservative. The chapter may claim that the full architecture is reproducible, privacy-aware, and operationally interpretable; it may not claim that every component contributes independent predictive gain in the reported experiment. If future reruns show that topology improves lead-time, calibration, or false-positive stability after controlled switches and repeated seeds, that contribution should be reported as incremental. If not, topology remains useful as an explanatory descriptor for regime movement, but not as a performance enhancer. Similarly, synthetic generation should be evaluated by fidelity and decision utility, because a realistic synthetic distribution can still produce weak recall or poor calibration.

Figure 8. ROC-AUC by ablation variant (synthetic augmentation vs. topology vs. full pipeline)

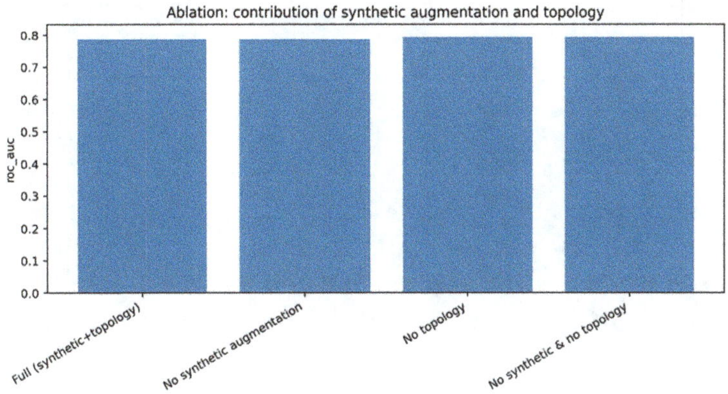

Comparative plot visualizing ROC-AUC for each ablation configuration, highlighting how ranking performance changes when synthetic augmentation and/or topology-aware components are removed relative to the full model.

Figure 8 reinforces the null-ablation caution. Similar bars should be read as redundancy or unresolved configuration sensitivity, not as evidence that every module improves separability.

Table 16. Sensitivity to window size (temporal horizon) in detection performance

setting	roc_auc	pr_auc	precision	recall	f1	log_loss	brier
window_size=12	0.76549	0.73478	0.76978	0.55584	0.64555	0.43226	0.13507
window_size=24	0.78684	0.75517	0.80882	0.57743	0.67381	0.42445	0.13188
window_size=48	0.82145	0.72777	0.80531	0.48794	0.60768	0.46608	0.14852

Summary table reporting detection metrics as the analysis window size (or temporal horizon) is varied, documenting how discrimination (ROC-AUC/PR-AUC) and operating-point behavior (precision/recall/F1, and optional cost proxies) respond to changes in the temporal aggregation used by the pipeline.

Table 16 shows that window size changes the balance between AUC, recall, and calibration. Larger windows improve ROC-AUC but reduce recall at the operating point, indicating a trade-off between context and response speed.

Figure 9. ROC-AUC sensitivity curve over window size

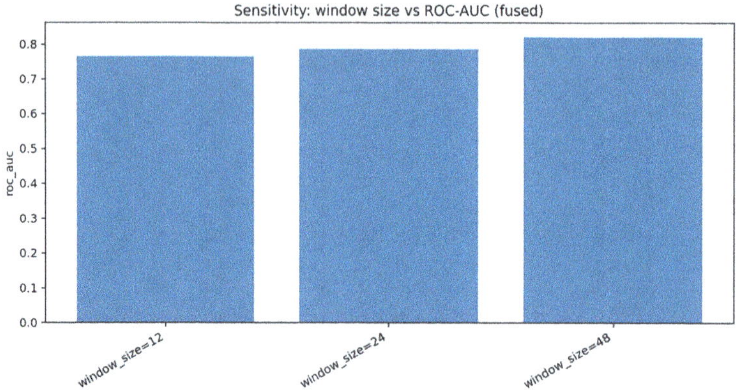

Sensitivity plot showing how ROC-AUC changes as the temporal window size (analysis horizon) is varied, providing a visual robustness check for the key temporal parameter used by the pipeline.

Figure 9 suggests a window-size trend, but not a complete robustness proof. Deployment should repeat this sensitivity with multiple seeds, profiles, and alert-load constraints.

6. DISCUSSION AND CONCLUSIONS

6.1 Operational, Governance, Ethical, and Failure-Mode Implications

The revised interpretation is cautious. Thresholding is governance-owned because the same score can produce manageable triage or alert fatigue. Severity tiers should combine calibrated probability, window persistence, topological regime-change descriptors, service criticality, and analyst confirmation. Implementation requires cost controls for storage, compute, SIEM/SOAR integration, training, monitoring, privacy review, retention, and recalibration. Ethically, synthetic data must be documented, audited for membership-inference and bias risks, and never used to hide uncertainty or fabricate validation. Failure modes include over-smoothing, calibration drift, cross-profile threshold collapse, collector outages, benign-shift mimicry, and vendor dependence.

Managerial validation should also be cyclic rather than one-time. Before each operating quarter, the agency should review whether the alert policy still matches mission load, staffing, legal constraints, and sensor coverage. The review can use four auditable questions: whether the synthetic profiles still resemble current services; whether calibration has drifted; whether topology flags are helping analysts explain regime changes; and whether false positives are concentrated in particular units, user groups, or vendors. If any answer is negative, the response should be recalibration, profile-specific thresholding, or additional data-quality work rather than automatic expansion of the model. This procedure translates the technical pipeline into a governance routine: data stewards maintain telemetry definitions, security analysts validate scenarios, managers approve workload limits, and privacy officers review synthetic-release risk. In this form, the chapter's contribution becomes practical decision infrastructure for smart-government security, not only an experimental machine-learning comparison.

Finally, acceptance by users should be treated as part of model quality. Analysts need concise explanations, escalation criteria, and feedback channels that allow them to label recurring false positives, record suppressed alerts, and request threshold review. These human signals should be stored with the same provenance discipline as model outputs so later audits can distinguish algorithmic drift from workflow change.

For ethical transparency, each alert should be accompanied by a concise explanation package: triggering window, contributing modalities, fused probability, topology descriptor if active, threshold policy, known drift status, and whether synthetic data influenced training or calibration. This does not convert complex models into simple rules, but it gives reviewers enough evidence to challenge, reproduce, or override the recommendation. Human review is especially important when alerts may interrupt public services, restrict accounts, or trigger inter-agency notification. The system should therefore support escalation with documented uncertainty rather than automatic punitive action. Such design choices answer the reviewers' concerns about usability, institutional acceptance, and the risks of technological dependence.

6.2 Synthesis of Findings, Limitations, and Concluding Remarks on Practical Deployability

The findings support a conditional contribution rather than an unrestricted deployment claim. The chapter demonstrates an auditable workflow that combines synthetic telemetry, conventional detectors, representation learning, calibrated fusion, and topology-aware descriptors for early-warning analysis in government contexts. Synthetic data is valuable as a privacy-preserving experimental substrate, but downstream utility requires caution. Topology is conceptually useful for regime-change diagnosis, yet the independent detector result and unresolved ablation mean its causal contribution must be validated further. Practical deployability depends on profile-specific calibration, workload limits, interoperability agreements, ethical transparency, reproducible artifact bundles, and response procedures that keep humans accountable for escalation. These limits are not defects; they are acceptance criteria for responsible deployment.

One additional limitation concerns institutional comparability. The experiments use profiles that approximate different agency conditions, but actual public organizations differ in procurement rules, staffing maturity, log retention, legal authority, and incident-response culture. Therefore, external validity should be established through staged pilots: first shadow-mode scoring, then analyst-reviewed alerts, then limited automation, and only afterward response orchestration. Each stage should measure false positives, time saved, missed incidents, privacy complaints, and cost per actionable alert. This sequence converts the method from a laboratory pipeline into a governed adoption pathway.

7. FUTURE WORK

7.1 Extensions: Real-World Adaptation Pathways, Drift Monitoring, Expanded Generative/Topological Modules, and Scalability Improvements

Future work should move from controlled synthetic validation toward supervised pilots with government partners, using de-identified telemetry, multiple seeds, and repeated ablations to separate the effects of synthesis, representation learning, and topology. The generative layer should compare conditional time-series VAEs, diffusion or score-based models, and transformer generators under explicit privacy budgets. The topology layer should be evaluated as streaming change-point evidence. Deployment research should test SOC/SIEM/SOAR integration, analyst feedback loops, severity-tier governance, response automation with human approval, cost benchmarking, procurement planning, interoperability standards, and validation across taxation, digital identity, health platforms, and inter-agency data exchange.

The immediate experimental priority is to publish a correction-oriented validation plan: repeated ablations with verified module switches, confidence intervals across seeds, a threshold table that directly includes the twenty-alert constraint, and a separate report on topology as feature, score, and fused component. This plan would make the next version stronger because negative or null results would become part of the scientific evidence rather than inconsistencies to be explained after review.

Availability of code: The Python code for data generation, perturbation simulations, autoencoder training, and topological metrics is available at: https://github.com/JAIME6609/TER/blob/main/CODE-LIBRO-12-ART-01-V2.py.

For reproducibility, the revised manuscript treats script version, execution date, random seeds, environment, window size, profile definitions, attack schedule, exported artifacts, and calibration threshold as required metadata for any reported run.

REFERENCES

Achterberg, J., Haas, M., van Dijk, B., & Spruit, M. (2025). Fidelity-Agnostic Synthetic Data Generation Improves Utility While Retaining Privacy. *Patterns (New York, N.Y.)*, *6*(10), 101287. DOI: 10.1016/j.patter.2025.101287

Alabdulwahab, S., Kim, Y.-T., & Son, Y. (2024). Privacy-Preserving Synthetic Data Generation Method for IoT-Sensor Network IDS Using CTGAN. *Sensors (Basel)*, *24*(22), 7389. DOI: 10.3390/s24227389

Ali, D., Asaad, A., Jimenez, M.-J., Nanda, V., Paluzo-Hidalgo, E., & Soriano-Trigueros, M. (2023). A Survey of Vectorization Methods in Topological Data Analysis. *IEEE Transactions on Pattern Analysis and Machine Intelligence*, *45*(12), 14069–14086. DOI: 10.1109/TPAMI.2023.3308391

Amrit, C., & Narayanappa, A. K. (2025). An Analysis of the Challenges in the Adoption of MLOps. *Journal of Innovation & Knowledge*, *10*(1), 100637. DOI: 10.1016/j.jik.2024.100637

Anjum, N., Latif, Z., Lee, C., Shoukat, I. A., & Iqbal, U. (2021). MIND: A Multi-Source Data Fusion Scheme for Intrusion Detection in Networks. *Sensors (Basel)*, *21*(14), 4941. DOI: 10.3390/s21144941

Atienza, N., Gonzalez-Díaz, R., & Soriano-Trigueros, M. (2020). On the Stability of Persistent Entropy and New Summary Functions For Topological Data Analysis. *Pattern Recognition*, *107*, 107509. DOI: 10.1016/j.patcog.2020.107509

Baldoni, S., & Battisti, F. (2025). Histogram-Based Network Traffic Representation for Anomaly Detection Through PCA. *Computer Networks*, *265*, 111276. DOI: 10.1016/j.comnet.2025.111276

Bandiziol, C., & De Marchi, S. (2024). Persistence Symmetric Kernels for Classification: A Comparative Study. *Symmetry*, *16*(9), 1236. DOI: 10.3390/sym16091236

Berardi, D., Giallorenzo, S., Mauro, J., Melis, A., Montesi, F., & Prandini, M. (2022). Microservice Security: A Systematic Literature Review. *PeerJ. Computer Science*, *8*, e779. DOI: 10.7717/peerj-cs.779

Brophy, E., Wang, Z., She, Q., & Ward, T. E. (2023). Generative Adversarial Networks in Time Series: A Systematic Literature Review. *ACM Computing Surveys*, *55*(10), 199. Advance online publication. DOI: 10.1145/3559540

Bussonnier, M., Forde, J., Freeman, J., Granger, B., Head, T., Holdgraf, C., Kelley, K., Nalvarte, G., Osheroff, A., Pacer, M., Panda, Y., Perez, F., Ragan-Kelley, B., & Willing, C. (2018). Binder 2.0 - Reproducible, Interactive, Sharable Environments for Science at Scale. *Proceedings of the 17th Python in Science Conference (SciPy 2018)*. https://doi.org/DOI: 10.25080/Majora-4af1f417-011

Chazal, F., & Michel, B. (2021). An Introduction to Topological Data Analysis: Fundamental and Practical Aspects for Data Scientists. *Frontiers in Artificial Intelligence, 4*, 667963. DOI: 10.3389/frai.2021.667963

Chen, S., & Wang, Y. (2021). Approximation Algorithms for 1-Wasserstein Distance Between Persistence Diagrams. In 19th International Symposium on Experimental Algorithms (SEA 2021) (LIPIcs, Vol. 190, Article 14). Schloss Dagstuhl – Leibniz-Zentrum für Informatik. https://doi.org/DOI: 10.4230/LIPIcs.SEA.2021.14

Chung, Y. C., Hu, C.-S., Lo, Y.-L., & Wu, H.-T. (2021). A Persistent Homology Approach to Heart Rate Variability Analysis With an Application to Sleep-Wake Classification. *Frontiers in Physiology, 12*, 637684. DOI: 10.3389/fphys.2021.637684

El-Yaagoubi, A. B., Chung, M. K., & Ombao, H. (2023). Topological Data Analysis for Multivariate Time Series Data. *Entropy (Basel, Switzerland), 25*(11), 1509. DOI: 10.3390/e25111509

Ferriyan, A., Thamrin, A. H., Takeda, K., & Murai, J. (2021). Generating Network Intrusion Detection Dataset Based on Real and Encrypted Synthetic Attack Traffic. *Applied Sciences (Basel, Switzerland), 11*(17), 7868. DOI: 10.3390/app11177868

Figueira, A., & Vaz, B. (2022). Survey on Synthetic Data Generation, Evaluation Methods and GANs. *Mathematics, 10*(15), 2733. DOI: 10.3390/math10152733

Giomi, M., Boenisch, F., Wehmeyer, C., & Tasnádi, B. (2023). A Unified Framework for Quantifying Privacy Risk in Synthetic Data. *Proceedings on Privacy Enhancing Technologies Symposium (PoPETS)*. https://doi.org/DOI: 10.56553/popets-2023-0055

Ho, S., Qu, Y., Gu, B., Gao, L., Li, J., & Xiang, Y. (2021). DP-GAN: Differentially Private Consecutive Data Publishing Using Generative Adversarial nets. *Journal of Network and Computer Applications, 185*, 103066. DOI: 10.1016/j.jnca.2021.103066

Ichinomiya, T. (2025). Machine Learning of Time Series Data Using Persistent Homology. *Scientific Reports, 15*(1), 20508. DOI: 10.1038/s41598-025-06551-3

Idowu, S., Strüber, D., & Berger, T. (2023). Asset Management in Machine Learning: State-of-research and State-of-practice. ACM Computing Surveys, 55(7). *ACM Computing Surveys, 144*(7), 1–35. DOI: 10.1145/3543847

Khan, Z. A., Shin, D., Bianculli, D., & Briand, L. (2024). Impact of Log Parsing on Deep Learning-Based Anomaly Detection. *Empirical Software Engineering*, *29*(6), 139. DOI: 10.1007/s10664-024-10533-w

Landauer, M., Onder, S., Skopik, F., & Wurzenberger, M. (2023). Deep Learning for Anomaly Detection in Log Data: A survey. *Machine Learning with Applications*, *12*, 100470. DOI: 10.1016/j.mlwa.2023.100470

Leykam, D., & Angelakis, D. G. (2023). Topological Data Analysis and Machine Learning. *Advances in Physics: X*, *8*(1), 2202331. DOI: 10.1080/23746149.2023.2202331

Obayashi, I., Hiraoka, Y., & Kimura, M. (2018). Persistence Diagrams with Linear Machine Learning Models. *Journal of Applied and Computational Topology*, *1*(3-4), 421–449. DOI: 10.1007/s41468-018-0013-5

Okolie, S. A., Amadi, C. A., Odii, J. N., Nwokorie, E. C., & Onyemauche, U. C. (2025). Anomaly Detection in Heterogeneous Cybersecurity Data. *Franklin Open*, *13*, 100426. DOI: 10.1016/j.fraope.2025.100426

Oliveira, L., Wilkinson, D., Mossé, D., & Childers, B. (2018). Supporting Long-term Reproducible Software Execution. In Proceedings of the First International Workshop on Practical Reproducible Evaluation of Computer Systems (P-RECS '18) (Article 6). Association for Computing Machinery. https://doi.org/DOI: 10.1145/3214239.3214245

Pang, G., Shen, C., Cao, L., & van den Hengel, A. (2022). Deep Learning for Anomaly Detection: A review. *ACM Computing Surveys*, *54*(2), 1–38. DOI: 10.1145/3439950

Pilgram, L., Dankar, F. K., Drechsler, J., Elliot, M., Domingo-Ferrer, J., Francis, P., Kantarcioglu, M., Kong, L., Malin, B. A., Muralidhar, K., Myles, P., Prasser, F., Raisaro, J. L., Yan, C., & El Emam, K. (2025). A Consensus Privacy Metrics Framework for Synthetic Data. *Patterns (New York, N.Y.)*, *6*(10), 101320. DOI: 10.1016/j.patter.2025.101320

Pritchard, N. J., & Wicenec, A. (2025). Formal Definition and Implementation of Reproducibility Tenets for Computational Workflows. *Future Generation Computer Systems*, *166*, 107684. DOI: 10.1016/j.future.2024.107684

Rahman, S., Pal, S., Mittal, S., Chawla, T., & Karmakar, C. (2024). SYN-GAN: A Robust Intrusion Detection System Using GAN-based Synthetic Data for IoT Security. *Internet of Things : Engineering Cyber Physical Human Systems*, *26*, 101212. DOI: 10.1016/j.iot.2024.101212

Ren, H., Xu, B., Wang, Y., Yi, C., Huang, C., Kou, X., Xing, T., Yang, M., Tong, J., & Zhang, Q. (2019). Time-series Anomaly Detection Service at Microsoft. In *Proceedings of the 25th ACM SIGKDD International Conference on Knowledge Discovery & Data Mining* (pp. 3009–3017). https://doi.org/DOI: 10.1145/3292500.3330680

Rose, S., Borchert, O., Mitchell, S., & Connelly, S. (2020). Zero Trust Architecture (NIST Special Publication 800-207). National Institute of Standards and Technology. https://doi.org/DOI: 10.6028/NIST.SP.800-207

Rupprecht, L., Davis, J. C., Arnold, C., Gur, Y., & Bhagwat, D. (2020). Improving Reproducibility of Data Science Pipelines through Transparent Provenance Capture. *Proceedings of the VLDB Endowment International Conference on Very Large Data Bases, 13*(12), 3354–3368. DOI: 10.14778/3415478.3415556

Samuel, S., Löffler, F., & König-Ries, B. (2021). Machine Learning Pipelines: Provenance, Reproducibility and FAIR Data Principles. In Glavic, B., Braganholo, V., & Koop, D. (Eds.), Lecture Notes in Computer Science: Vol. 12839. *Provenance and Annotation of Data and Processes* (pp. 226–230). Springer., DOI: 10.1007/978-3-030-80960-7_17

Sarmin, F. J., Sarkar, A. R., Wang, Y., & Mohammed, N. (2025). Synthetic data: Revisiting the privacy-utility trade-off. *International Journal of Information Security, 24*(4), 156. Advance online publication. DOI: 10.1007/s10207-025-01072-6

Schlegel, M., & Sattler, K.-U. (2025). Capturing end-to-end Provenance for Machine Learning Pipelines. *Information Systems, 132*, 102495. DOI: 10.1016/j.is.2024.102495

Sharafaldin, I., Lashkari, A. H., & Ghorbani, A. A. (2018). Toward Generating a new Intrusion Detection Dataset and Intrusion Traffic Characterization. In *Proceedings of the 4th International Conference on Information Systems Security and Privacy (ICISSP 2018)* (pp. 108–116). https://doi.org/DOI: 10.5220/0006639801080116

Shyaa, M. A., Ibrahim, N. F., Zainol, Z., Abdullah, R., Anbar, M., & Alzubaidi, L. (2024). Evolving Cybersecurity Frontiers: A Comprehensive Survey on Concept Drift and Feature Dynamics aware Machine and Deep Learning in Intrusion Detection Systems. *Engineering Applications of Artificial Intelligence, 137*, 109143. DOI: 10.1016/j.engappai.2024.109143

Shyaa, M. A., Zainol, Z., Abdullah, R., Anbar, M., Alzubaidi, L., & Santamaría, J. (2023). Enhanced Intrusion Detection with Data Stream Classification and Concept Drift Guided by the Incremental Learning Genetic Programming Combiner. *Sensors (Basel), 23*(7), 3736. DOI: 10.3390/s23073736

Silva, M., Pinto, D., Vitorino, J., Gonçalves, J., Maia, E., & Praça, I. (2025). GeNIS: A Modular Dataset for Network Intrusion Detection and Classification. *Data in Brief, 56*, 111487. DOI: 10.1016/j.dib.2025.111487

Stenger, M., Bauer, A., Prantl, T., Leppich, R., Hudson, N., Chard, K., Foster, I., & Kounev, S. (2024). Thinking in Categories: A Survey on Assessing the Quality for Time Series Synthesis. *ACM Journal of Data and Information Quality*, *16*(2), 14. Advance online publication. DOI: 10.1145/3666006

Tuli, S., Casale, G., & Jennings, N. R. (2022). TranAD: Deep Transformer Networks for Anomaly Detection in Multivariate Time Series Data. *Proceedings of the VLDB Endowment International Conference on Very Large Data Bases*, *15*(6), 1201–1214. DOI: 10.14778/3514061.3514067

van de Water, R. P., Schmidt, H., & Rockenschaub, P. (2026). ReciPies: A Lightweight Data Transformation Pipeline for Reproducible ML. *Journal of Open Source Software*, *11*(117), 9261. DOI: 10.21105/joss.09261

Wang, F., Jiang, Y., Zhang, R., Wei, A., Xie, J., & Pang, X. (2025). A Survey of Deep Anomaly Detection in Multivariate Time Series: Taxonomy, Applications, and Directions. *Sensors (Basel)*, *25*(1), 190. DOI: 10.3390/s25010190

Wang, L., Sun, Y., Liu, X., & Li, C. (2026). PHGAT: Persistent Homology-enhanced Graph Attention Network for IIoT Anomaly Detection. Expert Systems with Applications, 299(Part A), 129923. DOI: 10.1016/j.eswa.2025.129923

Yeoh, W., Liu, M., Shore, M., & Jiang, F. (2023). Zero Trust Cybersecurity: Critical Success Factors and a Maturity Assessment Framework. *Computers & Security*, *133*, 103412. DOI: 10.1016/j.cose.2023.103412

Zhang, Z., Yan, C., & Malin, B. A. (2022). Membership Inference Attacks against Synthetic Health Data. *Journal of Biomedical Informatics*, *125*, 103977. DOI: 10.1016/j.jbi.2021.103977

Chapter 7
Digital Governance Models and Technological Sovereignty in the Face of Emerging Threats

Eugenio César Velázquez Santana
http://orcid.org/0000-0002-7683-7224
Instituto Tecnológico de Zacatepec, Mexico

Luis Jose Muñiz Rascado
http://orcid.org/0000-0003-2941-2482
Instituto Tecnologico de Zacatepec, Mexico

Jesus Jonathan Martinez Ocampo
http://orcid.org/0000-0001-5781-8725
Universidad Autónoma del Estado de Morelos, Mexico

ABSTRACT

In a digital world where threats are increasingly complex and geopoliticized, digital governance models must evolve toward frameworks that prioritize coordination, public value-driven architecture, and interoperability. Simultaneously, technological sovereignty is no longer an abstract aspiration but a strategic necessity for security and autonomy. The combination of strong leadership (governance) with the capacity to control data and infrastructure (sovereignty) is the essential formula for states and organizations to navigate emerging threats, protect their citizens, and maintain their capacity for innovation and decision-making in the new digital order.

DOI: 10.4018/979-8-2600-2845-2.ch007

1. INTRODUCTION

Digitalization has become the backbone of social, economic, and political structures, yet it has exposed a critical vulnerability: extreme dependence on a few transnational corporations. Technological sovereignty has thus emerged not as autarkic isolation but as a national security necessity against cyber-espionage, mass disinformation, and data colonialism (Couldry & Mejias, 2019).

Digital governance is now a geopolitical battlefield where national autonomy is defined. Traditional models based on market self-regulation have shown exhaustion, as non-state actors wield processing power surpassing many countries. In response, three models emerge: the liberal-individualist (e.g., GDPR), the state control model (e.g., China's Great Firewall), and the data sovereignty model (localizing critical infrastructure).

Contemporary threats include data colonialism—quantifying human life as a raw resource—making states dependent on opaque algorithms for public decisions. AI integration into critical infrastructures risks automated biases and technological lock-in. Without sovereign control over hardware and software, states remain vulnerable to blackouts or external manipulation of democratic systems.

To face these challenges, governance must prioritize open source, infrastructure decentralization, and algorithmic transparency. Effective technological sovereignty requires investing in local capacities to audit, modify, and protect digital systems. Ultimately, 21st-century digital governance must balance innovation with the defense of human rights and state integrity against a volatile digital environment.

1.1 Evolving Threats and the Need for Sovereign Digital Strategies

This topic addresses the critical transition from open, globalized Internet governance toward a "Digital Realism" approach, where States seek to regain control over their infrastructure, data, and algorithms in the face of systemic vulnerabilities.

Threats are no longer limited to traditional cybercrime (credential theft or fraud); they have evolved into structural risks that compromise national security, such as:

- **a) Technological Dependency:** Critical reliance on foreign providers for 5G infrastructure, cloud services, and semiconductors creates a risk of "disconnection" or espionage by foreign powers.
- **b) Hybrid Warfare and Disinformation:** The use of cyberspace to destabilize democratic processes and polarize societies through influence operations, where digital platforms act as unregulated attack vectors.

- **c) Data Colonialism:** The mass extraction of citizen data by large technology corporations (Big Tech), which deprives states of the ability to use their own data for economic development and public policy formulation.

To mitigate these threats, Sovereign Digital Strategies have emerged; governance models are shifting toward Digital Sovereignty, understood as a State's capacity to act autonomously in the digital world. Key strategies include:

- **a) Regulatory Sovereignty (The EU Model):** Implementation of robust legal frameworks (such as the GDPR or the EU AI Act) that impose ethical and security standards on any actor operating in their territory, exporting their norms globally (the "Brussels Effect").
- **b) Infrastructure Sovereignty (Hardware and Cloud):** Strategic investments to re-shore the production of critical technologies (e.g., the Chips Act in the US and Europe) and the development of sovereign clouds (such as Gaia-X) to ensure that sensitive data does not leave the country's legal jurisdiction.
- **c) Operational Sovereignty (Cybersecurity):** Development of proprietary offensive and defensive capabilities, reducing reliance on foreign security software that could contain "backdoors."

Table 1 contrasts the digital threat (the problem) with the governance model that each threat seeks to undermine, and the sovereign strategy required to mitigate it.

Table 1. Comparative: Evolving Threats and Digital Sovereignty Strategies

Evolving Digital Threat	Risk to National Sovereignty	Governance Model Affected	Required Sovereign Digital Strategy
1. Supply Chain Attacks	Exposure of critical infrastructure (e.g., energy, finance) to hostile actors through third-party software or hardware.	Infrastructure Sovereignty	Provider Diversification (Anti-Dependency): Investment in source code auditing and local production of critical components (e.g., semiconductors).
2. Data Colonialism	Massive and asymmetric extraction of value (data) by foreign platforms, depriving the local economy of the raw material for AI.	Economic and Data Sovereignty	Data Localization and Sovereign Clouds: Local storage requirements and development of proprietary AI stacks (e.g., India Stack).
3. Disinformation and Algorithmic Polarization	Manipulation of public discourse, undermining electoral processes and social cohesion.	Democratic and Cognitive Sovereignty	Platform Liability and Algorithmic Transparency (DSA): Mandating the disclosure of algorithmic parameters and the diligent removal of illegal content.
4. Extraterritorial Jurisdiction (CLOUD Act)	Legal access by foreign governments to data of national citizens and companies stored in the cloud, even within the State's territory.	Legal and Regulatory Sovereignty	Ex-Ante Regulation (DMA): Imposing strict legal jurisdiction and encryption control over data (Operational Sovereignty).
5. Platform Monopolies (Gatekeepers)	Stifling of competition and the local ecosystem due to the dominance of large tech corporations (e.g., self-preferencing).	Market Sovereignty	Structural Antitrust Laws: Imposing interoperability and conduct prohibitions on Gatekeepers (e.g., EU Digital Markets Act).

Own elaboration.

Modern digital governance posits that without technological sovereignty, there is no political sovereignty. States that fail to develop strategies to control their physical layers (cables, servers), logical layers (protocols), and content layers will remain vulnerable to external leverage and the deterioration of their democratic institutions.

1.2 Geopolitical Shifts in the Digital Order

This topic analyses the transition from a utopian vision of a global internet (the "global village") toward a reality of digital fragmentation (or Splinternet), driven by the systemic rivalry between major powers, especially the United States and China.

The current digital order is understood as the Narrative of Bipolar Competition, defined by the collision of two opposing visions seeking to establish global standards:

- **a) The "Open World" Narrative (Led by the US/West):** Promotes a model based on free markets, cross-border data flows, and multi-stakeholder governance. Paradoxically, however, this vision is now used to exclude actors deemed "untrustworthy" (as seen in restrictions on Chinese semiconductors or 5G networks).
- **b) The "Closed World" Narrative (Led by China/Russia):** Emphasizes strict cyber-sovereignty, where the State holds the absolute right to control infrastructure, data, and content within its digital borders to ensure national security and social stability.

The result is a Fragmentation into Technological Blocks, where the digital order is fracturing into "spheres of technological influence." Third-party countries (often referred to as the "Global South" or swing states) find themselves pressured to choose between two incompatible ecosystems of hardware, software, and standards (for example, choosing between Huawei infrastructure or Western providers like Ericsson/Nokia), leading to a technological decoupling.

These Geopolitical Narratives show that the conflict is not only material (chips, cables) but ideological. Powers use strategic narratives to legitimize their actions:

- **Realism:** Technology is viewed as a weapon of national power and security.
- **Liberalism:** Technology is presented as a tool for cooperation and democratic development.
- **Critical (Global South):** Denounces a "digital colonialism" where powers extract data and value without offering real development.

Table 2 conceptualizes the struggle between the three dominant models seeking to impose their vision on internet and technology governance globally. The conflict is based on the element that each block considers the Supreme Sovereign of cyberspace: the Market, the State, or the Citizen.

Table 2. Geopolitical Narratives of Digital Sovereignty

Geopolitical Narrative	Primary Sovereign	Strategic Objective	Sought Domain/Control
1. Market Globalism	The Corporation / The Market	Innovation and Free Data Flow (for economic growth).	Control over Internet Architecture and Software (through technical standards).
2. State Cyber-Sovereignty	The State	Stability and Political Control (prevention of foreign interference).	Control over Infrastructure (filters, firewalls, cables) and Data Localization.
3. Humanistic Regulatory Sovereignty	The Citizen / The Law	Protection of Fundamental Rights (Privacy, Non-Discrimination).	Control over Market Rules and Algorithmic Accountability (through ex-ante legislation).

Own elaboration.

1.3 Chapter Objectives and Roadmap

This foundational section establishes the purpose of this chapter: to demonstrate that technological sovereignty is not a protectionist end in itself, but a necessary condition for preserving democracy and security in the 21st century.

Objectives of the Approach (The "What" and "Why"): The central objective is to deconstruct the traditional (territorial) notion of sovereignty to adapt it to cyberspace. Specific objectives typically include:

- **a) Diagnosing Asymmetry:** To highlight the power gap between States and technology corporations (Big Tech), where the latter act as "de facto sovereign powers" by establishing the rules of the game.
- **b) Redefining Sovereignty:** To move beyond hardware control to include data sovereignty (who owns it), algorithmic sovereignty (who decides how it is processed), and identity sovereignty (who certifies digital citizenship).
- **c) Proposing a Resilience Framework:** To design governance models that allow countries to withstand external shocks (cyberattacks, supply chain disruptions) without disconnecting from the global internet.

The Roadmap (The Logical Structure): The "roadmap" outlines the analytical path followed to validate the need for new governance models:

- **a) Contextualization Phase (State of the Art):** Analysis of how the digital *laissez-faire* of the 1990s led to current monopolies and security vulnerabilities.
- **b) Comparative Phase (Models in Conflict):** Evaluation of the three major current approaches:

1. The Libertarian-Corporate model (USA).
2. The Authoritarian-State model (China/Russia).
3. The Regulatory-Humanist model (European Union/GDPR).

- **c) Propositional Phase (Implementation Strategies):** Development of concrete steps to achieve autonomy, such as the localization of critical infrastructure, the promotion of open-source software, and digital diplomacy.

Figure 1 represents a high-level scheme showing how challenges (Threats and Dependencies) translate into actions (Governance) to achieve strategic objectives (Sovereignty).

Figure 1. Objectives and Roadmap of Sovereign Digital Governance

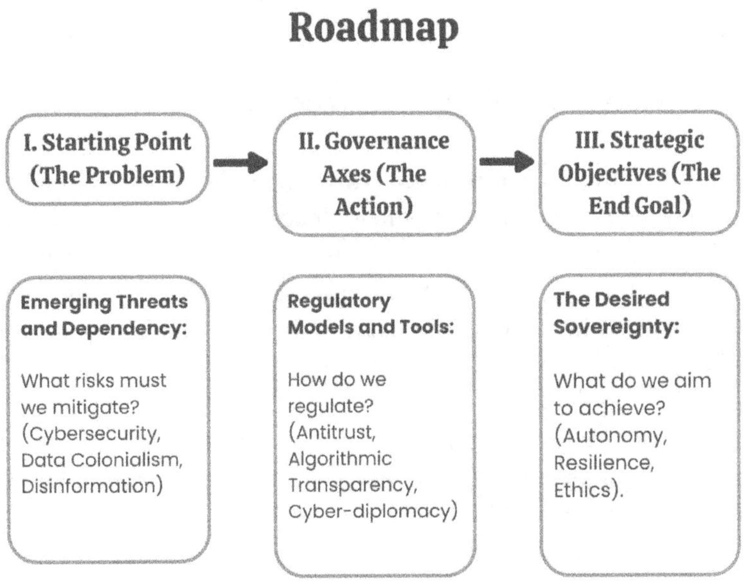

Own elaboration

Research Methodology and Analytical Framework

To ensure the credibility, transparency, and scientific robustness of the analysis presented in this chapter, a rigorous methodological framework has been designed.

This framework moves beyond normative argumentation and comparative description toward an empirically grounded evaluation of digital governance models and technological sovereignty. The methodology is structured around three interconnected components: a mixed-methods research design, a concrete analytical model (the Adaptive Sovereign Resilience Model), and an embedded case study with explicit validation protocols.

Research Design and Approach

The study uses a sequential explanatory mixed-methods design in three phases. First, a qualitative comparative analysis of three governance models (liberal-individualist, state-control, regulatory-humanist) using legal instruments like GDPR, DMA, CLOUD Act, and China's Data Security Law. Second, a quantitative index measuring technological sovereignty across nations. Third, integration through a case study validating the analytical model. The non-experimental design includes cross-sectional comparison and a longitudinal trace of policy evolution over the past decade.

The Adaptive Sovereign Resilience Model (ASRM)

The Adaptive Sovereign Resilience Model (ASRM) is an original analytical framework proposed in this chapter, built on theoretical foundations from Couldry and Mejias (2019) on data colonialism, Floridi (2020) on digital sovereignty, and Pohle and Thiel (2020) on sovereignty as capacity. The ASRM views technological sovereignty not as a binary condition but as a dynamic continuum determined by four dimensions:

1. Infrastructural sovereignty: control over physical and logical digital infrastructure (data centers, cables, semiconductors), measured by the ratio of domestically controlled nodes adjusted for foreign dependency.
2. Data sovereignty: legal and technical control over data storage, processing, and access, including localization requirements and immunity from extraterritorial laws like the U.S. CLOUD Act.
3. Algorithmic sovereignty: capacity to audit and regulate automated systems, measured by auditable system proportion and open-source adoption.
4. Operational sovereignty: ability to respond autonomously to cyber incidents, measured by recovery time, national CERT authority, and reliance on foreign security software.

The overall sovereignty score (ST) is a weighted sum of the four normalized sub-scores (0–1). Weights are derived from expert consultation. States are classified into four levels: critical dependency (0.00–0.25), limited sovereignty (0.26–0.50), functional sovereignty (0.51–0.75), and strategic sovereignty (0.76–1.00).

Embedded Case Study: Brazil and the Pursuit of Digital Autonomy

To validate the ASRM empirically, the chapter undertakes an intensive case study of Brazil. This case is selected for three strategic reasons. First, Brazil possesses one of the most advanced legal frameworks for digital governance in the Global South, including the Marco Civil da Internet (2014) and the Lei Geral de Proteção de Dados (LGPD, 2018), which closely mirrors the European GDPR. Second, Brazil has experienced direct threats to its technological sovereignty, most notably the U.S. National Security Agency surveillance operations exposed in 2013, which catalysed domestic policy responses. Third, Brazil exhibits a paradox of high normative ambition coexisting with persistent infrastructural dependency, making it an ideal test case for the ASRM's capacity to capture gradations of sovereignty.

The case study addresses three research questions: (1) At what level of the ASRM does Brazil currently reside? (2) What strategies has Brazil deployed to reduce critical dependencies on foreign digital infrastructure? (3) What gaps persist between Brazil's regulatory framework and its operational capabilities?

Data collection follows a triangulation protocol with four sources: (1) legal documents (Marco Civil, LGPD, decrees, Anatel resolutions); (2) technical data (Anatel reports, cloud provider disclosures, data center surveys); (3) algorithmic governance evidence (TSE public audits, academic evaluations); and (4) operational indicators (CERT.br incident reports, cybersecurity indices). Additionally, ten semi-structured interviews are conducted with stakeholders from government, legal experts, private sector, and academia. Interview data are anonymized and analyzed using thematic coding.

Validation and Quality Criteria

The chapter ensures robustness via four criteria: credibility (triangulation of documents, statistics, interviews; independent coding with Cohen's kappa), transferability (thick Brazilian case description; boundary conditions for Global South application), dependability (transparent audit trail, public protocol, annotated matrices), and confirmability (reflexive journal, anonymized raw data). Evidence strength is graded as strong, requires convergence among at least three independent sources, including quantitative public data and consensual perceptions across interviews, moderate (two sources without contradiction), or weak (single source or unvalidated perceptions), applied systematically to claims about Brazil's ASRM dimensions.

Contribution and Scope of the Methodology

The methodological framework described above transforms the chapter's contribution from a purely theoretical or comparative exercise into an empirically validated analysis of digital governance and technological sovereignty. The ASRM offers a replicable instrument for diagnosing sovereign capabilities, while the Brazilian case study provides concrete evidence of how a middle-power state navigates the tension between integration into global digital networks and the pursuit of autonomous governance. The findings derived from this methodology are presented in the relevant sections of this chapter, particularly in the comparative analysis of governance models and in the discussion of digital autonomy in the Global South. By making its procedures explicit and its evidence auditable, this chapter aspires to contribute not only to academic debates on digital sovereignty but also to policy deliberations in states seeking to chart their own digital futures.

2. FOUNDATIONS OF DIGITAL GOVERNANCE

Digital governance is defined as the critical framework of norms, institutions, and processes that regulate behavior in the digital space and the management of technological resources, where it has ceased to be a merely technical issue to become a fundamental sociopolitical pillar in the information age. Unlike traditional network management, digital governance is defined as the set of processes, institutions, and norms that regulate the creation, exchange, and use of data and technologies in the transnational space.

According to Couldry and Mejias (2019), this phenomenon must be understood through the lens of power structures, where digital infrastructure is not neutral but acts as a new mechanism for the appropriation of human life for economic purposes.

To understand its foundations, it is necessary to analyze three critical dimensions:

- Data Sovereignty: The conflict between the free flow of information and the need for States to protect privacy and national security.
- Algorithmic Transparency: The ethical requirement that artificial intelligence systems and automated decision-making be auditable and explain their inherent biases.

- Inclusion and the Digital Divide: Governance regulates not only the "what" but also the "who," seeking to mitigate inequalities in access that perpetuate new forms of social exclusion.

A contemporary critical foundation is the resistance to data colonialism. Under this framework, governance seeks to balance the scales of power against "platform capitalism," where a handful of global companies dictate the rules of social and economic interaction. Effective digital governance proposes moving from a model of unilateral extraction to one of digital agency, where the user regains control over their digital footprint and informative self-determination.

2.1 Centralized vs. Distributed Governance Models

This topic delves into the architectural and political dichotomy defining the current conflict over digital sovereignty. It contrasts the efficiency and control of centralization against the resilience and innovation of decentralization.

- **a) Centralized Governance (Multilateral / State-Led Approach):** This model, favored by powers such as China and Russia (and increasingly by European regulators), transfers the hierarchical structure of the Nation-State into cyberspace. The State serves as the central node that validates, filters, and regulates traffic. It is based on hard digital borders.
  - **Perceived Advantage (Security):** Facilitates surveillance, enforcement of local laws, and coordinated defense against national cyberattacks.
  - **Threat (Single Point of Failure):** Creates "Honey Pots" (large centralized data repositories) that are attractive and vulnerable targets for hackers. Additionally, it enables mass censorship and internet "kill switches."
- **b) Distributed Governance (Multi-stakeholder / Polycentric Approach):** This is the original model of the internet, defended by technical bodies (ICANN, IETF). Authority does not reside in a single entity but is distributed among multiple actors (civil society, technicians, companies, and governments). Its characteristics include decision-making by technical consensus, mesh network architecture, and free data flow.
  - **Perceived Advantage (Resilience):** Since there is no central head, the network is difficult to destroy. If a node fails, traffic is rerouted. it fosters rapid innovation.
  - **Threat (Difficulty of Attribution):** The lack of a central controller makes it difficult to prosecute cybercrimes, combat disinformation,

or hold malicious actors accountable when they hide behind network anonymity.

The Current Paradox is Private vs. Public Centralization

The analysis highlights a critical emerging threat: although the internet was designed to be distributed, in practice, it has re-centralized in the hands of a few private corporations (Google, Amazon, Meta). This has led governments to attempt to impose "State Centralized Governance" to counteract "Corporate Centralized Governance," creating a clash of sovereignties.

Case Studies: Governance Models in Action

This section analyzes how different philosophies of digital sovereignty translate into specific legal and technical mechanisms:

- **a) Authoritarian-State Model: The Golden Shield Project (China).** Represents "Hard Cyber-Sovereignty." This is the most sophisticated example of a national intranet. China has not only regulated the internet but has created a complete parallel ecosystem.
- **b) Technical Mechanism:** The "Great Firewall" utilizes Deep Packet Inspection (DPI) and IP blocking to filter cross-border traffic in real-time.
- **c) Governance Implication:** The State has direct access ("backdoor") to the data of any company operating on its soil. The Data Security Law (2021) mandates that companies share data with the government if national security requires it.
    - **Result:** Absolute sovereignty over the cognitive space and citizen data, at the expense of civil liberties.
- **d) Regulatory-Humanist Model: The Digital Markets Act (European Union).** Represents "Regulatory Sovereignty." Since the EU lacks its own major tech giants, it uses its massive legislative power to subdue foreign corporations (the "Brussels Effect").
- **e) Legal Mechanism:** The Digital Markets Act (DMA) designates large platforms (Google, Apple, Meta) as "Gatekeepers."
- **f) Governance Implication:** It prohibits them from favoring their own services (e.g., Google cannot prioritize its maps in search results) and mandates interoperability (e.g., WhatsApp must be able to receive messages from other apps).

- **Result:** Creates "consumer sovereignty," returning power to local users and businesses against foreign monopolies without the need to build a technical wall.

- **g) Libertarian-Corporate Model: Section 230 (United States).** Represents "Market Sovereignty." Historically, the US has delegated governance to private companies to foster rapid innovation.
- **h) Legal Mechanism:** Section 230 of the Communications Decency Act. It establishes that platforms are not editorially responsible for the content published by their users.
- **i) Governance Implication:** Allows companies like Facebook or X (Twitter) to self-regulate, deciding what is "truth" or "falsehood" without direct state intervention.
    - **Result:** Explosive economic growth in the tech sector, but with a loss of state sovereignty to corporations that now wield their own geopolitical power (such as Starlink in military conflicts).

Table 3 contrasts the two philosophical paradigms competing for control of cyberspace, which underpin the geopolitical narratives of major powers (China vs. US/EU).

Table 3. Comparative: Centralized vs. Distributed Governance Models

Feature	Centralized / Statist Governance Model	Distributed / Multi-stakeholder Governance Model
Primary Sovereign	The State	The Ecosystem (Market, Civil Society, Academia, State)
Key Philosophy	**Absolute Cyber-Sovereignty:** State control over internal information is paramount for stability.	**Multi-stakeholder Governance:** The Internet is global, and its management must be shared.
Primary Objective	Political Stability and National Security (Controlling internal risk).	Innovation, Openness, and Human Rights (Maximizing economic value and freedom).
Control Mechanism	**Infrastructure Control (Filters):** Censorship, forced data localization, network monitoring, and national firewalls.	**Conduct Regulation (Laws):** Application of antitrust laws, algorithmic transparency, and data protection (e.g., GDPR, DMA).
Security Focus	**Regime Security:** Priority on surveillance and the prevention of dissent.	**System Security:** Priority on resilience, network defense, and information sharing.
Geopolitical Examples	China, Russia, Iran (Emphasis on "Cyber-Sovereignty").	European Union, United States, Canada (Emphasis on "Internet Governance").

2.2 Public-Private Collaboration and Multi-stakeholderism

This topic focuses on the need to move beyond governance models that are strictly state-led (centralized) or purely private (self-regulated). The complexity of emerging threats forces a multi-stakeholder approach where the State and the private sector share responsibilities and resources.

- **a) The Need for Collaboration:** Digital threats (ransomware, supply chain attacks) possess two critical characteristics that compel collaboration:

  1. **Shared Vulnerability:** Much of a country's critical infrastructure (energy, telecommunications, banking) is operated by private companies. A cyber-attack on a private company can have national security consequences.
  2. **Information Asymmetry:** Private tech companies possess the necessary operational information and technical expertise (90% of internet traffic is operated by them), while the State possesses legal authority and threat intelligence (often classified). Neither can resolve a crisis alone.

- **b) Public-Private Partnership (PPP) Models:** PPPs are the primary mechanism for mobilizing resources, adopting different forms:

  1. **Information Sharing:** The creation of Information Sharing and Analysis Centers (ISACs) where the private sector can anonymously share real-time threat data with government agencies, improving the defense of both parties.
  2. **Regulatory Incentives:** The State offers benefits (such as liability waivers) to companies that implement high security standards, mitigating the cost of cybersecurity investments.
  3. **Strategic Partnerships:** Direct collaboration on key infrastructure projects (e.g., joint development of a sovereign cloud or protection of undersea cables).

- **c) Multi-stakeholder Governance:** The concept expands to include civil society, academia, and the technical community (engineers, open-source developers). This approach ensures that digital governance is not only secure (State and Businesses) but also open and ethical, preventing security frameworks from being used to suppress dissent or innovation.

2.3 From Open Government to Digital Resilience

There has been a digital transformation within the public sector, evolving from a paradigm focused on initiation and efficiency toward a new strategic approach based on the State's capacity to confront and overcome cyberattacks and technological disruptions. This shift reflects the maturity of digital governance in the face of emerging threats.

The Open Government Paradigm (Emphasis on Transparency): Open Government was the first major model of digital reform (during the 2000s and 2010s). It was based on three fundamental pillars:

- **Transparency:** Publication of Open Data and accountability.
- **Participation:** Use of digital platforms for citizens to influence political decisions.
- **Collaboration:** Partnership between the government, civil society, and the private sector.

While this model improved trust and efficiency, its primary deficiency was underestimating the threat to the operational continuity of digital infrastructures. Openness and interconnectivity, without adequate security, created new attack surfaces.

The Transition to Digital Resilience (Emphasis on Continuity): Facing the proliferation of ransomware threats targeting municipalities, hospitals, and critical infrastructure, the focus has shifted toward Digital Resilience as an element of sovereignty.

- **Definition of Resilience:** It is not only the capacity to defend oneself but the ability of the government system to maintain the functionality of critical services (e.g., electricity, payments, emergency care) even during a sustained cyberattack or a technological disaster.
- **Integration of Cybersecurity:** Cybersecurity ceases to be a technical IT component and becomes a strategic asset integrated into risk management at the executive level.
- **Operational Sovereignty:** Involves ensuring that essential services do not depend on systems or platforms with known vulnerabilities or those controlled by foreign jurisdictions.

Modern governance merges both paradigms: it utilizes technology for openness (transparency) but within a robust framework of security and resilience (sovereignty). Digital governance must be agile to respond to technological disruption and ensure that the trust gained through Open Government is not lost due to a catastrophic security failure.

Figure 2. Evolution of Public Governance: From Open Government to Digital Resilience (Transition Framework).

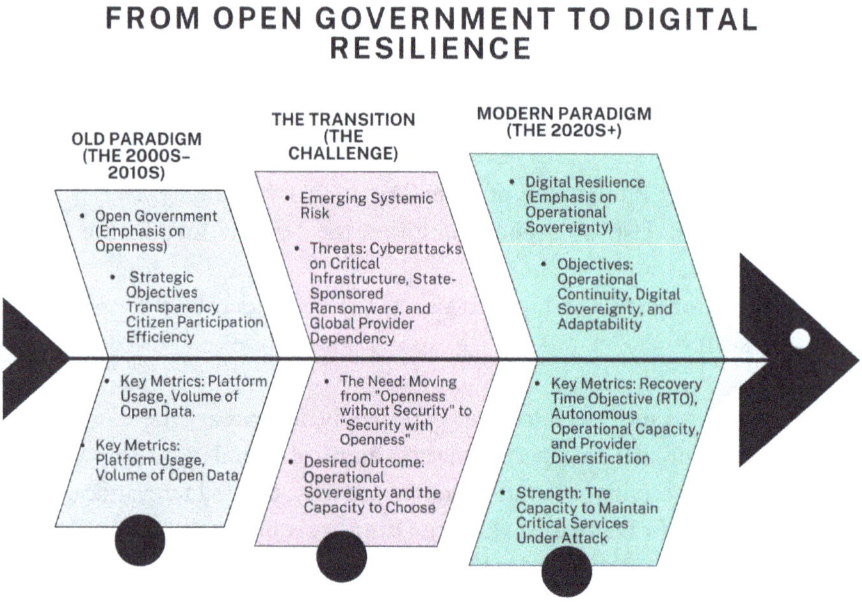

Own elaboration.

Figure 2 represents a transition of priorities driven by experience.

- **Open Government (Openness):** This model focused on improving the relationship between the State and the citizen. Its pillars (Transparency and Participation) facilitated democracy but increased the attack surface due to widespread interconnection.
- **Emerging Systemic Risk (The Shock):** The massive digitalization of government encountered an escalation of cyber threats (such as ransomware attacks targeting health, judicial, or energy systems). This phase demonstrated that the loss of an essential service due to a cyberattack is a threat to sovereignty as serious as a military conflict.
- **Digital Resilience (Sovereignty):** The new paradigm focuses on the continuity of the State. Modern governance demands that the government maintain

the capacity to operate (operational sovereignty) and to recover quickly (resilience) from any shock, prioritizing security-by-design in all digital services.

3. TECHNOLOGICAL SOVEREIGNTY AND CLOUD GEOPOLITICS

Historically, sovereignty was exercised over physical borders. Today, data is the new sovereign asset, but its storage is not ethereal; it resides in data centers subject to specific laws.

Technological sovereignty refers to the capacity of a State or community to decide autonomously on its digital infrastructure, software, and data management without structural dependencies on third parties. The Geopolitics of the Cloud is the study of how global powers use control over network infrastructure and data processing to project power and secure strategic advantages.

Currently, the cloud ecosystem is dominated by an oligopoly distributed mainly between the United States (Amazon AWS, Microsoft Azure, Google Cloud) and China (Alibaba Cloud, Huawei Cloud). This creates three main challenges:

- Extraterritoriality of the Law: The ability of a country to access data stored on foreign servers if the parent company resides on its soil.
- Vendor Lock-in: The technical and economic difficulty of migrating national critical infrastructures from one private cloud to another, limiting the State's autonomy of decision.
- Infrastructure Vulnerability: Control over undersea cables and Internet Exchange Points (IXPs).

Europe has led the theoretical and practical response through projects such as Gaia-X, which seeks to create a federated and secure data ecosystem that reduces dependence on American and Chinese "hyperscalers." The goal is not only technical but regulatory: to impose EU values of privacy and transparency over pure technical efficiency.

3.1 Data Localization and Sovereign Clouds

This topic analyses infrastructure and data sovereignty strategies, where governance focuses on the physical control of critical information. The goal is to reduce dependency on cloud services from foreign providers and ensure that data is subject exclusively to national laws.

- **The Imperative of Data Localization:** Data localization is a legal requirement that mandates companies to store specific data (personal, financial, health-related) within the national jurisdiction.
  - **National Security Motivation:** Preventing access by foreign governments. Laws such as the U.S. CLOUD Act allow American authorities to access data stored by their companies globally, regardless of the physical server's location, creating a direct threat to the sovereignty of third-party countries.
  - **Regulatory Motivation:** Ensuring that data can be audited, regulated, and, if necessary, seized by national authorities for law enforcement purposes.

Sovereign Clouds are positioned as the solution. A "Sovereign Cloud" is a cloud computing infrastructure that guarantees that both data and management operations (metadata, logs, encryption keys) reside and are strictly controlled under the laws of a nation or economic bloc (such as the EU).

It features key characteristics such as:

- **Data Residency:** Physical storage occurs within national borders.
- **Operational Control:** Access to and management of the infrastructure (and software updates) are carried out by trusted local entities.
- **Legal Protection:** Jurisdiction and legal contracts are strictly tied to the national legal framework, precluding the application of foreign laws.

Regarding the Economic Dilemma, data localization and the cloud present a tension between sovereignty and efficiency, particularly concerning costs and market fragmentation. Investments in local infrastructure and redundancy requirements significantly increase operating costs for companies, which can slow down the adoption of advanced technologies. Furthermore, excessive localization requirements can lead to global data fragmentation, hindering the cross-border flows necessary for research and multinational corporate operations.

Table 4 breaks down the core concept of data localization, the different implementation models, and how these relate to the need to build Sovereign Clouds as a strategic asset.

Table 4. Data Localization and Sovereign Clouds

Key Concept	Description and Definition	Implications for Digital Sovereignty
Data Localization	A legal requirement mandating companies (national or foreign) to store or process specific types of data within the physical borders of a State.	Mitigates the risk of extraterritorial jurisdiction (e.g., U.S. CLOUD Act) and ensures legal access to data by national authorities.
Localization Models	Full Localization: Total prohibition of transferring sensitive data abroad (e.g., health or financial data). Partial Localization: Requirement to maintain a copy of the data within the country, allowing the original to flow.	Partial Localization (the most common model) seeks a balance between national security and the efficiency of digital trade.
Sovereign Cloud	A cloud computing service designed to meet the strictest security and legal compliance requirements of a nation or economic bloc (e.g., European Cloud).	Guarantees Operational Autonomy: Ensures that infrastructure, software, and, crucially, encryption keys are under national legal control, even if the underlying technology is foreign.
Dependency Effect	If critical data resides in foreign clouds, the country is subject to the laws and policies of that nation, creating an asymmetric dependency.	The development of Sovereign Clouds is a strategic move of controlled decoupling to reclaim sovereignty over the State's data infrastructure.
Main Challenge	The risk of Internet fragmentation (Splinternet) and increased costs for companies that must replicate data centers across multiple jurisdictions.	Governance must distinguish between national security data (requiring strict localization) and commercial data (which can flow freely under privacy rules).

3.2 Cross-Border Data Flows and Digital Dependencies

This topic focuses on the analysis of the fundamental tension between promoting the free flow of data for economic growth and the need to control that flow to protect national sovereignty and privacy. Governance is facing the challenge of regulating a resource that flows without respecting physical borders.

- **The Geopolitical Value of Data Flow:** Cross-border data is not merely information; it is the "engine" of the digital economy and the raw material for Artificial Intelligence.
    - o **Economic Dominance:** Massive data flows tend to be unilateral, moving predominantly from peripheral and developing economies toward a few global technological hubs (mainly the US and China). This creates an extractive dependency, where the value of processing and monetizing the data occurs outside the country of origin.
    - o **Supply Chain Control:** Digital platforms (from e-commerce to cloud services) require uninterrupted data flows. The ability to limit or block

these flows becomes a tool for geopolitical containment, creating a critical dependency.

- **Regulatory Sovereignty and Legal Conflict:** The greatest conflict arises when the laws of different jurisdictions collide in cyberspace.
    - o **The Globalist Standard (USA):** Promotes free flow to maximize the efficiency and profit of its companies, using trade agreements to lobby against data localization restrictions.
    - o **The Privacy Standard (EU):** Uses the General Data Protection Regulation (GDPR) to establish that data flows to third countries are only legal if those countries guarantee an adequate level of protection, creating a regulatory barrier.
    - o **The Legal Challenge:** The lack of harmonization in how countries define data ownership, privacy, and security creates legal uncertainty and hinders international cooperation in the fight against cybercrime.
- **Implications for Governance:** To mitigate these dependencies, States must negotiate Data Rules of Origin—similar to trade in goods—establishing rules on where the value of the data is generated and processed. They must also invest in Local Infrastructure, reducing reliance on foreign cables and services for data transit.

Table 5 synthesizes three key indicators that define the geopolitical landscape of data: volume growth, value concentration, and critical dependency on cloud infrastructure.

Table 5. Statistics: Cross-Border Data Flows and Digital Dependencies

Indicator 1: Growth and Asymmetry of Data Flows (The Global Tension)		
Variable	**Statistical Trend**	**Geopolitical Implication**
Cross-Border Data Volume	Exponential increase (doubles every 4-5 years).	The speed of the flow exceeds the capacity of States to regulate them.
Asymmetric Data Flow	For every unit of data outgoing from the Global South, there are 5-10 units flowing toward data centers in the Global North (USA, China).	**Reinforces Data Colonialism**: Developing countries act a source of raw data, but they do not capture the value of
Indicator 2: Value Concentration (Cloud Dominance)		
Variable	**Percentage (Market Concentration)**	**Implication for Technological Sovereignty**
Cloud Market Share (IaaS)	**~70% - 80%** of global infrastructure is controlled by AWS, Azure, and Google Cloud.	**Critical Dependency:** If these providers are interrupted (b attack or legal decision), a large part of the global econom comes to a standstill. This demands the creation of **Sovereign Clouds.**
"Big Tech" Market Value	The top 5 tech companies represent **more than 20%** of the S&P 500 stock index value (USA).	Their economic power translates into regulatory power (lobbying) that hinders the implementation of national laws (e.g., privacy or antitrust).
Indicator 3: The Regulatory Response (The Cost of Sovereignty)		
Variable	**Cost Type**	**Strategic Implication**
Regulatory Compliance Cost	Estimated **15% - 25%** increase in operating costs for companies when complying with data localization and GDPR.	Demonstrates that sovereignty has an economic cost tha States must weigh against security and autonomy.
Number of Data Localization Laws	Growth of **~300%** since 2015.	Indicates a clear trend toward **Internet fragmentation** dr by geopolitical mistrust and the need to protect legal jurisdiction.

Own elaboration.

3.3 Cybersecurity as a Strategic Asset

Cybersecurity has transcended its traditional technical role (firewall protection) to become a pillar of national security and economic competitiveness. It is conceived as a strategic asset that allows a State to operate autonomously and defend its interests in a hostile digital environment.

- **From Network Protection to National Resilience:** The focus has shifted from simple "perimeter defense" to systemic resilience. A State is strategically secure not only when it avoids an attack but when it can recover quickly from a major incident without its critical functions collapsing.

- **Integration with National Security:** Cybersecurity is no longer just the responsibility of IT agencies; it is now integrated with intelligence (attack attribution), military defense, and foreign policy (digital diplomacy).
- **Protection of the Economic Base:** The defense of Intellectual Property, trade secrets, and innovation data are now primary tasks of state cybersecurity, as cyber theft has become a form of economic warfare.

Regarding Cybersecurity as a component of technological sovereignty, it can be said that a country is not sovereign if its critical systems are designed, operated, or defended by foreign entities.

- **Proprietary Offensive and Defensive Capabilities:** This strategic asset includes the ability to develop in-house security tools, reduce dependence on foreign software (which may contain known or unknown vulnerabilities), and train high-level local talent.
- **Norm Shaping:** A State with strong cyber capabilities can project power by influencing international cybersecurity standards and norms, ensuring that global protocols align with its security interests.

In terms of attribution and deterrence, strategic cybersecurity implies the ability to attribute cyberattacks to their authors with sufficient certainty to impose economic or diplomatic consequences. This is key to deterrence:

- **Deterrence by Denial:** Strengthening defenses so that the cost of attacking becomes prohibitive for the adversary.
- **Deterrence by Punishment:** Having the capability to respond to an attack with reprisals (either cybernetic or conventional).

Figure 3 is a mental map organized into four main nodes, demonstrating the importance of cybersecurity in national strategy.

Figure 3. Cybersecurity as a Strategic Asset. Own elaboration.

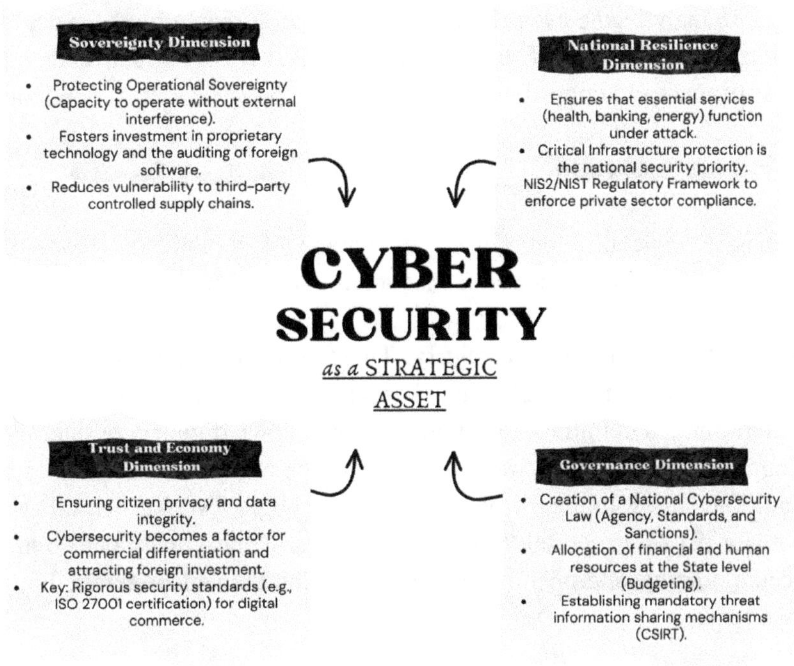

4. REGULATING BIG TECH AND PLATFORM POWER

The expansion of the companies known as "Big Tech" (Google, Amazon, Meta, Apple, and Microsoft) has transformed the global economic structure, consolidating a model of platform capitalism. This phenomenon is characterized by algorithmic intermediation and the massive extraction of data, which has generated concerns regarding the abuse of dominant positions and the erosion of privacy.

Unlike traditional industries, platforms operate under network effects, where their value grows exponentially with the number of users, creating natural monopolies that are difficult to dismantle. The current regulatory trend (e.g., the EU Digital Markets Act) seeks to act ex-ante, establishing prior rules for "gatekeepers" instead of waiting for the harm to occur.

4.1 Anti-monopoly and Content Moderation Laws

This topic analyzes the two primary regulatory tools that States have deployed to counteract the concentration of power in Big Tech platforms: control over their market power (**Antitrust**) and control over their discourse power (Content Moderation).

1. The Problem of Market Power Concentration

The massive concentration of users and data in a few platforms (Google, Meta, Amazon) creates digital monopolies that act as "Gatekeepers."

- **Threat to Economic Sovereignty:** These companies can stifle competition, impose unfair conditions on local businesses, and extract significant rents, undermining a country's ability to develop its own digital ecosystem.
- **Regulatory Response (Antitrust Laws):** The modern response goes beyond traditional fines. In the European Union, the Digital Markets Act (DMA) imposes a list of structural "dos and don'ts" on Gatekeepers before an abuse occurs, forcing interoperability and preventing the self-preferencing of their own services.

2. Content Moderation and the Democratic Challenge

The ability of platforms to unilaterally decide what information is amplified or suppressed grants private companies immense political power and poses a direct threat to the sovereignty of public discourse.

- **Threat to Democratic Sovereignty:** The uncontrolled spread of disinformation, electoral manipulation, and extremist content can destabilize democratic processes and exacerbate social polarization.
- **Regulatory Response (Content Laws):** The response is the regulation of liability. The EU's Digital Services Act (DSA) and similar laws in other jurisdictions (such as the NetzDG in Germany) mandate that platforms be more transparent about their recommendation algorithms and act with greater diligence to remove illegal or harmful content.

3. Tension and the Future of Governance

The main tension lies in how to regulate content moderation without the State becoming a censor. The goal of contemporary digital governance is to establish a framework of accountability and transparency that forces platforms to answer for their actions, thereby reclaiming regulatory sovereignty over key spaces of the economy and the public sphere.

4.2 EU's Digital Markets Act and U.S. Antitrust Cases

This topic focuses on the practical application of antitrust and competition laws as key tools of regulatory sovereignty, contrasting the different philosophies that the EU and the US employ to control digital monopolies and their consequent threats to competition and democracy.

The EU's Structural and Proactive Approach (DMA): The European Union's Digital Markets Act (DMA) represents the most ambitious paradigm of regulatory sovereignty. Its goal is to change the rules of the game before abuse occurs.

- **Designation of Gatekeepers:** The DMA designates platforms that meet certain revenue and user thresholds as Gatekeepers.
- **Ex-Ante Regulation:** It imposes a list of structural obligations and prohibitions (*dos and don'ts*) that Gatekeepers must permanently follow. For example, they must allow interoperability for messaging services, stop favoring their own products in their stores (**self-preferencing**), and give users more control over app installation.
- **Purpose of Sovereignty:** The DMA seeks to restore market sovereignty by fostering the growth of smaller European tech companies and ensuring fair competition.

The US Corrective and Legal Approach (Antitrust): Historically, US antitrust law has focused on consumer welfare, pursuing companies only after a tangible harm to the consumer (often measured by price increases) is proven.

- **Federal and State Litigation:** Cases are built on the Sherman Antitrust Act and the Clayton Act (20th-century laws). Notable cases (such as litigation against Google for search and digital advertising or against Meta for the acquisition of Instagram/WhatsApp) are long, costly, and focused on dismantling or modifying existing business practices.
- **Focus on Consumer Harm:** The challenge is that digital services are often "free" for the user (e.g., social networks), making it difficult to prove "consumer harm" in terms of price.
- **Purpose of Sovereignty:** The primary goal is to maintain competition and innovation, though the process is inherently slower and more reactive than the EU's.

Geopolitical Implications and Impact:

- **"The Brussels Effect":** EU regulations (like the DMA) often become the de facto global standard, as companies prefer a single set of rules to operate in a large market.
- **Risk of Decoupling:** The US legal approach can lead to forced decoupling (asset divestiture), whereas the EU approach seeks structural behavioural changes within its borders.

Figure 4 presents a structure designed to compare the two regulatory powers (EU vs. US) and how their approaches converge towards market sovereignty.

Figure 4. Control of Digital Monopolies and Market Sovereignty. Own elaboration.

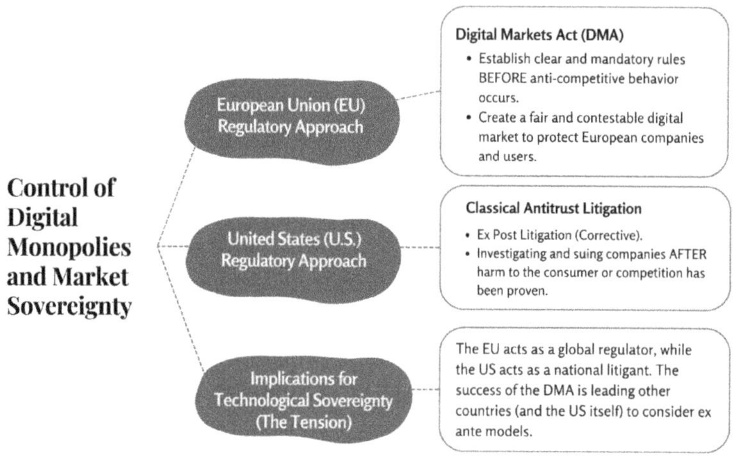

4.3 Platform Responsibility and Algorithmic Transparency

This topic focuses on the debate regarding the legal and ethical responsibility of large digital platforms for the content they host, amplify, or suppress, and the necessity for States to impose algorithmic transparency to mitigate bias and manipulation.

- **Platform Liability (The "Common Carrier" Dilemma):** Historically, Section 230 of the U.S. Communications Decency Act established that platforms were not liable for third-party content published by their users. While this allowed for massive growth, it generated a negative social externality.

- o **The Passivity vs. Activity Challenge:** Platforms argue they are merely "passive" (neutral carriers of information), but their recommendation algorithms make them "active" (de facto editors). They amplify extremist content, misinformation, or hate speech to maximize engagement and profits.
- o **Regulatory Response:** The European model, through the Digital Services Act (DSA), attempts to resolve this dilemma: platforms are held accountable for due diligence (they must act with speed and transparency) rather than having direct editorial responsibility for every piece of content, thereby creating a framework of systemic liability.

- **Algorithmic Sovereignty and Transparency:** Recommendation algorithms are opaque "black boxes," even to States. This opacity poses a threat to social sovereignty:
  - o **Threat to Human Rights:** Algorithms can apply racial, gender, or economic biases in critical decision-making (credit, employment), violating fundamental rights.
  - o **Threat to Cognitive Sovereignty:** By controlling what a citizen sees, the algorithm shapes public debate and perceived reality, wielding political power superior to that of many governments.
  - o **Transparency as a Governance Tool:** States seek to compel platforms to reveal the key parameters of their recommendation systems (especially for high-impact systems), allowing for external auditing and regulatory oversight.
- **The Ethical Framework and Technological Sovereignty:** Modern digital governance postulates that sovereignty is not just about infrastructure and data, but about the principles governing social interaction.
  - o **Trustworthy AI:** Initiatives like the EU AI Act seek to classify artificial intelligence systems by risk level. High-risk systems (such as those used in biometrics or critical infrastructure) can only be deployed if they guarantee human oversight, explainability, and conformity with human rights.

5. INTERNATIONAL CYBER ALLIANCES AND NATIONAL DOCTRINES

Global cybersecurity has shifted toward digital geopolitics, where alliances like Five Eyes and NATO now pursue governance standards and collective deterrence, not just technical cooperation. National doctrines have evolved from defensive stances to "persistent engagement" (U.S.) or "digital sovereignty" (China/Russia). This creates tension between the liberal vision (open, interoperable internet) and the sovereignist vision (state control over data). Future conflicts will depend on coordinated rapid responses to zero-day attacks and disinformation campaigns, redefining traditional sovereignty.

5.1 NATO, OECD, and ASEAN Cybersecurity Policies

This topic compares the cybersecurity approaches adopted by three key organizations, each with a distinct geopolitical and economic focus, demonstrating how multilateral cooperation has become essential for digital defense.

- **NATO: Collective Security in Cyberspace.** The North Atlantic Treaty Organization (NATO) approaches cybersecurity from a military defense and collective security perspective. NATO considers cyberspace an operational domain (alongside land, sea, and air).
    - o **Strategic Doctrine:** NATO doctrine allows for the invocation of Article 5 (an attack against one is an attack against all) in response to a cyberattack, provided it reaches the threshold of an armed conflict. This elevates cybersecurity to the highest level of military strategy. It promotes the interoperability of national cyber defenses and the exchange of critical information among members.
- **OECD: Economic Governance and Trust Standards.** The Organisation for Economic Co-operation and Development (OECD) focuses on cybersecurity from an economic, regulatory, and market trust perspective.
    - o **Resilience and Trade:** Its work centers on developing policy frameworks that promote economic resilience and protect cross-border data flows. The OECD promotes a "security culture" (risk management responsibility for businesses) and establishes guidelines for information security risk management. Its goal is to ensure that cyber incidents do not undermine confidence in the digital economy or hinder international trade.
- **ASEAN: Regional Capacity and Regulatory Harmonization.** The Association of Southeast Asian Nations (ASEAN) focuses on capacity building and harmonizing responses among its diverse Member States, many of which have varying levels of digital development.
    - o **Regional Cooperation:** ASEAN promotes trust and technical information sharing (via CERTs and CSIRTs) through structures such as the ASEAN Ministerial Conference on Cybersecurity (AMCC). Its key

challenge is balancing the need for common security standards with respect for each nation's digital sovereignty. Its policies aim to protect regional connectivity as an economic driver, avoiding regulatory fragmentation that would inhibit investment.

Figure 5 compares how these different international organizations define and manage cyberspace security according to their core mandates.

Figure 5. Cybersecurity Policies of NATO, OECD, and ASEAN. Own elaboration.

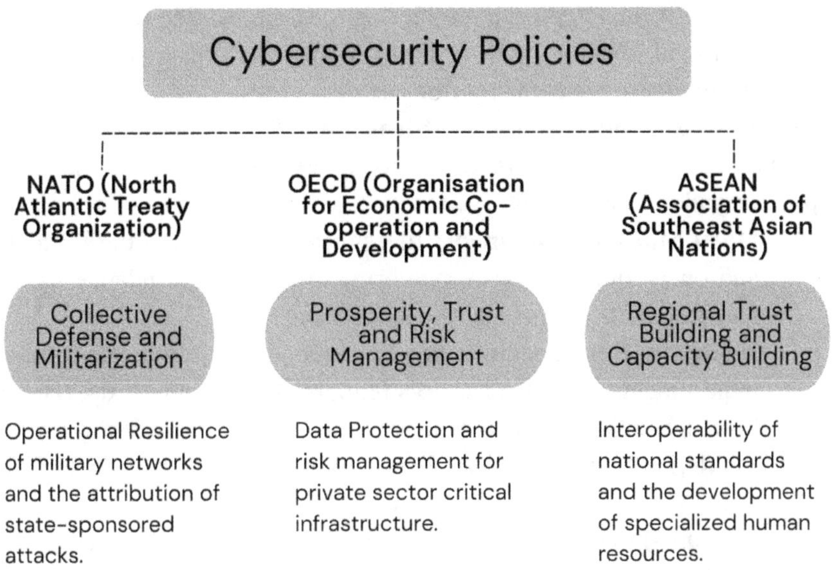

5.2 Digital Autonomy in Latin America, India, and Africa

This topic examines how regions in the Global South approach sovereignty and digital autonomy from a different perspective than that of the US, China, or the EU. Their primary challenge is not creating regulations for their own tech giants, but mitigating dependence on external actors for infrastructure, software, and data flows.

- **The Challenge of Asymmetric Dependency:** Developing countries are characterized by asymmetric digital dependence. They not only rely on foreign providers for infrastructure (cloud services, 5G) but also lack the technical and economic capacity to establish an independent governance alternative.
  - o **Latin America:** A struggle between adopting open data models (promoted by the US) and the need to protect citizen privacy (inspired by the EU's GDPR). Chinese investment in telecommunications infrastructure creates a geopolitical security dilemma.
  - o **Africa:** Faces "digital colonialism," where connectivity infrastructure (subsea cables, data centers) and mobile financial platforms are controlled by external powers, limiting economic sovereignty.
  - o **India:** A dual approach: promoting local innovation (the "India Stack" or digital identity stack) while facing pressure from large platforms to maintain unregulated cross-border data flows.
- **Models of Regional Autonomy (Strategies):** Digital autonomy in these regions focuses less on *ex-ante* regulation and more on building their own capacities and infrastructures:
  - o **Open Stack Development:** Investment in sovereign digital identities and open-source software platforms to reduce dependence on foreign commercial licenses (e.g., the India Stack).
  - o **Moderate Data Localization:** Implementing specific data localization requirements for critical sectors (e.g., banking or health data) to ensure legal control while allowing other data flows to avoid stifling innovation.
  - o **Strategic Alliances:** South-South cooperation (among developing nations) and collaboration with the EU (adopting their privacy regulatory standards) to seek a counterweight to the dominant influence of the US and China.
- **The Goal of Autonomy:** For these regions, digital autonomy is defined as the ability to make sovereign decisions regarding infrastructure, data markets, and innovation policies without coercion from foreign actors. This is a prerequisite for ensuring that digitalization benefits local economic development rather than just global corporations.

5.3 Cyber Diplomacy and Global Norms

This topic focuses on the use of diplomacy as a tool to manage emerging threats, attempting to forge an international consensus on the rules of war and peace in cyberspace. Cyber-diplomacy is the projection of a State's digital sovereignty through the negotiation of global norms.

- **The Conflict over Governance: Norms and Principles:** The main challenge of cyber-diplomacy is the lack of a unified international legal framework, leading to a clash between governance models:

    1. **The Western Model (Multi-stakeholder):** Advocates for the application of existing international laws (including human rights) to cyberspace and promotes a governance approach that includes companies, civil society, and governments.
    2. **The Absolute Sovereignty Model (State-led):** Led by China and Russia, it promotes total State sovereignty over its internal cyberspace, defending the need for a new binding international treaty that legitimizes State control over information.

- **Key Forums for Cyber-diplomacy:** Negotiations take place across multiple stages, reflecting the fragmentation of global power:

    1. **UN Group of Governmental Experts (GGE):** Focused on applying international law to information and communication technologies. Its work has been crucial in establishing that the laws of war (International Humanitarian Law) are applicable to cyber conflicts.
    2. **UN Open-Ended Working Group (OEWG):** A more inclusive forum that has achieved consensus on a set of Norms of Responsible State Behavior (RBC), such as refraining from attacking critical infrastructure or incident response centers.

- **The Strategic Goal of Cyber-diplomacy:** The ultimate goal is deterrence. By agreeing on behavioral norms, States seek to:

    1. **Reduce the Risk of Escalation:** Establishing clear "red lines" to prevent cyber incidents from escalating into conventional military conflicts.
    2. **Project Influence:** Each country or bloc (US, EU, China) uses diplomacy to ensure their governance models (whether free data flow or strict control) become the global normative standard, securing their long-term technological sovereignty.

Table 6 below breaks down the areas of consensus and conflict that define the multilateral effort to establish peace and stability in cyberspace.

Table 6. Research Results on Cyber-diplomacy and Global Norms

Research Area	Key Result (Consensual Achievement)	Persistent Limitation or Conflict Area	Implication for Technological Sovereignty
Applicability of International Law (IL)	UN Consensus (GGE and OEWG) that existing International Law (including the UN Charter) is fully applicable to cyberspace.	**Attribution and Threshold of Wrongful Acts:** No agreement on when a specific cyberattack crosses the threshold of "use of force" or "armed attack."	Strengthens the legal capacity of States to respond to cyberattacks but leaves the specific response ambiguous.
Norms of Responsible State Behavior (RBC)	Agreement on a set of 11 Voluntary Norms including: not damaging critical infrastructure, cooperating in incident investigations, and respecting human rights.	**Non-Binding Nature:** RBCs are voluntary, not mandatory. Some States (China, Russia) continue to promote a binding treaty to legitimize state control.	Fosters deterrence through transparency and trust but does not provide a legal enforcement mechanism.
The Role of Non-State Actors	Recognition of the need to include the private sector and civil society in cybersecurity debates (**Multi-stakeholder model**).	**Geopolitical Divide:** Centralized countries limit the participation of non-state actors, favoring exclusive State control over security.	Drives **Distributed Sovereignty** (democracies) which relies on collaboration with tech companies for network defense.
Capacity Building	UN and regional programs (OAS, EU) helping developing countries create CERTs (Cyber Emergency Response Teams) and legal frameworks.	**Persistent Capacity Gap:** Global South countries lack the human and financial resources to implement RBCs effectively, perpetuating dependency.	Cyber-diplomacy is used as a tool to mitigate dependency and promote a more equitable cyberspace.
Discussion on a New Treaty	The proposal for a new global treaty remains a subject of active debate at the UN (driven by Russia).	**Western Opposition:** Western countries oppose this, fearing a new treaty would impose a state-control structure and undermine Internet freedom.	Represents a struggle for the future governance model: **Centralized State vs. Open Internet**.

Own elaboration.

6. CONCLUSION

Quantum Computing: An Emerging Governance Challenge

The prospective arrival of practical quantum computing introduces systemic vulnerabilities that existing digital governance frameworks are not equipped to address. A sufficiently powerful quantum computer could break the cryptographic protocols (RSA, ECC) that underpin secure communications, digital signatures, and authentication systems (Mosca, 2018). This creates a "harvest now, decrypt later" risk: encrypted data transmitted today may be decrypted retroactively, rendering current data protection laws insufficient for long-term confidentiality.

Three governance challenges emerge. First, dependency on foreign post-quantum cryptographic standards may reproduce existing technological hierarchies (Khanal et al., 2024). Second, differential transition capacities between wealthy and developing nations could create a "quantum divide." Third, existing norms of responsible state behavior do not address quantum-specific attack vectors, including the potential for undetectable decryption of historical communications.

For technological sovereignty, quantum preparedness requires three anticipatory actions: mandating cryptographic agility in regulatory frameworks, investing in domestic quantum research and development, and initiating multilateral discussions on quantum-specific norms (Floridi, 2020; Mossé & Sòstres, 2023). States that defer action risk finding their digital infrastructure transparent to quantum-capable adversaries within a decade.

Governance Must Evolve With Technological Disruption

The analysis of digital governance models and technological sovereignty demonstrates an inescapable truth: technological disruption is inherently faster than legislation and diplomacy. Therefore, the ultimate goal of governance cannot be to create a static set of rules, but to establish a dynamic and flexible framework capable of adapting to yet-unconceived threats (such as quantum computing, synthetic biology, or next-generation AI).

The principal conclusion is that effective digital sovereignty is defined by resilience and responsiveness, not by the capacity for absolute control. Governance must adopt iterative design principles and regulatory sandboxes (controlled testing environments) so that policies can be tested, evaluated, and adjusted in real time, rather than waiting years for the passage of a law that is born obsolete.

Successful models, such as the EU AI Act, demonstrate that the appropriate response to new technologies is not to prohibit them, but to classify risk (unacceptable, high, limited) and impose requirements proportional to the potential harm. Furthermore, the reliance on the private sector for infrastructure and technical expertise means that Public-Private Partnerships (PPP) have shifted from being an option to a strategic necessity for national security. No State can achieve sovereignty alone.

The evolution of governance requires discarding the concept of "total sovereignty" (the Great Firewall model) in favor of an open and participatory sovereignty that balances security with openness:

- **Sovereignty of Principles:** Priority must be given to sovereignty over values (Ethics, Human Rights) and autonomy in decision-making, rather than the physical location of every byte of data.
- **Investment in Capacity:** True digital autonomy lies in strategic investment in local talent, research, and open-source development, thereby reducing dependence on the closed technologies and licenses of foreign powers.

Technological disruption will not stop. The governance models that succeed will be those that understand sovereignty not as a protective wall, but as an adaptive capacity that allows the nation to operate with confidence and autonomy in an inherently volatile and competitive cyberspace. The neutrality of technology has ended; governance is now the geopolitical battlefield.

National Autonomy Without Isolationism

The exploration of digital governance models establishes that the strategic response to emerging threats and technological dominance is not digital isolationism (such as the closed intranet model), but the active pursuit of national autonomy. This autonomy is defined as a State's ability to make sovereign decisions and operate resiliently in cyberspace without being vulnerable to external coercion or disruption.

The isolationist model is strategically unviable for most economies due to:

- **Economic Costs:** Disconnecting from the global data flow halts innovation, slows digital trade, and undermines competitiveness. The cost of building a parallel digital ecosystem is prohibitive.
- **Ineffectiveness Against Threats:** Isolation does not prevent state-sponsored attacks or internal threats. In fact, it reduces exposure to global security best practices and essential collaboration in fighting cybercrime.

Digital autonomy must focus on the capacity to choose and to resist, achieved through three pillars:

1. **Diversification (Anti-Dependency):** Reducing critical reliance on a single foreign provider or power for key infrastructure (5G, cloud services).
2. **Interoperability and Open Standards:** Investing in open-source technologies to ensure that entities are not trapped by vendor lock-in and can migrate between platforms.
3. **Sovereignty of Operational Control:** Ensuring that even if data is stored in the cloud, the control over encryption keys, access policies, and legal jurisdiction remains in national hands.

Global Cooperation for Cyber Peace and Stability

The security of a nation is inseparable from the security of the global network. Peace and stability cannot be achieved through unilateral action; they require active and consensual multilateral governance.

- **The Failure of Unilateral Deterrence:** Deterrence based solely on a single State's offensive or defensive capacity is insufficient, as attribution is difficult and cyber-retaliation can escalate unpredictably.
- **The Imperative of Collaboration:** The only effective defense against organized cybercrime and state-sponsored attacks is the exchange of technical information and the harmonization of response capabilities (as seen in NATO, OECD, or ASEAN).

Cyber stability depends on States adhering to internationally accepted norms of behavior, managed through cyber-diplomacy:

- **Norm-Setting:** UN forums (GGE/OEWG) have been crucial in confirming that International Law (including the UN Charter and International Humanitarian Law) is fully applicable to cyberspace.
- **Responsible State Behavior (RBC):** Promoting the universal adoption of RBCs, such as the prohibition of attacking civilian critical infrastructure (health, energy) and the obligation to cooperate in incident investigations.

Cyber stability is a global public good. Autonomy is built by investing in one's own capacity while using regulatory power to compel global actors to respect national sovereignty.

Navigating Digital Sovereignty from the Global South

For nations with limited infrastructure, digital sovereignty cannot mean autarky. The resource and expertise constraints render complete decoupling from foreign providers impractical. Instead, these states must pursue *strategic interdependence*: selectively localizing critical data (health, finance, elections) while accepting reliance on global cloud and AI services for non-sensitive functions. Sovereignty thus becomes a matter of negotiating leverage—through procurement conditions, data protection laws, and regional alliances—rather than achieving technical independence. The goal is not to eliminate dependency but to make it negotiated, transparent, and reversible when necessary.

REFERENCES

Couldry, N., & Mejias, U. A. (2019). *The Costs of Connection: How Data Is Colonizing Human Life and Appropriating It for Capitalism.* Stanford University Press., https://www.sup.org/books/title/?id=28816

European Parliament & Council of the European Union. (2022). Regulation (EU) 2022/1925 of the European Parliament and of the Council of 14 September 2022 on contestable and fair markets in the digital sector (Digital Markets Act). *Official Journal of the European Union, L, 265*, 1–66.

European Parliament & Council of the European Union. (2022). Regulation (EU) 2022/2065 of the European Parliament and of the Council of 19 October 2022 on a Single Market For Digital Services (Digital Services Act). *Official Journal of the European Union, L, 277*, 1–102.

Floridi, L. (2020). The Fight for Digital Sovereignty: What It Is, and Why It Matters, Especially for the EU. *Philosophy & Technology, 33*(3), 369–378. DOI: 10.1007/s13347-020-00423-6 PMID: 35194548

Khanal, A., Adhikari, S., Bista, R., Shrestha, S., & Dahal, K. (2024). A systematic review on AI sovereignty: Challenges, opportunities, and future directions. *International Journal of Information Security*. Advance online publication. DOI: 10.1007/s10207-024-00888-6

Mosca, M. (2018). Cybersecurity in an era of quantum computing: What risks and what responses? *IEEE Security & Privacy*, *16*(5), 38-41. https://doi.org/DOI: 10.1109/MSP.2018.3761723

Mossé, M., & Sòstres, M. (2023). Quantum computing and digital sovereignty: A geopolitical perspective. *European Journal of Futures Research*, *11*(1), 1-12. https://doi.org/DOI: 10.1186/s40309-023-00218-4

Pohle, J., & Thiel, T. (2020). Digital sovereignty. *Internet Policy Review*, *9*(4). Advance online publication. DOI: 10.14763/2020.4.1532

Soriano, J. P. (2025). Geopolitics in the digital age: the U.S.-China competition through their narratives on digital technologies. IDP Revista de Internet Derecho y Política. https://ddd.uab.cat/record/310822

Zhu, Q., & Edelmann, N. (2017). Editorial 9(2). JeDEM - EJournal of EDemocracy and Open Government, 9(2), i - iii. https://doi.org/DOI: 10.29379/jedem.v9i2.487

Chapter 8

International and Local Legal Frameworks for Cybersecurity and Regulatory Advances and Gaps

Ricardo A. Barrera-Cámara
http://orcid.org/0000-0002-3170-4671
Universidad Autónoma del Carmen, Mexico

David H. Fuque-Ehuan
http://orcid.org/0009-0005-5032-8076
Universidad Autónoma del Carmen, Mexico

Alejandro Fuentes-Penna
http://orcid.org/0000-0002-4303-3852
El Colegio de Morelos, Mexico

Fernando E. Sánchez-Martinez
http://orcid.org/0000-0003-4458-5402
Universidad Autónoma del Carmen, Mexico

ABSTRACT

The increase of digital threats and the uneven development of regulations in distinct parts of the world generate significant challenges in data management, the creation of standards for new technologies, and the protection of infrastructure. These differences affect global goals linked to sustainable development objectives, as well as addressing issues related to the safe and responsible use of digital technologies.

DOI: 10.4018/979-8-2600-2845-2.ch008

The study employs qualitative documentary research to analyze laws, regulations, frameworks, and technical standards. The results of the analysis show advances in technological security regulations, as well as the existence of areas that need greater attention to meet the challenges that new technologies demand. Congruent, flexible, and ethical regulatory frameworks are required to strengthen cyber resilience and global sustainability.

INTRODUCTION

The growing development and use of new technologies, digital services, computing, and cloud services has led to an increase in technological threats and risks, as well as inequalities in cybersecurity legal frameworks, both in their design and implementation, affecting data governance.

Regulation is not keeping pace with technological innovation (Zukis, 2022). Instead of collaborating to strengthen security and resilience, countries are developing fragmented regulations (Obioha-Val, 2025). While there have been advances in technical and legal standards, implementation gaps persist due to the speed of technological change and the challenges of digital sovereignty (Farrand & Carrapico, 2022). This reality requires analyzing the relationship between regulatory frameworks and technologies from a cybersecurity perspective.

Ethical principles, technical standards, institutional capacities, and legal frameworks are challenges that must be aligned to ensure effective cybersecurity governance. International regulatory developments regarding cybersecurity governance and the gaps in their implementation in Mexico and Latin America constitute an important contribution to this chapter, showing that fragmented governance, coupled with uneven institutional capacity and emerging technologies, creates risks to data protection, critical infrastructure, and cyberrights.

Given this situation, two research questions arise: What are the main advances and regulatory gaps in data protection and cybersecurity and their impact on international and regional rights and critical infrastructure? How are technical security standards integrated into regulations and legal procedures for their evaluation and compliance, and what challenges do Mexico and Latin America face with the increase in technological and digital risks?

The objective is to analyze models, legal frameworks, national and international regulations, standards for security management, risk management, and AI, in order to identify advances or legal gaps in security management, risk management, data protection, and artificial intelligence, and the situation in Mexico and Latin America.

The study is directly linked to SDG 9, SDG 16, and SDG 17. For Mexico, it contributes to the fulfillment of the 2025-2030 National Development Plan in the areas of governance, well-being, economy and sustainability, protection of rights, international cooperation. and public innovation for national technological development (Presidencia de la República, 2025). It is also linked to the National Strategic Programs by considering regulatory compliance, critical infrastructure, digital services, and data governance in strategic sectors.

The study follows qualitative documentary research (Sumartono et al., 2024), conducting a critical and comparative analysis of the legal framework and technical standards, trends, and emerging technologies related to cybersecurity, data protection, and artificial intelligence.

BACKGROUND

Related Works

The growing use and development of new technologies makes it necessary to establish, create and update regulatory frameworks for data and infrastructure protection at local and international levels.

The creation of an international legal framework is proposed for the protection of digital attacks through technologies that connect countries with each other, which should be strengthened for both public and private sectors through four principles: modernization of cybersecurity laws, uniformity of legal requirements, coordination of cooperation incentives and coercive regulations, and supply chain security (Chatinakrob, 2024; Kosseff, 2018).

Although cyberattacks are categorized in international frameworks to coordinate responses, biases and legal loopholes persist (Rahman & Das, 2024). Therefore, a mandatory and detailed international law is proposed to regulate cybersecurity, protecting the population, humanitarian activities, and infrastructure through strategies for possible war scenarios.

In (Ali, 2024), guides the development of a critical analysis of legal frameworks and cybersecurity standards, including ISO/27001, NIST, the Budapest Convention, and laws in the US, India, the UK, the EU, and Australia. The results indicate that legislation must be adaptable to ongoing development, harmonized internationally, and promote training and privacy to ensure security and resilience.

With (Llamas Covarrubias, 2025), identifies gaps in current proposals that undermine infrastructure and SMEs, proposing a national law to combat cybercrime. For his part, (Almeida, 2025) evaluates European Union frameworks for addressing discrepancies in cybersecurity skills, seeking inclusive standardization applicable to emerging technologies (AI) and small and medium-sized enterprises.

The study (Sehrawat et al., 2025) analyze cybersecurity legislation in the United States, India, and China. Through real-life cases and comparative analysis, they identify legal gaps in the scope, enforcement, and territorial cooperation between these countries.

The literature highlights three key points. First, international laws must be binding and applicable to everyone. Second, security should be based on technical practices rather than binding laws, as it is easier to update a standard than a law. Third, in Latin America, a lack of resources, regulatory shortcomings, and institutional fragmentation hinder the proper implementation of both technical standards and laws.

FOUNDATIONS OF CYBERSECURITY LAW AND REGULATION

The legal architecture of cyberspace is built on the transformation of technical concepts into regulatory obligations. Below, we analyze the legal foundations that determine legal preparedness, examining how the security triad becomes a legal duty, how conflicting laws are categorized, and what international principles limit state power.

Core Legal Concepts: Confidentiality, Integrity, Availability

The technical triad of CIA (Confidentiality, Integrity, and Availability) forms the operational basis of cybersecurity. However, in the contemporary regulatory environment, these concepts are no longer engineering goals but have become enforceable legal obligations. Noncompliance with these standards gives rise to specific criminal, civil, and contractual liabilities.

– Confidentiality has evolved from simple data custody to a legal duty of care, where leaks may be treated as negligence when reasonable safeguards are absent (Snail ka Mtuze & Musoni, 2023; Watney, 2024).

– Integrity confers evidentiary value on information and is essential for the regulation of cybercrimes, as data manipulation can constitute a separate offense; however, the lack of standardized parameters can complicate claims for damages (Nugraha & Martin, 2022; Watney, 2024).

– Availability, understood as a duty of continuity, is essential for protecting critical infrastructure, although prioritizing accessibility over security may increase confidentiality risks (Nugraha & Martin, 2022; Watney, 2024).

Categories of Regulation: Privacy, Cybercrime, Digital Surveillance

The tension between privacy (individual rights) and product security (code robustness) requires a dual legal strategy to manage systems that are technically secure but invasive with regard to data (Ruohonen et al., 2025). In contrast, cybercrime regulation operates under a punitive logic, empowering the state to investigate and cooperate internationally (Watney, 2024).

International Legal Principles: Legality, Necessity, Proportionality

The application of intrusive surveillance technologies requires principles of legitimacy. Legality and necessity prohibit unauthorized secondary uses (such as mass surveillance) and require data minimization under the privacy by design approach (Ruohonen et al., 2025). Likewise, proportionality requires balancing security and rights, measuring the effectiveness of the state in combating cybercrime without nullifying constitutional guarantees (Watney, 2024).

SUPRANATIONAL NORMS AND REGIONAL REGULATIONS

Cybersecurity governance ranges from the regulatory centralization of the European model to voluntary sectoral cooperation in the United States. Faced with this divergence, emerging regions in Asia are seeking a strategic balance between digital sovereignty and the need to maintain cross-border data flows.

The European Union: GDPR and NIS2 Directive

Europe is transitioning from privacy protection (GDPR) to socioeconomic resilience and operational continuity (NIS2). Analysis of the 'Weimar Triangle' reveals that, despite regulatory expansion into new strategic sectors, implementation varies: Germany's institutional strength contrasts with legislative delays in Poland, showing that legal preparedness depends heavily on the maturity of each state (Sałek & Fajdek, 2025).

United States: CCPA, HIPAA, and Federal Approaches

Unlike European centralism, the United States has a fragmented regulatory mosaic due to the absence of comprehensive federal legislation. State initiatives such as the

CCPA, although inspired by the GDPR, prioritize market and consumer logic over human rights, creating internal friction for companies (Khan & Goswami, 2025). At the federal level, reliance on sectoral agencies consolidates a reactive model that, while favoring innovation, leaves gaps in protection and hinders transatlantic cooperation due to legal uncertainty (Ludvigsen, 2024).

Latin America: Brazil's LGPD and Regional Cooperation

Latin America replicates the European model 'Brussels Effect' to ensure data flow, as seen in Brazil's LGPD. However, this mimicry clashes with underfunded infrastructure and weak enforcement capacity, resulting in legal frameworks that are robust on paper but fragile in practice (Khan & Goswami, 2025).

Asia and Africa: Emerging Frameworks and Harmonization Efforts

Asia and Africa are developing hybrid models that subordinate individual privacy to data sovereignty and national security. In East Asia, China is leading the way in data sharing subject to strict location controls (Wan & Ye, 2025). At the same time, ASEAN faces the complexity of harmonizing diverse legal cultures with the digital economy, delaying a common framework (Polii et al., 2025). This asymmetric implementation is replicated in Africa, where initiatives such as the Malabo Convention depend on the pragmatic adaptation of European standards by regional leaders such as South Africa.

TECHNICAL STANDARDS AND LEGAL IMPLEMENTATION

Technical standards are a set of recommendations, specifications, and regulations developed by internationally or nationally recognized organizations with the purpose of making available a general framework that enables risk management, safety assurance, and responsible use of technologies in a global environment.

ISO/IEC Standards in Management of Security, Risk and Artificial Intelligence

Within the ISO/IEC 27000 series, ISO/IEC 27001, establishes requirements for implementing and improving information security management systems, enabling organizations to demonstrate control and governance over security practices(International Organization for Standardization, 2022b). ISO/IEC 27002 complements this standard by providing information security controls and implementation guidelines based on best practices (International Organization for Standardization, 2022c). ISO/IEC 27032 extends this governance approach to cybersecurity by offering guidance for organizations that use the internet, addressing common risks, stakeholder roles, and the relationship between internet, web, network, and cybersecurity (International Organization for Standardization, 2023b).

Other ISO/IEC standards strengthen governance by addressing incident management, risk-based cybersecurity policy, cyber insurance, and privacy. ISO/IEC 27035 provides guidance for preparing for and responding to information security incidents(International Organization for Standardization, 2023b). ISO/IEC 27102 and ISO/IEC 27103 support risk-based cybersecurity policy management and cyber-insurance-related information sharing to protect critical digital assets and manage the impact of cyber incidents (International Organization for Standardization, 2026). ISO/IEC 27701 establishes requirements for a Personal Information Management System, helping controllers and processors align privacy governance with personal data protection and accountability obligations (International Organization for Standardization, 2025).

ISO also addresses the governance of artificial intelligence through a series of standards that contribute to the responsible management of AI. ISO/IEC 22989 specifies the terminology and concepts of artificial intelligence as a basis for governance of artificial intelligence and standardization (International Organization for Standardization, 2022a). ISO/IEC 23894 offers guidance for any organization and context regarding risk management in the development, production, deployment, or use of artificial intelligence products, systems, and services (International Organization for Standardization, 2023a). It also provides processes for effectively integrating and implementing artificial intelligence risk management. ISO/IEC 42001 specifies requirements for the establishment, implementation, maintenance, and continuous improvement of an artificial intelligence management system for any organization, regardless of size or activity, that provides or uses artificial intelligence system products or services; it supports traceability, transparency, and reliability (International Organization for Standardization, 2023c).

Table 1 lists the ISO international technical standards discussed in this chapter, along with their titles, categories, and the specific regulatory areas to which they pertain: security management, cybersecurity, incident response, data protection, and artificial intelligence governance.

Table 1. Technical standards related to security, cybersecurity, incident and artificial intelligence management.

Standard	Category	Specification
ISO/IEC 27001	Security Management	Information Security Management System
ISO/IEC 27002	Security Management	Information security controls
ISO/IEC 27032	Cybersecurity	Network and application risk management
ISO/IEC 27102	Security Management	Cybersecurity insurance
ISO/IEC 27103	Security Management	Cybersecurity insurance
ISO/IEC 27035	Incident Management	Information security incident management
ISO/IEC 27701	Data Protection	Data Privacy
ISO/IEC 42001	Artificial Intelligence	Artificial Intelligence Management System
ISO/IEC 23894	AI and Risk Management	Risk Management in Artificial Intelligence
ISO/IEC 22989	Artificial Intelligence	Fundamental Concepts

Source. Author's own elaboration

ISO/IEC standards are of great importance not only for their technical focus, but also because they serve as a bridge that supports the transition from mandatory legal requirements to practical audits. Accountability and risk management through ISO/IEC 27001 and ISO/IEC 27002, incident management through ISO/IEC 27035, privacy and data protection through ISO/IEC 27701, and ISO/IEC 42001 and ISO/IEC 23894 to document artificial intelligence risk management, responsible use, and transparency. These standards serve as a bridge between mandatory legal requirements and their implementation within organizations.

Sector-Specific Standards: Healthcare, Banking, Critical Infrastructure

The ISO/IEC 2700 family of standards provides the foundations for information security management for any type of organization; however, each organization has its own characteristics and activities, each one requires specific standards linked to the organization's line of business.

– Health. Personal and clinical data are strongly linked to confidentiality, privacy, integrity and availability of data as services.
– Banking. In banking and financial services, they strengthen risk management, transaction security in the face of possible fraud, and operational resilience. In addition, artificial intelligence can be used to evaluate credit risk, increasing the importance of artificial intelligence risk management (ISO/IEC 23894).

– Critical infrastructure. All the services that make it possible for information technologies to function require availability, contingency plans and operational response to possible attacks involving managers, authorities and regulatory entities.

Integration of Technical Norms in National Legislation

The incorporation of technical standards into legislation takes the form of direct references or national adaptations within regulatory frameworks. By linking to mandatory certification and data protection rights, this integration harmonizes policies and risk management, establishing verifiable compliance mechanisms based on best practices.

Digital platforms, services, data, technologies, and technological infrastructures operate beyond national borders, which is why it is important to examine digital sovereignty and jurisdiction in cyberspace.

DIGITAL SOVEREIGNTY AND JURISDICTION IN CYBERSPACE

According to (Mohichehra, 2024), digital sovereignty is the way in which the state exercises its authority in digital environments, and jurisdiction is the authority to apply laws and digital control in environments without physical boundaries. In (Pierucci, 2025), it is stated that sovereignty is control of data and infrastructure, while jurisdiction refers to the scope of laws in digital contexts (digital platform) and persons or entities involved.

Territorial Conflicts in Data Storage and Access

States generate conflicts when they claim right and authority over data, information or infrastructure by considering the physical location of service providers' data centers based on their laws or the laws' own scope (Kaya & Shahid, 2025), the location of data centers the most important point on which the current state the state.

Brief case illustration: The "Warrant Case", where the US government forced Microsoft to hand over data (emails) stored in another country (Ireland) based on the Stored Communications Act (de Hert & Thumfart, 2020). On the other hand, the government of the United States of America and the European Union analyzed various situations and policies to establish a series of restrictions and laws for TikTok based on security concerns and data protection (Cristiano & Monsees, 2025).

The Rise of Sovereign Clouds and Data Localization Laws

A sovereign cloud is a type of cloud designed to comply with laws of a country or region, to ensure storage, processing, management in defined borders that guarantee security, sovereignty and jurisdiction of information (Solanke, 2024).

Data localization laws require that certain data be stored, processed and retained in a certain place; to reduce foreign dependence, improve jurisdictional access, combat security and privacy (Organisation for Economic Co-operation and Development, 2023). On the other hand (Messenger, 2024), it argues that these provisions may affect economic efficiency and international digital trade commitments.

Global Regulatory Fragmentation and Its Risks

Regulatory fragmentation refers to multiple legal initiatives for data protection, platforms, cybersecurity and even data governance, but from a local or national perspective, without following a global and unified perspective (Dunayev & Lugovenko, 2024).

Global regulatory fragmentation can generate several risks (Burri & Kugler, 2024; Guo & Li, 2025): legal uncertainty and regulatory problems, increased compliance costs and barriers to digital trade, weakened cybersecurity and operational resilience, problems in international cooperation and law enforcement, technical fragmentation and reduced interoperability of the digital environment, risks and fragmentation in the protection of fundamental rights and guarantees.

Emerging technologies such as artificial intelligence, the Internet of Things, and neurotechnology are developing and advancing more rapidly than regulatory frameworks, creating risks of regulatory fragmentation.

LEGAL CHALLENGES OF EMERGING TECHNOLOGIES

Technological advancement and the constant use of new technologies present legal challenges (artificial intelligence, biotechnology, cybersecurity, big data, blockchain, IoT, privacy) and problems (loopholes, jurisdiction, liability) when technology advances too fast in relation to the laws that regulate them or there is an absence of these.

Artificial Intelligence: Legal Accountability and Risk

The adoption of autonomous systems reveals a 'responsibility gap' in tort law. Algorithmic opacity and autonomy challenge classic concepts of fault and causality

(Sullivan & Schweikart, 2019) especially in 'black box' systems such as autonomous vehicles or healthcare. This complexity makes it impossible to establish a clear causal link between human action and harm, creating a legal vacuum regarding ultimate liability (Custers et al., 2025).

Brief case illustration: Artificial intelligence can discriminate or cause harm, and as a result, it is difficult to determine who is responsible. The affected party is unable to determine who is responsible for the error, so when something goes wrong, they must be able to identify the responsible party, making human oversight and continuous traceability essential.

Despite ex ante mitigation attempts (such as the EU AI Act), the literature points to a misalignment with ex post civil liability mechanisms. Compliance with administrative standards does not guarantee redress for harm, creating a scenario of sub-deterrence for developers (Chamberlain, 2022). In response to this crisis, the following solutions are proposed:

- Strict liability proposes regulating high-risk AI through mandatory strict and safe regimes, equating it with dangerous activities (Soyer & Tettenborn, 2022; Weil, 2024). This approach is necessary to correct information asymmetry; otherwise, requiring the victim to prove faults in a 'black box' would constitute a probatio diabolica, leaving them defenseless in the face of the technical impossibility of auditing the algorithm (Weil, 2024).
- AI as a Subject of Law. A more radical proposal suggests granting a corporate personality to AI systems, similar to an LLC, allowing them to own assets and insurance of their own to concentrate liability (Lai, 2021).
- Controlling person principle. Alternatively, a residual responsibility is proposed for whoever has the obligation to exercise human control over the system, ensuring that there is always a responsible human agent in the chain.

The academic trend suggests the adaptation of tort law through hybrid mechanisms that contemplate traditional negligence with presumptions of causation and shared liability.

Blockchain and Smart Contracts: Regulation by Design

Blockchain architecture conflicts with data protection rights, particularly in the tension between Article 17 of the GDPR and blockchain immutability. Pseudonymization, hashes, and public keys do not necessarily constitute full anonymization; therefore, they may still be treated as personal data (Politou et al., 2019). There is another governance issue when there is no central authority capable of enforcing evacuation orders, leaving those affected without legal recourse (Tatar et al., 2020).

Smart contracts can validate the initial agreement, but they struggle to apply complex legal principles, such as good faith, during their execution. This can lead to irreversible outcomes and subsequent litigation, limiting their viability as legal instruments (Drummer & Neumann, 2020; Giancaspro, 2017).

Similarly, the fact that DAOs lack legal personality can expose their members to unlimited liability. Furthermore, their decentralized structure makes it more difficult to determine which jurisdiction applies and how to serve legal summonses (Guillaume, 2024).

Metaverse, IoT and Neurotech: Normative Blind Spots

Current frameworks such as the GDPR are insufficient to protect neural data, as they underestimate the risk of cognitive intervention. It is therefore imperative to create 'neuro-rights' that guarantee mental integrity in the face of external interference (Lenca & Andorno, 2017). Given the technological capacity to decode thought, urgent constitutional barriers are needed to preserve human autonomy in the face of the advance of neurocapitalism (Szoszkiewicz & Yuste, 2025).

The expectation of ownership in the metaverse clashes with its revocable license nature. To provide economic security, the law must recognize these assets as full property (Buletsa, 2022) overcoming the Terms of Service regime that currently allows for their unilateral removal without compensation (Hutson et al., 2023).

Security obsolescence in the IoT requires a redefinition of civil liability, classifying software vulnerabilities as manufacturing defects (Crootof, 2019) For the IoMT, given the possibility of physical harm or death, preventive cybersecurity regulation is mandatory, replacing any user disclaimer (Thomasian & Adashi, 2021).

Table 2 summarizes the critical regulatory frictions identified throughout this topic, as well as the solutions proposed to overcome them.

Table 2. Regulatory obsolescence matrix and doctrinal proposals on emerging technologies.

Technology	Traditional Legal Principle (Status Quo)	Technological Friction	Proposed Solution
Inteligencia Artificial	Negligence and Linear Causality	Black box: opacity and autonomy break the causal link. The victim faces a diabolical test.	Objective liability and compulsory insurance to correct asymmetry (Soyer & Tettenborn, 2022; Weil, 2024)
Blockchain	Right to be forgotten (GDPR, Art. 17)	Immutability: Technical impossibility of deleting data without breaking the chain. Absence of a "Data Controller".	Law by design or off-chain storage of personal data (Politou et al., 2019; Tatar et al., 2020)
Smart Contracts	Voluntariness of the parties and contractual fairness.	Code rigidity: Binary inability to handle ambiguity, force majeure, or good faith.	Hybrid governance: Insertion of escape clauses in the code or ex post judicial review (Giancaspro, 2017)
DAOs	Juristic personality and limited liability.	Decentralization: The lack of formal registration results in unlimited and joint liability for the partners.	Digital Personality: Recognition of new types of companies (digital LLC) or algorithmic personality (Guillaume, 2024; Sims, 2019)
Neurotechnology	Data Privacy (Medical Approach)	Mental Decoding: Technical ability to read and manipulate the "internal forum" (thoughts).	Neuro rights: New human rights to protect cognitive freedom and mental integrity (Lenca & Andorno, 2017; Szoszkiewicz & Yuste, 2025)

Source. Prepared internally based on a review of the literature and doctrine.

The integration of various technologies and the lack of regulatory standards put businesses and individuals at risk, making the protection of critical infrastructure vital to maintaining services.

LEGAL PROTECTION OF CRITICAL INFRASTRUCTURE AND NATIONAL CYBERDEFENSE

The technological assets and infrastructure of organizations and countries must be protected physically and digitally through the establishment of standards, laws, policies and strategies against any possible threat.

ICS, SCADA Systems and National Cybersecurity Strategies

The application of IT standards (such as ISO 27001) in critical infrastructures is ineffective and risky, as SCADA architecture prioritizes physical availability over confidentiality, and standard technical requirements can destabilize real-time processes (Nazir et al., 2017).

Brief case illustration: SCADA industrial architecture was designed to operate without interruptions and did not account for cybersecurity; therefore, security measures must be implemented gradually to avoid disrupting the system's operation and the sector to which it belongs.

The obsolescence of hardware in legacy systems creates an unsolvable legal conflict: critical infrastructures operate with decades-old technology without native security. Modern directives such as NIS2 demand standards that are technically unattainable for this equipment without a total overhaul, causing a critical gap between regulatory requirements and operational capacity (Naval et al., 2025; Teichmann, 2025).

There is a market failure where low fines make it rational to prioritize the payment of penalties (OpEx) over costly SCADA system upgrades (CapEx). This financial decision discourages risk mitigation and leaves the state vulnerable to systemic attacks (Falco et al., 2018).

Legal Instruments for Incident Response and Resilience

Regulatory Divergence and Administrative Overload

The effectiveness of incident response is compromised by global regulatory divergence. Faced with inconsistent definitions and contradictory regimes (GDPR, nFADP, SEC), multinational companies must divert technical resources toward compliance bureaucracy, incurring high operating costs and legal uncertainty risks (Ecabert et al., 2024; Marotta & Madnick, 2023).

The Risk of Civil Self-Incrimination

The lack of procedural protection makes cooperation with authorities a double-edged sword: forensic reports can be used as evidence in civil trials. In ransomware incidents, this risk of self-incrimination creates a perverse incentive to limit transparency to the strict legal minimum (Teichmann & Wittmann, 2023).

Evolution of the Corporate Standard of Care

Cybersecurity is a core fiduciary duty where technological ignorance is not a valid defense. Directors face direct personal liability for supervisory failures or delays in disclosure, transforming what was once a technical risk into an existential corporate risk (Trautman & Ormerod, 2017).

International Cooperation and Cyber Treaties

The speed of cybercrime has rendered the slow diplomatic processes of MLATs obsolete. To overcome this barrier, the Second Additional Protocol to the Budapest Convention introduces a mechanism for direct cooperation between authorities and private service providers, "bypassing" traditional state bureaucracy to secure digital evidence before it disappears (Conversano, 2024).

The new UN Convention adopted in 2024 complicates geopolitical order by creating a parallel legal system that is less rigorous than the Budapest Convention. Its weakness in protecting human rights and excessive delegation to local law mark a setback in the global standardization of cybersecurity (Bannelier, 2025; Watney, 2025).

The global regulatory divides the scene into two camps (Table 3): the rights-based model (Budapest) versus strict cyber sovereignty (UN). This polarization traps multinationals in an unsolvable legal dilemma, where complying with data requests under the UN framework carries the risk of violating the privacy standards and fundamental rights of the Budapest camp (Novo, 2025; Tropina, 2024; Watney, 2025).

Table 3. Comparative Analysis of Regulatory Divergence: Budapest Convention vs UN Convention

Dimension of Analysis	Budapest Convention (2001)	UN Convention (2024)
Human rights safeguards	Explicit and robust. Article 15 makes cooperation conditional on compliance with international standards (such as the ECHR or the ICCPR).	Depending on local law. Although it mentions human rights, it delegates interpretation and application to the domestic legislation of each State, weakening global protection.
Scope of Jurisdiction	Targeted. It is mainly limited to specific cybercrimes defined in the treaty.	Expansive. Evidence-gathering powers apply to any serious crime, not just cybercrimes, broadening the risk of surveillance.
Risk of Political Abuse	Low. Designed between states with relatively convergent democratic standards.	Stop. Critics warn that its vague wording allows for the legitimization of "information control" and the persecution of dissent under the guise of cybercrime.
Impact on Governance	It acts as a standard for harmonization and reference even for non-signatories.	Causes a risk of "legal bifurcation" and fragmentation, forcing a choice between two contradictory regimes.

Source. Own work based on (Bannelier, 2025; Novo, 2025; Tropina, 2024; Watney, 2025).

EVALUATION MECHANISMS AND LEGAL COMPLIANCE

Audits, Data Protection Impact Assessments (DPIAs), and Sanctions

Demonstrable accountability demands more than formal compliance; it requires the integration of technical audits, impact assessments, and analyses of the risks of penalties. The impact of the GDPR shows that compliance increases operating costs and affects profitability; audits must go beyond legal checklists and focus on the effectiveness of security controls (Frey & Presidente, 2024).

Uneven publication of sanctions by European authorities creates information asymmetries, limiting companies' ability to identify sanctioned behaviors and forcing auditors to adopt a cautious risk approach (Baquero et al., 2025).

PIA and DPIA methodologies still face standardization problems, as they often lack empirical validation and weakly integrate legal requirements with technical controls. Hybrid frameworks should link Article 35 of the GDPR with information security standards to support objective risk measurement (Wairimu et al., 2024).

Compliance Maturity Models and Legal Readiness

The adoption of maturity models such as CMMC or ISO presents a serious asymmetry: although small and medium-sized enterprises are the backbone of the economy, they face critical structural barriers. Even though one in five global cyber threats attacks an SME, international standards are generic and require hundreds of technical controls that exceed their financial and operational capacity (Pawar & Palivela, 2025).

Limited resources and a lack of expertise perpetuate a state of technical defenselessness that, far from achieving managed maturity, prevents organizations from complying with strict legal mandates such as the GDPR due to vulnerabilities such as obsolete software (Ali et al., 2025).

Costs and inadequate infrastructure hinder the adoption of new security tools (Oldemeyer et al., 2024) Therefore, requiring CMMC 2 or 3 maturity levels without adapted frameworks such as the BDSLCCI model could exclude a large part of the market, forcing companies to choose between the cost of compliance or legal risk (Pawar & Palivela, 2025).

Given the difficulty in interpreting abstract standards and the slow implementation of the schemes under Article 42 of the GDPR, the ISO/IEC 27701 standard has established itself as the de facto global compliance mechanism. This functional replacement of legal certification poses a critical duality defined as both a threat and an opportunity (Lachaud, 2020):

1. Opportunity. It offers organizations a ready-made solution that operationalizes vague legal requirements into auditable controls, allowing them to demonstrate due diligence in multiple jurisdictions simultaneously.
2. Threat. It creates the risk of establishing a parallel, privatized compliance regime, where the validation of fundamental rights depends on commercial auditors rather than authorities, which could lead to the "commodification" of rights guarantees.

Although there are theoretical tensions, the practical usefulness of the standards is undeniable. The mapping of controls carried out in recent literature confirms a substantial, though not total, alignment between technical standards and legal obligations. According to the analysis of ISO 27701 controls against the GDPR, it is evident that information security controls (Annex A of ISO 27001) satisfactorily cover the requirements of Article 32 of the GDPR (Security of processing).

Legal preparedness transcends technology. ISO 27701 integrates governance controls, such as rights management and privacy by design, which act as a bridge to regulatory compliance. While its adoption does not provide absolute legal certainty, it constitutes the most robust evidence of proactive responsibility for operating in the global market.

In Table 4, it shows the legal requirements for auditable technical artifacts, including ambiguity, ISO/IEC 27701 control, and artifacts/evidence.

Table 4. Operationalization of legal requirements in auditable technical artefacts.

Legal Requirement (GDPR)	Ambiguity Challenge	ISO/IEC 27701 Control (Tool)	Artifact/Specific Evidence (What is Delivered)
Art. 33. Notification of security breaches (<72 hours).	The law does not define how to detect the breach or how to measure 72 hours.	Clause 6.13.1: Management of information security incidents.	Audit Logs (SIEM): Records with immutable timestamps that show the exact time of detection vs. the time of reporting.
Article 25. Privacy by Design and by Default.	Article 25: Privacy by Design and by Default.	Clause 6.14.1.2: Security in the development of lifecycle.	DPIA (Data Protection Impact Assessment) Report: Document signed prior to the launch of the software detailing the data flow and mitigated risks.
Art. 28. Management of Data Processors (Suppliers).	Difficulty monitoring the security of third parties/ suppliers.	Clause 7.2.2: Agreements with PII (Personal Information) managers.	Responsibility Matrix (RACI): Technical contractual annex that defines who encrypts, who backs up, and who deletes data.
Art. 17. Right to Erasure ("Right to be Forgotten").	Technical difficulty in deleting data in immutable backups.	Clause 6.6.2: Secure disposal and erasure of media.	Data Destruction Certificate: A cryptographic or physical report that validates the irretrievable overwriting of information.

Source. Author's own work, based on the analysis of controls (Lachaud, 2020) and documentation requirements (Anwar & Gill, 2020; Carneiro et al., 2025).

Table 4 is a representation of the GDPR requirements in relation to the ISO/IEC 27701 standard; the articles represent key areas where legal obligations demand auditable technical evidence: data breaches, privacy by design, processor management, and the right to erasure. It illustrates how abstract legal obligations can be operationalized by applying specific technical measures; this does not replace a specific legal assessment for each jurisdiction.

Public-Private Collaboration for Regulatory Enforcement

The complexity of cyberspace has overwhelmed the unilateral surveillance capabilities of states. As a result, regulatory enforcement is shifting toward a hybrid model of public-private partnership (PPP), where responsibility for compliance is shared between authorities and infrastructure operators.

The critical challenge of public-private collaboration lies in enabling the regulatory flow of data in sensitive environments such as Health Information Exchanges (HIEs) and Trusted Research Environments (TREs). Given that contracts are insufficient in these ecosystems, it is imperative to implement Data Protection by Design (DPbD) to integrate governance directly into the architecture. This transforms exchange mechanisms into auditable infrastructures where the law is translated into code, enabling research without compromising the privacy required by the GDPR (Conley & Pocs, 2018).

Given the inability of regulators (DPAs) to conduct mass audits, the state tacitly delegates oversight into the private sector, using the ISO/IEC 27701 standard as evidence of compliance. Although this creates a private certification market that risks leaving the interpretation of the law in corporate hands, this symbiosis is emerging as the only sustainable model for global data governance (Lachaud, 2020).

Analysis of assessment and compliance mechanisms reveals that legal preparedness in 2024 is no longer a binary state of compliance, but rather a continuous process of risk management:

1. Economically, as demonstrated (Frey & Presidente, 2024), the cost of compliance is material and affects competitiveness, acting as a barrier to entry that purifies the market.
2. Technically, the adoption of maturity models and standards such as ISO 27701 has become indispensable for translating abstract legal mandates into concrete operations, especially in the absence of uniform transparency in sanctions (Baquero et al., 2025).
3. Strategically, public-private collaboration is no longer optional; secure interoperability between state and commercial infrastructures (Conley & Pocs, 2018) is the new standard for regulatory enforcement.

MEXICO AND LATIN AMERICA: LOCAL REGULATIONS IN A GLOBAL CONTEXT

The protection of personal data in Latin America is fundamental to digital governance and cybersecurity, although the region lacks regulations that integrate these aspects holistically. Instead, regulatory fragmentation prevails, with each country adapting national models based on fundamental rights or general standards.

The evolution of new technologies, coupled with the digitization of data, raises ethical and legal concerns about storage, access, automatic processing, biases in artificial intelligence models, processing, transparency, and even the lack of regulations on artificial intelligence and cybersecurity.

The protection of personal data in legislation for the public and private sectors is one of the actions for which Mexico is recognized. However, local regulations on personal data protection, cybersecurity, and artificial intelligence are highly influenced by international standards, trends, and models.

The Mexican Data Protection Framework and the Role of INAI

Mexico, based on human rights as its foundation, updated its constitution to protect personal data. Articles 6 and 16 of the constitution are examples of this. Article 6 guarantees the right to information and free access to it, as well as the right of reply and access to information and communication technologies; Article 16 (Diario Oficial de la Federación, 2009) was added and updated to protect people's rights, giving them control and rights over their personal data.

Under the approach to personal data protection, two laws have been enacted, one aimed at the private sector and the other at the public sector: the Federal Law on Protection of Personal Data Held by Private Parties (LFPDPPP) and the General Law on Protection of Personal Data Held by Obligated Subjects (LGPDPPSO):

– The Federal Law on Protection of Personal Data Held by Private Parties regulates the processing of information in the private sector to guarantee privacy and informational self-determination (Diario Oficial de la Federación, 2025a). The purpose of this law is to protect personal data held by private parties (companies or various organizations), to regulate its controlled and informed processing, and to guarantee individuals' privacy and right to informational self-determination. In other words, individuals must be informed of the use of their data, give their authorization, and ensure their rights of access, rectification, cancellation, and opposition. The failure to protect personal data and the unauthorized access and misuse of data are directly related to cybersecurity. Artificial intelligence models process and treat data to build profiles or models for making decisions that may affect individuals' right to access certain products and services.

– General Law on the Protection of Personal Data Held by Obligated Subjects (Diario Oficial de la Federación, 2025b). This law aims to protect, regulate the processing and use of personal data held by public bodies or obligated subjects at all levels of government (federal, state, municipal), state powers, autonomous bodies, and political parties. This allows for equitable processing and ensures that individuals can exercise their ARCO rights.

Complementarily, the General Law on Transparency and Access to Information (Diario Oficial de la Federación, 2025c) aims to ensure that citizens have access to information in a transparent manner and promotes accountability, and access to all public information documented or in the possession of obligated entities.

The National Transparency System brings together agencies to guarantee the right to know, accountability, and data protection at all three levels of government, facilitating requests through its National Platform. However, the Organic Simplification

Decree abolishes the INAI (formerly autonomous) (Diario Oficial de la Federación, 2024) Its functions are transferred: data protection to the Anti-Corruption and Good Governance Secretariat, and access to information to the new decentralized body Transparency for the People.

Independent authorities and international cooperation are essential for auditing artificial intelligence and cybersecurity algorithms to protect human rights (Febles Pozo & Nieto Rojas, 2025). Protection and transparency bodies that depend on the executive branch jeopardize transparency, accountability, and the protection of digital rights (Semanate Esquivel & Recalde Herrera, 2023).

Legislative Challenges: Harmonization, Capacity, Institutional Coordination

Latin American countries have a diversity of regulations with a local focus, which makes it difficult to create regulations for cybersecurity and smart technologies (Antequera, 2023). Although Brazil, Mexico, Chile, and Uruguay are models in personal data laws, the lack of regional integration highlights the absence of common and robust standards. Currently, Mexico, Peru, and Chile are developing key reforms for information management (Garrigues, 2025).

Technical and economic constraints hinder the implementation of security and surveillance models for emerging technologies in Colombia, Peru, Ecuador, and Argentina, creating inequality in institutional capacity (ALSur, 2024). However, the Argentine government continues to prioritize initiatives related to artificial intelligence, data protection, and transparency (Agencia de Acceso a la Información Pública, 2024).

The lack of cooperation and coordination between regulatory bodies and cybersecurity incident response teams create legal loopholes. This has a negative impact on data protection and individual rights, encourages algorithmic bias, and affects incident management (OECD/CAF, 2023).

The Table 5 shows legal frameworks or regulations related to personal data, cybersecurity, and artificial intelligence in Latin American countries.

Table 5. Legal frameworks for data protection, cybersecurity, and artificial intelligence in Latin American countries.

Country	Law or framework	Comments
México	Political Constitution of the United Mexican States (Articles 6 and 16).	Excludes cybersecurity and artificial intelligence.
	Federal Law on Protection of Personal Data Held by Private Parties (LFPDPPP).	Includes general security, excluding AI and cybersecurity.
	General Law on the Protection of Personal Data Held by Obligated Subjects (LGPDPPSO)	Public sector is without regulations and sanctions.
	National Institute for Transparency, Access to Information, and Protection of Personal Data: Resolutions and its successor body	Uncertainty in autonomy of the new body.
Brasil	Lei Geral de Proteção de Dados Pessoais (LGPD) Lei nº 13.709/2018.	Aligned to RGPD; omits AI and minimizes cybersecurity (Gobierno Federal de Brasil, n.d.).
	Marco Civil da Internet (Lei nº 12.965/2014).	Internet rights, AI and cybersecurity loophole (Presidência da República, 2014).
Argentina	Law No. 25326: Protection of Personal Data.	Protects personal data, omits Big Data and AI (Ministerio de Justicia, 2020).
	Proposed amendments to the Personal Data Protection Act and regulation of AI.	Uncertain legal transition due to lack of oversight in AI, cybersecurity and personal data (Agencia de Acceso a la Información Pública, 2023; Honorable Cámara de Diputados de la Nación, 2025; Poder Ejecutivo Nacional, 2023).
Colombia	Ley Estatutaria 1581, Decreto 1377.	Protection of personal data (Congreso de la República de Colombia, 2012).
Chile	Law No. 19,628: Protection of Privacy	It is aimed at protecting personal data (Congreso Nacional de Chile, 1999).
	Law No. 21719: Protection of Personal Data	Personal data protection (Congreso Nacional de Chile, 2024).
Perú	Law No. 29733: Personal Data Protection Law.	Focuses on personal data protection, creation of the Data Protection Agency (Congreso de la República del Perú, 2011), transparent use IA (Poder Ejecutivo del Perú, 2024).
	Peru's Digital Rights Charter	Right of access to the Internet and ICT (Presidencia del Consejo de Ministros, 2022).
Ecuador	Organic Law on Personal Data Protection	Privacy and protection of personal Data (Asamblea Nacional del Ecuador, 2021).

continued on following page

Table 5. Continued

Country	Law or framework	Comments
Uruguay	Law No. 18,331 on Personal Data Protection and Habeas Data Action	Privacy and protection of personal data in public or private repositories (Parlamento del Uruguay, 2008).
	Decree No. 451/009	Creation of a national computer security incident response center (Poder Ejecutivo de Uruguay, 2009).
	Artificial Intelligence Strategy for Digital Government	Responsible and ethical use of AI in the public Sector (Agencia de Gobierno Electrónico y Sociedad de la Información y del Conocimiento, 2021).
Latin America	Laws of each country based on the General Data Protection Regulation	Lack of cooperation, collaboration, and organization for the creation of regulations or standards.

Source: Own work.

Proposals for a Latin American Digital Rights Charter

The Ibero-American Charter of Principles and Rights in Digital Environments is an initiative approved by several Latin American countries that includes policies aimed at technological development, the development of digital societies, the protection of people's rights in digital environments, digital divides, artificial intelligence, inclusion, and equity (Secretaría General Iberoamericana, 2023). It is based on 10 Basic principles: Person-centeredness; Digital inclusion and connectivity; Privacy, trust, data security and cybersecurity; Full access to education, culture and health in inclusive and secure digital environments; Special attention to children and adolescents; Social, economic and political participation in fair and sustainable digital environments; Digital public administration; Fair, inclusive and secure digital economy; Approach to emerging technologies that does not renounce the centrality of people; Ibero-American assistance and cooperation for digital transformation.

CONCLUSION

The progress and challenges in cybersecurity are reflected in the implementation of the GDPR, NIST2 Directive, standards, artificial intelligence governance models, and data protection laws. Unfortunately, proper implementation is hindered by a lack of international and institutional cooperation, adequate regulatory harmonization, and the protection of digital rights. The ISO/IEC and NIST CSF 2.0 standards are useful for interpreting legal aspects in auditable controls such as risk management or accountability. The results depend largely on technical capacity, legal enforcement, and harmony and coordination between the public and private sectors. It is essential that legal aspects be verifiable through technical mechanisms. Technical mechanisms must be implemented to verify legal compliance.

Accelerated technological development requires proactive, flexible, and ethical regulations to manage risks and protect critical infrastructures and strengthening citizen trust.

FUTURE RESEARCH DIRECTIONS

Artificial intelligence is a changing and challenging field. The study of standards and specifications related to intelligent agents and systems should be continued. The responsibilities that providers or generators of products and services offer to users should also be considered, as well as the possible design of a framework in this context.

INTEREST CONFLICT

The authors declare that they have no conflict of interest in the publication of this chapter.

REFERENCES

Agencia de Acceso a la Información Pública. (2023). *Resolución N.º 161/2023: Programa de transparencia y protección de datos personales en el uso de la inteligencia artificial.* https://www.argentina.gob.ar/normativa/nacional/resolución-161-2023-389231

Agencia de Acceso a la Información Pública. (2024). *Guía para entidades públicas y privadas en materia de transparencia y protección de datos personales para una inteligencia artificial responsable.* https://www.argentina.gob.ar/sites/default/files/guia_ai-final-2025.pdf

Agencia de Gobierno Electrónico y Sociedad de la Información y del Conocimiento. (2021, April 23). *Estrategia de Inteligencia Artificial.* https://www.gub.uy/agencia-gobierno-electronico-sociedad-informacion-conocimiento/comunicacion/publicaciones/estrategia-inteligencia-artificial

Ali, A. B. A., Ayyasamy, R. K., Akbar, R., Jebna, A. K., & Adnan, K. (2025). Cybersecurity infrastructure compliance key factors to detect and mitigate malware attacks in SMEs: A systematic literature review. *SAGE Open*, *15*(1), 21582440251314671. Advance online publication. DOI: 10.1177/21582440251314671

Ali, M. J. (2024). Cybercrime and Cybersecurity: A Critical Analysis of Legal Frameworks and Enforcement Mechanisms. *Bharati International Journal of Multidisciplinary Research & Development*, *2*(8), 137–154. DOI: 10.70798/Bijmrd/020800017

Almeida, F. (2025). Comparative analysis of EU-based cybersecurity skills frameworks. *Computers & Security*, *151*, 104329. DOI: 10.1016/j.cose.2025.104329

ALSur. (2024). *The Regulatory Pathways for AI in Latin America.* https://www.alsur.lat/sites/default/files/2024-09/ALSUR%20-%20IA%20en%20Latam%20%5BENG%5D.pdf

Antequera, C. (2023, June 19, 2023). *Data protection in Latin American countries. ClarkeModet.* https://www.clarkemodet.com/en/articles/data-protection-in-latin-american-countries

Anwar, M., & Gill, A. (2020). Developing an integrated ISO 27701 and GDPR based information privacy compliance requirements model. In *ACIS 2020 Proceedings Article 20.* https://aisel.aisnet.org/acis2020/20

Asamblea Nacional del Ecuador. (2021). *Ley Orgánica de Protección de Datos Personales.* https://www.finanzaspopulares.gob.ec/wp-content/uploads/2021/07/ley_organica_de_proteccion_de_datos_personales.pdf

Bannelier, K. (2025). Risks and opportunities of the UN Cybercrime Convention for the UNODC & the fight against transnational organised crime: A first assessment. *Transnational Criminal Law Review*, *4*(1), 140–155. DOI: 10.22329/tclr.v4i1.9468

Baquero, P. M., Wang, A., & Amariles, D. R. (2025). Unveiling transparency in data protection enforcement across the EU: Assessing the level and quality of disclosure of GDPR fines by data protection authorities. *European Law Journal*, *31*(3), 177–202. DOI: 10.1111/eulj.70008

Buletsa, S. (2022). Virtualne maino u metavsesviti yak obiekt cyvilnykh prav. *Uzhhorod National University Herald. Series. Law*, *72*, 21. DOI: 10.24144/2307-3322.2022.72.21

Burri, M., & Kugler, K. (2024). Regulatory autonomy in digital trade agreements. *Journal of International Economic Law*, *27*(3), 397–423. DOI: 10.1093/jiel/jgae025

Carneiro, F. D., Rampasso, I. S., de Matos Mello, S. L., Sigahi, T. F. A. C., Lespay, H., & Anholon, R. (2025). A flexible ISO 27701-based framework for assessing cybersecurity maturity: A proposition and a case application. *Computers & Security*, *158*, 104645. DOI: 10.1016/j.cose.2025.104645

Chamberlain, J. (2022). The risk-based approach of the European Union's proposed artificial intelligence regulation: Some comments from a tort law perspective. *European Journal of Risk Regulation*, *14*(1), 1–13. DOI: 10.1017/err.2022.38

Chatinakrob, T. (2024). Interplay of International Law and Cyberspace: State Sovereignty Violation, Extraterritorial Effects, and the Paradigm of Cyber Sovereignty. *Chinese Journal of International Law*, *23*(1), 25–72. DOI: 10.1093/chinesejil/jmae005

Conley, E., & Pocs, M. (2018). GDPR compliance challenges for interoperable health information exchanges (HIEs) and trustworthy research environments (TREs). *European Journal for Biomedical Informatics*, *14*(3), 7. Advance online publication. DOI: 10.24105/ejbi.2018.14.3.7

Conversano, M. (2024). Il fattore temporale nell'acquisizione transfrontaliera delle e-evidence: Il bilanciamento operato nel secondo Protocollo addizionale alla Convenzione di Budapest. *La Nuova Giuridica*, *6*(2), 62–76. DOI: 10.36253/lng-3409

Cristiano, F., & Monsees, L. (2025). Beyond the ban: TikTok and the politics of digital sovereignty in the EU and US. *Politics and Governance*, *13*, e10461. DOI: 10.17645/pag.10461

Crootof, R. (2019). The Internet of torts: Expanding civil liability standards to address corporate remote interference. *Duke Law Journal*, *69*(3), 583–667.

Custers, B., Lahmann, H., & Scott, B. (2025). From liability gaps to liability overlaps: Shared responsibilities and fiduciary duties in AI and other complex technologies. *AI & Society*, *40*(5), 4035–4050. DOI: 10.1007/s00146-024-02137-1

de Hert, P., & Thumfart, J. (2020). The Microsoft Ireland case, the CLOUD Act and the cyberspace sovereignty trilemma: Post-territorial technologies and companies question regulatory state monopolies. In Hötzendorfer, W., Tschohl, C., & Kummer, F. (Eds.), *International trends in legal informatics: Festschrift for Erich Schweighofer* (pp. 373–417)., DOI: 10.38023/47fd0a3f-c62a-4cd6-840e-e8ea89bdea68

de la República de Colombia, C. (2012). *Ley Estatutaria 1581 de 2012 por la cual se dictan disposiciones generales para la protección de datos personales.* https://www.funcionpublica.gov.co/eva/gestornormativo/norma.php?i=53646

de la República del Perú, C. (2011). *Ley N.º 29733, Ley de protección de datos personales.* https://www.minsa.gob.pe/Recursos/OGTI/SINADEF/Ley-29733.pdf

Diario Oficial de la Federación. (2009). *Decreto por el que se adiciona un párrafo segundo al artículo 16 de la Constitución Política de los Estados Unidos Mexicanos.* https://dof.gob.mx/nota_detalle.php?codigo=5092143&fecha=01/06/2009#gsc.tab=0

Diario Oficial de la Federación. (2024). *Decreto de simplificación orgánica (December 20, 2024).* https://www.dof.gob.mx/nota_detalle.php?codigo=5745905&fecha=20/12/2024

Diario Oficial de la Federación. (2025a). *Ley Federal de Protección de Datos Personales en Posesión de los Particulares (última reforma publicada el 14 de noviembre de 2025).* https://www.diputados.gob.mx/LeyesBiblio/pdf/LFPDPPP.pdf

Diario Oficial de la Federación. (2025b). *Ley General de Protección de Datos Personales en Posesión de Sujetos Obligados (reforma publicada el 14 de noviembre de 2025).* https://www.diputados.gob.mx/LeyesBiblio/pdf/LGPDPPSO.pdf

Diario Oficial de la Federación. (2025c). *Ley General de Transparencia y Acceso a la Información Pública (last amended March 20, 2025).* https://www.diputados.gob.mx/LeyesBiblio/pdf/LGTAIP.pdf

Drummer, D., & Neumann, D. (2020). Is code law? Current legal and technical adoption issues and remedies for blockchain-enabled smart contracts. *Journal of Information Technology*, *35*(4), 337–360. DOI: 10.1177/0268396220924669

Dunayev, I., & Lugovenko, N. (2024). The state and personal data in the post-GDPR world: Towards a global consensus or regulatory fragmentation? *Theory and Practice of Public Administration*, *2*(79), 28–62. DOI: 10.26565/1727-6667-2024-2-02

Ecabert, T., Muhly, F., & Zimmermann, V. (2024). Implications of cyber incident reporting obligations on multinational organizations headquartered in Switzerland. *International Cybersecurity Law Review*, *5*(4), 585–614. DOI: 10.1365/s43439-024-00129-x

Falco, G., Caldera, C., & Shrobe, H. (2018). IIoT Cybersecurity Risk Modeling for SCADA Systems. *IEEE Internet of Things Journal*, *5*(6), 4486–4495. DOI: 10.1109/JIOT.2018.2822842

Farrand, B., & Carrapico, H. (2022). Digital sovereignty and taking back control: From regulatory capitalism to regulatory mercantilism in EU cybersecurity. *European Security*, *31*(3), 435–453. DOI: 10.1080/09662839.2022.2102896

Febles Pozo, N., & Nieto Rojas, P. (2025). *Inteligencia artificial y protección de datos: desafíos en la era digital*. Colex., DOI: 10.69592/979-13-7011-111-3

Frey, C. B., & Presidente, G. (2024). Privacy regulation and firm performance: Estimating the GDPR effect globally. *Economic Inquiry*, *62*(3), 1074–1089. DOI: 10.1111/ecin.13213

Garrigues. (2025, January 7). *Data protection evolving regulation in Latin America and their impact on labor relations*. https://www.garrigues.com/en_GB/new/data-protection-evolving-regulation-latin-america-and-their-impact-labor-relations

Giancaspro, M. (2017). Is a 'smart contract' really a smart idea? Insights from a legal perspective. *Computer Law & Security Review*, *33*(6), 825–835. DOI: 10.1016/j.clsr.2017.05.007

Gobierno Federal de Brasil. (n.d.). *Lei Geral de Proteção de Dados Pessoais (LGPD)*. Retrieved November 25, 2025, from https://www.gov.br/esporte/pt-br/acesso-a-informacao/lgpd

Guillaume, F. (2024). Decentralized autonomous organizations (DAOs) before state courts: How can private international law keep up with global digital entities? In Perestrelo de Oliveira, M., & Garcia Rolo, A. (Eds.), *Decentralised Autonomous Organisation (DAO) Regulation: Principles and Perspectives for the Future* (pp. 135–168). Mohr Siebeck., DOI: 10.1628/978-3-16-163701-8

Guo, S., & Li, X. (2025). Cross-border data flow in China: Shifting from restriction to relaxation? *Computer Law & Security Review*, *56*, 106079. DOI: 10.1016/j.clsr.2024.106079

Honorable Cámara de Diputados de la Nación. (2025). *Proyecto de ley: Marco legal para el desarrollo, implementación y uso responsable de sistemas de inteligencia artificial (IA) en Argentina.* https://rest.hcdn.gob.ar/web/tramites-parlamentarios/render/adjunto/6893e15373329.pdf

Hutson, J., Banerjee, G., Kshetri, N., Odenwald, K., & Ratican, E. (2023). Architecting the metaverse: Blockchain and the financial and legal regulatory challenges of virtual real estate. *Journal of Intelligent Learning Systems and Applications, 15*(1), 1–23. DOI: 10.4236/jilsa.2023.151001

International Organization for Standardization. (2022a). *ISO/IEC 22989:2022 Information technology — Artificial intelligence — Artificial intelligence concepts and terminology* (ISO/IEC 22989:2022). https://www.iso.org/standard/74296.html

International Organization for Standardization. (2022b). *ISO/IEC 27001:2022 Information security, cybersecurity and privacy protection — Information security management systems — Requirements* (ISO/IEC 27001:2022). https://www.iso.org/standard/27001

International Organization for Standardization. (2022c). *ISO/IEC 27002:2022 Information security, cybersecurity and privacy protection — Information security controls* (ISO/IEC 27002:2022). https://www.iso.org/standard/75652.html

International Organization for Standardization. (2023a). *ISO/IEC 23894:2023 Information technology — Artificial intelligence — Guidance on risk management* (ISO/IEC 23894:2023). https://www.iso.org/standard/77304.html

International Organization for Standardization. (2023b). *ISO/IEC 27035-1:2023 Information technology — Information security incident management — Part 1: Principles and process* (ISO/IEC 27035-1:2023). https://www.iso.org/standard/78973.html

International Organization for Standardization. (2023c). *ISO/IEC 42001:2023 Information technology — Artificial intelligence — Management systems* (ISO/IEC 42001:2023). https://www.iso.org/standard/81230.html

International Organization for Standardization. (2025). *ISO/IEC 27701:2025 Information security, cybersecurity and privacy protection — Privacy information management systems — Requirements and guidance* (ISO/IEC 27701:2025). https://www.iso.org/standard/27701

International Organization for Standardization. (2026). *ISO/IEC TS 27103:2026 Cybersecurity — Guidance on using ISO and IEC standards in a cybersecurity framework* (ISO/IEC TS 27103:2026). https://www.iso.org/es/norma/27103

Kaya, M., & Shahid, H. (2025). Cross-border data flows and digital sovereignty: Legal dilemmas in transnational governance. *Interdisciplinary Studies in Society, Law, and Politics*, *4*(2), 219–233. DOI: 10.61838/kman.isslp.4.2.20

Khan, M. N. I., & Goswami, D. (2025). Cybercrime and contractual liability: A systematic review of legal precedents and risk mitigation frameworks. *Journal of Sustainable Development and Policy*, *1*(1), 1–24. DOI: 10.63125/x3cd4413

Kosseff, J. (2018). Developing collaborative and cohesive cybersecurity legal principles. In *2018 10th International Conference on Cyber Conflict (CyCon). (283–298)*. IEEE. DOI: 10.23919/CYCON.2018.8405022

Lachaud, E. (2020). ISO/IEC 27701 standard: Threats and opportunities for GDPR certification. *European Data Protection Law Review*, *6*(2), 194–210. DOI: 10.21552/edpl/2020/2/7

Lai, A. (2021). Artificial intelligence, LLC: Corporate personhood as tort reform. *Detroit College of Law at Michigan State University Law Review*, *2021*(2), 597–654.

Lenca, M., & Andorno, R. (2017). Towards new human rights in the age of neuroscience and neurotechnology. *Life Sciences, Society and Policy*, *13*(1), 5. DOI: 10.1186/s40504-017-0050-1

Llamas Covarrubias, J. Z. (2025). Cybersecurity in Mexico: An in-depth analysis of a fragmented regulatory landscape. *Mexican Law Review*, *18*(1), 69–115. DOI: 10.22201/iij.24485306e.2025.1.19686

Ludvigsen, K. R. (2024). Creating cybersecurity regulatory mechanisms, as seen through EU and US law. In Phallack, K., & Honnet, T. (Eds.), *Regulating personal data protection and cybersecurity* (pp. 123–130). Konrad-Adenauer Stiftung., https://www.kas.de/en/web/kambodscha/single-title/-/content/the-law-talk-publication-2023

Marotta, A., & Madnick, S. E. (2023). Regulating cyber incidents: A review of recent reporting requirements. In *Proceedings of the 20th International Conference on Security and Cryptography (SECRYPT 2023)* (pp. 410–416). SciTePress. DOI: 10.5220/0012086000003555

Messenger, G. (2024). Mitigating the rise of unilateralism: Lessons from forestry management. *Journal of International Economic Law*, *27*(2), 223–240. DOI: 10.1093/jiel/jgae018

Ministerio de Justicia. (2020, Octuber 20). *Ley 25.326 de protección de los datos personales*. Retrieved November 29, 2025, from https://servicios.infoleg.gob.ar/infolegInternet/anexos/60000-64999/64790/norma.htm

Mohichehra, R. (2024). Sovereignty And Jurisdiction In Cyberspace. *Eurasian Journal of Humanities and Social Sciences, 29*, 14–21. https://geniusjournals.org/index.php/ejhss/article/view/5699

Nacional de Chile, C. (1999). *Ley N° 19.628 Protección de la vida privada*. https://www.dipres.gob.cl/598/articles-51683_Otrasleyes_ley19628.pdf

Nacional de Chile, C. (2024). *Ley N.º 21.719 que regula la protección y el tratamiento de los datos personales y crea la Agencia de Protección de Datos Personales*. https://www.bcn.cl/leychile/navegar?idNorma=1209272

Naval, M., Perjons, E., & Hacks, S. (2025). Cybersecurity challenges in critical infrastructure: A perspective on regulations and competence in Luxembourg. In *Proceedings of the 11th International Conference on Information Systems Security and Privacy:* Volume 1*: ICISSP* (Vol. 1, pp. 15–26). SciTePress. DOI: 10.5220/0013091500003899

Nazir, S., Patel, S., & Patel, D. (2017). Assessing and augmenting SCADA cyber security: A survey of techniques. *Computers & Security*, *70*, 436–454. DOI: 10.1016/j.cose.2017.06.010

Novo, L. (2025). In or out? Managing risks from the UN Cybercrime Convention. In *Proceedings of the 17th International Conference on Cyber Conflict (CyCon 2025)* (pp. 1-18). IEEE. DOI: 10.23919/CyCon65856.2025.11103714

Nugraha, Y., & Martin, A. (2022). Cybersecurity service level agreements: Understanding government data confidentiality requirements. *Journal of Cybersecurity*, *8*(1), tyac004. Advance online publication. DOI: 10.1093/cybsec/tyac004

Obioha-Val, O. A. (2025). Bridging gaps in cybersecurity governance: Leveraging collaborative digital solutions. *Asian Journal of Research in Computer Science, 18*(2), 82–100. OECD/CAF. (2023). *Digital Government Review of Latin America and the Caribbean: Building inclusive and responsive public services*. OECD Publishing. https://doi.org/DOI: 10.9734/ajrcos/2025/v18i2564

Oldemeyer, L., Jede, A., & Teuteberg, F. (2024). Investigation of artificial intelligence in SMEs: A systematic review of the state of the art and the main implementation challenges. *Management Review Quarterly*, *75*(2), 1185–1227. DOI: 10.1007/s11301-024-00405-4

Organisation for Economic Co-operation and Development. (2023). *The nature, evolution and potential implications of data localisation measures* (No. 278). OECD Publishing. DOI: 10.1787/18166873

Parlamento del Uruguay. (2008). *Ley N.º 18.331 de protección de datos personales y acción de habeas data*. https://www.ohchr.org/sites/default/files/Documents/Issues/Privacy/Uruguay.pdf

Pawar, S., & Palivela, H. (2025). Need of paradigm shift in cybersecurity implementation for small and medium enterprises (SMES). *International Journal of Cybersecurity Intelligence & Cybercrime*, *8*(1), 39–75. DOI: 10.52306/2578-3289.1184

Pierucci, F. (2025). Sovereignty in the Digital Era: Rethinking Territoriality and Governance in Cyberspace. *Digital Society : Ethics, Socio-Legal and Governance of Digital Technology*, *4*(1), 27. DOI: 10.1007/s44206-025-00189-4

Poder Ejecutivo de Uruguay. (2009). *Decreto N.º 414/009: Reglamentación de la Ley N.º 18.331, relativo a la protección de datos personales*. https://www.impo.com.uy/bases/decretos/451-2009

Poder Ejecutivo del Perú. (2024). *Decreto Supremo N.º 016-2024-JUS que aprueba el Reglamento de la Ley N.º 29733, Ley de Protección de Datos Personales*. https://www.gob.pe/institucion/smv/normas-legales/6426760-016-2024-jus

Poder Ejecutivo Nacional. (2023). *Proyecto de ley de protección de datos personales (Mensaje N.º 87/2023)*. https://www.argentina.gob.ar/sites/default/files/mensajeyproyecto_leypdp2023.pdf

Polii, V., Julius, D., & Looka Banaya, C. (2025). Legal protection of personal data privacy in the digital era: A comparative study between Indonesia and ASEAN countries. *Jurnal Ilmu Hukum dan Sosial, 3*(2), 1194-1206. DOI: 10.51903/yjyvvy47

Politou, E., Casino, F., Alepis, E., & Patsakis, C. (2019). Blockchain Mutability: Challenges and Proposed Solutions. *IEEE Transactions on Emerging Topics in Computing*, *9*(4), 1972–1986. DOI: 10.1109/TETC.2019.2949510

Presidência da República. (2014, April 23). *Lei nº 12.965/2014 (Marco Civil da Internet)*. Retrieved November 28, 2025, from https://www.planalto.gov.br/ccivil_03/_ato2011-2014/2014/lei/l12965.htm

Presidencia de la República. (2025). *Plan Nacional de Desarrollo 2025-2030*. Diario Oficial de la Federación. https://sidof.segob.gob.mx/notas/docFuente/5755162

Presidencia del Consejo de Ministros. (2022). *Carta Peruana de Derechos Digitales*. https://www.gob.pe/institucion/pcm/informes-publicaciones/3302991-carta-peruana-de-derechos-digitales

Rahman, M. M., & Das, T. K. (2024). Countering cyberattacks: Gaps in international law and prospects for overcoming them. *Journal of Digital Technologies and Law, 2*(4), 973–1002. DOI: 10.21202/jdtl.2024.46

Ruohonen, J., Hjerppe, K., & Kang, E.-Y. (2025). A mapping analysis of requirements between the CRA and the GDPR. In *2025 IEEE 33rd International Requirements Engineering Conference Workshops (REW)* (pp. 215-222). IEEE. DOI: 10.1109/REW66121.2025.00034

Sałek, K., & Fajdek, P. (2025). Analysis of the implementation of the NIS2 directive in the Weimar Triangle countries. *Central European Review of Economics & Finance, 50*(1), 41–52. DOI: 10.24136/ceref.2025.003

Secretaría General Iberoamericana. (2023). *Carta Iberoamericana de Principios y Derechos en los Entornos Digitales* https://segib.org/es/publicacion/carta-iberoamericana-de-principios-y-derechos-en-entornos-digitales/

Sehrawat, A., & Katiyar, A. S. (2025). Cybersecurity laws in the digital age: Gaps and recommendations. *Journal of Informatics Education and Research, 5*(2), 3839–3850. DOI: 10.52783/jier.v5i2.2862

Semanate Esquivel, A., & Recalde Herrera, L. L. (2023). El estado y la defensa de ciberespacio. *Revista de la Academia del Guerra del Ejército Ecuatoriano, 16*(1), 99–109. DOI: 10.24133/AGE.VOL16.N01.2023.07

Sims, A. (2019). Blockchain and decentralised autonomous organisations (DAOs): The evolution of companies? *SSRN, 28*, 423–458. DOI: 10.2139/ssrn.3524674

Snail ka Mtuze, S., & Musoni, M. (2023). An overview of cybercrime law in South Africa. *International Cybersecurity Law Review, 4*(3), 299–323. DOI: 10.1365/s43439-023-00089-8

Solanke, A.ADEDAMOLA ABIODUN SOLANKE. (2024). Sovereign cloud implementation: Technical architectures for data residency and regulatory compliance. *International Journal of Science and Research Archive, 11*(2), 2136–2147. DOI: 10.30574/ijsra.2024.11.2.0502

Soyer, B., & Tettenborn, A. (2022). Artificial intelligence and civil liability—Do we need a new regime? *International Journal of Law and Information Technology, 30*(4), 385–397. DOI: 10.1093/ijlit/eaad001

Sullivan, H., & Schweikart, S. (2019). Are current tort liability doctrines adequate for addressing injury caused by AI? *AMA Journal of Ethics, 21*(2), E160–E166. DOI: 10.1001/amajethics.2019.160

Sumartono, E., Harliyanto, R., Situmeang, S., Siagian, D., & Septaria, E. (2024). The legal implications of data privacy laws, cybersecurity regulations, and AI ethics in a digital society. *The Journal of Academic Science*, *1*(2), 103–110. DOI: 10.59613/29qypw51

Szoszkiewicz, Ł., & Yuste, R. (2025). Mental privacy: Navigating risks, rights and regulation. *EMBO Reports*, *26*(14), e3469. DOI: 10.1038/s44319-025-00505-6

Tatar, U., Gokce, Y., & Nussbaum, B. (2020). Law versus technology: Blockchain, GDPR, and tough tradeoffs. *Computer Law & Security Review*, *38*, 105454. DOI: 10.1016/j.clsr.2020.105454

Teichmann, F. (2025). Cybersecurity of critical infrastructure in europe: The NIS2 directive in focus. *International Cybersecurity Law Review*, *6*(3), 207–220. DOI: 10.1365/s43439-025-00154-4

Teichmann, F. M. J., & Wittmann, C. (2023). When is a law firm liable for a data breach? An exploration into the legal liability of ransomware and cybersecurity. *Journal of Financial Crime*, *30*(6), 1491–1498. DOI: 10.1108/JFC-04-2022-0093

Thomasian, N. M., & Adashi, E. Y. (2021). Cybersecurity in the Internet of Medical Things. *Health Policy and Technology*, *10*(3), 100549. DOI: 10.1016/j.hlpt.2021.100549

Trautman, L., & Ormerod, P. (2017). Corporate directors' and officers' cybersecurity standard of care: The Yahoo data breach. *SSRN*, *66*(5), 1231–1272. DOI: 10.2139/ssrn.2883607

Tropina, T. (2024). 'This is not a human rights convention!': The perils of overlooking human rights in the UN cybercrime treaty. *Journal of Cyber Policy*, *9*(2), 200–220. DOI: 10.1080/23738871.2024.2419517

Wairimu, S., Iwaya, L. H., Fritsch, L., & Lindskog, S. (2024). On the evaluation of privacy impact assessment and privacy risk assessment methodologies: A systematic literature review. *IEEE Access : Practical Innovations, Open Solutions*, *12*, 56623–56639. DOI: 10.1109/ACCESS.2024.3360864

Wan, G., & Ye, X. (2025). East Asian personal data protection laws and international medical data sharing: Pathways for coordination. *International Journal of Multidisciplinary Research and Growth Evaluation*, *6*(5), 109–113. DOI: 10.54660/.IJMRGE.2025.6.5.109-113

Watney, M. (2024). Exploring South Africa's cybersecurity legal framework regulating information confidentiality, integrity, and availability. In *Proceedings of the 19th International Conference on Cyber Warfare and Security, ICCWS 2024* (Vol. 19, No. 1, pp. 430–437). Academic Conferences & Publishing International Limited. DOI: 10.34190/iccws.19.1.1999

Watney, M. (2025). The legal pitfalls to ratification of the United Nations Convention against Cybercrime. In Lipps, C., & Han, B. (Eds.), *Proceedings of the 24th European Conference on CyberWarfare and Security, ECCWS 2025* (Vol. 24, No. 1, pp. 713–719). Curran Associates Inc. DOI: 10.34190/eccws.24.1.3381

Weil, G. (2024). Tort Law as a Tool for Mitigating Catastrophic Risk from Artificial Intelligence. SSRN *Electronic Journal*. DOI: 10.2139/ssrn.4694006

Zukis, B. (2022). Digital and Cybersecurity Governance Around the World. *Annals of Corporate Governance*, *7*(1), 1–92. DOI: 10.1561/109.00000032

KEY TERMS AND DEFINITIONS

ARCO Rights: Human rights of individuals to access, rectify, cancel, and oppose the use of their personal data.

Cybersecurity: Combination of technologies, procedures, rules, and standards for the protection of infrastructure and personal data, as well as recovery plans.

Compilation of References

Abbasi, M. (2020). Security in Cyberspace in the Field of International Relations. *J Arch Mil Med.*, *8*(4), e114485. DOI: 10.5812/jamm.114485

Abdullah Sani, H. A., & Jaafar, N. I. (2025a). A bibliometric and content analysis of internet of things (IoT) in the public sector. *Journal of Science and Technology Policy Management.*

Abdullah Sani, H. A., & Jaafar, N. I. (2025b). *Exploring the impact of IoT on governance and public service transformation: evidence from Malaysia's public sector.* Smart and Sustainable Built Environment.

Abir, S. A. A., Anwar, A., Choi, J., & Kayes, A. (2021). Iot-enabled smart energy grid: Applications and challenges. *IEEE Access : Practical Innovations, Open Solutions*, *9*, 50961–50981. DOI: 10.1109/ACCESS.2021.3067331

Achterberg, J., Haas, M., van Dijk, B., & Spruit, M. (2025). Fidelity-Agnostic Synthetic Data Generation Improves Utility While Retaining Privacy. *Patterns (New York, N.Y.)*, *6*(10), 101287. DOI: 10.1016/j.patter.2025.101287

Agencia de Acceso a la Información Pública. (2023). *Resolución N.º 161/2023: Programa de transparencia y protección de datos personales en el uso de la inteligencia artificial.* https://www.argentina.gob.ar/normativa/nacional/resolución-161-2023-389231

Agencia de Acceso a la Información Pública. (2024). *Guía para entidades públicas y privadas en materia de transparencia y protección de datos personales para una inteligencia artificial responsable.* https://www.argentina.gob.ar/sites/default/files/guia_ai-final-2025.pdf

Agencia de Gobierno Electrónico y Sociedad de la Información y del Conocimiento. (2021, April 23). *Estrategia de Inteligencia Artificial.* https://www.gub.uy/agencia-gobierno-electronico-sociedad-informacion-conocimiento/comunicacion/publicaciones/estrategia-inteligencia-artificial

Agius, J., Karagiannis, G. M., Pescaroli, G., Galbusera, L., Theocharidou, M., Krausmann, E., & Chaudhari, K. 'Critical Infrastructures', in: Casajus Valles, A., Marin Ferrer, M., Poljanšek, K., Clark, I. (eds.), Science for Disaster Risk Management 2020: acting today, protecting tomorrow, EUR 30183 EN, Publications Office of the European Union, Luxembourg, 2020, ISBN 978-92-76-18182-8, , JRC114026. DOI: 10.2760/571085

Ajitha, N., Ashwin, G., Divakar, S., & Dhanushree, M. (2025). Machine Learning-based Panic Syncsight: An IoT-Integrated Panic Attack Detection System for Enhanced Therapeutic Insights. 2025 5th International Conference on Soft Computing for Security Applications (ICSCSA).

Alabdulwahab, S., Kim, Y.-T., & Son, Y. (2024). Privacy-Preserving Synthetic Data Generation Method for IoT-Sensor Network IDS Using CTGAN. *Sensors (Basel), 24*(22), 7389. DOI: 10.3390/s24227389

Alahi, M. E. E., Sukkuea, A., Tina, F. W., Nag, A., Kurdthongmee, W., Suwannarat, K., & Mukhopadhyay, S. C. (2023). Integration of IoT-enabled technologies and artificial intelligence (AI) for smart city scenario: recent advancements and future trends. Sensors (Basel), 23(11), 5206.

Alam, Q. M., Kolar, V., & Thottan, M. (2024). Towards AI/ML-driven network traffic engineering. *Proceedings of the 4th International Conference on AI-ML Systems*, 1-8. DOI: 10.1145/3703412.3703436

Alam, T. (2021). Cloud-based IoT applications and their roles in smart cities. *Smart Cities*, *4*(3), 1196–1219. DOI: 10.3390/smartcities4030064

Alam, T. (2023). Blockchain and big data-based access control for communication among iot devices in smart cities. *Wireless Personal Communications*, *132*(1), 433–456. DOI: 10.1007/s11277-023-10617-8

Alcaraz, C., & Zeadally, S. (2013). Critical control system protection in the 21st century. *Computer*, *46*(10), 74–83. DOI: 10.1109/MC.2013.69

Aldehim, G., Shahzad, T., Khan, M. A., Ghadi, Y. Y., Jiang, W., Mazhar, T., & Hamam, H. (2025). Balancing sustainability and security: A review of 5G and IoT in smart cities. *Digital Communications and Networks*, *11*(6), 1722–1737. DOI: 10.1016/j.dcan.2025.06.007

Ali, A. B. A., Ayyasamy, R. K., Akbar, R., Jebna, A. K., & Adnan, K. (2025). Cybersecurity infrastructure compliance key factors to detect and mitigate malware attacks in SMEs: A systematic literature review. *SAGE Open*, *15*(1), 21582440251314671. Advance online publication. DOI: 10.1177/21582440251314671

Ali, D., Asaad, A., Jimenez, M.-J., Nanda, V., Paluzo-Hidalgo, E., & Soriano-Trigueros, M. (2023). A Survey of Vectorization Methods in Topological Data Analysis. *IEEE Transactions on Pattern Analysis and Machine Intelligence*, *45*(12), 14069–14101. DOI: 10.1109/TPAMI.2023.3308391 PMID: 37647183

Ali, M. J. (2024). Cybercrime and Cybersecurity: A Critical Analysis of Legal Frameworks and Enforcement Mechanisms. *Bharati International Journal of Multidisciplinary Research & Development*, *2*(8), 137–154. DOI: 10.70798/Bijmrd/020800017

Ali, M., & Sun, W. (2024). *Securing Critical Infrastructures: Restoration from Cyber-Physical Attacks in Active Distribution Grids. 2024 IEEE Power & Energy Society General Meeting*. PESGM., DOI: 10.1109/PESGM51994.2024.10688621

Almalki, F. A., Alsamhi, S. H., Sahal, R., Hassan, J., Hawbani, A., Rajput, N. S., Saif, A., Morgan, J., & Breslin, J. (2021). Green IoT for eco-friendly and sustainable smart cities: Future directions and opportunities. *Mobile Networks and Applications*, *28*(1), 178–202. DOI: 10.1007/s11036-021-01790-w

Almeida, F. (2025). Comparative analysis of EU-based cybersecurity skills frameworks. *Computers & Security*, *151*, 104329. DOI: 10.1016/j.cose.2025.104329

Almulhim, A. I. (2025). A Conceptual Framework for Integrating IoT and Blockchain for Smart and Sustainable Urban Development. *Smart Cities*, *8*(6), 209. DOI: 10.3390/smartcities8060209

Almulla, Z. T., & Rahman, H. (2025). The Role of Network Segmentation and Micro-Segmentation in Operational Technology Security. 2025 International Conference on Artificial Intelligence in Information and Communication (ICAIIC), Fukuoka, Japan, pp. 0342-0347, DOI: 10.1109/ICAIIC64266.2025.10920695

Almuqrin, A., Mutambik, I., Alomran, A., Gauthier, J., & Abusharhah, M. (2022). Factors Influencing Public Trust in Open Government Data. *Sustainability (Basel)*, *14*(15), 9765. DOI: 10.3390/su14159765

Alshantti, A., Rasheed, A., & Westad, F. (2025). Privacy Re-identification Attacks on Tabular GANs. *Security and Privacy*, *8*(1), e469. DOI: 10.1002/spy2.469

ALSur. (2024). *The Regulatory Pathways for AI in Latin America*. https://www.alsur.lat/sites/default/files/2024-09/ALSUR%20-%20IA%20en%20Latam%20%5BENG%5D.pdf

Amershi, S., Begel, A., Bird, C., DeLine, R., Gall, H., Kamar, E., Nagappan, N., Nushi, B., & Zimmermann, T. (2019). Software Engineering for Machine Learning: A Case Study. *Proceedings of the 41st International Conference on Software Engineering: Software Engineering in Practice (ICSE-SEIP '19)*, 291–300. https://doi.org/DOI: 10.1109/ICSE-SEIP.2019.00042

Amrit, C., & Narayanappa, A. K. (2025). An Analysis of the Challenges in the Adoption of MLOps. *Journal of Innovation & Knowledge*, *10*(1), 100637. DOI: 10.1016/j.jik.2024.100637

Anjum, N., Latif, Z., Lee, C., Shoukat, I. A., & Iqbal, U. (2021). MIND: A Multi-Source Data Fusion Scheme for Intrusion Detection in Networks. *Sensors (Basel)*, *21*(14), 4941. DOI: 10.3390/s21144941

Antequera, C. (2023, June 19, 2023). *Data protection in Latin American countries. ClarkeModet.* https://www.clarkemodet.com/en/articles/data-protection-in-latin-american-countries

Anwar, M., & Gill, A. (2020). Developing an integrated ISO 27701 and GDPR based information privacy compliance requirements model. In *ACIS 2020 Proceedings Article 20.* https://aisel.aisnet.org/acis2020/20

Asamblea Nacional del Ecuador. (2021). *Ley Orgánica de Protección de Datos Personales.* https://www.finanzaspopulares.gob.ec/wp-content/uploads/2021/07/ley_organica_de_proteccion_de_datos_personales.pdf

Asiri, M., Saxena, N., Gjomemo, R., and Burnap, P. (2023). Understanding Indicators of Compromise against Cyber-attacks in Industrial Control Systems: A Security Perspective. ACM Trans. Cyber-Phys. Syst. 7, 2, Article 15, 33 pages. DOI: 10.1145/3587255

Ata, A., Khan, M. A., Abbas, S., Ahmad, G., & Fatima, A. (2019). Modelling smart road traffic congestion control system using machine learning techniques. *Neural Network World*, *29*(2), 99–110. DOI: 10.14311/NNW.2019.29.008

Atienza, N., González-Díaz, R., & Soriano-Trigueros, M. (2020). On the Stability of Persistent Entropy and New Summary Functions for Topological Data Analysis. *Pattern Recognition*, *107*, 107509. DOI: 10.1016/j.patcog.2020.107509

Atlam, H. F., Walters, R. J., & Wills, G. B. (2018). Fog computing and the Internet of Things: A review. *Big Data and Cognitive Computing*, *2*(2), 10. DOI: 10.3390/bdcc2020010

Aziboledia Frederick, B., & Egerton Taylor, O. (2023). Analysis on Cybersecurity Control and Monitoring Techniques in Industrial IoT: Industrial Control Systems. *Internet of Things and Cloud Computing*, *11*(1), 1–17. DOI: 10.11648/j.iotcc.20231101.11

Baldoni, S., & Battisti, F. (2025). Histogram-Based Network Traffic Representation for Anomaly Detection Through PCA. *Computer Networks*, *265*, 111276. DOI: 10.1016/j.comnet.2025.111276

Bandiziol, C., & De Marchi, S. (2024). Persistence Symmetric Kernels for Classification: A Comparative Study. *Symmetry*, *16*(9), 1236. DOI: 10.3390/sym16091236

Banerjee, A. (2025). Securing the future: AI-driven data transmission in IoT-powered smart cities. *Soft computing fusion with applications*, *2*(1), 33-53.

Bannelier, K. (2025). Risks and opportunities of the UN Cybercrime Convention for the UNODC & the fight against transnational organised crime: A first assessment. *Transnational Criminal Law Review*, *4*(1), 140–155. DOI: 10.22329/tclr.v4i1.9468

Baquero, P. M., Wang, A., & Amariles, D. R. (2025). Unveiling transparency in data protection enforcement across the EU: Assessing the level and quality of disclosure of GDPR fines by data protection authorities. *European Law Journal*, *31*(3), 177–202. DOI: 10.1111/eulj.70008

Barker, M., Chue Hong, N. P., Katz, D. S., Lamprecht, A.-L., Martinez Ortiz, C., Psomopoulos, F., Harrow, J., Castro, L. J. G., Gruenpeter, M., Martinez, P. A., & Honeyman, T. (2022). Introducing the FAIR Principles for Research Software. *Scientific Data*, *9*(1), 622. DOI: 10.1038/s41597-022-01710-x PMID: 36241754

Barnes, D., Polanco, L., & Perea, J. A. (2021). A Comparative Study of Machine Learning Methods for Persistence Diagrams. *Frontiers in Artificial Intelligence*, *4*, 681174. DOI: 10.3389/frai.2021.681174 PMID: 34396089

Batty, M., Axhausen, K. W., Giannotti, F., Pozdnoukhov, A., Bazzani, A., Wachowicz, M., Ouzounis, G., & Portugali, Y. (2012). Smart cities of the future. *The European Physical Journal. Special Topics*, *214*(1), 481–518. DOI: 10.1140/epjst/e2012-01703-3

Bekzhanov, A., Sadykova, A., & Mukhamedi, Y. (2024). Enhancing Cybersecurity Through AI-Driven Intrusion Detection Systems in Industrial Control Systems. *International Journal of Information Engineering and Science*, *1*(2), 26–32. DOI: 10.62951/ijies.v1i2.91

Bellini, P., Nesi, P., & Pantaleo, G. (2022). IoT-enabled smart cities: A review of concepts, frameworks and key technologies. *Applied Sciences (Basel, Switzerland), 12*(3), 1607. DOI: 10.3390/app12031607

Bello, A., Jahan, S., Farid, F., & Ahamed, F. (2023). A Systemic Review of the Cybersecurity Challenges in Australian Water Infrastructure Management. *Water (Basel), 15*(1), 168. DOI: 10.3390/w15010168

Berardi, D., Giallorenzo, S., Mauro, J., Melis, A., Montesi, F., & Prandini, M. (2022). Microservice Security: A Systematic Literature Review. *PeerJ. Computer Science, 8*, e779. DOI: 10.7717/peerj-cs.779

Berry, E., Chen, Y.-C., Cisewski-Kehe, J., & Fasy, B. T. (2020). Functional Summaries of Persistence Diagrams. *Journal of Applied and Computational Topology, 4*(2), 211–262. DOI: 10.1007/s41468-020-00048-w

Bjerkevik, H. B. (2021). On the Stability of Interval Decomposable Persistence Modules. *Discrete & Computational Geometry, 66*(1), 92–121. DOI: 10.1007/s00454-021-00298-0

Boopathi Raja, G. (2021). *An intelligent approach for detecting and preventing heart attacks using wearable technology. Handbook of Research on Lifestyle Sustainability and Management Solutions Using AI Big Data Analytics, and Visualization*. IGI Gobal.

Brophy, E., Wang, Z., She, Q., & Ward, T. E. (2023). Generative Adversarial Networks in Time Series: A Systematic Literature Review. *ACM Computing Surveys, 55*(10), 199. Advance online publication. DOI: 10.1145/3559540

Bubenik, P., & Elchesen, A. (2022). Universality of Persistence Diagrams and the Bottleneck and Wasserstein Distances. *Computational Geometry, 105–106*, 101882. DOI: 10.1016/j.comgeo.2022.101882

Bubenik, P., & Wagner, H. (2020). Embeddings of Persistence Diagrams into Hilbert Spaces. *Journal of Applied and Computational Topology, 4*(3), 339–351. DOI: 10.1007/s41468-020-00056-w

Buletsa, S. (2022). Virtualne maino u metavsesviti yak obiekt cyvilnykh prav. *Uzhhorod National University Herald. Series. Law, 72*, 21. DOI: 10.24144/2307-3322.2022.72.21

Burri, M., & Kugler, K. (2024). Regulatory autonomy in digital trade agreements. *Journal of International Economic Law, 27*(3), 397–423. DOI: 10.1093/jiel/jgae025

Bussonnier, M., Forde, J., Freeman, J., Granger, B., Head, T., Holdgraf, C., Kelley, K., Nalvarte, G., Osheroff, A., Pacer, M., Panda, Y., Perez, F., Ragan-Kelley, B., & Willing, C. (2018). Binder 2.0 - Reproducible, Interactive, Sharable Environments for Science at Scale. *Proceedings of the 17th Python in Science Conference (SciPy 2018)*. https://doi.org/DOI: 10.25080/Majora-4af1f417-011

Canonico, R., & Sperlì, G. (2023). Industrial cyber-physical systems protection: A methodological review. *Computers & Security*, *135*, 103531. DOI: 10.1016/j.cose.2023.103531

Carneiro, F. D., Rampasso, I. S., de Matos Mello, S. L., Sigahi, T. F. A. C., Lespay, H., & Anholon, R. (2025). A flexible ISO 27701-based framework for assessing cybersecurity maturity: A proposition and a case application. *Computers & Security*, *158*, 104645. DOI: 10.1016/j.cose.2025.104645

Chamberlain, J. (2022). The risk-based approach of the European Union's proposed artificial intelligence regulation: Some comments from a tort law perspective. *European Journal of Risk Regulation*, *14*(1), 1–13. DOI: 10.1017/err.2022.38

Chatinakrob, T. (2024). Interplay of International Law and Cyberspace: State Sovereignty Violation, Extraterritorial Effects, and the Paradigm of Cyber Sovereignty. *Chinese Journal of International Law*, *23*(1), 25–72. DOI: 10.1093/chinesejil/jmae005

Chatterjee, S., Kar, A. K., & Mustafa, S. Z. (2021). Securing IoT devices in smart cities of India: From ethical and enterprise information system management perspective. *Enterprise Information Systems*, *15*(4), 585–615. DOI: 10.1080/17517575.2019.1654617

Chauhan, S., Malik, N., & Vig, R. (2025). AI/ML techniques in servicing LDCT reconstruction: A systematic literature review. *Discover Artificial Intelligence*, *5*(1), 229. Advance online publication. DOI: 10.1007/s44163-025-00419-1

Chazal, F., & Michel, B. (2021). An Introduction to Topological Data Analysis: Fundamental and Practical Aspects for Data Scientists. *Frontiers in Artificial Intelligence*, *4*, 667963. DOI: 10.3389/frai.2021.667963 PMID: 34661095

Chen, S., Dey, T. K., Li, J., & Wang, Y. (2021). Approximation Algorithms for 1-Wasserstein Distance Between Persistence Diagrams. In SEA 2021 (LIPIcs, Vol. 190, Article 14). Schloss Dagstuhl – Leibniz-Zentrum für Informatik. https://doi.org/DOI: 10.4230/LIPIcs.SEA.2021.14

Chen, D., Wawrzynski, P., & Lv, Z. (2021). Cyber security in smart cities: A review of deep learning-based applications and case studies. *Sustainable Cities and Society*, *66*, 102655. DOI: 10.1016/j.scs.2020.102655

Chiang, M., & Zhang, T. (2016). Fog and IoT: An overview of research opportunities. *IEEE Internet of Things Journal, 3*(6), 854–864. DOI: 10.1109/JIOT.2016.2584538

Chirra, D. R. (2024). AI-Enabled Cybersecurity Solutions for Protecting Smart Cities Against Emerging Threats.

Chong, C.-Y., & Kumar, S. P. (2003). Sensor networks: Evolution, opportunities, and challenges. *Proceedings of the IEEE, 91*(8), 1247–1256. DOI: 10.1109/JPROC.2003.814918

Chung, Y. C., Hu, C.-S., Lo, Y.-L., & Wu, H.-T. (2021). A Persistent Homology Approach to Heart Rate Variability Analysis With an Application to Sleep-Wake Classification. *Frontiers in Physiology, 12*, 637684. DOI: 10.3389/fphys.2021.637684

Ciekanowski, Z., Gruchelski, M., Nowicka, J., Żurawski, S., & Pauliuchuk, Y. (2023). Cyberspace as a Source of New Threats to the Security of the European Union. *European Research Studies, XXVI*(3), 782–797. DOI: 10.35808/ersj/3249

Claroty. (2023). The global state of industrial cybersecurity 2023: New technologies, persistent threats, and maturing defenses. https://web-assets.claroty.com/claroty-industrial-survey-report-dec-2023.pd

Cloete, M. (2024). Cyber criminals targeting UK manufacturing industry in 2024. Moore Kingston Smith. 01-16-2024 Retrieved from: https://mooreks.co.uk/insights/cyber-criminals-targeting-uk-manufacturing-industry-in-2024/

Cohen, A., & Nissim, K. (2020). Towards Formalizing the GDPR's Notion of Singling out. *Proceedings of the National Academy of Sciences of the United States of America, 117*(15), 8344–8352. DOI: 10.1073/pnas.1914598117 PMID: 32234789

Conley, E., & Pocs, M. (2018). GDPR compliance challenges for interoperable health information exchanges (HIEs) and trustworthy research environments (TREs). *European Journal for Biomedical Informatics, 14*(3), 7. Advance online publication. DOI: 10.24105/ejbi.2018.14.3.7

Conversano, M. (2024). Il fattore temporale nell'acquisizione transfrontaliera delle e-evidence: Il bilanciamento operato nel secondo Protocollo addizionale alla Convenzione di Budapest. *La Nuova Giuridica, 6*(2), 62–76. DOI: 10.36253/lng-3409

Cook, W. (2020, March 29). Many U.S. Workers in critical occupations in the fight against COVID-19 (Revised). Retrieved March 17, 2026, from https://www.lmiontheweb.org/more-than-half-of-u-s-workers-in-critical-occupations-in-the-fight-against-covid-19/

Cormode, G., Maddock, S., Ullah, E., & Gade, S. (2025). Synthetic Tabular Data: Methods, Attacks and Defenses. *Proceedings of the VLDB Endowment International Conference on Very Large Data Bases, 18*(12), 5448–5450. DOI: 10.14778/3750601.3750692

Couldry, N., & Mejias, U. A. (2019). *The Costs of Connection: How Data Is Colonizing Human Life and Appropriating It for Capitalism.* Stanford University Press., https://www.sup.org/books/title/?id=28816

Cristiano, F., & Monsees, L. (2025). Beyond the ban: TikTok and the politics of digital sovereignty in the EU and US. *Politics and Governance, 13*, e10461. DOI: 10.17645/pag.10461

Crootof, R. (2019). The Internet of torts: Expanding civil liability standards to address corporate remote interference. *Duke Law Journal, 69*(3), 583–667.

Cui, L., Xie, G., Qu, Y., Gao, L., & Yang, Y. (2018). Security and privacy in smart cities: Challenges and opportunities. *IEEE Access : Practical Innovations, Open Solutions, 6*, 46134–46145. DOI: 10.1109/ACCESS.2018.2853985

Custers, B., Lahmann, H., & Scott, B. (2025). From liability gaps to liability overlaps: Shared responsibilities and fiduciary duties in AI and other complex technologies. *AI & Society, 40*(5), 4035–4050. DOI: 10.1007/s00146-024-02137-1

Cybersecurity and Infrastructure Security Agency. (2024, 17 de enero). CISA releases 2023 year in review showcasing efforts to protect critical infrastructure. https://www.cisa.gov/news-events/news/cisa-releases-2023-year-review-showcasing-efforts-protect-critical-infrastructure

Das, D. K. (2024). Exploring the symbiotic relationship between digital transformation, infrastructure, service delivery, and governance for smart sustainable cities. *Smart Cities, 7*(2), 806–835. DOI: 10.3390/smartcities7020034

de Hert, P., & Thumfart, J. (2020). The Microsoft Ireland case, the CLOUD Act and the cyberspace sovereignty trilemma: Post-territorial technologies and companies question regulatory state monopolies. In Hötzendorfer, W., Tschohl, C., & Kummer, F. (Eds.), *International trends in legal informatics: Festschrift for Erich Schweighofer* (pp. 373–417)., DOI: 10.38023/47fd0a3f-c62a-4cd6-840e-e8ea89bdea68

de la República de Colombia, C. (2012). *Ley Estatutaria 1581 de 2012 por la cual se dictan disposiciones generales para la protección de datos personales.* https://www.funcionpublica.gov.co/eva/gestornormativo/norma.php?i=53646

de la República del Perú, C. (2011). *Ley N.º 29733, Ley de protección de datos personales.* https://www.minsa.gob.pe/Recursos/OGTI/SINADEF/Ley-29733.pdf

Department for Science. Innovation and Technology. (2023). UK cyber security sectoral analysis 2023. UK Government. https://www.gov.uk/government/publications/cyber-security-sectoral-analysis-2023/uk-cyber-security-sectoral-analysis-2023

Diario Oficial de la Federación. (2009). *Decreto por el que se adiciona un párrafo segundo al artículo 16 de la Constitución Política de los Estados Unidos Mexicanos*. https://dof.gob.mx/nota_detalle.php?codigo=5092143&fecha=01/06/2009#gsc.tab=0

Diario Oficial de la Federación. (2024). *Decreto de simplificación orgánica (December 20, 2024)*. https://www.dof.gob.mx/nota_detalle.php?codigo=5745905&fecha=20/12/2024

Diario Oficial de la Federación. (2025a). *Ley Federal de Protección de Datos Personales en Posesión de los Particulares (última reforma publicada el 14 de noviembre de 2025)*. https://www.diputados.gob.mx/LeyesBiblio/pdf/LFPDPPP.pdf

Diario Oficial de la Federación. (2025b). *Ley General de Protección de Datos Personales en Posesión de Sujetos Obligados (reforma publicada el 14 de noviembre de 2025)*. https://www.diputados.gob.mx/LeyesBiblio/pdf/LGPDPPSO.pdf

Diario Oficial de la Federación. (2025c). *Ley General de Transparencia y Acceso a la Información Pública (last amended March 20, 2025)*. https://www.diputados.gob.mx/LeyesBiblio/pdf/LGTAIP.pdf

Drummer, D., & Neumann, D. (2020). Is code law? Current legal and technical adoption issues and remedies for blockchain-enabled smart contracts. *Journal of Information Technology*, *35*(4), 337–360. DOI: 10.1177/0268396220924669

Dunayev, I., & Lugovenko, N. (2024). The state and personal data in the post-GDPR world: Towards a global consensus or regulatory fragmentation? *Theory and Practice of Public Administration*, *2*(79), 28–62. DOI: 10.26565/1727-6667-2024-2-02

Ecabert, T., Muhly, F., & Zimmermann, V. (2024). Implications of cyber incident reporting obligations on multinational organizations headquartered in Switzerland. *International Cybersecurity Law Review*, *5*(4), 585–614. DOI: 10.1365/s43439-024-00129-x

El Emam, K., Mosquera, L., Fang, X., & El-Hussuna, A. (2022). Utility Metrics for Evaluating Synthetic Health Data Generation Methods: Validation study. *JMIR Medical Informatics*, *10*(4), e35734. DOI: 10.2196/35734 PMID: 35389366

Elmaghraby, A. S., & Losavio, M. M. (2014). Cyber security challenges in smart cities: Safety, security and privacy. *Journal of Advanced Research*, *5*(4), 491–497. DOI: 10.1016/j.jare.2014.02.006 PMID: 25685517

El-Yaagoubi, A. B., Chung, M. K., & Ombao, H. (2023). Topological Data Analysis for Multivariate Time Series Data. *Entropy (Basel, Switzerland)*, *25*(11), 1509. DOI: 10.3390/e25111509

ENE. I. and SAVU, D. (2023). Cybersecurity – A Permanent Challenge for the Energy Sector. Romanian Cyber Security Journal, ISSN 2668-6430, vol. 5(1), pp. 107-119. DOI: 10.54851/v5i1y202310

European Parliament & Council of the European Union. (2022). Regulation (EU) 2022/1925 of the European Parliament and of the Council of 14 September 2022 on contestable and fair markets in the digital sector (Digital Markets Act). *Official Journal of the European Union, L, 265*, 1–66.

European Parliament & Council of the European Union. (2022). Regulation (EU) 2022/2065 of the European Parliament and of the Council of 19 October 2022 on a Single Market For Digital Services (Digital Services Act). *Official Journal of the European Union, L, 277*, 1–102.

European Union Agency for Cybersecurity. (2024). *2024 report on the state of cybersecurity in the Union*. ENISA.

European Union. (2022). Directive (EU) 2022/2555 of the European Parliament and of the Council of 14 December 2022 on measures for a high common level of cybersecurity across the Union. Official Journal of the European Union, L 333, 80-152.

Fabrègue, B. F. G., & Bogoni, A. (2023). Privacy and security concerns in the smart city. *Smart Cities*, *6*(1), 586–613. DOI: 10.3390/smartcities6010027

Fagan, M., Megas, K. N., Scarfone, K., & Smith, M. (2021a). *IoT device cybersecurity guidance for the federal government: Establishing IoT device cybersecurity requirements (NIST SP 800-213)*. National Institute of Standards and Technology., DOI: 10.6028/NIST.SP.800-213

Fagan, M., Megas, K. N., Scarfone, K., & Smith, M. (2021b). *IoT device cybersecurity guidance for the federal government: IoT device cybersecurity requirement catalog (NIST SP 800-213A)*. National Institute of Standards and Technology., DOI: 10.6028/NIST.SP.800-213A

Faheemuddin, S. (2025). IoT-Enabled Urban Infrastructure: A Framework for Smart City Development.

Falco, G., Caldera, C., & Shrobe, H. (2018). IIoT Cybersecurity Risk Modeling for SCADA Systems. *IEEE Internet of Things Journal*, *5*(6), 4486–4495. DOI: 10.1109/JIOT.2018.2822842

Farrand, B., & Carrapico, H. (2022). Digital sovereignty and taking back control: From regulatory capitalism to regulatory mercantilism in EU cybersecurity. *European Security*, *31*(3), 435–453. DOI: 10.1080/09662839.2022.2102896

Febles Pozo, N., & Nieto Rojas, P. (2025). *Inteligencia artificial y protección de datos: desafíos en la era digital*. Colex., DOI: 10.69592/979-13-7011-111-3

Ferriyan, A., Thamrin, A. H., Takeda, K., & Murai, J. (2021). Generating Network Intrusion Detection Dataset Based on Real and Encrypted Synthetic Attack Traffic. *Applied Sciences (Basel, Switzerland)*, *11*(17), 7868. DOI: 10.3390/app11177868

Figueira, A., & Vaz, B. (2022). Survey on Synthetic Data Generation, Evaluation Methods and GANs. *Mathematics*, *10*(15), 2733. DOI: 10.3390/math10152733

Fiore, U., Florea, A., & Pérez Lechuga, G. (2019). An interdisciplinary review of smart vehicular traffic and its applications and challenges. *Journal of Sensor and Actuator Networks*, *8*(1), 13. DOI: 10.3390/jsan8010013

Floridi, L. (2020). The Fight for Digital Sovereignty: What It Is, and Why It Matters, Especially for the EU. *Philosophy & Technology*, *33*(3), 369–378. DOI: 10.1007/s13347-020-00423-6 PMID: 35194548

Fonseca, J., & Bação, F. (2023). Tabular and Latent Space Synthetic Data Generation: A Literature Review. *Journal of Big Data*, *10*(1), 115. DOI: 10.1186/s40537-023-00792-7

Fovino, I. N., Coletta, A., & Masera, M. (2021). Cyber-physical security of critical infrastructures. In M. T. H. (Ed.), Handbook of Computer Networks and Cyber Security (pp. 729–752). Springer. https://doi.org/DOI: 10.1007/978-3-030-72369-9_30

Frey, C. B., & Presidente, G. (2024). Privacy regulation and firm performance: Estimating the GDPR effect globally. *Economic Inquiry*, *62*(3), 1074–1089. DOI: 10.1111/ecin.13213

Gao, C., Wang, F., Hu, X., & Martinez, J. (2023). Research on sustainable design of smart cities based on the Internet of things and ecosystems. *Sustainability (Basel)*, *15*(8), 6546. DOI: 10.3390/su15086546

Garau Guzman, J., & Baeza, V. M. (2023). Enhancing urban mobility through traffic management with UAVs and VLC technologies. *Drones (Basel)*, *8*(1), 7. DOI: 10.3390/drones8010007

Garg, T., Gupta, S., Obaidat, M. S., & Raj, M. (2024). Drones as a service (DaaS) for 5G networks and blockchain-assisted IoT-based smart city infrastructure. *Cluster Computing*, *27*(7), 8725–8788. DOI: 10.1007/s10586-024-04354-1

Garrigues. (2025, January 7). *Data protection evolving regulation in Latin America and their impact on labor relations*. https://www.garrigues.com/en_GB/new/data-protection-evolving-regulation-latin-america-and-their-impact-labor-relations

Gebru, T., Morgenstern, J., Vecchione, B., Vaughan, J. W., Wallach, H., Daumé, H.III, & Crawford, K. (2021). Datasheets for Datasets. *Communications of the ACM*, *64*(12), 86–92. DOI: 10.1145/3458723

Georgiev, P. and Dimitrova, K. (2024) IIoT and cyber security in industrial enterprises. SECURITY & FUTURE. Vol. 8 (2024), Issue 2, pg(s) 53-56.

Ghadami, R.. (2025). An intrusion detection system in the Internet of Things with deep learning and an improved arithmetic optimization algorithm and sine cosine algorithm. *Scientific Reports*, *15*(1), 22074. Advance online publication. DOI: 10.1038/s41598-025-22074-3 PMID: 41173998

Giancaspro, M. (2017). Is a 'smart contract' really a smart idea? Insights from a legal perspective. *Computer Law & Security Review*, *33*(6), 825–835. DOI: 10.1016/j.clsr.2017.05.007

Giomi, M., Boenisch, F., Wehmeyer, C., & Tasnádi, B. (2023). A Unified Framework for Quantifying Privacy Risk in Synthetic Data. *Proceedings on Privacy Enhancing Technologies. Privacy Enhancing Technologies Symposium*, *2023*(2), 312–331. DOI: 10.56553/popets-2023-0055

Giraldo, J., Sarkar, E., Cardenas, A. A., Maniatakos, M., & Kantarcioglu, M. (2018). Security and privacy in cyber-physical systems: A survey of surveys. *IEEE Design & Test*, *34*(4), 7–17. DOI: 10.1109/MDAT.2017.2709310

Gobierno Federal de Brasil. (n.d.). *Lei Geral de Proteção de Dados Pessoais (LGPD)*. Retrieved November 25, 2025, from https://www.gov.br/esporte/pt-br/acesso-a-informacao/lgpd

Goncalves, A., Ray, P., Soper, B., Stevens, J., Coyle, L., & Sales, A. P. (2020). Generation and Evaluation of Synthetic Patient Data. BMC Medical Research Methodology, 20(1), 108. https://doi.org/ https://doi.org/DOI: 10.1186/s12874-020-00977-1

Gong, R., Groshen, E., & Vadhan, S. (2022). Harnessing the Known Unknowns: Differential Privacy and the 2020 Census. Harvard Data Science Review (Special Issue: Differential Privacy for the 2020 U.S. Census). https://doi.org/DOI: 10.1162/99608f92.cb06b469

Govea, J., Gaibor-Naranjo, W., & Villegas-Ch, W. (2024). Transforming Cybersecurity into Critical Energy Infrastructure: A Study on the Effectiveness of Artificial Intelligence. *Systems*, *12*(5), 165. DOI: 10.3390/systems12050165

Goyal, M., & Mahmoud, Q. H. (2024). A Systematic Review of Synthetic Data Generation Techniques Using Generative AI. *Electronics (Basel), 13*(17), 3509. DOI: 10.3390/electronics13173509

Gubbi, J., Buyya, R., Marusic, S., & Palaniswami, M. (2013). Internet of Things (IoT): A vision, architectural elements, and future directions. *Future Generation Computer Systems, 29*(7), 1645–1660. DOI: 10.1016/j.future.2013.01.010

Guerrero-ibanez, J. A., Zeadally, S., & Contreras-Castillo, J. (2015). Integration challenges of intelligent transportation systems with connected vehicle, cloud computing, and Internet of things technologies. *IEEE Wireless Communications, 22*(6), 122–128. DOI: 10.1109/MWC.2015.7368833

Guillaume, F. (2024). Decentralized autonomous organizations (DAOs) before state courts: How can private international law keep up with global digital entities? In Perestrelo de Oliveira, M., & Garcia Rolo, A. (Eds.), *Decentralised Autonomous Organisation (DAO) Regulation: Principles and Perspectives for the Future* (pp. 135–168). Mohr Siebeck., DOI: 10.1628/978-3-16-163701-8

Guo, S., & Li, X. (2025). Cross-border data flow in China: Shifting from restriction to relaxation? *Computer Law & Security Review, 56*, 106079. DOI: 10.1016/j.clsr.2024.106079

Harris, S. (2014). Securing big data in our future intelligent cities. *IET Conference on Future Intelligent Cities*, 8 (4.)-8 (4.). https://doi.org/DOI: 10.1049/ic.2014.0049

Hassebo, A., & Tealab, M. (2023). Global models of smart cities and potential IoT applications: A review. *IoT, 4*(3), 366–411. DOI: 10.3390/iot4030017

Hawes, M. B. (2020). Implementing Differential Privacy: Seven Lessons from the 2020 United States Census. *Harvard Data Science Review, 2*(2). Advance online publication. DOI: 10.1162/99608f92.353c6f99

Heidari, A., Navimipour, N. J., & Unal, M. (2022). Applications of ML/DL in the management of smart cities and societies based on new trends in information technologies: A systematic literature review. *Sustainable Cities and Society, 85*, 104089. DOI: 10.1016/j.scs.2022.104089

Hemsley, K. E., & Fisher, R. E. (2018). *History of Industrial Control System Cyber Incidents*. Idaho National Laboratory., DOI: 10.2172/1505628

Hernandez, M. H. M., Osorio-Marulanda, P. A., Catalina, M., Loinaz, L., Epelde, G., & Aginako, N. (2025). Comprehensive Evaluation Framework for Synthetic Tabular Data in Health: Fidelity, Utility and Privacy Analysis of Generative Models with and without Privacy Guarantees. *Frontiers in Digital Health*, *7*, 1576290. Advance online publication. DOI: 10.3389/fdgth.2025.1576290 PMID: 40343213

Hittmeir, M., Mayer, R., & Ekelhart, A. (2020). A Baseline for Attribute Disclosure Risk in Synthetic Data. In CODASPY '20 (pp. 133–143). https://doi.org/DOI: 10.1145/3374664.3375722

Honorable Cámara de Diputados de la Nación. (2025). *Proyecto de ley: Marco legal para el desarrollo, implementación y uso responsable de sistemas de inteligencia artificial (IA) en Argentina.* https://rest.hcdn.gob.ar/web/tramites-parlamentarios/render/adjunto/6893e15373329.pdf

Ho, S., Qu, Y., Gu, B., Gao, L., Li, J., & Xiang, Y. (2021). DP-GAN: Differentially Private Consecutive Data Publishing Using Generative Adversarial nets. *Journal of Network and Computer Applications*, *185*, 103066. DOI: 10.1016/j.jnca.2021.103066

Hosseini, S., Barker, K., & Ramirez-Marquez, J. E. (2016). A review of definitions and measures of system resilience. *Reliability Engineering & System Safety*, *145*, 47–61. DOI: 10.1016/j.ress.2015.08.006

Houichi, M., Jaidi, F., & Bouhoula, A. (2024). Cyber security within smart cities: A comprehensive study and a novel intrusion detection-based approach. *Computers, Materials & Continua*, *81*(1), 393–441. DOI: 10.32604/cmc.2024.054007

Hu, H., Salcic, Z., Sun, L., Dobbie, G., Yu, P. S., & Zhang, X. (2022). Membership Inference Attacks on Machine Learning: A survey. ACM Computing Surveys, 54(11s). *ACM Computing Surveys*, *235*(11s), 1–37. DOI: 10.1145/3523273

Hutson, J., Banerjee, G., Kshetri, N., Odenwald, K., & Ratican, E. (2023). Architecting the metaverse: Blockchain and the financial and legal regulatory challenges of virtual real estate. *Journal of Intelligent Learning Systems and Applications*, *15*(1), 1–23. DOI: 10.4236/jilsa.2023.151001

Ichinomiya, T. (2025). Machine Learning of Time Series Data Using Persistent Homology. *Scientific Reports*, *15*(1), 20508. DOI: 10.1038/s41598-025-06551-3

Idowu, S., Strüber, D., & Berger, T. (2023). Asset Management in Machine Learning: State-of-research and State-of-practice. ACM Computing Surveys, 55(7). *ACM Computing Surveys*, *144*(7), 1–35. DOI: 10.1145/3543847

International Organization for Standardization. (2022a). *ISO/IEC 22989:2022 Information technology — Artificial intelligence — Artificial intelligence concepts and terminology* (ISO/IEC 22989:2022). https://www.iso.org/standard/74296.html

International Organization for Standardization. (2022b). *ISO/IEC 27001:2022 Information security, cybersecurity and privacy protection — Information security management systems — Requirements* (ISO/IEC 27001:2022). https://www.iso.org/standard/27001

International Organization for Standardization. (2022c). *ISO/IEC 27002:2022 Information security, cybersecurity and privacy protection — Information security controls* (ISO/IEC 27002:2022). https://www.iso.org/standard/75652.html

International Organization for Standardization. (2023a). *ISO/IEC 23894:2023 Information technology — Artificial intelligence — Guidance on risk management* (ISO/IEC 23894:2023). https://www.iso.org/standard/77304.html

International Organization for Standardization. (2023b). *ISO/IEC 27035-1:2023 Information technology — Information security incident management — Part 1: Principles and process* (ISO/IEC 27035-1:2023). https://www.iso.org/standard/78973.html

International Organization for Standardization. (2023c). *ISO/IEC 42001:2023 Information technology — Artificial intelligence — Management systems* (ISO/IEC 42001:2023). https://www.iso.org/standard/81230.html

International Organization for Standardization. (2025). *ISO/IEC 27701:2025 Information security, cybersecurity and privacy protection — Privacy information management systems — Requirements and guidance* (ISO/IEC 27701:2025). https://www.iso.org/standard/27701

International Organization for Standardization. (2026). *ISO/IEC TS 27103:2026 Cybersecurity — Guidance on using ISO and IEC standards in a cybersecurity framework* (ISO/IEC TS 27103:2026). https://www.iso.org/es/norma/27103

International Society of Automation. (n.d.). *ISA/IEC 62443 series of standards*. ISA.

Irshad, R. R., Hussain, S., Hussain, I., Ahmad, I., Yousif, A., Alwayle, I. M., & Badr, M. M. (2023). An intelligent buffalo-based secure edge-enabled computing platform for heterogeneous IoT network in smart cities. *IEEE Access : Practical Innovations, Open Solutions, 11*, 69282–69294. DOI: 10.1109/ACCESS.2023.3288815

Ismagilova, E., Hughes, L., Rana, N. P., & Dwivedi, Y. K. (2022). Security, privacy and risks within smart cities: Literature review and development of a smart city interaction framework. *Information Systems Frontiers*, *24*(2), 393–414. DOI: 10.1007/s10796-020-10044-1 PMID: 32837262

Jan, M. A., Nanda, P., Zheng, X., & Jamalipour, A. (2017). A survey on security and privacy issues in wireless sensor networks. *IEEE Communications Surveys and Tutorials*, *19*(2), 1346–1369. DOI: 10.1109/COMST.2016.2633620

Jayaraman, B., & Evans, D. (2022). Are Attribute Inference Attacks Just Imputation? *Proceedings of the 2022 ACM SIGSAC Conference on Computer and Communications Security (CCS '22)*, 3093–3107. https://doi.org/DOI: 10.1145/3548606.3560663

Jin, J., Gubbi, J., Marusic, S., & Palaniswami, M. (2014). An information framework for creating a smart city through Internet of things. *IEEE Internet of Things Journal*, *1*(2), 112–121. DOI: 10.1109/JIOT.2013.2296516

Jin, S., Palmer, H., Gat, I., Deja, K., Li, D., & Bao, Y. (2024). Implications of Data Topology for Deep Generative Models. *Frontiers of Computer Science*, *6*, 1260604. DOI: 10.3389/fcomp.2024.1260604

Joshi, S., Baviskar, A., & Rajmane, S. (2026). A review of cybersecurity in smart cities and intelligent transport systems. *Discover Internet of Things*, *6*(1), 41. Advance online publication. DOI: 10.1007/s43926-026-00312-y

Karnouskos, S. (2020). Stuxnet worm impact on industrial cyber-physical system security. In *IECON 2020 The 46th Annual Conference of the IEEE Industrial Electronics Society* (pp. 1–6). IEEE. DOI: 10.1109/IECON43393.2020.9254884

Kaspersky. (2026). Overview of Kaspersky's Industrial CyberSecurity Solutions [Image]. Kaspersky. https://cdn.kaspersky.com/fm/site-editor/ba/ba468099629797e8e17b64a2f9df3cce/processed/body-image-2-q93.png

Katal, N. (2024). Ai-driven healthcare services and infrastructure in smart cities. In *Smart cities* (pp. 150–170). CRC Press. DOI: 10.1201/9781003442660-7

Kaya, M., & Shahid, H. (2025). Cross-border data flows and digital sovereignty: Legal dilemmas in transnational governance. *Interdisciplinary Studies in Society, Law, and Politics*, *4*(2), 219–233. DOI: 10.61838/kman.isslp.4.2.20

Kayan, H., Nunes, M., Rana, O., Burnap, P., & Perera, C. (2022). Cybersecurity of industrial cyber-physical systems: A review. *ACM Computing Surveys*, *54*(11s), 229. Advance online publication. DOI: 10.1145/3510410

Kenny, C. T., Kuriwaki, S., McCartan, C., Rosenman, E. T. R., Simko, T., & Imai, K. (2021). The use of Differential Privacy for Census Data and its Impact on Redistricting: The case of the 2020 U.S. Census. *Science Advances*, *7*(41), eabk3283. Advance online publication. DOI: 10.1126/sciadv.abk3283 PMID: 34613778

Khalil, U., Malik, O. A., Uddin, M., & Chen, C.-L. (2022). A comparative analysis on blockchain versus centralized authentication architectures for IoT-enabled smart devices in smart cities: A comprehensive review, recent advances, and future research directions. *Sensors (Basel)*, *22*(14), 5168. DOI: 10.3390/s22145168 PMID: 35890848

Khan, A. U. R., & Ahmad, R. W. (2022). A blockchain-based IoT-enabled E-waste tracking and tracing system for smart cities. *IEEE Access : Practical Innovations, Open Solutions*, *10*, 86256–86269. DOI: 10.1109/ACCESS.2022.3198973

Khanal, A., Adhikari, S., Bista, R., Shrestha, S., & Dahal, K. (2024). A systematic review on AI sovereignty: Challenges, opportunities, and future directions. *International Journal of Information Security*. Advance online publication. DOI: 10.1007/s10207-024-00888-6

Khan, M. N. I., & Goswami, D. (2025). Cybercrime and contractual liability: A systematic review of legal precedents and risk mitigation frameworks. *Journal of Sustainable Development and Policy*, *1*(1), 1–24. DOI: 10.63125/x3cd4413

Khan, Z. A., Shin, D., Bianculli, D., & Briand, L. (2024). Impact of Log Parsing on Deep Learning-Based Anomaly Detection. *Empirical Software Engineering*, *29*(6), 139. DOI: 10.1007/s10664-024-10533-w

Kim, S. (2014). Cyber Security and Middle Power Diplomacy: A Network Perspective. *Korean Journal of International Studies*, *12*(2), 323–352. DOI: 10.14731/kjis.2014.12.12.2.323

Kindji, G. C. N., Rojas-Barahona, L. M., Fromont, É., & Urvoy, T. (2025). Tabular Data Generation Models: An in-depth Survey and Performance Benchmarks with Extensive Tuning. *Neurocomputing*, *658*, 131655. DOI: 10.1016/j.neucom.2025.131655

Knowles, W., Prince, D., Hutchison, D., Disso, J. F. P., & Jones, K. (2021). A survey of cyber security management in industrial control systems. *International Journal of Critical Infrastructure Protection*, *9*, 52–80. DOI: 10.1016/j.ijcip.2015.02.002

Kosseff, J. (2018). Developing collaborative and cohesive cybersecurity legal principles. In *2018 10th International Conference on Cyber Conflict (CyCon). (283–298).* IEEE. DOI: 10.23919/CYCON.2018.8405022

Krause, T., Ernst, R., Klaer, B., Hacker, I., & Henze, M. (2021). Cybersecurity in Power Grids: Challenges and Opportunities. *Sensors (Basel), 21*(18), 6225. DOI: 10.3390/s21186225 PMID: 34577432

Kurakova, A., & Homayouni, H. (2025). A Comprehensive Evaluation Framework for Synthetic Medical Tabular Data Generation. *Journal of Biomedical Informatics, 171*, 104939. DOI: 10.1016/j.jbi.2025.104939 PMID: 41101425

Lachaud, E. (2020). ISO/IEC 27701 standard: Threats and opportunities for GDPR certification. *European Data Protection Law Review, 6*(2), 194–210. DOI: 10.21552/edpl/2020/2/7

Lai, A. (2021). Artificial intelligence, LLC: Corporate personhood as tort reform. *Detroit College of Law at Michigan State University Law Review, 2021*(2), 597–654.

Landauer, M., Onder, S., Skopik, F., & Wurzenberger, M. (2023). Deep Learning for Anomaly Detection in Log Data: A survey. *Machine Learning with Applications, 12*, 100470. DOI: 10.1016/j.mlwa.2023.100470

Lenca, M., & Andorno, R. (2017). Towards new human rights in the age of neuroscience and neurotechnology. *Life Sciences, Society and Policy, 13*(1), 5. DOI: 10.1186/s40504-017-0050-1

Leykam, D., & Angelakis, D. G. (2023). Topological Data Analysis and Machine Learning. *Advances in Physics: X, 8*(1), 2202331. DOI: 10.1080/23746149.2023.2202331

Li, N. R. P., & Padwal, H. H. (2020). The importance of public support in the implementation of green transportation in smart cities using smart vehicle bicycle communication transport. *The Electronic Library, 38*(5/6), 997–1011. DOI: 10.1108/EL-07-2020-0210

Linkov, I., Bridges, T., Creutzig, F., Decker, J., Fox-Lent, C., Kroger, W., Lambert, J. H., Levermann, A., Montreuil, B., Nathwani, J., Nyer, R., Renn, O., Scharte, B., Scheffler, A., Schreurs, M., & Thiel-Clemen, T. (2014). Changing the resilience paradigm. *Nature Climate Change, 4*(6), 407–409. DOI: 10.1038/nclimate2227

Linkov, I., Eisenberg, D. A., Plourde, K., Seager, T. P., Allen, J., & Kott, A. (2013). Resilience metrics for cyber systems. *Environment Systems & Decisions, 33*(4), 471–476. DOI: 10.1007/s10669-013-9485-y

Li, Y., Yang, R., & Lu, Y. (2024). A Privacy Risk Identification Framework of Open Government Data: A mixed-method study in China. *Government Information Quarterly, 41*(1), 101916. DOI: 10.1016/j.giq.2024.101916

Llamas Covarrubias, J. Z. (2025). Cybersecurity in Mexico: An in-depth analysis of a fragmented regulatory landscape. *Mexican Law Review, 18*(1), 69–115. DOI: 10.22201/iij.24485306e.2025.1.19686

Ludvigsen, K. R. (2024). Creating cybersecurity regulatory mechanisms, as seen through EU and US law. In Phallack, K., & Honnet, T. (Eds.), *Regulating personal data protection and cybersecurity* (pp. 123–130). Konrad-Adenauer Stiftung., https://www.kas.de/en/web/kambodscha/single-title/-/content/the-law-talk-publication-2023

Makrakis, G. M., Kolias, C., Kambourakis, G., Rieger, C., & Benjamin, J. (2021). Industrial and Critical Infrastructure Security: Technical Analysis of Real-Life Security Incidents. *IEEE Access : Practical Innovations, Open Solutions, 9*, 165295–165325. DOI: 10.1109/ACCESS.2021.3133348

Marotta, A., & Madnick, S. E. (2023). Regulating cyber incidents: A review of recent reporting requirements. In *Proceedings of the 20th International Conference on Security and Cryptography (SECRYPT 2023)* (pp. 410–416). SciTePress. DOI: 10.5220/0012086000003555

Mazzolin, R. and Madni, A. (2022). An Overview of Cyber Security Considerations and Vulnerabilities in Critical Infrastructure Systems and Potential Automated Mitigation - A Review. Journal of Engineering Research and Sciences, 1(4), 09–21. DOI: 10.55708/js0104002

Mehmood, M. Y., Oad, A., Abrar, M., Munir, H. M., Hasan, S. F., & Muqeet, H. A. u., & Golilarz, N. A. (2021). Edge computing for IoT-enabled smart grid. *Security and Communication Networks, 2021*(1), 5524025.

Messenger, G. (2024). Mitigating the rise of unilateralism: Lessons from forestry management. *Journal of International Economic Law, 27*(2), 223–240. DOI: 10.1093/jiel/jgae018

Miller, B., & Rowe, D. C. (2012). A survey of SCADA and critical infrastructure incidents. In *Proceedings of the 1st Annual Conference on Research in Information Technology* (pp. 51-56). DOI: 10.1145/2380790.2380805

Ministerio de Justicia. (2020, Octuber 20). *Ley 25.326 de protección de los datos personales*. Retrieved November 29, 2025, from https://servicios.infoleg.gob.ar/infolegInternet/anexos/60000-64999/64790/norma.htm

Mitchell, M., Wu, S., Zaldivar, A., Barnes, P., Vasserman, L., Hutchinson, B., Spitzer, E., Raji, I. D., & Gebru, T. (2019). Model Cards for Model Reporting. *Proceedings of the Conference on Fairness, Accountability, and Transparency (FAT '19)*, 220–229. https://doi.org/DOI: 10.1145/3287560.3287596

Mohapatra, H. (2021). Socio-technical challenges in the implementation of smart city. *2021 International Conference on Innovation and Intelligence for Informatics, Computing, and Technologies (3ICT)*, 57-62. https://doi.org/DOI: 10.1109/3ICT53449.2021.9581905

Mohapatra, H. (2025). A comprehensive review on urban resilience via fault-tolerant IoT and sensor networks. *Computers, Materials & Continua*, *85*(1), 221–247. DOI: 10.32604/cmc.2025.068338

Mohapatra, H. (2026). Task offloading and edge computing in IoT—Gaps, challenges and future directions. *Computers, Materials & Continua*, *0*(0), 1–10. DOI: 10.32604/cmc.2026.076726

Mohapatra, H., & Rath, A. K. (2019). Fault tolerance in WSN through PE-LEACH protocol. *IET Wireless Sensor Systems*, *9*(6), 358–365. DOI: 10.1049/iet-wss.2018.5229

Mohapatra, H., & Rath, A. K. (2020). Fault-tolerant mechanism for wireless sensor network. *IET Wireless Sensor Systems*, *10*(1), 23–30. DOI: 10.1049/iet-wss.2019.0106

Mohapatra, H., & Rath, A. K. (2021). An IoT based efficient multi-objective real-time smart parking system. *International Journal of Sensor Networks*, *37*(4), 219. DOI: 10.1504/IJSNET.2021.119483

Mohapatra, H., Rath, A. K., & Panda, N. (2022). IoT infrastructure for the accident avoidance: An approach of smart transportation. *International Journal of Information Technology : an Official Journal of Bharati Vidyapeeth's Institute of Computer Applications and Management*, *14*(2), 761–768. DOI: 10.1007/s41870-022-00872-6

Mohichehra, R. (2024). Sovereignty And Jurisdiction In Cyberspace. *Eurasian Journal of Humanities and Social Sciences*, *29*, 14–21. https://geniusjournals.org/index.php/ejhss/article/view/5699

Mohsen, B. M. (2024). AI-driven optimization of urban logistics in smart cities: Integrating autonomous vehicles and IoT for efficient delivery systems. *Sustainability (Basel)*, *16*(24), 11265. DOI: 10.3390/su162411265

Mosca, M. (2018). Cybersecurity in an era of quantum computing: What risks and what responses? *IEEE Security & Privacy*, *16*(5), 38-41. https://doi.org/DOI: 10.1109/MSP.2018.3761723

Mosenia, A., & Jha, N. K. (2017). A comprehensive study of security of Internet-of-Things. *IEEE Transactions on Emerging Topics in Computing*, *5*(4), 586–602. DOI: 10.1109/TETC.2016.2606384

Mossé, M., & Sòstres, M. (2023). Quantum computing and digital sovereignty: A geopolitical perspective. *European Journal of Futures Research*, *11*(1), 1-12. https://doi.org/DOI: 10.1186/s40309-023-00218-4

Musa, A. A., Dulawat, S., Saleh, K. T., & Alhassan, I. A. (2022). Applicability of utilizing blockchain technology in smart cities development. *Smart City Infrastructure*, 317-339. https://doi.org/DOI: 10.1002/9781119785569.ch13

Nacional de Chile, C. (1999). *Ley N° 19.628 Protección de la vida privada*. https://www.dipres.gob.cl/598/articles-51683_Otrasleyes_ley19628.pdf

Nacional de Chile, C. (2024). *Ley N.º 21.719 que regula la protección y el tratamiento de los datos personales y crea la Agencia de Protección de Datos Personales*. https://www.bcn.cl/leychile/navegar?idNorma=1209272

Nafees, M.N., Saxena, N., Cardenas, A., Grijalva, S., Burnap, P. (2023). Smart Grid Cyber-Physical Situational Awareness of Complex Operational Technology Attacks: A Review. ACM Comput. Surv. 55, 10, 36 pages. Doi: DOI: 10.1145/3565570

National Institute of Standards and Technology. (2024). The NIST Cybersecurity Framework (CSF) 2.0 (NIST CSWP 29). DOI: 10.6028/NIST.CSWP.29

Naval, M., Perjons, E., & Hacks, S. (2025). Cybersecurity challenges in critical infrastructure: A perspective on regulations and competence in Luxembourg. In *Proceedings of the 11th International Conference on Information Systems Security and Privacy:* Volume 1*: ICISSP* (Vol. 1, pp. 15–26). SciTePress. DOI: 10.5220/0013091500003899

Nazir, S., Patel, S., & Patel, D. (2017). Assessing and augmenting SCADA cyber security: A survey of techniques. *Computers & Security*, *70*, 436–454. DOI: 10.1016/j.cose.2017.06.010

Nicholson, A., Webber, S., Dyer, S., Patel, T., & Janicke, H. (2012). SCADA security in the light of cyber-warfare. *Computers & Security*, *31*(4), 418–436. DOI: 10.1016/j.cose.2012.02.009

Niu, J., Liu, P., Zhu, X., Shen, K., Wang, Y., Chi, H., Shen, Y., Jiang, X., Ma, J., & Zhang, Y. (2024). A Survey on Membership Inference Attacks and Defenses in Machine Learning. *Journal of Information and Intelligence*, *2*(5), 404–454. DOI: 10.1016/j.jiixd.2024.02.001

Nizeyimana, E., Hanyurwimfura, D., Hwang, J., Nsenga, J., & Regassa, D. (2023). Prototype of monitoring transportation pollution spikes through the Internet of things edge networks. *Sensors (Basel), 23*(21), 8941. DOI: 10.3390/s23218941 PMID: 37960640

Novo, L. (2025). In or out? Managing risks from the UN Cybercrime Convention. In *Proceedings of the 17th International Conference on Cyber Conflict (CyCon 2025)* (pp. 1-18). IEEE. DOI: 10.23919/CyCon65856.2025.11103714

Nugraha, Y., & Martin, A. (2022). Cybersecurity service level agreements: Understanding government data confidentiality requirements. *Journal of Cybersecurity, 8*(1), tyac004. Advance online publication. DOI: 10.1093/cybsec/tyac004

Nxumalo, S. (2025). Leveraging AI in mitigating road accidents and alleviating traffic congestion: A South African perspective. *The Sustainable Mobility and Transportation Symposium 2025*, 79. https://doi.org/DOI: 10.3390/engproc2025113079

Obayashi, I., Hiraoka, Y., & Kimura, M. (2018). Persistence Diagrams with Linear Machine Learning Models. *Journal of Applied and Computational Topology, 1*(3-4), 421–449. DOI: 10.1007/s41468-018-0013-5

Obioha-Val, O. A. (2025). Bridging gaps in cybersecurity governance: Leveraging collaborative digital solutions. *Asian Journal of Research in Computer Science, 18*(2), 82–100. OECD/CAF. (2023). *Digital Government Review of Latin America and the Caribbean: Building inclusive and responsive public services.* OECD Publishing. https://doi.org/DOI: 10.9734/ajrcos/2025/v18i2564

Okika, N., Nwatuzie, G. A., Odozor, L., Oni, O., & Idoko, I. P. (2025). Addressing iot-driven cybersecurity risks in critical infrastructure to safeguard public utilities and prevent large-scale service disruptions. *International Journal of Innovative Science and Research Technology, 10*(2).

Okolie, S. A., Amadi, C. A., Odii, J. N., Nwokorie, E. C., & Onyemauche, U. C. (2025). Anomaly Detection in Heterogeneous Cybersecurity Data. *Franklin Open, 13*, 100426. DOI: 10.1016/j.fraope.2025.100426

Oladele, O. K. (2024). Internet of Things (IoT) integration and its impact on smart cities, automation, and data-driven decision-making. *Journal of Smart Infrastructure, 5*(2), 45–58.

Oldemeyer, L., Jede, A., & Teuteberg, F. (2024). Investigation of artificial intelligence in SMEs: A systematic review of the state of the art and the main implementation challenges. *Management Review Quarterly, 75*(2), 1185–1227. DOI: 10.1007/s11301-024-00405-4

Oliveira, L., Wilkinson, D., Mossé, D., & Childers, B. (2018). Supporting Long-term Reproducible Software Execution. In Proceedings of the First International Workshop on Practical Reproducible Evaluation of Computer Systems (P-RECS '18) (Article 6). Association for Computing Machinery. https://doi.org/DOI: 10.1145/3214239.3214245

Organisation for Economic Co-operation and Development. (2023). *The nature, evolution and potential implications of data localisation measures* (No. 278). OECD Publishing. DOI: 10.1787/18166873

Palash, M. N. H. (2025). The economic impact of cybersecurity threats on critical infrastructure: Evaluating U.S. policy effectiveness and private sector readiness. [IJAEM]. *International Journal of Advances in Engineering and Management*, *7*(5), 222–230. DOI: 10.35629/5252-0705222230

Pang, G., Shen, C., Cao, L., & van den Hengel, A. (2022). Deep Learning for Anomaly Detection: A review. *ACM Computing Surveys*, *54*(2), 1–38. DOI: 10.1145/3439950

Parlamento del Uruguay. (2008). *Ley N.º 18.331 de protección de datos personales y acción de habeas data*. https://www.ohchr.org/sites/default/files/Documents/Issues/Privacy/Uruguay.pdf

Pawar, S., & Palivela, H. (2025). Need of paradigm shift in cybersecurity implementation for small and medium enterprises (SMES). *International Journal of Cybersecurity Intelligence & Cybercrime*, *8*(1), 39–75. DOI: 10.52306/2578-3289.1184

Pemmasani, P. K., & Osaka, M. (2021). The future of smart cities: Cybersecurity challenges in public infrastructure management. *International Journal of Modern Computing*, *4*(1), 72–85.

Pierucci, F. (2025). Sovereignty in the Digital Era: Rethinking Territoriality and Governance in Cyberspace. *Digital Society : Ethics, Socio-Legal and Governance of Digital Technology*, *4*(1), 27. DOI: 10.1007/s44206-025-00189-4

Pilgram, L., Dankar, F. K., Drechsler, J., Elliot, M., Domingo-Ferrer, J., Francis, P., Kantarcioglu, M., Kong, L., Malin, B., Muralidhar, K., Myles, P., Prasser, F., Raisaro, J. L., Yan, C., & El Emam, K. (2025). A Consensus Privacy Metrics Framework for Synthetic Data. *Patterns (New York, N.Y.)*, *6*(10), 101320. DOI: 10.1016/j.patter.2025.101320 PMID: 41142908

Pinto, A., Herrera, L.-C., Donoso, Y., & Gutierrez, J. A. (2023). Survey on Intrusion Detection Systems Based on Machine Learning Techniques for the Protection of Critical Infrastructure. *Sensors (Basel)*, *23*(5), 2415. DOI: 10.3390/s23052415 PMID: 36904618

Pliatsios, D., Sarigiannidis, P., Lagkas, T., & Sarigiannidis, A. G. (2020). A Survey on SCADA Systems: Secure Protocols, Incidents, Threats and Tactics. *IEEE Communications Surveys and Tutorials*, *22*(3), 1942–1976. DOI: 10.1109/COMST.2020.2987688

Poder Ejecutivo de Uruguay. (2009). *Decreto N.º 414/009: Reglamentación de la Ley N.º 18.331, relativo a la protección de datos personales*. https://www.impo.com.uy/bases/decretos/451-2009

Poder Ejecutivo del Perú. (2024). *Decreto Supremo N.º 016-2024-JUS que aprueba el Reglamento de la Ley N.º 29733, Ley de Protección de Datos Personales*. https://www.gob.pe/institucion/smv/normas-legales/6426760-016-2024-jus

Poder Ejecutivo Nacional. (2023). *Proyecto de ley de protección de datos personales (Mensaje N.º 87/2023)*. https://www.argentina.gob.ar/sites/default/files/mensajeyproyecto_leypdp2023.pdf

Pohle, J., & Thiel, T. (2020). Digital sovereignty. *Internet Policy Review*, *9*(4). Advance online publication. DOI: 10.14763/2020.4.1532

Polii, V., Julius, D., & Looka Banaya, C. (2025). Legal protection of personal data privacy in the digital era: A comparative study between Indonesia and ASEAN countries. *Jurnal Ilmu Hukum dan Sosial*, *3*(2), 1194-1206. DOI: 10.51903/yjyvvy47

Politou, E., Casino, F., Alepis, E., & Patsakis, C. (2019). Blockchain Mutability: Challenges and Proposed Solutions. *IEEE Transactions on Emerging Topics in Computing*, *9*(4), 1972–1986. DOI: 10.1109/TETC.2019.2949510

Ponnusamy, S., Chourasia, H., Rathod, S. B., & Patil, D. (2024). AI-driven traffic management systems. *Smart Cities*, •••, 96–121. DOI: 10.1201/9781003442660-5

Powar, J., & Beresford, A. R. (2023). SoK: Managing Risks of Linkage Attacks on Data Privacy. *Proceedings on Privacy Enhancing Technologies. Privacy Enhancing Technologies Symposium*, *2023*(2), 97–116. DOI: 10.56553/popets-2023-0043

Presidência da República. (2014, April 23). *Lei nº 12.965/2014 (Marco Civil da Internet)*. Retrieved November 28, 2025, from https://www.planalto.gov.br/ccivil_03/_ato2011-2014/2014/lei/l12965.htm

Presidencia de la República. (2025). *Plan Nacional de Desarrollo 2025-2030*. Diario Oficial de la Federación. https://sidof.segob.gob.mx/notas/docFuente/5755162

Presidencia del Consejo de Ministros. (2022). *Carta Peruana de Derechos Digitales*. https://www.gob.pe/institucion/pcm/informes-publicaciones/3302991-carta-peruana-de-derechos-digitales

Pritchard, N. J., & Wicenec, A. (2025). Formal Definition and Implementation of Reproducibility Tenets for Computational Workflows. *Future Generation Computer Systems*, *166*, 107684. DOI: 10.1016/j.future.2024.107684

Pun, C. S., Lee, S. X., & Xia, K. (2022). Persistent-Homology-Based Machine Learning: A Survey and a Comparative Study. *Artificial Intelligence Review*, *55*(7), 5169–5213. DOI: 10.1007/s10462-022-10146-z

Rahman, M. M., & Das, T. K. (2024). Countering cyberattacks: Gaps in international law and prospects for overcoming them. *Journal of Digital Technologies and Law*, *2*(4), 973–1002. DOI: 10.21202/jdtl.2024.46

Rahman, S., Pal, S., Mittal, S., Chawla, T., & Karmakar, C. (2024). SYN-GAN: A Robust Intrusion Detection System Using GAN-based Synthetic Data for IoT Security. *Internet of Things : Engineering Cyber Physical Human Systems*, *26*, 101212. DOI: 10.1016/j.iot.2024.101212

Raja, G. B. (2022). Effective waste management system for smart cities. *Intelligent Green Technologies for Sustainable Smart Cities*, 33-52.

Raja, G. B., & Chakraborty, C. (2023). Internet of things based effective wearable healthcare monitoring system for remote areas. In *Implementation of Smart Healthcare Systems using AI, IoT, and Blockchain* (pp. 193-218). Elsevier. DOI: 10.1016/B978-0-323-91916-6.00004-7

Raja, G. B., Vigneashwaran, R., Rohan, M., Praveen, N., & Vijay, N. (2025). IoT-Based Sewage Atmosphere and Health Monitoring for Sanitation Workers with Alerting System. 2025 7th International Conference on Inventive Material Science and Applications (ICIMA).

Raja, G. B. (2021). Appliance control system for physically challenged and elderly persons through hand gesture-based sign language. In *Biomedical Signal Processing for Healthcare Applications* (pp. 173–193). CRC Press. DOI: 10.1201/9781003147817-8

Raja, G. B. (2025a). Advancements of IoT and sensor informatics in wearable, implantable, mobile, and remote healthcare. In *Innovations in Biomedical Engineering* (pp. 87–121). Elsevier. DOI: 10.1016/B978-0-443-30146-9.00003-4

Raja, G. B. (2025b). SmartCare—A comprehensive wearable sensor-based remote health monitoring and rehabilitation system. In *Rehabilitation Robotics and Healthcare Devices* (pp. 27–46). Elsevier. DOI: 10.1016/B978-0-443-21505-6.00011-6

Rao, P. M., Pedada, S., Jangirala, S., Das, A. K., & Rodrigues, J. J. (2024). Role of IoT in the ages of digital to smart cities: Security challenges and countermeasures. IEEE Internet of Things Magazine, 7(1), 56–64.

Reddy, P. (2025). How to Respond to a Cyber Security Incident. *International Journal of Innovative Research in Computer and Communication Engineering.*, *13*(1), 37–41. DOI: 10.15680/IJIRCCE.2025.1301005

Ren, H., Xu, B., Wang, Y., Yi, C., Huang, C., Kou, X., Xing, T., Yang, M., Tong, J., & Zhang, Q. (2019). Time-series Anomaly Detection Service at Microsoft. In *Proceedings of the 25th ACM SIGKDD International Conference on Knowledge Discovery & Data Mining* (pp. 3009–3017). https://doi.org/DOI: 10.1145/3292500.3330680

Roman, R., Zhou, J., & Lopez, J. (2013). On the features and challenges of security and privacy in distributed Internet of Things. *Computer Networks*, *57*(10), 2266–2279. DOI: 10.1016/j.comnet.2012.12.018

Rose, S., Borchert, O., Mitchell, S., & Connelly, S. (2020). Zero Trust Architecture (NIST Special Publication 800-207). National Institute of Standards and Technology. https://doi.org/DOI: 10.6028/NIST.SP.800-207

Ruohonen, J., Hjerppe, K., & Kang, E.-Y. (2025). A mapping analysis of requirements between the CRA and the GDPR. In *2025 IEEE 33rd International Requirements Engineering Conference Workshops (REW)* (pp. 215-222). IEEE. DOI: 10.1109/REW66121.2025.00034

Rupprecht, L., Davis, J. C., Arnold, C., Gur, Y., & Bhagwat, D. (2020). Improving Reproducibility of Data Science Pipelines through Transparent Provenance Capture. *Proceedings of the VLDB Endowment International Conference on Very Large Data Bases*, *13*(12), 3354–3368. DOI: 10.14778/3415478.3415556

Sałek, K., & Fajdek, P. (2025). Analysis of the implementation of the NIS2 directive in the Weimar Triangle countries. *Central European Review of Economics & Finance*, *50*(1), 41–52. DOI: 10.24136/ceref.2025.003

Salvi, A., Spagnoletti, P., & Noori, N. S. (2022). Cyber-resilience of critical cyber infrastructures: Integrating digital twins in the electric power ecosystem. *Computers & Security*, *112*, 102507. DOI: 10.1016/j.cose.2021.102507

Samuel, S., Löffler, F., & König-Ries, B. (2021). Machine Learning Pipelines: Provenance, Reproducibility and FAIR Data Principles. In Glavic, B., Braganholo, V., & Koop, D. (Eds.), Lecture Notes in Computer Science: Vol. 12839. *Provenance and Annotation of Data and Processes* (pp. 226–230). Springer., DOI: 10.1007/978-3-030-80960-7_17

Santangelo, G., Nicora, G., Bellazzi, R., & Dagliati, A. (2025). How Good is Your Synthetic Data? SynthRO, a Dashboard to Evaluate and Benchmark Synthetic Tabular Data. *BMC Medical Informatics and Decision Making*, *25*(1), 89. DOI: 10.1186/s12911-024-02731-9 PMID: 39966793

Sarmin, F. J., Sarkar, A. R., Wang, Y., & Mohammed, N. (2025). Synthetic data: Revisiting the privacy-utility trade-off. *International Journal of Information Security*, *24*(4), 156. Advance online publication. DOI: 10.1007/s10207-025-01072-6

Schlegel, M., & Sattler, K.-U. (2022). Management of Machine Learning Lifecycle Artifacts: A survey. *SIGMOD Record*, *51*(4), 18–35. DOI: 10.1145/3582302.3582306

Schlegel, M., & Sattler, K.-U. (2025). Capturing end-to-end Provenance for Machine Learning Pipelines. *Information Systems*, *132*, 102495. DOI: 10.1016/j.is.2024.102495

Seceon. (2026). Overview of Seceon's OTM Platform Components [Image]. Seceon. https://seceon.com/wp-content/uploads/2025/05/Cybersecurity-for-Critical-Infrastructure-in-the-Middle-East_-Why-a-Proactive-AI-Driven-Approach-Is-Essential-visual-selection.png

Secretaría General Iberoamericana. (2023). *Carta Iberoamericana de Principios y Derechos en los Entornos Digitales* https://segib.org/es/publicacion/carta-iberoamericana-de-principios-y-derechos-en-entornos-digitales/

Sehrawat, A., & Katiyar, A. S. (2025). Cybersecurity laws in the digital age: Gaps and recommendations. *Journal of Informatics Education and Research*, *5*(2), 3839–3850. DOI: 10.52783/jier.v5i2.2862

Sekonya, N., & Sithungu, S. (2023). An Analysis of Critical Cybersecurity Controls for Industrial Control Systems. *European Conference on Cyber Warfare and Security*. 22. 410-419. DOI: 10.34190/eccws.22.1.1157

Semanate Esquivel, A., & Recalde Herrera, L. L. (2023). El estado y la defensa de ciberespacio. *Revista de la Academia del Guerra del Ejército Ecuatoriano*, *16*(1), 99–109. DOI: 10.24133/AGE.VOL16.N01.2023.07

Shahid, K., Hassan, M., Husnain, A., & Mukhtar, S. (2023). *Information and communication technologies for new generation of sustainable smart cities*. Sustainable Smart Cities - A Vision for Tomorrow., DOI: 10.5772/intechopen.107251

Sharafaldin, I., Lashkari, A. H., & Ghorbani, A. A. (2018). Toward Generating a new Intrusion Detection Dataset and Intrusion Traffic Characterization. In *Proceedings of the 4th International Conference on Information Systems Security and Privacy (ICISSP 2018)* (pp. 108–116). https://doi.org/DOI: 10.5220/0006639801080116

Sharma, T., Bhati, B. S., & Gautam, M. (2022). A study on Internet of things: Applications, security and protection. 2022 9th International Conference on Computing for Sustainable Global Development (INDIACom), 820-824. DOI: 10.23919/INDIACom54597.2022.9763266

Shen, S., Zhang, K., Zhou, Y., Zhang, X., & Ci, S. (2020). Security in edge-assisted Internet of Things: Challenges and solutions. *Science China. Information Sciences*, *63*(12), 220302. DOI: 10.1007/s11432-019-2906-y

Shyaa, M. A., Ibrahim, N. F., Zainol, Z., Abdullah, R., Anbar, M., & Alzubaidi, L. (2024). Evolving Cybersecurity Frontiers: A Comprehensive Survey on Concept Drift and Feature Dynamics aware Machine and Deep Learning in Intrusion Detection Systems. *Engineering Applications of Artificial Intelligence*, *137*, 109143. DOI: 10.1016/j.engappai.2024.109143

Shyaa, M. A., Zainol, Z., Abdullah, R., Anbar, M., Alzubaidi, L., & Santamaría, J. (2023). Enhanced Intrusion Detection with Data Stream Classification and Concept Drift Guided by the Incremental Learning Genetic Programming Combiner. *Sensors (Basel)*, *23*(7), 3736. DOI: 10.3390/s23073736

Sicari, S., Rizzardi, A., Grieco, L. A., & Coen-Porisini, A. (2015). Security, privacy and trust in Internet of Things: The road ahead. *Computer Networks*, *76*, 146–164. DOI: 10.1016/j.comnet.2014.11.008

Silva, M., Pinto, D., Vitorino, J., Gonçalves, J., Maia, E., & Praça, I. (2025). GeNIS: A Modular Dataset for Network Intrusion Detection and Classification. *Data in Brief*, *56*, 111487. DOI: 10.1016/j.dib.2025.111487

Simola, J., Savola, R., Frantti, T., Takala, A., & Lehkonen, R. (2023). Developing Cybersecurity in an Industrial Environment by Using a Testbed Environment. *Proceedings of the 22nd European Conference on Cyber Warfare and Security, ECCWS 2023*, 2023, pp. 429-438, DOI: 10.34190/eccws.22.1.1362

Sims, A. (2019). Blockchain and decentralised autonomous organisations (DAOs): The evolution of companies? *SSRN*, *28*, 423–458. DOI: 10.2139/ssrn.3524674

Singh, P., Jain, P., Saini, V., Kumari, K., & Bajaj, P. K. (2024). Enhancing Smart City Infrastructure Through IoT-Enabled Predictive Maintenance and Real-Time Data Analytics. *2024 International Conference on Progressive Innovations in Intelligent Systems and Data Science (ICPIDS)*.

Smith, R., Janicke, H., He, Y., Ferra, F., & Albakri, A. (2021). The Agile Incident Response for Industrial Control Systems (AIR4ICS) framework. *Computers & Security*, *109*, 102398. DOI: 10.1016/j.cose.2021.102398

Snail ka Mtuze, S., & Musoni, M. (2023). An overview of cybercrime law in South Africa. *International Cybersecurity Law Review, 4*(3), 299–323. DOI: 10.1365/s43439-023-00089-8

Sobeslav, V., & Horalek, J. (2025). Cybersecurity baseline and risk mitigation for open data in IoT-enabled smart city systems: A case study of the Hradec Kralove Region. *Sensors (Basel), 25*(16), 4966. DOI: 10.3390/s25164966 PMID: 40871830

Solanke, A.ADEDAMOLA ABIODUN SOLANKE. (2024). Sovereign cloud implementation: Technical architectures for data residency and regulatory compliance. *International Journal of Science and Research Archive, 11*(2), 2136–2147. DOI: 10.30574/ijsra.2024.11.2.0502

Soriano, J. P. (2025). Geopolitics in the digital age: the U.S.-China competition through their narratives on digital technologies. IDP Revista de Internet Derecho y Política. https://ddd.uab.cat/record/310822

Soyer, B., & Tettenborn, A. (2022). Artificial intelligence and civil liability—Do we need a new regime? *International Journal of Law and Information Technology, 30*(4), 385–397. DOI: 10.1093/ijlit/eaad001

Sridhar, S., Hahn, A., & Govindarasu, M. (2012). Cyber–Physical System Security for the Electric Power Grid. *Proceedings of the IEEE, 100*(1), 210–224. DOI: 10.1109/JPROC.2011.2165269

Srivastav, A. D., Verma, S. B., & Pandey, A. K. (2025). Cybersecurity Strategies for Industrial Installations in the Critical Infrastructure Sector: *Challenges and Solutions International Conference on Networks and Cryptology (NETCRYPT)*, New Delhi, India, 2025, pp. 1564-1567, DOI: 10.1109/NETCRYPT65877.2025.11102534

Staves, A., Balderstone, H., Green, B., Gouglidis, A., & Hutchison, D. (2020). A Framework to Support ICS Cyber Incident Response and Recovery. Paper presented at the 17th International Conference on Information Systems for Crisis Response and Management, Blacksburg, United States.

Stenger, M., Bauer, A., Prantl, T., Leppich, R., Hudson, N., Chard, K., Foster, I., & Kounev, S. (2024). Thinking in Categories: A Survey on Assessing the Quality for Time Series Synthesis. *ACM Journal of Data and Information Quality, 16*(2), 14. Advance online publication. DOI: 10.1145/3666006

Stouffer, K., Pillitteri, V., Lightman, S., Abrams, M., & Hahn, A. (2020). Guide to operational technology (OT) security (NIST Special Publication 800-82, Rev. 3). National Institute of Standards and Technology. DOI: 10.6028/NIST.SP.800-82r3

Sullivan, H., & Schweikart, S. (2019). Are current tort liability doctrines adequate for addressing injury caused by AI? *AMA Journal of Ethics*, *21*(2), E160–E166. DOI: 10.1001/amajethics.2019.160

Sumartono, E., Harliyanto, R., Situmeang, S., Siagian, D., & Septaria, E. (2024). The legal implications of data privacy laws, cybersecurity regulations, and AI ethics in a digital society. *The Journal of Academic Science*, *1*(2), 103–110. DOI: 10.59613/29qypw51

Szoszkiewicz, Ł., & Yuste, R. (2025). Mental privacy: Navigating risks, rights and regulation. *EMBO Reports*, *26*(14), e3469. DOI: 10.1038/s44319-025-00505-6

Tao, X., Cheng, L., Zhang, R., Chan, W. K., Chao, H., & Qin, J. (2023). Towards green innovation in smart cities: Leveraging traffic flow prediction with machine learning algorithms for sustainable transportation systems. *Sustainability (Basel)*, *16*(1), 251. DOI: 10.3390/su16010251

Tatar, U., Gokce, Y., & Nussbaum, B. (2020). Law versus technology: Blockchain, GDPR, and tough tradeoffs. *Computer Law & Security Review*, *38*, 105454. DOI: 10.1016/j.clsr.2020.105454

Teichmann, F. (2025). Cybersecurity of critical infrastructure in europe: The NIS2 directive in focus. *International Cybersecurity Law Review*, *6*(3), 207–220. DOI: 10.1365/s43439-025-00154-4

Teichmann, F. M. J., & Wittmann, C. (2023). When is a law firm liable for a data breach? An exploration into the legal liability of ransomware and cybersecurity. *Journal of Financial Crime*, *30*(6), 1491–1498. DOI: 10.1108/JFC-04-2022-0093

Thomasian, N. M., & Adashi, E. Y. (2021). Cybersecurity in the Internet of Medical Things. *Health Policy and Technology*, *10*(3), 100549. DOI: 10.1016/j.hlpt.2021.100549

Transforming our world: The 2030 agenda for sustainable development. (2022). *Sustainable Development Goals*. https://doi.org/DOI: 10.5040/9781509934058.0025

Trautman, L., & Ormerod, P. (2017). Corporate directors' and officers' cybersecurity standard of care: The Yahoo data breach. *SSRN*, *66*(5), 1231–1272. DOI: 10.2139/ssrn.2883607

Trindade, M., Kaye, J., & De Cristofaro, E. (2024). Navigating Identity Disclosure Risk in Synthetic Data: outliers and vulnerabilities. arXiv. https://doi.org//arXiv.2406.02736DOI: 10.48550

Tropina, T. (2024). 'This is not a human rights convention!': The perils of overlooking human rights in the UN cybercrime treaty. *Journal of Cyber Policy*, *9*(2), 200–220. DOI: 10.1080/23738871.2024.2419517

Tuli, S., Casale, G., & Jennings, N. R. (2022). TranAD: Deep Transformer Networks for Anomaly Detection in Multivariate Time Series Data. *Proceedings of the VLDB Endowment International Conference on Very Large Data Bases*, *15*(6), 1201–1214. DOI: 10.14778/3514061.3514067

Umscheid, J., Schmitz, P., & Pape, S. (2022). Learning from security incidents in critical infrastructure: A systematic review. *Computers & Security*, *120*, 102821. DOI: 10.1016/j.cose.2022.102821

van de Water, R. P., Schmidt, H., & Rockenschaub, P. (2026). ReciPies: A Lightweight Data Transformation Pipeline for Reproducible ML. *Journal of Open Source Software*, *11*(117), 9261. DOI: 10.21105/joss.09261

Van Hoang, T. (2024). Impact of integrated artificial intelligence and internet of things technologies on smart city transformation. *Journal of technical education science, 19*(Special Issue 01), 64-73.

Villafranca, A., Thant, K. M., Tasic, I., & Cano, M.-D. (2025). AI-enabled IoT intrusion detection: Unified conceptual framework and research roadmap. *Machine Learning and Knowledge Extraction*, *7*(4), 115. DOI: 10.3390/make7040115

Wairimu, S., Iwaya, L. H., Fritsch, L., & Lindskog, S. (2024). On the evaluation of privacy impact assessment and privacy risk assessment methodologies: A systematic literature review. *IEEE Access : Practical Innovations, Open Solutions*, *12*, 56623–56639. DOI: 10.1109/ACCESS.2024.3360864

Walters, J. P., Liang, Z., Shi, W., & Chaudhary, V. (2007). Wireless sensor network security: A survey. In Security in Distributed, Grid, Mobile, and Pervasive Computing (pp. 367-409). DOI: 10.1201/9780429119347-20

Wang, L., Sun, Y., Liu, X., & Li, C. (2026). PHGAT: Persistent Homology-enhanced Graph Attention Network for IIoT Anomaly Detection. Expert Systems with Applications, 299(Part A), 129923. DOI: 10.1016/j.eswa.2025.129923

Wan, G., & Ye, X. (2025). East Asian personal data protection laws and international medical data sharing: Pathways for coordination. *International Journal of Multidisciplinary Research and Growth Evaluation*, *6*(5), 109–113. DOI: 10.54660/.IJMRGE.2025.6.5.109-113

Wang, F., Jiang, Y., Zhang, R., Wei, A., Xie, J., & Pang, X. (2025). A Survey of Deep Anomaly Detection in Multivariate Time Series: Taxonomy, Applications, and Directions. *Sensors (Basel)*, *25*(1), 190. DOI: 10.3390/s25010190

Wang, X., Ning, Z., Hu, X., Ngai, E. C., Wang, L., Hu, B., & Kwok, R. Y. (2018). A city-wide real-time traffic management system: Enabling Crowdsensing in social internet of vehicles. *IEEE Communications Magazine*, *56*(9), 19–25. DOI: 10.1109/MCOM.2018.1701065

Wang, Y., Attebury, G., & Ramamurthy, B. (2006). A survey of security issues in wireless sensor networks. *IEEE Communications Surveys and Tutorials*, *8*(2), 2–23. DOI: 10.1109/COMST.2006.315852

Wasserman, L. (2018). Topological Data Analysis. *Annual Review of Statistics and Its Application*, *5*(1), 501–532. DOI: 10.1146/annurev-statistics-031017-100045

Watney, M. (2024). Exploring South Africa's cybersecurity legal framework regulating information confidentiality, integrity, and availability. In *Proceedings of the 19th International Conference on Cyber Warfare and Security, ICCWS 2024* (Vol. 19, No. 1, pp. 430–437). Academic Conferences & Publishing International Limited. DOI: 10.34190/iccws.19.1.1999

Watney, M. (2025). The legal pitfalls to ratification of the United Nations Convention against Cybercrime. In Lipps, C., & Han, B. (Eds.), *Proceedings of the 24th European Conference on CyberWarfare and Security, ECCWS 2025* (Vol. 24, No. 1, pp. 713–719). Curran Associates Inc. DOI: 10.34190/eccws.24.1.3381

Weil, G. (2024). Tort Law as a Tool for Mitigating Catastrophic Risk from Artificial Intelligence. SSRN *Electronic Journal*. DOI: 10.2139/ssrn.4694006

World population prospects 2017 - Volume I: Comprehensive tables. (2021). *Statistical Papers - United Nations (Ser. A). Population and Vital Statistics Report*. Advance online publication. DOI: 10.18356/9789210001014

Yeoh, W., Liu, M., Shore, M., & Jiang, F. (2023). Zero Trust Cybersecurity: Critical Success Factors and a Maturity Assessment Framework. *Computers & Security*, *133*, 103412. DOI: 10.1016/j.cose.2023.103412

Zanella, A., Bui, N., Castellani, A., Vangelista, L., & Zorzi, M. (2014). Internet of Things for smart cities. *IEEE Internet of Things Journal*, *1*(1), 22–32. DOI: 10.1109/JIOT.2014.2306328

Zhang, Z., Yan, C., & Malin, B. A. (2022). Membership Inference Attacks Against Synthetic Health Data. *Journal of Biomedical Informatics*, *125*, 103977. DOI: 10.1016/j.jbi.2021.103977 PMID: 34920126

Zhu, Q., & Edelmann, N. (2017). Editorial 9(2). JeDEM - EJournal of EDemocracy and Open Government, 9(2), i - iii. https://doi.org/DOI: 10.29379/jedem.v9i2.487

Zinchenko, O. (2025). Cyber security in international relations: Risks and prospects. *Eximia*, *14*(1), 1–20. DOI: 10.47577/eximia.v14i1.526

Zukis, B. (2022). Digital and Cybersecurity Governance Around the World. *Annals of Corporate Governance*, *7*(1), 1–92. DOI: 10.1561/109.00000032

About the Contributors

Miguel Ángel Ruiz Jaimes is a Professor and Researcher at the Universidad Politécnica del Estado de Morelos (UPEMOR), Mexico. He holds a Ph.D. in Computer Systems Engineering and is a recognized member of the Mexican National System of Researchers (SNI Level I). Dr. Ruiz Jaimes has more than twenty years of experience in information technologies, cybersecurity, artificial intelligence, and digital governance. He has authored and co-authored multiple scientific articles and book chapters published by IGI Global, MDPI, and other international publishers. In addition, he serves as a peer reviewer and editorial board member for journals such as IJCoPI and BEEI. His current research focuses on AI ethics, cybersecurity in critical infrastructures, and emerging technologies applied to public sector innovation.

José Miguel Liceaga Ortiz De La Peña is an Engineer in Communications and Electronics from the Higher School of Mechanical and Electrical Engineering (ESIME) Culhuacán Unit of the IPN. Master of Science in Microelectronics Engineering from SEPI-ESIME UPC of the IPN. He is currently a student in the Doctorate in Advanced Sciences and Technologies (DCTA) program at the Polytechnic University of Pachuca (UPP). Full-time Research Professor at the Polytechnic University of Pachuca (UPP). Attached to the Department of Biomedical Engineering and previously to the Department of Telematics Engineering and Network and Telecommunications Engineering. He got the PRODEP Desirable Profile.

***

Jaime Aguilar-Ortiz holds a Ph.D. in Mathematical Sciences (CINVESTAV–IPN, Mexico) and serves as a professor and researcher in the fields of Mathematics, Artificial Intelligence, and Project Management, with academic involvement also extending to the Universidad Politécnica Metropolitana de Hidalgo. He additionally leads innovation-driven initiatives as Director General of CICAINTE and TEDNOVA GROUP, bridging rigorous academic work with applied technological development and institutional impact. His prior scholarly and editorial contributions include the preparation and/or editing of a substantial body of books and educational resources spanning mathematics education, financial mathematics, programming, and technology-based learning, complemented by the creation of audiovisual materials, educational platforms, and serious-game applications aimed at strengthening learning outcomes. His academic production further includes dozens of peer-reviewed articles and book chapters addressing themes at the intersection of smart cities, education, and AI, together with sustained experience in research mentoring, curriculum development, and interdisciplinary collaboration. These achievements, combined with recognized academic credentials and a consistent record of knowledge dissemination and capacity building, position him as a strong editor for a high-impact scholarly volume with methodological rigor, cross-sector relevance, and measurable educational and societal value.

Mohammad Al-Khaldy is an Assistant professor of Business Intelligence and Data Analytics at University of Petra, Jordan. He completed his PhD in Atrificial Intelligence and Data Science for the University of Hull -United Kingdom - 20017. Alkhaldy's research interests include data analytics, machine learning, predictive analytics, NLP, and decision support systems. His research has been published extensively in academic journals and conferences. Alkhaldy taught a variety of courses in Artificial intelligence and business intelligence, including Data Mining, Business Analytics, Computer Programming, Intelligent business systems, Data Visualization, and machine learning. Alkhaldy is a member of Jordan Computers Society, and Arab Robotics & AI Association. He also a reviewer for several other academic conferences and journals.

Amjad Aldweesh is a computer associate professor interested in the Blockchain and Smart contracts technology as well as cyber security. Amjad has a Bachelor degree in computer science. He has a MSc degree in advanced computer science and security from the University of Manchester with distinction. Amjad is the second in the UK and the first in the middle east to have a PhD in the Blockchain and Smart contracts technology from Newcastle University.

Ricardo Barrera-Cámara is in Computer Systems from the Universidad del Sur. Master in Informatics from the Universidad Autónoma of Carmen. Research professor at the Autonomous University of Carmen in Mexico. National System of Researchers level 1. Leader of the academic group of scientific and technological computing. Leader of the Academy of Administration and information processing.

His research areas are Scientific Computing, Data Science, Optimization, Quality and Information Technology, Sustainable Development Goals.

Ocotlán Diaz-Parra is a Professor and Researcher at Universidad Politécnica de Pachuca (UPP), a National Researcher under the Secretaria de Ciencia, Humanidades, Tecnología e Innovación program, and an Adjunct Researcher at the National Laboratory of Autonomous Vehicles and Exoskeletons (LANAVEX). His research interests include Smart Cities, Smart Water, Smart Education, Smart Government, Smart Healthcare, Smart Farming, Smart Energy, Smart Sports, Smart Food, Smart Tourism, Algorithmic Finance, Algorithmic Portfolio Management, Applications and Theory of Algorithms, Bio-inspired Algorithms, Combinatorial Optimization Problems, Compilers, Computational Intelligence, Computational Complexity Theory, Computational Financial Intelligence, Complexity of Algorithms, Complexity of Instances, Computational Statistics, Computer Networks, Computer Science Security, Cybercrimes, Data Mining, Education, Evolutionary Computation, Heuristic Optimization Techniques in Bioinformatics, Hybrid Evolutionary Algorithms, Hybrid Optimization Algorithms, Machine Learning, Meta-heuristics, Operations Research, Operations Management, Parallel & Distributed Computing, Production Planning and Logistics Optimization, Project Scheduling Problems, Software Engineering, and Transgenic Algorithms.

Carlos Domínguez-Mayorga holds a Ph.D. in Sciences specializing in Artificial Intelligence, with a foundational background in Physics and Mathematics. His research focuses on Deep Learning, NLP, neural networks, and the development of predictive models. He has an extensive track record in scientific publications and graduate program management, applying cutting-edge data science techniques to engineering and sustainability projects.

Rafael Figueroa-Díaz received PhD degree in Mechanical Engineering in National Center for Research and Technological Development, Cuernavaca, México, in 2012. His made a master science in mechatronics in 2007. His current research interests in modal balancing in rotating systems and fault diagnosis using vibration.

Alejandro Fuentes-Penna is a Mexican academic and researcher specializing in strategic planning, artificial intelligence, and educational technology. He earned his Ph.D. in Strategic Planning and Technology Management from the Universidad Popular Autónoma del Estado de Puebla (UPAEP) in 2012. Prior to that, he completed a Master's degree in Computer Science at the Instituto Tecnológico y de Estudios Superiores de Monterrey (ITESM), where he published two articles in international conferences and secured first place in the Technology category of the Third Banamex Award for Internet Evolution. Dr. Fuentes Penna has held various academic positions, including serving as a Full-Time Research Professor at the Escuela Superior de Tlahuelilpan of the Universidad Autónoma del Estado de Hidalgo (UAEH). His research interests encompass educational management, educational technology, complexity in social sciences, and bio-inspired intelligent scientific computing. He has contributed to multiple publications, including articles indexed in JCR and Scopus, as well as books in his areas of expertise. Throughout his career, Dr. Fuentes Penna has received numerous national and international recognitions for academic and research excellence. He has been awarded the PRODEP Profile (formerly PROMEP) three times, is a member of the State System of Researchers in Morelos, and was recently included in the National System of Researchers at the Candidate level. Additionally, he has collaborated with various universities and research institutes, including the Universidad Nacional Autónoma de México (UNAM) and the Mexican Institute of Transportation. Dr. Fuentes Penna has extensive experience in teaching at both undergraduate and graduate levels, in both face-to-face and online modalities. He has supervised theses, coordinated educational programs, and organized significant academic events such as the International Space Week and the National Science and Technology Week.

David H. Fuque-Ehuan is a Professor of Information Technology at Universidad Autónoma del Carmen. Develops technology solutions for enterprise and institutional process optimization, with research focus on Machine Learning, Database Systems, Computer Vision, and Internet of Things (IoT). Background includes graduate studies in Education.

Marco Antonio García-Márquez is a computer scientist, AI researcher, and professor with extensive experience in machine learning, computer vision, and data science. He holds a Master's degree in Computer Science and a PhD in Applied Engineering, he is a member of the academic body of Cybernetics and Applied Computing. With over 20 years of experience in higher education and academic leadership, he has played a key role in curriculum design, program accreditation, and student success strategies for universities and public institutions. His work focuses on the implementation of information systems, deep learning, image processing, and artificial intelligence, with practical applications in automated decision-making, pattern recognition, and IoT systems. He has developed and implemented AI-powered algorithms using Python, Keras, OpenCV, PyTorch, and Pandas, as well as real-time embedded systems with OpenCV, OpenGL, PHP, JavaScript, C, C++, Python, MicroPython, and Arduino. García Márquez is an active contributor to scientific research, academic quality assessment, and AI-powered solutions for education and industry. His commitment to interdisciplinary collaboration and technological advancements has positioned him as a key figure in Science computer.

Jesús Martínez-Ocampo obtained his Bachelor's degree in Sciences with a terminal area in Physics from the Autonomous University of the State of Morelos (UAEM) in 2018. In 2021, he earned a Master's degree in Engineering and Applied Sciences with honorable mention from UAEM. That same year, he was accepted as a doctoral student in Engineering and Applied Sciences at UAEM, where he is currently continuing his studies. In 2022, he began his participation in a basic science project titled "Amplification of random laser effects in nano solar cells with quantum dots in materials with percolation" through the National Council of Humanities, Sciences and Technologies (CONAHCYT). During 2022 and 2023, he conducted a research stay at the Institute of Physics at the Meritorious Autonomous University of Puebla (BUAP). He has taught exact and experimental sciences at basic, middle, high school, and master's levels, notably participating in science competitions with his students, achieving first place for the state of Morelos in the physics apparatus and experiments competition, and receiving an honorable mention at the national level. He has participated in national and international presentations at various conferences, has been a science communicator, and has served as a judge at scientific meetings. He is an author and co-author of various national and international scientific articles in the fields of quantum optics, complex systems, optical radiation, single-walled carbon nanotubes, electromagnetism, and computational physics.

Hitesh Mohapatra received the B.E. degree in Information Technology from Biju Patnaik University of Technology (BPUT), Odisha in 2006, and the MTech. Degree in CSE from Odisha University of Technology and Research (OUTR) University, Odisha in 2009. He received his Ph.D. in Computer Science & Engineering in 2021 from Veer Surendra Sai University of Technology (VSSUT), Burla, India. Dr. Mohapatra has published over 150+ research articles in SCI- and Scopus-indexed journals and conferences. He has 15 years of teaching experience both in industry and academia. He has served the research community with various capacities like session chair, technical chair, keynote speaker etc. His research interests include wireless sensor network, smart city, smart grid and smart water. Currently he is working as Associate Professor at School of Computer Engineering, KIIT (Deemed to be) University, Bhubaneswar, Odisha, India.

Luis Muñiz Rascado completed his undergraduate studies at the Instituto Tecnológico de Zacatepec, obtaining a Bachelor's degree in Computer Systems Engineering in 2002. As part of his degree requirements, he carried out a thesis research stay at the Instituto de Investigaciones Eléctricas. In 2007, he completed a Master's degree in Information Technologies at the Instituto Tecnológico de Zacatepec, conducting his thesis research stay within the Computational Genomics Program at the Center for Genomic Sciences (Centro de Ciencias Genómicas) of the National Autonomous University of Mexico (UNAM). From 2004 to 2023, he collaborated with the Computational Genomics Program at the Center for Genomic Sciences of UNAM as a member of the RegulonDB staff, participating in multiple research projects. He is currently pursuing a Ph.D. in Computer Science at the Centro Nacional de Investigación y Desarrollo Tecnológico (CENIDET), under the supervision of Dr. Noé Alejandro Castro Sánchez. Since 2013, he has served as a faculty member in the Department of Systems and Computing at the Instituto Tecnológico de Zacatepec.

Ziadoon Otaiwi has a PhD in Software Engineering. His areas of research interest Software Engineering.

Jazmín Rodríguez Flores has a PhD in Applied Engineering, specializing in systems analysis and design, has more than 17 years as a full time researcher at UPP, teaches undergraduate and graduate courses.

Jorge Ruiz-Vanoye is a Professor and Researcher at Universidad Politécnica de Pachuca (UPP), a National Researcher under the Secretaria de Ciencia, Humanidades, Tecnología e Innovación program, and an Adjunct Researcher at the National Laboratory of Autonomous Vehicles and Exoskeletons (LANAVEX). Additionally, he holds the title of Lecturer-level Researcher for the Agency for the Quality of the University System of Catalonia (Generalitat de Catalunya).

Fernando Sánchez-Martínez is a Professor at the Universidad Autónoma del Carmen, with 26 years' experience in teaching, research and academic management. He has collaborated in the design of curricula and the management of educational programmes, contributing to the strengthening of education in Information Technology and Computer Science. He is a member of the Academic Body of Scientific Computing, where he develops projects focused on solving organizational problems through technological applications. Throughout his career, he has been involved in educational innovation projects and the development of strategies to improve students' academic performance. His work has been presented at conferences and published in peer-reviewed journals, reinforcing his commitment to applied research in computing and technology.

Francisco R. Trejo-Macotela holds a Ph.D. in Electronics from INAOE and is Professor and Senior Researcher at Universidad Politécnica de Pachuca (UPP). He is a National Researcher of the Secretariat of Science, Humanities, Technology and Innovation (SECIHTI) of Mexico and adjunct member of LANAVEX. His prolific academic output comprises slightly more than 65 publications in domains including smart cities, embedded IoT systems, telecommunications, electronics, aquaculture, artificial intelligence, bio-inspired algorithms, combinatorial optimisation, and educational technologies.

Eugenio Velázquez Santana is an academic and researcher in information technology and strategic planning. He holds a doctorate from the Popular Autonomous University of Puebla and has been a full-time professor since 2002. He has also held positions as department head and graduate program coordinator. He has been a member of the State Research System of the State of Morelos.

Index

A

C

D

E

F

G

H

I

M

www.ingramcontent.com/pod-product-compliance
Lightning Source LLC
LaVergne TN
LVHW060003031026
849161LV00025B/1364